Kazuo Shinohara

Traversing the House and the City

Edited by Seng Kuan

Lars Müller Publishers

Harvard University
Graduate School of Design

KAZUO SHINOHARA

TRAVERSING THE HOUSE AND THE CITY

EDITOR'S NOTE:
Japanese personal names within this volume are listed family name first, given name second.

Foreword

This book on the work of Shinohara Kazuo is the third in a series of publications on postwar Japanese architects. Like the others in the series, on the works of Tange Kenzō and Kikutake Kiyonori, it has been produced in conjunction with a major exhibition at the Harvard University Graduate School of Design (GSD) and in collaboration with Lars Müller Publishers. The GSD has a long and productive connection with Japanese architecture. Exhibitions and publications such as those on the works of Tange, Kikutake, and Shinohara, as well as on contemporary architects, most recently Ishigami Junya and Atelier Bow-Wow, have enabled the school to gain a deeper understanding of the role of architecture within the broader framework of Japanese culture and society.

In addition, the GSD has recently become the home of the Tange Archives. This rare collection of drawings and models, now carefully catalogued, conserved, and digitized, will be of immense importance to those interested in studying the work of one of the twentieth century's most influential architects. Links with Japan extend further, to a number of endowed chairs, including a professorship in Tange's honor. The Tange Professorship has made it possible for the GSD to invite prominent international architects to Cambridge to teach studios, mount exhibitions, and deliver lectures.

Connections between the GSD and Japan go back to the time of Walter Gropius, who on completing his term as chair of the department of architecture made his only visit to Japan in 1954. There Gropius found in traditional Japanese domestic architecture the same hallmarks of the diversity of expression of modern architecture—the spirit of simplicity, modular construction, and the relation between the inside and the outside.

The aesthetic reciprocities between Japan and the West have their roots in the *Japonisme* movement of the nineteenth century, when European artists began to engage Japanese art, sculpture, and architecture. Architects and artists of the Bauhaus such as the Swiss painter Johannes Itten became interested in Japanese art and architecture long before Gropius's sojourn. In many ways, Gropius's appreciation of the simplicity of Japanese domestic architecture owes a debt to Bruno Taut, who came to Japan some twenty years before Gropius. The manner in which these architects saw direct parallels between the simplicity of Japanese domestic architecture and their own vision of modern architecture merits further study.

Shinohara Kazuo was also interested in traditional domestic architecture. But unlike the Europeans, who saw Japanese architecture as a precedent, and hence a form of legitimation for their own work, Shinohara seems to have viewed traditional Japanese buildings as material for transformation—perhaps less a source of direct inspiration, and more an artifact to be studied and acted upon the same way that a pathologist might dissect a body. Shinohara's early architectural "operations" produce a body of work based on forms of "distancing" from their original point of reference. In developing his work, he referred to the concept of *higōriteki* or "coordinates of irrationality" to designate an approach toward architecture that was more visceral and experiential than rational or symbolic.

A house assumes its uniqueness in comparison to traditional models through the way part of its roof is cut away, or by the logic of the structure of an umbrella applied to a roof, or by how a set of nearby electricity wires are registered in the way the house is formed—sculpted. Shinohara's domestic architecture pursues a mathematical spatial imagination, at times highly abstract. It often appears conventional or traditional in plan, but unconventional in section and structure, making the experience and use of the house radically different. As his famous dictum "A house is a work of art" suggests, his houses demand a response—even changes of habit—from their inhabitants.

Shinohara consciously and explicitly evolved his approach throughout his career, announcing these phases of his work as a series of "styles." In contrast to its meaning in Western architecture, his use of the term designates different "themes" or topics of interest or research. Nevertheless, it is hard not to draw parallels between the evolution of his Third (1974) and Fourth (1984) Styles, when he became more interested in chaos theory and the increasing influence of postmodernism in architectural discourse. It is a simplification, but Shinohara's houses of the First and Second Styles are more concerned with the interior and question of habitation, whereas the later houses demonstrate greater interest in the appearance of the building through their use of geometrical and graphic figures. Shinohara's architecture reached its expressive pinnacle with the completion of Centennial Hall (1987) at his alma mater, the Tokyo Institute of Technology (Tokyo Tech). Even though Shinohara intended to combine chaos and beauty, the curved volumetric element at the top of the building bears a resemblance to Claude-Nicolas Ledoux's famous unrealized project for the Inspector's House at the source of the Loue River (1773–79)—imagery that was very much present in architectural circles during the period of construction of Centennial Hall.

In his writings, Shinohara emphasized the importance of the experience of the city as a walker conscious of what he has seen and what lies ahead. "An image of my *city,*" he said, "evolves with the sight of the road." His conception of architecture as an "artistic" practice gave him greater freedom to experiment than his Metabolist contemporaries, who saw an indispensable relationship between architecture and the city, or perhaps more precisely between architecture and urban design. Therefore the chaos of the city of Tokyo, which excited him, seems to have been incorporated into his juxtapositions and the collision of multiple elements at Centennial Hall.

In Japan there are many followers of the so-called Shinohara School, architects who either worked or studied with him or his students at the Tokyo Institute of Technology. Hasegawa Itsuko worked with Shinohara during the early part of her career, and Itō Toyoo was considered a follower and belonging to the same circle. Both Hasegawa and Itō had also worked with Kikutake Kiyonori before turning to Shinohara. The combination of these experiences has played a significant role in shaping the path of both their careers. Current professors at Tokyo Tech, such as Okuyama Shin-ichi, Tsukamoto Yoshiharu, and Shiozaki Taishin, all represented in this volume, and all former students there, are proud bearers of the Shinohara legacy. Some years ago, the GSD hosted a series of lectures with the title "A New Innocence: Contemporary Trends in Japanese Architecture." This series brought together a group of Japanese practitioners from different generations, among them Itō Toyoo, Sejima Kazuyo, Nishizawa Ryūe, Fujimoto Sou, and Ishigami Junya. Part of the role of the series was to explore the question of lineage in architecture. Sejima, for example, had first worked for Itō, and Ishigami for Sejima when she set up her own firm. This is a longer story, but clearly, the architecture of Shinohara Kazuo continues to influence and shape multiple facets of contemporary Japanese architecture.

Mohsen Mostafavi
Alexander and Victoria Wiley Professor of Design and Harvard University Distinguished Service Professor
Harvard Graduate School of Design

Shinohara Kazuo in his Yokohama atelier, ca. 1993. Photo by Futagawa Yukio

TK

Shinohara Kazuo in Tanikawa House, ca. 1974. Photo by Taki Kōji

Introduction

Seng Kuan

Shinohara Kazuo created sublimely beautiful, purist houses that have reconfigured and enriched our understanding of domesticity, tradition, structure, scale, nature, and the city—the dwelling redefined as a space where meaning can be generated, based on a raw, private relationship between the inhabitant and the surrounding environment. Interest in Shinohara's work has been in steady ascendance in recent years, especially since his death in 2006 and the posthumous awarding of a Golden Lion at the 2010 Venice Architecture Biennale, which took him from being a cult figure for initiated connoisseurs to an architect who is now widely taught in schools around the world. As one surveys the state of architecture today, the aesthetic values he espoused and promoted with singular conviction appear more insightful and germane than ever.

Younger generations of Japanese architects, especially those who came of age after the collapse in 1991 of the so-called economic bubble, are indebted to Shinohara for new paths he forged and traversed in approaching the problems of form and context. In a similar manner, the appeal of Shinohara's architecture to young architects abroad lies in its potential for renewed faith in modernism after fatigue and disillusionment from the formal exuberances and moral relativism of recent decades.

Shinohara belonged to the remarkable generation of Japanese architects to come of age as Japan emerged from the trauma of war and began its course toward economic prosperity. Born in 1925, Shinohara began studying architecture at the Tokyo Institute of Technology (Tokyo Tech) in 1950, stayed on to join its architecture faculty, and remained until retirement from teaching in 1986. Having studied mathematics before turning to architecture and therefore being slightly older in age than Kikutake Kiyonori, Maki Fumihiko, Isozaki Arata, and Hara Hiroshi, Shinohara was nonetheless part of that cohort of Japanese architects and engaged in the same intense discursive confrontations with modernity and tradition and between the house and the city, helping to establish Japan as one of the foremost centers of international modernism of the last half century. Shinohara's many aphoristic pronouncements, such as "A house is a work of art" and "Inscribe eternity in space," represented a distinct vertex in the topography of modern Japanese architectural thought. Shinohara's key tenets, especially those from his early career, were often critiques of Japan's prevailing architectural practices and ideology, especially the strain of techno-rationalism centered at the University of Tokyo with Metabolism as its most emblematic offshoot. Throughout the 1960s he sharpened his polemical stance with concepts like house as art, eternity in space, autonomy of the architect, superfluous space, and symbolic space. While these ideas may appear contretemps to the ethos of postwar Japan's developmentalist economy and the bureaucratic state, the validity of Shinohara's architecture came into focus as the logic of growth and top-down organization, encapsulated in the architectural excesses of the 1980s, came to its sudden and disastrous close.

Most secondary literature on Shinohara has until now focused on a handful of the most iconic houses, especially House in White (1966), Tanikawa House (1974), and House in Uehara (1976), often presenting them as distinct, one-off phenomena by an elusive and mercurial architect. While Shinohara's writings are widely understood to be an integral part of his creative strategy—as Okuyama Shin-ichi's chapter in this volume addresses—even in their Japanese originals the vocabulary and language, always employed with precision and placed in a structured framework, are often deemed abstruse and inaccessible. Translating these terms faithfully and accurately has indeed been one of the major challenges of this project. Building on a series of archival exhibitions and symposia, the collection of new scholarly essays and translations of Shinohara's key texts included in this book reframes Shinohara's architectural achievements in terms of his oeuvre as a whole and situates them in the broader cultural and social contexts in Japan and globally. The inclusion of institutional-scale projects of the Fourth Style, which have been largely overlooked until now, is crucial to establishing Shinohara's insistence on the equivalation between the house and the city. More pointedly, the three key historiographical themes this volume attempts to address are (1) continuity and change through Shinohara's four successive styles; (2) a mathematical framework in his spatial imagination; and (3) his engagement with artists as clients and collaborators.

CONTINUITY AND CHANGE

A major historiographical contention in studying Shinohara concerns the significance of the four successive styles, whether shifts between the ordinal numbers represented more disruption or more coherence. As Shinohara pursued distinct formal, technological, and even ideological strategies in each of the four styles, the individual styles invariably attract their own constituencies and followers. Those interested in a more overt dialogue with Japanese tradition, executed with great finesse and elegance, are naturally drawn to the First Style, whereas others seeking forceful structural expressions tend to focus on the Third. Each of the styles also encompasses a significant span of time—a decade or more with the exception of the Second—and bears the imprint of the broader context of its era.

Several essays in this volume, especially those by Tsukamoto Yoshiharu and Shiozaki Taishin, underscore the coherence in Shinohara's creative process, which specifically allows for different formal or even conceptual approaches. Tsukamoto describes a series of matrices, inherent in Shinohara's method, as ontological spaces where specific design solutions can occur. Shiozaki's chapter examines the dialogue between the earthen slope in two of Shinohara's works, the famous Tanikawa House and the unrealized mountain cabin for his own family, which are separated by almost thirty years.

While Shinohara addressed the issue of style, or *yōshiki* in Japanese in his earliest writings, this nomenclature came with the Third Style, which emerged in the mid-1970s. He claims to have been inspired by Pablo Picasso's periodization, the blue and the rose, and so on. For Shinohara the significance of style is rooted in the potential of a clear, rigorous framework of operation: "The creation of any style will axiomatically encompass any force that is opposed to it and [the result] is the consequence of the struggle to resolve that opposition."[1] It is part of an ongoing process, an act that provides fresh nourishment to past achievements and affords the possibility of claiming as one's own some uncharted territory of the future. Interspersed throughout this volume are image folios of Shinohara's works. These drawings, sketches, and photographs are organized essentially chronologically, according to progression of the styles. Before delving into the thematic issues, it may be useful to introduce the key characteristics of the four styles here.

> "I would like for the houses I make to stand on this earth forever."
>
> —"A Theory of Residential Architecture," 1967[2]

THE FIRST STYLE

Shinohara's First Style is an exercise in conversing with Japan's architectural tradition, distilling compositional concepts such as frontality and division from his studies of prehistoric pit dwellings, *minka* commoner houses, and pedigreed *shoin*-style buildings like Katsura Villa and Jikō-in. Spanning one and a half decades, the First Style was the longest of the four phases. The first house in this series, House in Kugayama (1954), reveals a rudimentary interest in Ludwig Mies van der Rohe and response to prevailing attitudes toward tradition as shown in contemporary works of Tange Kenzō and Shinohara's teacher Seike Kiyoshi. Later works such as House in White and Suzushō House (1968) are far more abstract, as Shinohara turned to more symbolic aspects of space-making. The period also coincided with the peak of Metabolism's popularity as he countered with a rhetoric of permanence, expansiveness, irrationality, and the emotive desires for dwelling.

> "I believe the world flows ceaselessly through the small spaces of the house."
>
> —"Beyond Symbol Spaces," 1971[3]

THE SECOND STYLE

For a brief few years between The Uncompleted House (1970) and Prism House (1974), Shinohara explored a series of formal and semantic themes, turning his focus to a new reductive, formalist approach and appearing to favor a system based on a series of abstract operative terms. The rigorous geometry of Shinohara's Second Style emerged out of House of White's cubic volume, and the idea of fissure can be found in the interstitial space between North and South Houses in Hanayama (1965, 1968). The tension between expansiveness and divisions that defined the First Style gave way to sequences of movement and volumes that are choreographed with an almost baroque theatricality. Narrow double-height crevices lead into light-filled courtyards shimmering in bronze-colored walls. These changes also call for different representational tools, notably emphasis on axonometric drawings and new photographic techniques.

The Second Style was the briefest of the four styles, but the works from this period gave Shinohara his first major professional recognition and established his appeal to a rising generation of architects. In 1972 the annual prize from the Architectural Institute of Japan (AIJ), regarded as the most prestigious in Japan, was awarded to "the series of houses from The Uncompleted House onward." Prior to Shinohara, the only other occasion on which the AIJ awarded its top prize to private residences occurred seventeen years before, to the works of his teacher Seike Kiyoshi. The timing of this public recognition of Shinohara's architecture, following Osaka Expo '70 and the student protests of 1968–69, also signaled a profound shift in the discursive context of Japan's aesthetic culture.

> "In the city, the act of traversing has literal basic functions. I use traversing as a method of thinking simultaneously of the city and its antipode, the house."
>
> —"When Naked Space Is Traversed," 1976[4]

THE THIRD STYLE

In his design brief for a country house, written in verse, client Tanikawa Shuntarō described a summer room as "church for a pantheist." Architecture is reduced to its most basic terms, like a geometric tent that drapes over raw, sloping earth. The 45-degree pitch in the roof and column struts clash with the gentler incline of the ground plane, resulting in a deeply unsettling space inside. In the Third Style, Shinohara pushed the dialogue between the inhabitant and the spatial environment to new levels of intensity, as a series of bare, brute confrontations. The equivalation (*dōichishi*) of the city and the house, seeing them in identical terms, that first emerged in the discrete and interpenetrating volumes of the Second Style is now fully developed. During this period Shinohara made extended journeys abroad. Traveling through these foreign lands, he was drawn to the rigors of the urban environment—the bodies and movement of people as formal elements that constitute, in their aggregate, space itself. Nakedness is to dispense with everything that obfuscates and confounds the basic ideas and shapes underneath.

> "The greatest probability for anarchy to produce vitality and liveliness occurs when buildings designed and produced on the basis of the most advanced technology of the age and replete with totally decorous beauty submerged in the planlessness of street."
>
> —"Towards Architecture," 1981[5]

THE FOURTH STYLE AND MODERNNEXT

Beginning in the 1980s Shinohara took on a series of larger-scale, institutional commissions. At the same time he came to embrace more overtly the generative potential of urban chaos, which he first commented on in the 1960s during his First Style. The pairing of Centennial Hall at Tokyo Tech and his own house in Yokohama collectively manifest his idea of the "space machine" unmediated in its power and logic as a fighter jet. Shinohara's rising notoriety abroad, with solo exhibitions traveling through Europe and North America beginning in 1979 and teaching appointments at Yale University and the Technical University of Vienna, led him to a series of international design competitions. These often more expansive site conditions yielded designs that play with basic geometric forms, in contrast with the complex programs within.

This belated opportunity to intervene on an urban scale allowed Shinohara to realize fully his nuanced attitude toward the city. While this position was partly informed by his travels abroad, to Africa, the Americas, and Europe, it was also rooted in his earliest memories of suburban life in Tokyo, with his childhood home located in the environs of Shibuya Station. In an essay published in the journal *Kenchiku bunka* in 1988, Shinohara further introduced the term "ModernNext." As a counterpoint to postmodernism, ModernNext is a commentary on the "contemporary enormous village" that Tokyo had ballooned into, as the scale and intensity of urban activity reached unprecedented heights. ModernNext is a decisively forward-looking attitude. In the same way tradition formed the basis of innovation for the First Style, chaos and randomness are to instigate a new vitality for architecture and the city. The essay is translated into English in its entirety for this volume.

SHINOHARA AS MATHEMATICIAN

Shinohara Kazuo was first trained in mathematics at Tokyo College of Physics.[6] He turned to architecture in the immediate postwar years after a poignant moment of encounter with Tōshōdai-ji, one of the great ancient temples of Nara. Shinohara indeed looked back to mathematics for much of the architectural vocabulary he developed over time: division, transversality, discreteness, set theory, and chaos are the most salient appropriations. It is tempting for those in the Anglo-American world, where the writings of Rudolf Wittkower and Colin Rowe are widely taught, to draw parallels with the work of Andrea Palladio. This hypothesis becomes even more compelling as we consider Shinohara's houses from the Second Style, abstract spaces such as The Uncompleted House and Shino House (1970), which give a hint of sympathy with the Renaissance master. In another fragment of this superficial affinity, the Institute for Architectural and Urban Studies (IAUS) in New York hosted Shinohara's first solo exhibition in the United States in 1981. The title of Shinohara's 1964 essay, "The autonomy of house design,"[7] would have appealed to IAUS's leadership. Still, Shinohara was not overtly driven by Kantian aesthetics, rather he was speaking entirely within the context of Japan's postwar construction industry. Using the term *shutaisei*[8] to stand for autonomy, Shinohara referred to such precepts as freedom from urban master plans, avoidance of too much attention to site context, expansiveness, and independence from the client. More provocatively, the essay suggests that the realities of everyday life render detailed spatial planning of domestic interiors pointless; the architect's strategy should be to elevate design to abstraction and pursue beauty in the realm of fictive spaces, citing Mies's Farnsworth House as an example.

There is no record of Shinohara referring to the work of Palladio, nor that of Wittkower or Rowe. In the late 1950s, as Shinohara was developing his theory of Japanese residential tradition as based on principles of division and frontality, he looked to the Western tradition for comparison and contrast.[9] As he was mainly interested in defining certain cultural and formal archetypes, such as pit dwellings and elevated granaries, as the origins of the Japanese tradition, he referred to Tragic Poet's House and House of Pansa in Pompeii and even older houses of Priene and Olynthus. The archetypical Western example from the early modern period Shinohara cites is Montacute House, one of the so-called prodigy houses from Elizabethan England.

Shinohara makes no pronounced effort toward an absolute, "fictive" idea of natural order and mathematical beauty. His very first published writing was titled "A critique of the Modulor" stating that the modern age of atomic energy operates on abstract mathematics, whereas ratio-based theories based on natural observations like the golden ratio or Fibonacci sequence have little to contribute.[10] In his final book of architectural theory, *Toward a Super-Big Numbers Set City* (2001), Shinohara obliquely addressed the issue of architectural harmony in the musical sense—the topic of Wittkower's famous chapter in *Architectural Principles in the Age of Humanism* that situated Palladio's proportions in sixteenth-century musical theory.[11] In praising twentieth-century advances in atonal music, Shinohara saw the same beauty in contemporary Tokyo, as the cacophonous, atonal manifestation of its underlying confusion and turbulences.[12] As a mathematician, Shinohara embraced the irrationality (*higōriteki*) of things around him as a necessary condition, but also employed mathematical tools to come to terms with these realities. Transversality (*ōdansei*) is the most powerful of these tools. It is the cutting across of different lines, spaces, and ordering systems, producing fragments and sections, but transversals also describe moments of intersection. In House under High-Voltage Lines (1981) we see this transversal vividly captured in the two swooping curves in the sky.

ARCHITECTURE AND ART

When Shinohara made the pronouncement in 1962 that "a house is a work of art," it would have been immediately apparent to Japan's architectural community that the antagonist was the techno-rationalism of the mainstream construction industry. In the postwar period Shinohara was hardly alone in recognizing the importance of working with allied disciplines in the fine arts—painting, sculpture, poetry, drama, film, and so forth.[13] In 1949 the Shinseisaku Art Society expanded its membership to welcome architects, including Taniguchi Yoshirō, who was the éminence grise of Tokyo Tech; Tange Kenzō; and even Ikebe Kiyoshi, renowned for minimum dwelling prototypes for industrialized mass production. Throughout the 1950s, both Tange and Shinohara's teacher Seike Kiyoshi were also highly active in exhibition designs, working alongside other avant-garde practitioners in the arts.

Shinohara was more successful than his predecessors and peers in cultivating his artistic collaborators as patrons. This publication features interviews with some of the most loyal among Shinohara's remarkable coterie of clients: poet Tanikawa Shuntarō (Tanikawa Houses of 1958 and 1974), painter Nomiyama Gyōji (Sea Stairway, House in Itoshima), and the widow and son of photographer Ōtsuji Kiyoshi (House with an Earthen Floor, House in Uehara). As Christian Kerez's conversation with Tanikawa Shuntarō records, Tanikawa's father had originally suggested the eminent Taniguchi for his son's house, but was in turn referred to the slightly younger Seike, and the younger still Shinohara. Tanikawa, Ōtsuji, and Nomiyama all commissioned Shinohara with both a house in the city and one in the country. Shinohara's clients indulged him with extraordinary liberties in reinventing domestic arrangements. Many of them are considered *bunkajin,* or people of culture, referring to a broad spectrum of well-educated individuals engaged in the arts, writing, or education. Shinohara also maintained a long friendship with painter and stage set designer Asakura Setsu. Their collaborations, beyond the house Shinohara designed for her in 1964, also included *mingei*-inspired designs on the shōji screens in Umbrella House (1961) and a two-person exhibition held in 1964 on their individual works. The identities of these clients are sometimes imprinted onto Shinohara's designs in subtle ways, as in the shimmering bronze-color wallpaper in Shino House. Its owner was a publisher of encyclopedias.

One of the hallmarks of Japan's success in sustaining consistently high-quality architecture is the robustness of the infrastructure of architectural production and discourse—an extraordinary plethora of magazines, schools, design competitions, and professional organizations that defined and reinforced a strong community. Despite Shinohara's reputation as a severe personality, he actively participated in these professional activities, not only through writings and publication of his personal work, but also by joining and hosting roundtables and other forums of discussion. This generous exception to his otherwise introvert demeanor was especially evident even in his later, post–Tokyo Tech years in bringing together younger generations.

As the interviews make clear, the relationship between the architect and clients was not one of conventional patronage, as we understand princely commissions of the Renaissance or those from bourgeois industrialists in the nascent days of modernism. Despite the paucity of specific design briefs, there was no lack of communication from these clients in conveying their beliefs and aspirations. The roundtable discussion translated for this volume documents a forum moderated by Shinohara. His clients were his peers and partners, and these houses were modestly scaled, typically located in new emerging suburbs in Tokyo's periphery. What emerges from placing each of these houses in the context of its owners' lives is a remarkable view into not only this *bunkajin* community as it evolved in postwar Japan but also Tokyo's very urbanism.

With few exceptions, the images of Shinohara's houses presented in this volume are period photographs, meticulously staged with few visible traces of domestic life. Shinohara characterized architectural photographs as *false images* of spaces, but he noted that once we are accustomed to their conventions, "we are able to comprehend the true architectural spaces behind the *false* images."[14] Shinohara saw this true architectural space as a fictive space that becomes the new level of *reality.* Nomiyama Gyōji echoed this sentiment in the interview featured in this book: before he moved to France in 1952 he thought it was "a land that is not where humans lived" but existed only as the place of paintings by Paul Cézanne and Henri Matisse. Shinohara's clients were his collaborators in this act of fiction writing.

LEGACY

In 1979 the idea of a "Shinohara School" was first floated in the monographic issue of *SD* devoted to Shinohara's houses. The column "Notes on architecture in Japan" refers to Sakamoto Kazunari, Hasegawa Itsuko, and Itō Toyoo as representing a new generation in the propagation of Shinohara's architecture. All three were in their thirties at the time and had received much critical attention for their recent works.[15] Under the collective pen name Gruppo Specchio, the column was written by a handful of graduate students from the University of Tokyo, most notably Takeyama Kiyoshi Sey and Kuma Kengo. They were known for sharp, witty, and occasionally scathing commentaries, and one cannot help but suspect that the label "Shinohara School" was proposed with a little tongue-in-cheek, as its authors anxiously contemplated their own professional futures.[16]

Four decades after Gruppo Specchio's initial conjecture, we may ask: What would a Shinohara School look like today? Certainly Sakamoto, Hasegawa, and Itō, as well as other protégés of Shinohara, have cultivated their own followers, and different generations of architects, from different countries, have found lessons from Shinohara's work. Many Japanese architects now attribute the ideas of architects as auteurs and houses as art as truisms that were established almost single-handedly by Shinohara. Such adulation is perhaps overly enthusiastic, but there is no doubt that Shinohara was one of the true masters of the past half century, standing as a beacon of a particular conviction in space-making that remains relevant today. As Shibuya undergoes another round of transformation, there is no better time to revisit Shinohara and take a closer look.

1 Shinohara Kazuo, "Daisan no yōshiki," *Shinkenchiku* vol. 52, no. 1 (January 1977): 221–25. Translation used here from English version, "The Third Style, 1977," in *Kazuo Shinohara: Houses*, ed. David B. Stewart, Okuyama Shin-ichi, and Shiozaki Taishin, *2G*, no. 58/59 (2011): 268.

2 Shinohara Kazuo, "A Theory of Residential Architecture," *The Japan Architect* (October 1967): 39–45.

3 Shinohara Kazuo, "Beyond Symbol Spaces: An Introduction to Primary Spaces as Functional Spaces," *The Japan Architect* (April 1971): 81–88.

4 Shinohara Kazuo, "When Naked Space Is Traversed," *The Japan Architect* (February 1976): 64–72.

5 Shinohara Kazuo, "Towards Architecture," *The Japan Architect* (September 1981): 30–35.

6 The same school, now known as Tokyo University of Science, established its own architecture program in 1962.

7 Shinohara Kazuo, "Jūtaku sekkei no shutaise," *Kenchiku*, no. 44 (April 1964): 52–55.

8 Typically the term "*jiritsusei*" is used to stand for autonomy in the Kantian sense.

9 These studies were presented at successive meetings of the Architectural Institute of Japan and subsequently published in its bulletins: "Kūkan no bunkatsu to renketsu: Nihon kenchiku hōhō (7)," (June 1960); "Kūkan bunkatsu kara mita heimen kōsei: Nihon kenchiku hōhō (8)," (October 1960); "Seiō no heimen kōsei tono taihi" (October 1961).

10 Shinohara Kazuo, "Mojyurōru hihan," *Nihon kenchiku gakkai Kantō shibu dai 17 kai kenkyū happyōkai* (February 1955): 19–22.

11 Rudolf Wittkower, *Architectural Principles in the Age of Humanism* (1949; repr., New York: W.W. Norton, 1971), 132–42.

12 Shinohara Kazuo, *Chō taisū shūgo toshi he* "(Tokyo: A.D.A. EDITA, 2001), 127.

13 Seng Kuan, "Unity of the Arts at Sōgetsu Kaikan," in *Kenzō Tange: Architecture for the World*, ed. Seng Kuan and Yukio Lippit (Zurich: Lars Müller Publisher, 2012), 127–41.

14 Shinohara Kazuo, "The Mechanism of *Fiction* Never Stops Functioning, Exchange of Letters with Jacques Herzog and Pierre de Meuron," trans. Watanabe Hiroshi, *SD*, no. 401 (February 1998): 115 (Shinohara's italics).

15 Guruppo supekkio, "Shinohara sukūru no kenchiku," *SD*, no. 172 (January 1979): 223–28. The works cited in the column include Sakamoto's Machiya in Daita and House in Kumano-Nagareyama, Hasegawa's House in Kakio and Stationery Shop in Yaizu, and Itō's PMT Building and Hotel D. Of the trio, Sakamoto was the only one formally educated at Tokyo Tech. Hasegawa joined Shinohara's lab as a research student after working for Kikutake Kiyonori, whereas Itō lacked any formal affiliation with Tokyo Tech.

16 Takeyama Kiyoshi, "Kenchiku sekkei jimusho to iu 'ba' wo tsukuru," *traverse shinkenchiku-gaku kenkyū*, no. 14 (October 2013): 72–79.

Shinohara Kazuo, Cubic Forest, Kawasaki, Kanagawa Prefecture, 1971. Photos by Christian Kerez

Thoughts on Seven Houses I Have Visited

Christian Kerez

1 Kurosaka Akio, ed., "Anthology: Shinohara Kazuo, 1958–78," *SD*, no. 172 (January 1979): 81.

> "If there were only space for one small room, I would start by creating a room for the man and a room for the woman."
> —Shinohara Kazuo[1]

1 CUBIC FOREST, 1971
HOUSE IN HIGASHI-TAMAGAWA, 1973

In Le Corbusier's Unité d'Habitation the double-height living space is present in every part of each residential unit. Even the low, one-storey bedrooms on the far end of long, corridor-like extensions of the gallery relate to this living space and thus to the view into the distance beyond the double-height balcony façade.

The double-height room in Shinohara Kazuo's Cubic Forest, in contrast, appears introverted and self-contained; it is connected with the one-storey rooms only at its most remote corners, through sparse openings in the wall. And it is only here that this double-height spatial figure affords a view outward. This two-storey hall is configured as a sequence of three distinct spaces, allowing the unusual height of the room to be perceived in different ways. A small, narrow vertical corridor links two other spaces that can be experienced and described in opposite ways. In the middle of the first, shaft-like square hall's ceiling is a skylight, emphasizing its centrality and verticality. One would ordinarily assume that it is the center of the building, but it is actually here that visitors enter the house, abruptly and unexpectedly, because the front door is flush with the wall and thus entirely casual. The main living space at the end of the sequence extends through the entire width of the building. The solid walls lend the room a sense of scalelessness. It appears now above all to be big but not primarily tall. Only at the outermost edge do window-doors afford a view of the garden in front of the house. While the openings in the entrance hall have been cut out of a wall, the fixed glazing and the window-doors in this living space are set off from the façade and break up the corners of the building. These are not placed flat and pictorial, like the window and door openings in the entrance hall, but rather are sculptural and three-dimensional in design. This cutout is continued as a door opening inside the house and leads to the adjoining kitchen and work rooms. The stairs up to the bedrooms are right next to the main entrance at the other end of the house.

All the other rooms in this one-family house form the negative, as it were, of the inner spatial figure and the outer sculptural façade. The features of these curious, ramified rooms are the opposite of those in the main room. They are low and irregular. They have no clear beginning, no end, and no center. Yet it is these rooms that turn this home into a complex architectural entity based on complementary correspondences. In contrast to the uniform architectural idea underlying the above described flats in the Unité d'Habitation, a duality is generated by the unusual height of the living room. Here the architectural unity is based on spaces that correspond perfectly through mutual opposition. This relationship between a central double-height room and the adjoining rooms is repeatedly questioned and redefined in a series of houses, especially in this phase of Shinohara's oeuvre.

The main room in House in Higashi-Tamagawa seems less spacious and extensive than it is elongated and narrow. The double-height area of the house no longer figures as a

sequence of individual rooms but rather as one single, narrow, deep room that traverses the entire building. This narrow room appears fragmented, perhaps even somewhat incidental in shape. It slopes gently down to the garden, widening somewhat, and is slightly bent or rather broken toward the side. The actual living area is only one storey high. At the garden level, the tall, deep hall extends sideways to the outer wall and pushes its way behind the staircase back into the center of the building. The low living space is so directly linked to the double-height hall that it seems to be a niche-like extension of it. The kitchen that closes off the living-dining area is placed directly next to the entrance but cannot be entered from there. Here the double-height room is purely a place of transit. All the usable rooms are one storey high and located on either side of this hall. They are all clearly distinct in their relationship to the hall and in their contours. This informal arrangement also stands in extreme contrast to the symmetrical placement of the smaller rooms in Cubic Forest and to the outline of a perfect square. In this new house, a simple figure-ground reading is no longer possible. The completely open staircase rises in opposite direction to that of the front door. While the stairs are hidden in the previous example, here they demonstrably disrupt this central passage, and deep wall jambs emphasize the connections between the central main room and the neighboring smaller rooms. Meanwhile the doors to the street and the garden are both much taller than users would require and completely closed, so that the main room remains entirely introverted. As visitors enter the house from the garden or the street, the narrow passage opens up in its entire staggered depth, like a stage set. While the smaller rooms in Cubic Forest face away from the main room and only afford a view of it from the rear, here the smaller rooms directly facing the main room form a front view, illuminated by a sequence of skylights and without connection to the space outside.

While both buildings engage with a double-height main room in a private home, the difference between them does not represent a variation on a theme. Rather, architectural elements following a new architectural subject matter have been reassembled in a totally different setting, somewhat like the components of a scientific experiment. This radical modification of the basic premises of an architectural theme cannot be repeated ad libitum. Therefore, the end of one phase, or "style," as Shinohara named it, and the beginning of a new one are foreseeable, systemically imminent, and not biographically determined.

In Shinohara's buildings, the relationship between the rooms is much more important than the individual rooms themselves. Publications often show only fractions of a building. These parts have clearly been selected and assembled by Shinohara. The complexity of the extraordinarily dense spatial experience furnished by his buildings is rendered sectionwise as a diagrammatic translation. It provides an extremely indirect and rudimentary hint of what it is like to move about inside his houses and experience almost simultaneously the differences that distinguish these rooms.

2 TANIKAWA HOUSE, 1974
HOUSE IN ASHITAKA, 1977

The mighty roof at poet Tanikawa Shuntarō's home spans the earth in the middle of a forest. It does not seem as if this

Shinohara Kazuo, House in Higashi-Tamagawa, Setagaya Ward, Tokyo, 1973. Photos by Christian Kerez

main room is even meant to be entered, despite its setting of walls, windows, and roof. The quality and feel of the floor have absolutely nothing in common with the floors of stamped earth found in traditional farmhouses or in some of Shinohara's other projects. Meanwhile the slanted plane of the slightly sloping terrain reinforces the impression that all the architectural elements frame only an untouched portion of the landscape, without making the terrain as such usable.

The roof over this enclosed slope is symmetrical, corresponding to its construction of central wooden supports with lateral buttresses. This symmetry necessarily increases the height of the façade on the downhill (north) side so that it is exactly twice as high as the façade on the uphill (south) side. With their sturdy, cross-shaped wind braces (made out of wooden beams), the wooden frames lie on top of each other on the downhill side and next to each other uphill, thus underscoring their relationship. Only in the area of the smaller rooms does the gutter run as close to the ground as it does higher up on the slope. To maintain the 45-degree slope of the roof, the living area has been correspondingly lengthened in the downhill direction. With its small rooms, it looks more like an extension of the building.

The actual rooms for living, working, and sleeping occupy one of the four bays defined by the roof supports and its braces. These living quarters—the home—take up only a small part of the overall ground floor area. The façades under the gutter are entirely glazed, while the gable façades are largely closed walls. In side view, all the slopes of the space where neither floor nor ceiling is horizontal are revealed.

The contrast between the multilevel main room and the one-storey living quarters is taken to extremes—on one hand, through differences in scale, and on the other, through the juxtaposition of the raw, unfinished character of the main room and the comfortable livability of the private spaces.

The plot of land in the middle of a forest does not make the least impression of designated building land. There are no fences, no access driveway, and not even a clearly marked path. There is no front yard, no garden in this part of the forest, only this one, large roof. The forest floor consists of dark, sandy earth. Cleared of underbrush, ferns, and all other vegetation, the building's interior has a geometry that is flattened into a uniform black mass, into an inclined plane—all of this becomes part of the architecture itself. This existential reduction turns the surroundings into an extraordinary experience of architectural space.

There are hardly any site plans in the books that Shinohara has published of his buildings. Nonetheless, some of them refer explicitly to their surroundings. House in Itoshima (1976) frames the view of an island, while other houses are called House under High-Voltage Lines (1981) or House on a Curved Road (1978). In these cases, phenomena beyond the actual buildings become an architectural spatial experience in an entirely different way from what a conventional contextual design can offer. In retrospect, House in Higashi-Tamagawa could be viewed in the same sense. The main room describes the path from the street to the garden, and openings in the interior façade allow direct view from all the rooms onto this interior space, which is illuminated by several skylights. In this

way, the path from the street to the garden is exhibited, so to speak, and the relationship between street and garden is revealed only upon opening the doors, while the house on its confined plot does not permit any lateral views and catches only minimal light.

At Tanikawa House, context becomes architecture. Describing it is superfluous not only because the building was designed independent of its literal and incidental appearance but also because the context is stored and contained in the architectural space of the building.

In contrast to the light, almost vernacular wooden construction of the house in the middle of a forest, the roof of House in Ashitaka is monumental and heavy. And in contrast to the thin sheet-metal cladding at Tanikawa House, the large concrete panels imprinted by plywood shuttering create an impression of the monumental. The lateral forces of the hip roof are restrained by a powerful tension ring. Due to the deflecting of the lateral forces, the entire interior does not need any load-bearing or bracing support and could theoretically remain completely empty.

This monumental roof reaching down to the ground floor becomes an elemental event in its suburban environment of predominantly two-storey houses with small gabled roofs, most likely prescribed by a zoning ordinance to preserve a rural appearance. Even the elevation of the ground floor is but an elementary gesture to lift the roof. The ground floor consists only of discrete wall stelae, and the interval distance between these wall slabs is exactly the same as their own width. It thus appears that the sole purpose of the ground floor is to elevate the monumental body of the roof. The glazing can be pushed behind the concrete slabs. At night the windows can be covered from inside by white sliding panels that are barely distinguishable from the interior wall, and the glazing on the façade, which can otherwise contradict the building's archaic appearance, can thus be made to disappear from the inside at night and from the outside by day when the weather is beautiful.

This archaic gesture of reducing a one-family house to one single, monumental, pyramid-shaped roof is experienced in diametrically opposed ways in this home. One half of the house remains an empty, pure white room following the abstract shape of the exterior.

The private rooms that can be closed are not accessed directly from the main room as in other houses by Shinohara; instead, stairs and a long, circuitous corridor lead to these chambers. The corridor and all its doors establish a great sense of distance from the rooms of the family and of the community.

This half of the building in Ashitaka is subdivided in many different ways and leads a life of its own. A system of paths defines the assemblage of the rooms, and the kitchen belongs neither to the open nor to the subdivided area of the house. Placed in the exact center of the south façade, the front door opens into a small, narrow hall, behind which is the kitchen. In this way, access to the two halves of the building is mutually independent and completely equivalent.

Shinohara Kazuo, Tanikawa House, Naganohara, Gunma Prefecture, 1974. Photo by Christian Kerez

Shinohara Kazuo, House in Ashitaka, Numazu, Shizuoka Prefecture, 1977. Photo by Christian Kerez

While the living spaces in the house in the forest occupy a single section of the building between evenly placed roof supports, House in Ashitaka is divided into two halves: one empty, pure, and open, and the other consisting of many small, closed, irregular rooms. The effort made to create a unified, monumental shell is a prerequisite to linking two contrasting halves within one single building. In contrast, Tanikawa House's lightness, the additive character of its wooden construction, could also lead to interpreting the habitable section of the building as an extension. Complementary correspondences between the main room and the smaller rooms are found in most of Shinohara's buildings. Yet each time, this fundamental relationship between the main room and smaller rooms is articulated in a completely new and specific way.

One could predicate that the main room in Cubic Forest was the first to be defined and that the other, smaller rooms follow from it. The same could be said of House in Ashitaka. However, the gesture of exterior monumental unity and interior division into antithetical halves are mutually determinant, while the sculptural composition of the façade in Cubic Forest takes a stylistic approach in generating an entity and could be said to ignore the inner dichotomy. The building drawn earlier, Cubic Forest, embodies a more straightforward sense of unity in its design while the later building, in Ashitaka, represents an inextricable unity only in an ideational, conceptual sense. House in Ashitaka looks simpler although its underlying idea is much more complex. In the newer houses complementary correspondences are mutually determinant in a more holistic manner.

3 HOUSE WITH AN EARTHEN FLOOR, 1963
HOUSE IN WHITE, 1966

House with an Earthen Floor is a small weekend getaway. The sliding doors to the sleeping and living areas, which are covered with tatami mats, can be opened almost completely so that the entire house consists of a single room. Only the washing area behind the kitchen is fully enclosed into its own room. The two halves of the building, divided at the gable ridge, have contrasting characteristics. A wall of raw wooden planks divides the space on the lower area of stamped earth, with the open kitchen and closed bathroom placed behind it. This intervention adds an angular intrusion to the room so that it can no longer be taken in with a single glance. The tatami area, raised above a bench, is also divided. But the translucent sliding screens do not completely divide the room. In combination with the white panels of the wardrobe, they turn the room into a tranquil, completely enclosed and pure space.

The duality of Katsura Villa between garden design and architecture, ascribed by Tange Kenzō on the one hand to the Japanese archaic Jōmon period, and on the other to the classicist high culture of Yayoi,[2] is present in this house. Furthermore, the partition can be made to disappear almost entirely so that both halves of the room can be as much united as they can be separated. While in his projects Tange also hints at the two stylistic epochs in Japan, which are several centuries apart (although only in the contrast between surroundings and building or between shell and core), Shinohara Kazuo intimately interweaves these two aesthetic approaches by opening them up to each other, thus enabling them to be viewed back and forth in the same small room and under the same

2 Tange Kenzō, "Tradition and Creation in Japanese Architecture," in *Katsura: Tradition and Creation in Japanese Architecture*, ed. Tange Kenzō (New Haven, CT: Yale University Press, 1960), 14–36.

roof. The sliding panels are also a feature of the gable space, where they can barely be used. The bright, pure, raised room and the dark, earthy, irregular, and vernacular room determine each other through the division in the exact middle of the square floorplan different from any floorplan of a classic *minka*, where these two areas are placed side by side, more or less casually or pragmatically. While both houses are located in the outskirts of the highland resort town of Karuizawa, the way this building is subdivided by translucent shōji sliding screens is entirely different from the division of Tanikawa's weekend house described above. There the wall dividing the two parts of the house ends just under the roof and affords a view of the large hall from the upper-storey bedroom. A door connecting the two spaces is small and discreet, placed at the very bottom edge of the same wall. The distinction between primary and secondary rooms is, in turn, conspicuous and explicit. The division in House with an Earthen Floor, when the sliding screens are open, is typological and stylistic, while in the second case it is a solid division extending through the entire building, except for a few small recesses.

The division of House in White has still another, entirely different meaning. A wall divides the bedrooms from the living room, but it does not run through the middle of the building, exposing the central support like a surrealistic object in a high rectilinear room. The formal and structural connection with the pyramid-shaped roof above remains concealed in an attic space, and the slanted roof dominates the adjacent bedroom on the second floor. This bedroom is directly accessible from the main room as is the other bedroom underneath on the ground floor. The shape of the ground plan in this home is very similar to that of House with an Earthen Floor, both having a straight wall separating the house into living and sleeping areas. In one case the bedrooms are side-by-side; in the other they are stacked. The washroom and kitchen form a single body as in the house described above, but this body asserts an object-like presence in the large living room. Despite similarities in the geometry of the ground plan, the spatial experience here is entirely different. The compact body of the building is divided into varying spatial components—that is, it seems the small house is spatially fragmented, unlike in the previous case. These fragments show entirely different sections within the same simple overall volume. A long, narrow, almost corridor-like room lies next to the living room, which, being orthogonal, makes a very modernist impression, while the room above is dominated by the inclined roof, at the top of which there is a skylight. The basic division of this simple house has an abstractness that is underscored by the white, almost closed outside and inside walls—walls that reveal nothing about either their material or their construction and prompted the building's name. The fourth segment of the house, the garret, is not accessible.

Because of the irregular division, each of the three rooms at House in White relates to the simple volume of the building in a quite different way. Relations between rooms are in part misleading. The window placed exactly above the door leading to the ground-level bedroom is actually for the upper-level bedroom, which is accessible through the second door in the main room and via a steep staircase. Although it is the most important load-bearing element, the central support looks like a casually placed object. The remarkable span of living room ceiling and the canopy roof above are supported by hollow joists that remain hidden in the fourth, inaccessible room.

Shinohara Kazuo's attempt in his early work to derive basic architectural types from the vocabulary of a traditional style differs from the approach taken in later buildings where single elements of the architecture itself are subject to the same search for architectural basics. This syntax in his houses begins with the everyday, becomes abstract in a second series of experiments, and is subsequently reassembled anew.

Shinohara's writings are as much a part of his oeuvre as his buildings are. His texts do, of course, explore his work in multifarious ways, but they do not describe his buildings as such. They reflect questions that can be traced back to the designs of his buildings.

Many architectural phenomena such as frontality or division, which are given detailed theoretical attention in this example in order to describe the First Style, feature in all the later styles as well. In this sense, Shinohara's writings largely capture only individual aspects of his built work. As such, they are as constrained in their potential to convey a thorough understanding of his buildings as the photographs he selected.

4 HOUSE IN UEHARA, 1976

The ground floor of House in Uehara consists of an open carport, a photographic studio, and an adjoining darkroom with archive. Being almost flush with the wall, the supports on the ground floor disappear almost entirely in the three-part division of the simple, understated ground plan. Mighty struts are a monumental presence in the intimate living room above. The room-height diagonal columns on one side bear the load of the cantilevered building above the carport and are mirrored on the opposite side, while the adjacent, somewhat smaller pair of diagonal columns support the remaining part of the small house at the same right angle. For this reason the two pairs of buttresses differ in height and width. In contrast to these tall struts that dominate the entire room, the supports in the longitudinal direction are reinforced merely with small triangular ceiling discs. Only by truncating the size of these supports does it become possible to use this small house. As a result, the house is divided quite differently lengthwise and crosswise. The struts and supports on the plane of the façade step forward like pilasters, which gives them a strong sculptural presence in front of the white walls. They probably serve mainly to reinforce the slender concrete walls, and they complete the impression of a constructive thicket in which basically two freestanding supports with their mighty buttresses dominate the entire room, while all the other structural elements are subsumed into the peripheral walls. The differentiation of the supports and struts that emerges in this small house is taken to such extremes that not a single arrangement of struts is repeated on the top floor. In addition to this structural system, the photographer's studio on the ground floor and the living quarters above are distinguished by the spatial configuration and the arrangement of windows. While the division of rooms on the ground floor follows the placement of the supports, the dividing wall upstairs between sleeping and living area therefore retreats from the wide support; otherwise, it would not be possible to walk around it. Part of this setback has fixed glazing so that, for the second time, the wall is forcibly interrupted, and it acquires an object-like appearance from the side. The wall between the bedrooms is positioned in the middle of the house, on the axis of the two diagonal supports, but the symmetry in the niche is broken by the alternating bedroom doors and fixed room-height glazing on the sides and back of the niche.

The windows in the living quarters completely fill the triangular fields between struts and supports. In the living room, a single triangular window with fixed glazing affords a view of the street; the adjacent, symmetrically placed aluminum wing can be opened in summer. The monumental load-bearing structure is primarily illuminated from above, like a sculpture in the skylighted gallery of a museum. Large ceiling windows lie directly above the two staircases that connect the living room to the other floors. This eventful room can only be entered from above and below. The lower set of stairs ushers the outdoors into the interior living space, whereas the ladder to the upper floor is like a protrusion that extends the living space beyond the roof terrace.

The slight measurements of this small house underscore the rich, complex, spatial experience of all its architectural elements, juxtaposed in the smallest of spaces. This dense spatial experience has an intensity and simultaneity that would be deflected in a larger house.

In contrast to the diversity of openings in the living quarters, in the studio below the only window opens onto the carport, which becomes kind of a forecourt, with a staircase to the living quarters above. The division of this ground plan is as simple as the arrangement of the struts.

A self-supporting, vaulted attic space rises above the living quarters. Light in construction, it appears almost detached from the massive concrete construction underneath. Here a casual character is achieved with means that are entirely different from those on the ground floor. In that way, the eventful living area on the middle storey remains the center of this stacked building with its diversity of contrasting features.

The ground floor and the main room above, as well as the attic with the living area underneath, afford contrasting experiences of space, which determine each other at the same time, as in Shinohara's earlier buildings. The duality of the buildings in the earlier phase might be said to undergo multiplication or an increase in complexity. Here the density of spatial experience comes to a climax. House in Uehara does not belong to the Fourth Style but its object- and machine-like roof structure and the multiple storeys link it to that last phase of his architectural oeuvre. The formidable complexity of House in Uehara could be viewed as a prerequisite for transitioning to a larger scale, which preoccupied Shinohara Kazuo toward the end of his career.

This discussion of Shinohara's houses was first presented as part of the lecture series "Looking at Architecture, Describing Architecture" given at ETH Zurich in 2013–17. The author rewrote this text after a trip to Japan in spring 2020 that allowed for additional focus on the experience of four out of the seven houses. It will also be included in the forthcoming book *An Anthology of Space.*

Translated by Catherine Schelbert

Shinohara Kazuo, House in Uehara, Shibuya Ward, Tokyo, 1976. Photos by Christian Kerez

Shinohara Kazuo, House in Kugayama, Suginami Ward, Tokyo, 1954. Photo by Hirayama Chūji

The Small Japanese House

Seng Kuan

The small house (*shōjūtaku*) emerged in postwar Japan as one of the most important building types of architectural discourse and production. This is a surprising development, considering how Tange Kenzō and the Metabolist group first achieved notoriety internationally through their techno-rationalist, mass-based, and urban-scale visions.[1] Shinohara Kazuo worked solely in the single-family house type for the first three decades of his career, to the exclusion of institutional-scale work. This typological focus positioned him in diametric opposition to the Metabolists. Shinohara reinforced his outsider position through a series of polemical writings, most famously the declaration "A house is a work of art" made in 1962 at the height of the Metabolist boom.[2] As Shinohara strove to make clear, the single-family house (*jūtaku*) naturally belongs to the domain of art and is the outcome of authorship, as opposed to the factory (*kōjō*), which is to say the embodiment of a vast techno-industrial infrastructure behind it.

Following the two correlated trajectories of the *shōjūtaku* house type on the one hand, and the critical discourses of tradition on the other, this essay addresses the specific context in which Shinohara's engagement of houses began in the early 1950s. It recasts Shinohara's training in the laboratory of Seike Kiyoshi at the Tokyo Institute of Technology (Tokyo Tech), which had a unique focus on the single-family house type, and Shinohara's debut work, House in Kugayama of 1954, in the broader cultural debates and anxieties of its time. Shinohara emerged at the end of the decade having successfully reframed the terms of both *shōjūtaku* and tradition. Through a series of robust critical frameworks developed from his readings of architectural history and the contemporary city, Shinohara created entirely new paradigms of the modern house with significance that continues to reverberate to this day.

Shinohara's houses, particularly those belonging to the First Style in the 1950s and much of the '60s, were often compact. The two smallest were Umbrella House (1961) at 55 square meters and House with an Earthen Floor (1963) at 53.8 square meters. Others, such as the first Tanikawa House (1958) and House in Komae (1960), were somewhat larger, ranging between 61 and 62 square meters, respectively. In other words, the *shōjūtaku* type was a key operative model for Shinohara, especially in the First Style, even if he also took on larger projects contemporaneously and applied similar compositional principles without regard to building size, as in the case of House in Chigasaki (1960), which was unusually large at 235.6 square meters. The immediate cause of the *shōjūtaku* type's postwar boom was in a series of rationing laws, which initially limited the floor area for a family of five to 12 *tsubo,* or about 40 square meters (1 *tsubo* equals approximately 3.3 square meters).[3] This restriction was relaxed to 15 *tsubo,* or just under 50 square meters in 1948, which became the standard used during a particularly intense phase of architectural experimentation and theorization in the postwar period.[4] The journal *Shinkenchiku,* in a precursor to the well-known international residential design competitions, organized a series of concours beginning in 1947 on the 15-*tsubo* type. Yoshizaka Takamasa, Seike Kiyoshi, and Ikebe Kiyoshi were some of the protagonists of this activity and served as juries for many of these design competitions.

1 Metabolism was an architectural movement based on the idea that there are natural and innate life-cycles in the different constituent parts of buildings and cities. It was launched at the World Design Conference held in Tokyo in 1960, with architects Ōtaka Masato, Kikutake Kiyonori, Maki Fumihiko, Kurokawa Kishō, critic Kawazoe Noboru, and designers Awazu Kiyoshi and Ekuan Kenji represented in the manifesto pamphlet. Tange Kenzō and Arata Isozaki were also closely related to the group. Tange, Maki, Isozaki, and Kurokawa were the earliest Japanese architects to achieve global acclaim and recognized by international awards such as the RIBA Gold Medal and the Pritzker Architecture Prize.

2 Shinohara Kazuo, "Jūtaku wa geijutsu de aru," *Shinkenchiku* vol. 37, no. 5 (May 1962): 77–78.

3 For an excellent overview of the sociological aspects of housing in postwar Japan, see Ann Waswo, *Housing Postwar Japan: A Social History* (London: RoutledgeCurzon, 2003).

4 Namba Kazuhiko, *Sengo modanizumu kenchiku no kyokuhoku: Ikebe Kiyoshi shiron* (Tokyo: Shōkokusha, 1999), 47–72; Hayakawa Masao, "Sengo," in *Jūtaku kindai shi: jūtaku to kagu*, ed. Ōta Hirotarō (Tokyo: Yūsankaku, 1969), 151–8[illegible].

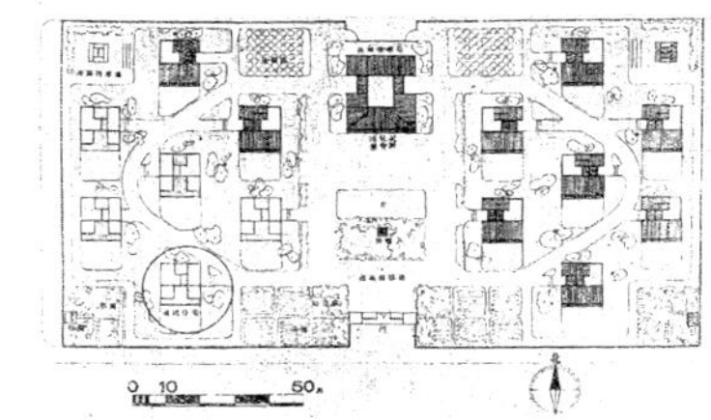

5 See Sekino Masaru, *Nihon jūtaku shōshi* (Tokyo: Sagami shobo, 1942).

6 Dōjunkai was founded in the aftermath of the Great Kantō earthquake of 1923 as a quasi-official agency to help provide emergency shelters and housing relief. The agency soon started experimenting with reinforced-concrete apartment blocks that would be more resilient to fire and earthquake and appealed to the new urban, salaried class. See Ueda Makoto, *Shūgō jūtaku monogatari* (Tokyo: Misuzu, 2004). In the 1930s Dōjunkai was mainly sponsoring research projects related to housing. An important outcome was the publication of a compendium of Western residential district designs: Kishida Hideto and Takayama Eika, *Gaikoku ni okeru jūtaku shikichiwari ruireishū* (Tokyo: Zaidan hōjin dōjunkai, 1936).

7 Internationale Kongresse für Neues Bauen, ed., *Seikatsu saishōgen no jūtaku*, trans. Tsuge Yoshio (Tokyo: Kōseisha shobo, 1930).

8 Timothy Benton, "Le Corbusier and the Loi Loucheur," *AA Files, no. 7* (1984): 54–60.

The *shōjūtaku* small-house type, which is closely associated with the postwar economic recovery and expansion of the middle class in Japan, has its formal and technological origins in *kokumin jūtaku,* or people's housing, developed at the height of the war effort.[5] *Kokumin jūtaku* itself evolved out of a somewhat accidental convergence of the European concept of *Existenzminimum* (minimum dwellings), prefabrication technology, and the culture of *minka* rural commoner housing, all of which were conditioned by exigencies of the war. This focus had the establishment's blessing, especially from Uchida Yoshizō, the éminence grise of Japan's architectural community. His laboratory at Tokyo Imperial University doubled as the design office for Dōjunkai in the recovery efforts after the Great Kantō Earthquake and produced a series of collective housing prototypes using reinforced concrete toward the end of the 1920s.[6] These efforts by Japanese architects in the prewar period resonated with the call sounded in Europe for a new approach to mass housing as advanced at the second conference of the International Congresses for Modern Architecture (CIAM) held in Frankfurt in 1929. A key member of Uchida's team, Tsuge Yoshio, managed to publish a Japanese translation of *Die Wohnung für das Existenzminimum* in May 1930, barely five months after that of the original report in German.[7] More important still was the involvement of Maekawa Kunio, who graduated from Tokyo Imperial University and worked in Le Corbusier's atelier in 1928–29. During his time in Paris, Maekawa was assigned to the Maisons Loucheur project, a residential prototype that responded to a new law for mass housing in rural France, and he presented the project at CIAM II in Frankfurt.[8] Two identical units of 45 square meters each, elevated off the ground, are conjoined by a masonry party wall. The floor plans are centered around a bathroom core, and living spaces are equipped with flexible furnishings that can be converted to different uses for daytime or night. As Maekawa would recall, "You know, when I was with Le Corbusier, I was put on the 'Maison Minimum' project. I was constantly fiddling with this right up until showing it at CIAM. During that time, Le Corbusier once said this to me—'This may be all right as a plan for the "Maison Minimum," but it won't do just leaving it at that. This will just be the core—it will develop in various directions, and not just for housing. If it's not something that can generate variation of architectural space, then it's useless.' For some reason these words stuck in my head. Looking back, I think that everything I've done had its beginnings in that moment."[9] While the Maisons Loucheur is often overlooked in Le Corbusier's large oeuvre of residential projects, in Japan its influence cannot be exaggerated. The prototype profoundly shaped the course of techno-rationalist architecture that led to the Metabolist movement[10] while also providing the square-plan small house with an international pedigree.

With the war's escalation and rising rhetoric of nationalism in Japan, these research efforts on the *Existenzminimum* and neighborhood planning led by Uchida Yoshizō and Dōjunkai evolved into *kokumin jūtaku,* which came from a direct translation of the German word *Volkswohnung.*[11] In 1941 the Architectural Institute of Japan set up a subcommittee on standardized housing (*kokumin hyōjun jūtaku*), counting among its members a new generation of architects such as Uchida Yoshizō's son Yoshifumi, Tange Kenzō, and the historian Sekino Masaru, all of them at the time graduate students at

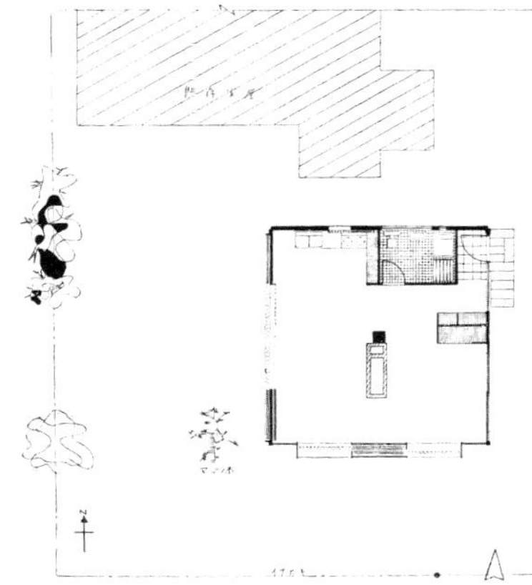

Uchida Yoshifumi, Architectural Institute of Japan's *kokumin jūtaku* competition scheme, first prize, 1941.

Banshōya Gyōji, Square House, Toshima Ward, Tokyo, 1953.

Tokyo Imperial University. New laws were written to standardize dwelling size, amenities, and neighborhood density.[12] Uchida Yoshifumi and Sekino Masaru previously collaborated on designing housing prototypes for the master plan of the northern Chinese city of Datong, a project led by Uchida the elder in 1938.[13] Notably, they endeavored to reconcile local housing traditions of northern China's Loess Plateau with Japanese domestic elements and new residential district planning ideas from Europe and the United States. Uchida Yoshifumi went on to win first prize in the 1941 competition for *kokumin jūtaku,* organized by the Architectural Institute of Japan, and published a series of nine research reports on this topic, on themes ranging from construction techniques and material to living arrangements and furnishings.[14] These design efforts by the younger Uchida proceeded in parallel with historiographical efforts by Sekino Masaru, who was writing the book *A Short History of Japanese Housing* with the stated purpose of helping guide Japan's national housing policy.[15] Uchida Yoshifumi and the circle of neophyte architects around him further situated standardized housing into a continuum of design and planning that stretched into the realm of regional and national land planning, culminating in the exhibition and publication *New Metropolis,* which produced a series of schemes each covering three scales: housing, neighborhood units, and metropolitan Tokyo.[16] These activities manifest not only the thorough internalization of CIAM's urbanism ideals, which were transmitted through their mentor Sakakura Junzō, who worked in Le Corbusier's atelier in 1930–37, but reflect the general approach to planning and housing in wartime and colonial efforts in Manchuria and elsewhere in continental Asia.

9 Maekawa's text is from Julian Worrall's translation of Yamana Yoshiyuki, "The Projects and Drawings that Mayekawa Was in Charge of at Le Corbusier's Atelier," in *Seitan 100 nen, Maekawa Kunio kenchiku ten zuroku*, ed. Matsukuma Hiroshi et al., exh. cat. (Tokyo: Bijutsu shuppansha, 2005), 308.

10 Seng Kuan, "Corbusianism in Japan," in forthcoming exhibition catalogue for *Ando and Le Corbusier: Masters of Architecture* presented at Wrightwood 659, Chicago, 2018, ed. Eric Mumford (Chicago: Alphawood Exhibitions, 2021).

11 The Japanese term was attributed to Hayakawa Fumio, an architect at the Ministry of Health and Welfare (*kōsei-shō*) in September 1940, in an article in *Kenchiku zasshi*.

12 One of the most consequential and controversial aspects of the Ministry of Health and Welfare's housing standards was the spatial separation of sleeping and eating functions (*shinshoku bunri*).

13 Whereas the younger Uchida oversaw the design of housing prototypes, Takayama Eika, one of the founding figures of urban planning as an academic discipline in Japan, was in charge of the design of residential districts. See Uchida Yoshizō, "Daidō toshi kenkakuan ni tsuite," *Kenchiku zasshi*, no. 657 (October 1938): 1,281–82; and Takayama Eika, "Daidō toyū keikaku oboekaki," *Gendai kenchiku*, no. 8 (January 1940): 48–57.

14 See Takeuchi Kōji et al., "Kenchikuka Uchida Yoshifumi no 'kokumin jūtaku' kōsō ni kansuru kenkyū," *Jūtaku sōgō kenkyū ronbunshū*, no. 36 (2009): 177–88. Uchida Yoshifumi's reports were serialized in the journal *Jūtaku* from January 1942 to April 1943.

15 Sekino Masaru, *Nihon jūtaku shōshi* (Tokyo: Sagami shobo, 1942). Three years later in 1945 Sekino Masaru completed the doctoral dissertation "Genealogy of building the Japanese house and the development of urban housing" (*Nihon jūtaku kensetsu no genryū to tojō jūtaku no seiritsu*), (D. Eng. diss., Tokyo Imperial University, 1945). This text was followed in 1948 by Ōta Hirotarō's book *A Pictorial History of the Japanese House* (*Zūsetsu Nihon no jūtaku*) (Tokyo: Shōkokusha, 1948). Sekino Masaru and Ōta Hirotarō's books were widely read, and referenced by Shinohara, for their relevance to contemporary practice.

16 Seng Kuan, "A Short Genealogy of Tange Kenzō's Modernist City," in *Metaborizumu no mirai toshi ten: sengo Nihon ima yomegaeru fukkō no yume to bizyon*, ed. Maeda Naotake et al., exh. cat. (Tokyo: Mori Art Museum, 2011), 226–34.

17 Tange Kenzō, "Konpe no jidai," interview by Fujimori Terunobu, *Kenchiku zasshi*, no. 1,229 (January 1985): 21–25. In 1941, as he was concluding his three-year apprenticeship under Maekawa Kunio, Tange joined two competitions for *kokumin jūtaku*, organized by Dōjunkai and the Architectural Institute of Japan, respectively. Tange received an honorable mention in the first competition, but his scheme for the second was not recognized.

18 Kuan, "Corbusianism in Japan," 162–63.

19 Banshōya's Square House was first published in *Shinkenchiku* vol. 33, no. 5 (May 1953): 18–22. For an overview of his early career, see Matsubara Kōsuku, "Banshōya Shōji no seinenki ni okeru kokunai gyōseki," *Nihon kenchiku gakkai keikakukei ronbunshū*, no. 674 (April 2012): 931–40. Matsubara suggests that Banshōya owes his interest in Heian-period culture to his father, Eiichi, who wrote a play inspired by *The Tale of Genji*.

It is evident that Tange Kenzō's House in Seijō, completed in 1953, loomed large in Shinohara's mind as he was designing House in Kugayama. As Tange later acknowledged, this unusual design originated in his own work on the *kokumin jūtaku* competitions of 1941.[17] No documentation on Tange's schemes from 1941 survives, as his were not selected for awards, but Uchida Yoshifumi's top-ranked design illustrates the aspirations of these neophyte architects working under the spell of Corbusian modernism while simultaneously grappling with new conceptions of domesticity and cultural identity. Sakakura Junzō's seminal work at the Japan Pavilion of the Paris World's Fair in 1937 was a major influence, as was Kishi Memorial Athletics Hall of 1941 by Maekawa Kunio with Tange Kenzō as project architect. Kishi Hall's remarkable front elevation, in its ingenious handling of wooden-construction details to monumental and classicizing effect, is clearly legible in Uchida Yoshifumi's housing scheme.[18]

The 1954 feature issue of *Shinkenchiku* that included Shinohara Kazuo's House in Kugayama also showcased recent achievements from the laboratory of Seike Kiyoshi at Tokyo Tech. Shinohara's work is shown alongside those of four other members of the Seike lab. Before we turn our attention to Shinohara, let us first look at the work presented by his classmate Banshōya Gyōji. The Square House (*seihōkei no ie*) was a bachelor pad of 52 square meters for the architect's older brother, situated on the south lawn at their parents' house.[19] Based on a perfect square plan, the scheme includes a structural pillar in the center supporting a pyramidal timber-frame roof. Banshōya refers to this chassis as *karakasa,* or paper umbrella. The house's open plan is organized around the central pillar, as a rotating sequence of four distinct zones. This symmetry is further manifest on the south and west elevations, which are more privileged for views and sunlight.

The square plan would persist as an important leitmotif in the design of modern Japanese houses,[20] with such distinguished examples as Kikutake Kiyonori's Sky House (1958) and Sakamoto Kazunari's House in Sanda (1969). Even Sejima Kazuyo's Plum Grove House (2003) should be considered as part of this lineage. It goes without saying that over half of Shinohara's houses from the First Style—encompassing Umbrella House, House with an Earthen Floor, and House in White (1966), all featured in this volume—are variants of this same type. In fact the square plan continues to surface through the Second Style and makes a final appearance at House in Uehara (1976) during the Third Style. It is helpful therefore to unpack briefly the particular typological development of the square house and tease out its historical contingencies and methodological implications.

Banshōya's square plan brings together two key typological threads of domestic architecture in modern Japan, the *Existenzminimum* of the European avant-garde on the one hand and Japan's own architectural patrimony on the other. In November 1953 the French journal *L'Architecture d'Aujourd'hui* ran a feature issue on residential designs. This publication bore directly out of CIAM IX, held in Aix-en-Provence a few months prior, with the goal of producing a "Charter of Habitat" as a postwar redux of CIAM II on minimum dwellings.[21] In his essay "L'Habitation individuelle minimum," the Corbusian protégé and Unité d'Habitation project architect

Sano Toshikata, own house, 1922.

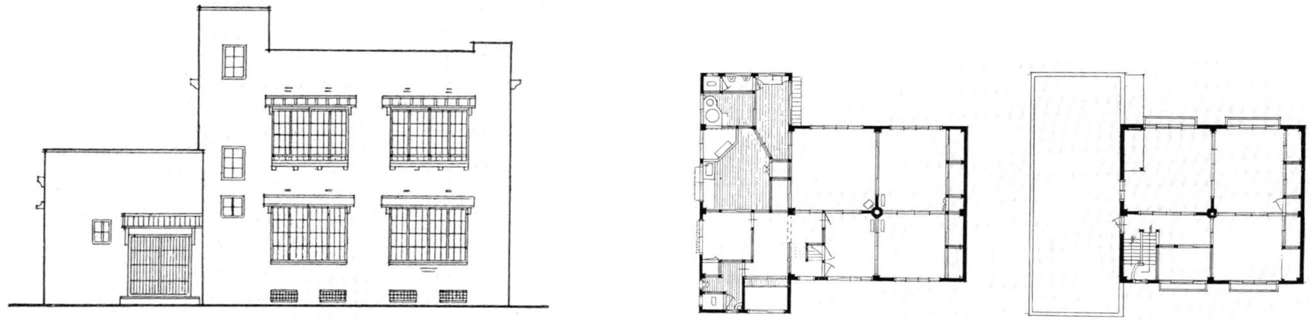

20 See Okuyama Shin-ichi and Yamada Hidenori, "Seihōkei heimen wo motsu jūtaku sakuhin ni okeru naibu keishiki, gaibu keishiki," *Nihon kenchiku gakkai gakujutsu kōen kōgaishū* (Kyūshū, September 1999): 553–54. According to a study, 78 of 707 plans that were awarded citations in annual *Shinkenchiku* residential competitions between 1947 and 2010 are based on the square plan: Ishigaki Takashi and Irie Masayuki, "Shinkenchiku konpe ni okeru sakuhin teisai to nyusennan no puran taipu bunseki," *Nihon kenchiku gakkai keikakukei ronbunshū*, no. 712 (June 2015): 1,493–1,502.

21 Eric Mumford, *The CIAM Discourse on Urbanism, 1928–1960* (Cambridge, MA.: MIT Press, 2000), 225–38.

22 Georges Candilis, "L'Habitation individuelle minimum," *L'Architecture d'Aujourd'hui* vol. 24, no. 49 (October 1953): 0–1.

Georges Candilis was emphatic that Banshōya's Square House belonged to the specific tradition of the minimum dwelling as it evolved within the framework of international modernism.[22] Banshōya's plan is clearly a genealogical descendent of the Maisons Loucheur, sharing a square configuration with a structural core in the center and more importantly, both taking advantage of the open plan with flexible living spaces.[23]

Banshōya's quadripartite plan also finds its antecedent in the *tanoji* type of Japanese *minka* rural commoner houses. *Ta-no-ji* means "character of 田" referring to the *kanji* ideogram that literally translates as field, or more specifically, rice paddies. It is one of the archetypal layouts of *minka* architecture, referring to the arrangement of a suite of four formal living spaces around a central post, the *daikokubashira.* Indeed the *tanoji* plan was invoked by none other than Sano Toshikata, the father of modern architecture in Japan, in building his own house in 1922.[24] Sano's two-storey main living space is divided into four quadrants by a heating stack disguised as a central pillar. The same two-by-two grid is imprinted on the south and north elevations as four identical windows. Services are relegated to one side of the house, as would be typical of the *doma,* referring to the more utilitarian part of the *minka* named for its earthen, at-grade floor.

As *L'Architecture d'Aujourd'hui* describes Banshōya's Square House, "One finds in this house several elements of traditional Japanese style that recall the tendencies of ancient Japan. However, the architect did not intend to realize a residence of the past; on the contrary, he strove to create a form of living that strictly adapts to the needs of life in Japan today."[25] It must be noted the *tanoji* type of *minka* houses did not necessitate a square plan. The quadripartite layout of the formal living space is coupled with the informal *doma,* which invariably results in an oblong block. The geometric precision in Banshōya's Square House, with its prominent roof, also descends from the more rarefied pedigree of monumental architecture of ancient Japan. *Taisha-zukuri,* the style of Shinto architecture associated with Izumo Grand Shrine, typically has a square plan for the main hall. In the Buddhist tradition, especially Pure Land Buddhism most prominent during the Heian period (794–1185), the Amida Hall is often configured as a square plan. The best-known example of this type is the so-called Golden Hall at Chūson-ji in Hiraizumi (1124), configured as a three-by-three grid and topped with a pyramidal roof, or *hōgyō-zukuri,* with deep eaves and protruding overhangs on all four sides. The slightly later Amida Hall at Jōdo-ji (1194) in Hyōgo Prefecture, referenced by Shinohara,[26] also follows this model.

The note of classicism is unmissable in Banshōya's interpretation of the *Existenzminimum:* "Within Japan's classical elegance [*kotenteki na fūgasa*] hangs the taste of modernity, and the designer's youthful desires are hidden in silence and solitude [*seijyaku*]."[27] The language in *Shinkenchiku*'s commentary similarly strikes a note of *mono no aware,* the aesthetic quality associated with Heian-period art and literature. Banshōya Gyōji, together with Shinohara Kazuo, was trained at the laboratory of Seike Kiyoshi at Tokyo Tech.[28] As architectural historian Fujioka Hiroyasu has pointed out, Seike's Dr. Mori House (1951) represented the first instance in the

postwar context of *"Nihonteki na mono,"* or the "pure Japanese thing."[29] In his own introductory essay to Mori House, Seike invoked the term *shitsurai,* an archaism describing the distribution and layout of various rituals and associated furnishings and accoutrements as practiced during "dynastic times."[30] In the prewar period of the 1930s there was burgeoning interest among Japan's modern architects in the early-modern (*kinsei*) period, particularly the architecture of tea from the sixteenth and seventeenth centuries,[31] but the concept of *shitsurai* and the implications of spatial homogeneity evoked by Seike after World War II were remarkable for their associations with the much more ancient Heian period and domestic practices of the court nobility. At the same time, Seike describes the layout of Mori House, especially the centering of two large tatami rooms in the plan, as creating "unified space (*ittaiteki na kūkan*)." It is a compact, single-storey house for a couple with one child. Seike took great care to sculpt a geometrically precise interior volume. Ceilings are made flush with the underside of deep eaves, and floors are laid out on a continuous plane. The house is lifted a few inches off the ground, with the footing recessed to create the illusion of a floating, abstract volume. The central location of the two tatami rooms reinforces the ideas of spatial fluidity and flexibility in the heart of the building. As explained by Fujioka, Seike Kiyoshi's use of the *shitsurai* concept can be traced to the particular research and teaching of architectural history at Tokyo Tech.[32] The historians at this school, Maeda Matsuoto and Fujioka Michio, took special interest in residential architecture, the former being a pioneer in the study of Heian-period *shinden* architecture associated with court aristocracy.[33] Seike brought this classical penchant into

23 In the Maisons Loucheur the main living space is further elevated from the ground and is largely supported by the bathroom core located in the center, allowing the *pilotis* space down below to be used as a workshop, anticipating later works by the Metabolists such as Kikutake's Sky House and Kurokawa Kishō's Mushroom House.

24 Sano Toshikata, *Jūtaku ron* (Tokyo: Bunka seikatsu kenkyūkai, 1925). It is also discussed in Sekino Masaru, *Nihon jūtaku shōshi*, 138.

25 Special issue "Habitations," ed. Renée Diamant-Berger, *L'Architecture d'Aujourd'hui* vol. 24, no. 49 (October 1953): 3.

26 Shinohara Kazuo, *Jūtaku kenchiku* (Residential architecture) (Tokyo: Kinokuniya shoten, 1964), 61–63.

27 "Seihōkei no ie," *Shinkenchiku* vol. 33, no. 5 (May 1953): 18–19.

28 Seike Kiyoshi (also styled as Kiyosi, 1918–2005) was educated at the Tokyo School of Fine Arts and the Tokyo Institute of Technology (Tokyo Tech). At Tokyo School of Fine Arts, Seike counted among his teachers Mizutani Takehiko, who studied at the Bauhaus in the late 1920s. As a graduate student at Tokyo Tech, Seike benefited from the mentorship of Taniguchi Yoshirō and the aforementioned historian Fujioka Michio.

29 Fujioka Hiroyasu, "Seike Kiyoshi no kenchiku: sono monozukuri ga toikakeru koto," in *Seike Kiyoshi* (Tokyo: Shinkenchiku-sha, 2006), 68–97 (English translation: 401–15). Cherie Wendelken's translation of "*Nihonteki na mono*" as "the Pure Japanese thing" is literal and conveys of the awkwardness of the idea even in the Japanese original. See Cherie Wendelken, "Pan-Asianism and the Pure Japanese Thing: Japanese Identity and Architecture in the Late 1930s," *positions: east asian cultures critique* vol. 8, no. 3 (2000): 819–28.

30 Dynastic times here is a euphemism for the Heian period and the Nara period that preceded it, when there was a high degree of centralized power in the imperial court. Seike Kiyoshi, "Mori hakushi no ie," *Shinkenchiku* vol. 31, no. 9 (September 1951): 280–87.

31 The representative figure in this revival of the *sukiya*-style architecture and the broader culture of tea was Horiguchi Sutemi. In 1940 he edited a special issue of *Gendai Kenchiku* (no. 13) devoted to the late sixteenth-century tea master Sen no Rikyū, which he developed into a major monograph *Rikyū no chashitsu* (1949).

32 Fujioka, "Seike Kiyoshi no kenchiku," 71–72.

33 See Maeda Matsuoto, "Shinden-zukuri no kōkyū," *Kenchiku zasshi*, no. 491 (1927:01): 1–38; and Maeda Matsuoto, *Kinsei jūtaku: Jūtaku no kōkyū* vol. 21., ed. Uchida Seizō, *Jūtaku kenchiku bunken shūsei* (Tokyo: Kashiwa shobo, 2003).

Seike Laboratory at Tokyo Institute of Technology, ca. 1954. Left to right: Shinohara Kazuo, Yamada (later Hayashi) Masako, Seike Kiyoshi, Banshōya Gyōji, Miyasaka Shūkichi.

Seike Kiyoshi, Dr. Mori House, Bunkyō Ward, Tokyo, 1951. Photo by Hiryama Chūji

Seike Kiyoshi, Prof. Saitō House, Ōta Ward, Tokyo, 1952. Photo by Hirayama Chūji

his design laboratory where the students made a series of large 1:10-scale models of *shinden*-style buildings of the late Heian period.[34]

In spring 1954 Walter Gropius, together with his wife Ise, visited Japan to attend the opening of the exhibition *Gropius and the Bauhaus* at the National Museum of Modern Art. During their visit, the Gropiuses were treated to a packed itinerary of ancient sites in Kyoto and Nara, but on one free afternoon Walter Gropius made a request to see some small houses he had seen in magazines. His Japanese chaperone, Hamaguchi Ryūichi (whom we will soon meet again), quickly figured out he was referring to works by Seike and arranged a visit the same day.[35] Gropius's widely read essay "Architecture in Japan" written upon his return to the United States, refers specifically to Seike's trilogy of small houses—Mori House, Saitō House (1952), and Miyagi House (1953)—as having "skillfully synthesized Japan's tradition with modern technology."[36] These modest postwar residences were illustrated side by side with some of the greatest historical monuments of Japan, including Ise Shrine, Tōdai-ji, and Katsura Villa.

The series of houses by Seike Kiyoshi and his protégés, together with Tange Kenzō's own house in Seijō and related projects—endorsed internationally by powerful figures like Gropius, Arthur Drexler, and John D. Rockefeller III—helped precipitate what became known as the Tradition Debate, or *dentō ronsō,* of the mid-1950s in the Japanese architectural community. The critic Kawazoe Noboru hastened this development with an editorial in the January 1955 issue of *Shinkenchiku* titled "Tange Kenzō's Japanese character."[37] Kawazoe's essay situates Tange's earlier, rationalist designs in rigid-frame *Rahmen* reinforced concrete structures, in Japan's historical space-making and construction techniques, while referencing historic sites such as Ise and Shōsō-in. As art historian and critic Kitazawa Noriaki has reminded us, while the Tradition Debate commonly refers to Kawazoe's characterization of Tange's architecture of the mid-1950s, in fact it derived from historicist currents of the avant-garde that first emerged in the 1930s and resurfaced in the early postwar period, developing as largely independent of architects.[38]

In the early 1950s several events in the Japanese art world signaled a broad attempt to reexamine and repurpose Japan's cultural patrimony, manifesting most notably in the exhibitions on Tawaraya Sōtatsu and Ogata Kōrin's so-called Rinpa school and on Japan's ancient cultures, both held in 1951 at the newly reorganized National Museum of Tokyo.[39] The first exhibition, on Rinpa, was devoted to the work of two painters from the seventeenth century later heralded as the progenitors of a uniquely Japanese pictorial style. The exhibition on Japan's ancient cultures, prominently featuring recent archeological finds, rekindled interest in the origins of Japan's *sui generis* plastic arts culture. Notably, it was inspiration from the ancient cultures exhibition that led artist Okamoto Tarō to propose his influential theory on the Jōmon and Yayoi, published in the art journal *Mizue* in December 1952, more than three years before Kawazoe's instigation.[40] This cultural and aesthetic turn must also be contextualized in Japan's geopolitical realignment as a US ally brought by the onset of the Korean War and Treaty of San Francisco. In 1953, just as Seike's series of early houses and Tange's House in Seijō

34 Hayashi Shōji, "Seike Kiyoshi to gendai no jūkyō desain," *Shinkenchiku* vol. 34, no. 11 (November 1954): 6–10

35 Hamaguchi Ryūichi "Seike Kiyoshi to Guropiusu: Nihon no kenchikuka Amerika he iku," *Geijutsu shinchō* vol. 16, no. 2 (February 1955): 78–80.

36 Walter Gropius, "Architecture in Japan," *Perspecta*, no. 3 (1955): 8–21.

37 Iwata Kazuo (Kawazoe Noboru writing as), "Tange Kenzō no Nihon-teki seikaku: tokun raamen kōzō no hatten wo tōshite," *Shinkenchiku* vol. 35, no. 1 (January 1955): 62–69.

38 Kitazawa Noriaki, "Dentō ronsō: 60 nendai avangyarudo he no airo," in *Bijutsu hihyō to sengo bijutsu*, ed. Bijutsu hihyō ka renmei (Tokyo: Buryukke, 2007), 103–22.

39 The two exhibitions were *Sōtasu Kōrin-ha ten* (April 4–May 6, 1951) and *Nihon kodai bunka ten* (October 10–November 25, 1951), both held at the National Museum of Tokyo.

40 Okamoto Tarō, "Yongjigen to no taiwa: Jōmon toki ron," *Mizue* (February 1952).

were being completed, the historicist refrain of revitalizing modernism with lessons from ancient Japan came to be embraced by Drexler and Rockefeller, who sought to introduce it to the Museum of Modern Art in New York (MoMA).[41] The Japanese Exhibition House, or Shōfu-sō, designed by Yoshimura Junzō after the seventeenth-century *shoin*-style structure Kōjō-in at Shiga Prefecture's Mii-dera and built by Itō Heizaemon, the eleventh-generation scion of a master builder family, stood in MoMA's courtyard on Fifty-Fourth Street and attracted a quarter of a million visitors in 1954–55.

Two months before Kawazoe's editorial in *Shinkenchiku* on Tange's alleged historicism, the same journal carried an article by the left-wing architectural critic Hamaguchi Ryūichi—who was once Tange and Uchida Yoshifumi's classmate and also a key member among Sakakura Junzō's coterie of protégés—titled "The Small-House Auteur: Ikebe Kiyoshi,"[42] Hamaguchi identified six broader socioeconomic reasons for the recent ascendance of the *shōjūtaku* small-house type: (1) demise of the absolute monarchy and decline in old elite's patronage of lavish mansions; (2) tendency to favor independent dwellings over social or cooperative housing in capitalist economies; (3) severe housing shortage after the war's end prompting widespread interest in residential architecture; (4) pressure to lower building costs in a broken economy; (5) transition from "feudal clans (*hōkenteki na daikazoku*)" to nuclear families; and (6) new ideas of living arrangements from abroad.[43] More importantly, Hamaguchi recognized a new postwar generation of architects who had developed highly sophisticated methods and styles of the *shōjūtaku* type with the aid of mass media. The small houses are showcased in various popular magazines and professional journals, often accompanied by critical commentaries, as *sakuhin,* or as works of artistic or literary merit. Their architects assumed the mantle of *sakka,* or auteur, a term that emerged out of French film criticism in the early 1950s and was quickly embraced in Japan. The *sakka* architect's design process privileged an aesthetic objective beyond the mere pleasure of its inhabitants, or "the conventional meaning of architectural activity (*futsū no imi no kenchikuō*)."[44] In other words, Hamaguchi appears to suggest the *sakka*'s pursuit is discursive and internal to the discipline.

Hamaguchi Ryūichi also singles out the work of Seike Kiyoshi as contributing, adversely, to the development of the small-house type through architectural journalism. Hamaguchi describes Seike's Mori House as emblematic of a regressive turn in Japanese political culture: "The onset of the Korean War provided the occasion for a reversal in Japan's democratization process, recession from the overcoming of feudalism, and bathing in stage light of nationalistic tradition (*kokuminteki dentō toiu koto ga kyakkō wo abihajimeta*)."[45] As if Hamaguchi's damnation was not sufficiently clear, he adds, "compared to Seike Kiyoshi's work, Ikebe Kiyoshi's work gives a feeling of strained aloofness (*gisu gisu*). At the same time, Seike Kiyoshi's work exudes the fragrance of effeminate beauty (*tanbiteki na kaori*), or stench to those who don't like it."[46]

One month after Kawazoe Noboru's editorial on the Tradition Debate, the same journal *Shinkenchiku* offered a counterpoint by Ikebe Kiyoshi titled "How to Tackle the Pure Japanese Thing."[47] Slightly younger in age than Tange and Seike, Ikebe

41 John D. Rockefeller III played a central role in building the postwar US-Japan alliance, both in negotiating the Treaty of San Francisco and through his patronage of MoMA, Asia Society, and Japan Society. Arthur Drexler was curator and later director of the Department of Architecture and Design at MoMA. For an account of Shōfu-sō's construction, see Sean Anderson, "Postscript, It/Then: On the Building of the Japanese Exhibition House," in *Structured Lineages: Learning from Japanese Structural Design*, ed. Guy Nordenson (New York: Museum of Modern Art, 2019), 199–215

42 Hamaguchi Ryūichi, "Shōjūtaku sakka-ron, Ikebe Kiyoshi," *Shinkenchiku* vol. 34, no. 11 (November 1954): 73–76.

43 Ibid., 73.

44 Ibid., 73–76.

45 Ibid., 75.

46 Ibid.

47 Ikebe Kiyoshi, "'Nihonteki desain' to ikani torikumuka," *Shinkenchiku* vol. 35, no. 2 (February 1955): 41–43.

Ikebe Kiyoshi, House No. 3 "3-Dimensional Minimum Dwelling," Shinjuku Ward, Tokyo, 1950. Photo by Hirayama Chūji

Tange Kenzō, House in Seijō, Setagaya Ward, Tokyo, 1953. Photo by Hirayama Chūji

belonged to the same generation educated just prior to the height of World War II, and he emerged in the postwar period as one of the most radical and politicized members of the avant-garde.[48] Among the more than a hundred small houses realized over Ikebe's career, the project most thorough in its embodiment of his approach is House No. 3, otherwise known as Three-Dimensional Minimum Dwelling, completed in 1950. At 15 *tsubo,* the compact house is a tour de force of rationalization, achieving a compelling flow through different zones of the house while maintaining the use of Western-style furnishings without resorting to multipurpose tatami flooring.

In the final years of the war, Ikebe worked with Sakakura Junzō on a prefabrication system for a timber-based, panel-frame housing prototype.[49] The initial concept was the Japanese adaptation into timber, commissioned by Japan's navy, of the SCAL prototype of rapid panel-frame system jointly developed in 1939 by Jean Prouvé, Pierre Jeanneret, and Charlotte Perriand.[50] Ikebe worked with more than twenty factories all over Japan, producing some 100,000 square meters of housing based on various adaptations of this module.[51] The evolution of *kokumin jūtaku* into *shōjūtaku* houses in the postwar period as independent, standalone structures devoid of any broader urbanistic coordination, in contrast to the collective framework spearheaded by Uchida Yoshifumi and Tange Kenzō during the war, must be considered in the context of the harsh realities of the war's end. As Japan became increasingly defensive, the national government implemented a policy of *sokai,* evacuating hundreds of thousands of people, especially children, away from urban centers. The *Existenzminimum* type took on new significance as makeshift shelters. Shortly after the war ended, Ikebe Kiyoshi joined the Number 2 campus of Tokyo Imperial University's Faculty of Engineering, established in nearby Chiba Prefecture as part of the war effort, where many of the rising generation of elite architects and engineers had clustered. Politically, Ikebe stood much further to the left of Tange and Seike and was active in the short-lived New Architects Union (NAU), which was closely aligned with the Japanese Communist Party.[52] In NAU's journal, Ikebe Kiyoshi introduced to the Japanese audience Henry-Russell Hitchcock's influential essay "The Architecture of Bureaucracy and the Architecture of Genius."[53] Hitchcock's prediction, that the defining theme of architectural development in the postwar era would be based on the economy of production rather than form and style, reaffirmed Ikebe's belief in a technological and industrial solution to Japan's housing crisis.

Ikebe and Seike frequently served alongside each other as juries for the *Shinkenchiku* residential design competitions.[54] In the background of these design exercises, which were mainly directed at recent graduates, was the reexamination of the idea of the family as the basic unit of social organization and architectural planning. The dismantling of the patriarchal *ie* system and promotion of women's rights, together with land reform and breaking up of the *zaibatsu* business conglomerates, were some of the most profound measures imposed by the US-led occupation. The basic unit of housing design evolved from the *ie* to the *katei,* or the modern nuclear family.[55] Ikebe Kiyoshi, having established his own laboratory at the University of Tokyo in 1949, focused on the idealization of movement of the human body, the housewife in particular,

48 The authoritative account of Ikebe's life and work can be found in Namba Kazuhiko, *Sengo modanizumu kenchiku no kyokuboku: Ikebe Kiyoshi no shiron* (Tokyo: Shōkokusha, 1999).

49 Yamana Yoshiyuki, "Sensō kumitachi kenchiku," *Jūtaku kenchiku*, no. 411 (July 2009): 30–33. An account of Ikebe's work in English, focusing on his theory of the module, can be found in Kuroishi Izumi, "Mathematics for/from Society: The Role of the Module in Modernizing Japanese Architectural Production," *Nexus Network Journal* vol. 11, no. 2 (2009): 201–15.

50 SCAL is the acronym for *Société centrale des alliages legers* (Light Alloy Company). Perriand left France for Japan in spring 1940 upon Sakakura's invitation and brought a comprehensive set of drawings described as "Batiments de la guerre," which included the SCAL prototype.

51 "Sengo jūtaku no besuto 10," *Shitsunai*, no. 248 (August 1975): 15–45.

52 The Japanese name is *Shin-Nihon kenchikuka shūdan*. See Honda Shōichi, *Kindai Nihon kenchiku undō shi* (Tokyo: Domesu, 2003).

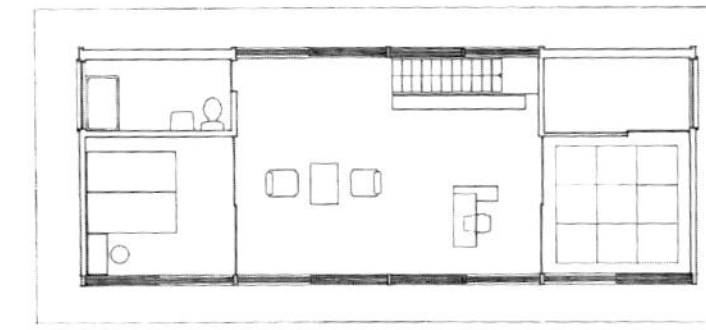

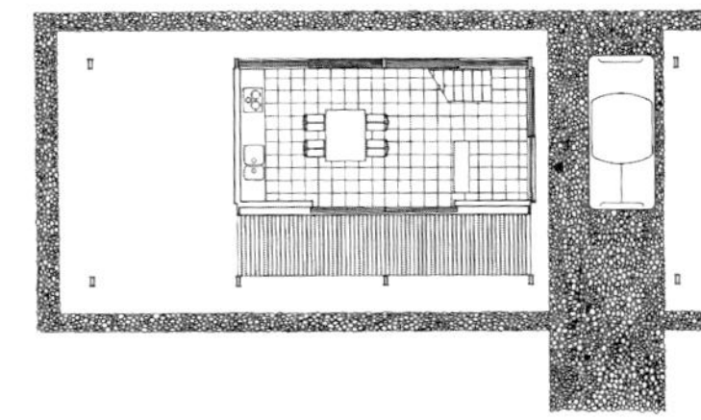

through this minuscular space. Hamaguchi Miho's *The Feudalism of the Japanese House,* published in 1949, inculcated in the postwar generation of architects the premise of gender roles in spatial organization. Ikebe himself joined an op-ed piece in the journal *Fujin Kōron* (Women's forum), authored together with Maekawa Kunio and Hamaguchi Ryūichi—the latter being Hamaguchi Miho's husband—titled "Women's Liberation and the Housing Question: Focusing on Domestic Labor."[56]

Ikebe Kiyoshi's 1955 response to Kawazoe's stance on tradition listed several reasons for the rising interest in *Nihonteki na mono,* or the Pure Japanese Thing. While he mentioned well-known factors such as the postwar reassessment of narrow interpretations of functionalism and rationalism and clear resonances between Japan's classical (*kotenteki*) architecture and modernism, he also pointed to the cultural aspects of postwar decolonization and rise of nationalism, as well as the corollary of Socialist Realist aesthetics in the Communist world.[57] In the specific context of Japan, Ikebe suggested that the nostalgic sentimentality in *Nihonteki na mono* also reflected disillusionment with postwar Japanese politics and the lack of more profound reforms in the infrastructure of architectural production. As he pointed out, Katsura Imperial Villa resulted from uniquely local (*fūdoteki*) cooptation of popular customs (*minshūteki dentō*) to suit the lifestyles of the seventeenth-century aristocracy. In other words, *Nihonteki na mono* was a misguided and facile response, aesthetically and politically, to the true needs of the people (*minshū*).

In Gropius's 1954 article "Architecture in Japan," a photo of Tange's House in Seijō is coyly placed in between an interior and an exterior view of Katsura's main *shoin*-style palace, appearing as if indistinguishable from the seventeenth-century building. The elevated posture of the Seijō house, exterior veranda (*engawa*) running the length of the south elevation, and wooden slanted roof all suggest overtures to Japan's residential tradition. In his introductory essay to the project, however, Tange describes the house in entirely contemporary, functionalist terms.[58] The text refers to three principles: *pilotis,* cores, and proportions. The former two, *pilotis* and cores, were the main research topics of his laboratory at the University of Tokyo, both of which he interpreted as aspects of universal, generic spaces: *pilotis* for the social, public aspect, and cores for the functionalist.[59] In describing his design of House in Seijō, Tange contextualizes the elevated posture of the house, locating all substantive programming to the upper floor, in terms of the territorial relationship of the house and family to the neighborhood and community. The openness of the ground floor, achieved with *pilotis,* provides contiguity with the open garden, unbound by fences and hedges and inviting neighborhood children to come play freely. The idea of an architectural core here, as Tange admits, is rudimentary and naïve. By clustering the services and circulation in the center on the plan, he nonetheless achieves a sense of spatial flexibility and ambiguity (*mugenteisei*) that he was striving for in the larger, institutional-scale buildings. Tatami flooring and *fusuma* sliding partitions further reinforce these aspirations toward generic space.

53 Ikebe Kiyoshi, "Hichikokku 'Byūrōkurashii no kenchiku to tensai no kenchiku' ni tsuite," *NAUM: shakai to henchiku to kenchikuka*, no. 1 (1949): 21–24. Hitchcock's original essay appeared as "The Architecture of Bureaucracy and the Architecture of Genius," *Architectural Review* vol. 101, no. 601 (January 1947): 3–6.

54 For instance, two competitions were held in 1948, the first one on "new housing that focuses on reduces domestic labor" and the other "15-*tsubo* single-family house, focusing on childrearing." The winning schemes together with comments and editorials from the jury were published in the August and November/December issues respectively.

55 See the excellent study by anthropologist Nishikawa Yūko, "Nihonkei kindai kazoku to sumai no hensen," *Ritsumeikan engo bunka kenkyū* vol. 6, no. 1 (July 1997): 25–63.

56 Maekawa Kunio, Hamaguchi Ryūichi, Ikebe Kiyoshi, "Fujin kaihō to jūtaku mondai: kaji rōdō wo chūshin toshite," *Fūjin kōron*, no. 33 (February 1948): 42–48.

57 Ikebe, "'Nihonteki desain' to ikani torikumuka," 41.

Shinohara Kazuo, House in Kugayama, upper-floor *hiroma* and Japanese room. Photo by Hirayama Chūji

Shinohara's first built work, House in Kugayama, bears unmistakable resemblance to Tange's House in Seijō. House in Seijō represented for Tange a discursive idea, the *kokumin jūtaku,* which was transplanted from the early 1940s when he was still in graduate school. His private, domestic arrangements provided the occasion for its realization a dozen years later in 1953, but there would be no more single-family houses associated with his name for the remainder of his long and prolific career. In contrast Shinohara was searching for a point of departure to set in motion new methodological trajectories. Adhering more closely to the language of Ludwig Mies van der Rohe, Shinohara's simple, symmetrical plan belies the lavish ornamentation and sensuality inside. Interior walls were upholstered with rich, dark-blue textiles, and ceilings were covered in golden Japanese *washi* paper. It was Shinohara's struggle with the aristocratic, *shoin*-style residential architecture exemplified in Katsura Villa and Jikō-in in Nara Prefecture. While it may be argued that many of Shinohara's later preoccupations, such as divisions and connections of space, frontality, expansiveness, abstraction, sensoriality, and tectonic expression, are already present in House in Kugayama, there is an unmistakable naïveté and tentativeness in this design. One can see evidence of intent, but not yet a method.

It seems fortuitous that Shinohara's maiden work captured the moment of Japan's return to the world stage. Adulations from overseas accorded to Seike and Tange's houses and Yoshimura's Exhibition House at MoMA were built on a longstanding view as propounded by Bruno Taut and others that there were innate affinities between modernism and ancient Japan, such as shared values of structural clarity, modular composition, honesty of material, and fluidity of space.[60] Indeed, the other key operative trajectory of modern architecture in Japan, the *shōjūtaku* small-house type, evolved out of an equally axiomatic transplantation of the European idea of the *Existenzminimum* as we have followed. By the middle of the 1950s both of these trajectories were reaching an impasse, and Tange and Seike would turn their respective creative energies toward other directions.

Shinohara's next house was House in Kugayama No. 2, completed in 1958 on a site adjacent to the first. The interval between the two houses, four years, would be the longest in his career. This gap also captures a number of profound shifts in the discursive environment for house design. Just as the second Kugayama house was being completed, the publication of a short essay, "Small House *Bansai,*" sent shockwaves through Japan's architectural community with its broadreaching critique of the *shōjūtaku* type. Written by Hatta Riya, the collective *nom de plume* of Isozaki Arata, Itō Teiji, and Kawakami Hideaki, this text declared the expiration of *shōjutaku's* avant-garde mandate. Japan's rapid economic expansion since the Korean War had pushed the discourse and social image of the small house into profane discussions of real estate values and middle-class comfort.[61] The three authors were all young graduate students at the University of Tokyo and belonged to the same generation as Shinohara. The always mercurial Isozaki Arata was focusing on what would become the joint-core system in the *Plan for Tokyo 1960*, working as a member of Tange's laboratory. More pertinent to our story here is the work of Itō Teiji, who was a protégé of Sekino Masaru, the historian of residential architecture

58 Tange Kenzō, "Jūkyō," *Shinkenchiku* vol. 35, no. 1 (January 1955): 19–25.

59 Ōki Taneo, Tarashima Akira, Kamiya Kōji, Nagashima Masamitsu, Isozaki Arata, Mogi Keiichirō, "Koa shisutemu—kukan no mugendeisei," *Shinkenchiku* vol. 35 no. 1 (January 1955): 50–57; Ōtani Sachio, Otsuki Kanichi, Mitsuyoshi Kenji, Sugi Shigehiko, Yoshikawa Takeshi, Mawatari Toshikuni, "Piroti: shakai no kūkan," *Shinkenchiku* vol. 35, no. 1 (January 1955): 58–61.

60 The German architect Bruno Taut took refuge in Japan in 1933–36 and wrote several texts on Katsura Villa, the Tokugawa mausolea in Nikkō, and other architectural topics. See for example Bruno Taut, *Houses and People of Japan* (Tokyo: Sanseidō, 1937).

61 Hatta Riya, "Shōjūtaku bansai," in *Gendai kenchiku gusakuron* (Tokyo: Shōkokusha, 1961), 19–45. The essay was originally published in *Kenchiku bunka*, no. 138 (April 1958): 4–10.

62 Futagawa Yukio, *Nihon no minka*, 10 vols. (Tokyo: Bijutsu shuppansha, 1957–59). Itō Teiji wrote the introductory essays. For a discussion of this series in English, see Claire Zimmerman and Eve Zimmerman, "Ethnographic Architectural Photography: Futagawa Yukio and *Nihon no minka*," *The Journal of Architecture* vol. 20, no. 4 (2015): 715–50.

63 The series began with Shinohara Kazuo, "Kaihōteki na kūkan to iu imi: Nihon kenchiku no seikaku I," *Nihon kenchiku gakkai ronbunshū*, no. 57 (July 1957): 429–43.

mentioned above. In 1954 Itō began studying sixteenth- and seventeenth-century commoner houses, most notably in Imai-chō in Nara Prefecture. In exactly the same time frame the young photographer Futagawa Yukio embarked on a multi-year journey to document rural commoner houses across the Japanese archipelago, which he published as the monumental ten-volume series *Nihon no minka* beginning in 1957.[62]

During the interim between the two Kugayama houses, Shinohara likewise immersed himself in the study of historic architecture, covering a diverse range of sites such as prehistoric pit dwellings (*tateana*) and ruins of Pompeii; raised-floor (*takayuka*) shrine and storage structures like Ise Shrine and Shōsō-in, Shishin-den and Higashi-Sanjō-dono in *shinden*-style palaces; group form complexes like Nikkō, the Athenian Acropolis, and Rome's Campidoglio; grand residences from the early modern period like Kyoto's Nijō Castle and Montacute House in England; as well as more recent *minka* examples. These findings were published as scientific papers in the journals of the Architectural Institute of Japan beginning in 1957—exactly concurrent with Futagawa's *Nihon no minka* album series.[63] In each of the twelve installments—the first two subtitled as "Characters of Japanese Architecture" and subsequently as "Methods of"—Shinohara put forth specific compositional and design strategies distilled from these historical lessons, such as open vs. non-open space, a building's relationship with the ground, division and connection, and perspective and frontality.

The incorporation of commoner *minka* motifs, perhaps the most recognizable feature of this more mature phase of Shinohara's First Style both in his design work and polemical writing, was not a postwar innovation. Sano Toshikata's house with the *tanoji* plan mentioned earlier was soon followed by a pair of houses by Horiguchi Sutemi: Koide House (1925) and Shien-sō (1926). They exhibit influence of the Dutch Wendingen movement in their geometric precision and expressiveness, but as informal retreats for their sophisticated clients these houses also benefited from an unusual freedom to take on a rustic and pastoral demeanor. Le Corbusier's two Japanese protégés, Sakakura Junzō and Maekawa Kunio, also drew from the *minka* language in designing Iihashi House (1941, by Sakakura) and Maekawa's own house (1942). Both were built at the height of the war effort when steel and concrete were inaccessible to civilians. In examining Shinohara's works from the First Style it would be difficult to overlook their formal affinities to these prewar antecedents, especially Horiguchi's Koide House and Maekawa's own house, where the kernels of Shinohara's ideas might be found. In the center of Maekawa's house is a white cubic space anchored by a row of monumental, unfinished round columns. But as Shinohara pursued his historical investigations during the interval between the two houses in Kugayama in the late 1950s, he began to construct a new framework of architectural creation through a matrix of *shoin*-inspired and *minka*-inspired features, always seeking tension between them. Tanikawa House (1958) and the House in Komae continued this new, *minka*-inspired trajectory that embodied "the presence of life" manifesting as a series of tightly organized living arrangements with provocative adjacencies, views, finishes, and structures. As Tsukamoto Yoshiharu's essay in this volume describes, each of Shinohara's four styles can be seen as an

Maekawa Kunio, own house, Shinagawa Ward, Tokyo, 1942 (now at Edo-Tokyo Open Air Architecture Museum, Koganei City, Tokyo). Photo by Taniuchi Hisataka, courtesy of Panasonic

Shinohara Kazuo, House in Chigasaki, Kanagawa Prefecture, *hiroma,* 1960. Photo by Saeki Yoshikatsu

enactment of these tensions based on a new matrix, creating criticality within a discursive space he has created. In other words, in the late 1950s Shinohara was to break away from an earlier naïveté to harmonize Miesian modernism with those elements from Katsura that happened to be the most compatible and sympathetic, and instead took modernism as a starting point—and as the site where creative impulses extracted from premodern Japan would be played out. This is not the validation of Japan's patrimony with contemporary relevance, nor a political correction to embrace the more common, allegedly more democratic roots of *minka.* In *minka* Shinohara was not seeking a formal language, like the *tanoji* quadripartite plan, that can be axiomatically appropriated and modernized, but rather certain ideal types, such as the *minka's* darkness, sense of enclosure, and attachment to earth, to create new ways of living and imagining space.[64]

In a similar vein, Shinohara sought to overcome the modern *shōjūtaku's* humble origin in the *Existenzminimum* and subvert its intrinsic smallness. In 1959–61 he designed two of the smallest and two of the largest houses of the First Style, alternating between small and large. The design phases of House in Komae (small) and House in Chigasaki (large) largely overlapped, and Umbrella House (small) began as Chigasaki (large) was being finalized. House with a Big Roof (1961, large) completed this relay.[65] Shinohara's new ideas of division and connection of space, developed from his historical investigations, were put to test most clearly in this series without regard to overall size of the house. The main living space (*hiroma*) in Chigasaki encompassed 71 square meters and was one of the largest domestic interior spaces in Japan. It was with the publication of this project Shinohara launched his frontal attack on Japan's mainstream techno-rationalist architectural culture and its posterchild Metabolism, which was barely a few months old at this time, by proposing the concept of superfluous space (*muda na kūkan,* also translated as wasteful space), declaring "I want to build and live in such a house that when I stand in a room the wall I face seems to be lying at a great distance."[66] It was an appeal to natural, innate human desires for space, to seek emotional comfort in expansiveness and distance. Whereas Tange defined the core of his House in Seijō as the clustering of bathroom, kitchen and staircase, Shinohara blithely called the large living space in House in Chigasaki its core.[67] Functions that cater to more mundane needs are cast away to the margins.

In examining the series of houses that started with the second House in Kugayama, it is important to recognize how Shinohara had thoroughly internalized the specific operative and discursive frameworks of the small house on the one hand and tradition on the other. He overcame their limitations with innovations that pushed the development of the modern Japanese house in entirely new directions, helping to create new paradigms of house design that continue to prove their relevance to architectural production to this day. Shinohara liked to describe *minka* as mushrooms, as a natural phenomenon that emerges from the ground if given the right conditions. Their significance then is an existential and contingent one rather than one of forms—and one that liberates the architect to follow new stimulations.

64 Shinohara Kazuo, "Minka ron," in *Jūtaku kenchiku* (Tokyo: Kunokuniya shoten, 1964), 50–61.

65 House in Komae, design May to November 1959, completion February 1960; House in Chigasaki, design January 1959 to February 1960, completion December 1960; Umbrella House, design December 1959 to September 1960, completion March 1961; House with a Big Roof, design August 1960 to May 1961, completion November 1961. Dates from Ishidō Takeshi et al. eds, *Shinohara Kazuo: Jūtaku zumen* (Tokyo: Shōkokusha, 2008), 137.

66 Originally published as "Seikatsu kūkan no atarashii shiten wo motomete," accompanying House in Chagasaki's debut, in January 1961 issue of *Shinkenchiku*. Retitled "Muda na kūkan" in Shinohara's anthologized writings *Jūtaku ron* (Residential theory) (Tokyo: Kajima shuppankai, 1970), 67–77.

67 Shinohara Kazuo, "Chigasaki no ie," *Shinjūtaku*, no. 169 (June 1961): 19.

Shinohara Kazuo, Umbrella House, Nerima Ward, Tokyo, 1961, roof chassis under construction. Photo by Murai Osamu

Variations on the Square: Shinohara's Umbrella House

Ken Tadashi Oshima

"This is the smallest house I have designed (area 55m²), but it is intimately connected in my mind with the largest I have designed (240m²), and it is a case in point in my argument that small and large houses should not be considered as completely separate categories. It also constitutes one of the factors that have led me to believe that in designing houses we must not confine ourselves to the requirements of the individual residence, but attempt to develop principles of residential architecture that have *wider social applications and implications.*"
—Shinohara Kazuo[1]

"The square is as high and as wide as a man with his arms outstretched. In the most ancient writings, and in the rock inscriptions of early man, it signifies the idea of enclosure, of house, of settlement."
—Bruno Munari[2]

Shinohara Kazuo published both his early masterwork Umbrella House (*karakasa no ie*) and his subsequent essay declaring, "A house is a work of art" in 1962.[3] A central artistic form of Shinohara's design—the square—is seen in the photographs by Murai Osamu that accompanies the essay. Featuring Umbrella House's interior, the image includes a ladder that visually leads the viewer to an illuminated square light atop the radiating rafters. Beyond the overall square plan of the house and base of the umbrella rafters, the square also frames a painting by Asakura Setsu hung on the back wall, and print design on the adjacent *fusuma* sliding panels, as literal works of art. Umbrella House thus prompts questions about the meanings of the square in the house's design and Shinohara's pursuit of the house as a work of art in local and global contexts.

Such a predilection toward this platonic shape can be attributed to Shinohara's training as a mathematician and his teaching of descriptive geometry at the Tokyo Institute of Technology. His mentor Seike Kiyoshi's own house featured a movable square tatami platform as a focal point of the design. Square tatami and shōji screen frames appear in Shinohara's maiden design of House in Kugayama (1954) and House in Kugayama No. 2 (1958), which is also roughly square in plan. The square tatami, lacking side bands, offered the advantage of being able to equally and efficiently accommodate many different configurations.

On a broader level, the square can be seen to be central to a modernist's conceptual zeitgeist. While 1962 marked the English publication of *Discovery of the Square* by Bruno Munari,[4] the basic geometric form was the Suprematist pursuit of Kazimir Malevich in works such as his 1915 oil painting *Black Square,* which evokes "the supremacy of pure artistic feeling" rather than the visual depiction of objects. The square, both in abstract concept and exact dimensions, was central to the Purist ideals of Le Corbusier and the precise geometries and square-gridded designs of Ludwig Mies van der Rohe.

Shinohara's Umbrella House also builds on precedents of the Japanese House. Namely, Shinohara's design, which he started in 1959, followed the 1954–55 Japanese Exhibition House on display at the Museum of Modern Art (MoMA) in New York. The Japanese House, designed by Yoshimura Junzō based on

1 Shinohara Kazuo, "Umbrella House," *The Japan Architect* (February 1963): 69–79.

2 Bruno Munari, *Discovery of the Square* (New York: George Wittenborn, 1965), 5. Originally published in Italian as *Il Quadrato,* 1960.

3 Shinohara Kazuo, "*Jūtaku wa geijutsu de aru*" (A house is a work of art), *Shinkenchiku* vol. 37, no. 5 (May 1962): 77–78. Republished in Shinohara Kazuo, *Jūtaku ron* (Residential theory) (Tokyo: Kajima shuppankai, 1970), 78–105.

4 Munari, *Discovery of the Square.*

5 Arthur Drexler, *The Architecture of Japan* (New York: Museum of Modern Art, 1955), 262–86.

6 Richard Haag, "Memo to Japanese Designers," *Shinkenchiku* vol. 30, no. 2 (February 1955): n.p.

7 Shinohara Kazuo, "A Theory of Residential Architecture," *The Japan Architect* (October 1967): 39.

8 Ibid., 46.

the seventeenth-century precedent of the Kōjō-in *shoin* design at Mii-dera, highlighted the parallels between Japanese traditions and modernist ideals, including the geometry of the square and flexible living space.[5] Moreover, as an exhibit at MoMA the house was literally "a work of art."

However, Umbrella House marks a shift to more common vernacular traditions in contrast to the elite traditions represented by the Katsura Villa, as expressed in Tange Kenzō's own house in Seijō (1953) and Shinohara's House in Kugayama—and following designer Richard Haag's "Memo to Japanese Designers" to pursue domestic vernacular models rather than imported Western ones:

> Japan is sick. This nation suffers from a chronic case of indigestion resulting from the over-consumption of undercooked foreign recipes and half-baked ideas.... Throughout Japan, the domestic architecture exhibits many forgotten but important lessons. Most of these lessons are worthy of universal application.[6]

For Shinohara, this observation resonated on a fundamental level, as he later explained:

> If modern highly industrial society continues to reveal its personality more and more clearly, deep-level human emotional processes will concentrate because they must intensify to oppose industrialization.... It is an undeniable fact that a pronouncement made against the background of our powerful modern industrial society is the only real strength.[7]

> The architect, existing outside of the bureaucracy, must criticize society and act as a last-line defense of humanity in crisis. To do this he must sincerely devote himself to the development of personal architecture and to forcing that architecture into society. In other words, he is sure that the superficiality and the inhumanity of modern civilization is on the increase. The architect must protect and emphasize the personal and inner life of the individual and family.[8]

Shinohara thus synthesized lessons from the everyday primordial elements of the umbrella and the farmhouse/*minka.* In Umbrella House, Shinohara transformed the circular structure of an umbrella to fit a square plan. Like an umbrella, the house's rafters fan out from the center anchored with a flat steel frame with the weight of the roof distributed evenly among the rafters. As Shinohara described, "I wished to express the force of space contained in the *doma* (earthen-floor room) of an old Japanese farmhouse by means of the geometric design of a *karakasa* (paper umbrella)." More explicitly, Umbrella House built on the design of the Edo-period Kasatei (Umbrella Pavilion) at Kōdai-ji in Kyoto. While retaining the precedent's exposed rafter structure, Shinohara removed the central supporting member to expose the illuminated square above. Moreover, he expanded the eight-mat pavilion to the scale of a home and used a crisp, geometric steel roof at a shallower pitch rather than using thatch.

Shinohara further reinterpreted domestic precedents according to geometric rigor to enhance the play of light and space. As he detailed:

Kannon Hall, Kasamori Temple, Chōnan, Chiba Prefecture, 1028, rebuilt in late sixteenth century. Photo by Seng Kuan

Kikutake Kiyonori, Sky House, Bunkyō Ward, Tokyo, 1958. Photo by Kawasumi Akio

In the space under the high roof of geometric form, I attempted to provide as broad a visual scope as possible. At the same time, I wished to set off the bedroom and the bath in a partitioned section. There is a large opening on the south side of the living room, and here I raised the level of the threshold somewhat to that of the room with tatami mats, which is higher than the floor of the living room. The result was that there is a shadow over the living room floor that answers the deep shadows under the ceiling. The general aim in the living room was to achieve an effect similar to that of the broad un-floored space found at one end of the typical Japanese farmhouse. As a matter of fact, throughout the designing of this house I had in mind a plan that I regard as an early form of the farmhouse. Though it is generally said that Japanese farmhouses are laid out on a rectangular plan bisected in two directions, I suspect that this is a developed form. It seems likely to me that the farmhouse, having originated as a single room, was first bisected in one direction only, and that in the next step one of the two halves was further partitioned into two. This form would be similar to that of the present house. One of its principal advantages is that it allows for considerable play of light and shadow within a relatively small space.[9]

Shinohara in fact based his theory of houses, *"Jūtaku ron,"* on the collective evolution of Japanese tradition (*Nihon dentō ron*).[10] In discussing iconic *minka* such as Kusakabe House in Hida Takayama, he argued that they maintained the primordial character of the Jōmon-period *tateana* pit dwelling defined by living on the *doma* (earthen floor) under a pronounced roof enclosure. These precedents expressed the structure within while maintaining light and ventilations through openings in the roof. Thus Umbrella House's illuminated square at the top of the rafters can be seen to evoke these fundamental qualities.

Yet in contrast to the large, multigenerational historic ideal of the *minka,* Umbrella House provides a model of a minimal postwar dwelling for a nuclear family. The client, Kawai Shōzō, was an employee of the KDD company building the basically one-room house for his family, his wife and three children.[11] While the impressive size and scope of Kusakabe House was beyond reach for Kawai, he could attain its essence in Umbrella House, built along rapidly developing suburban Tokyo, just west of Ikebukuro Station.

A contrasting variation of Shinohara's square-plan postwar Japanese minimal dwelling can be found in Kikutake Kiyonori's Sky House. Begun a year before Umbrella House, Sky House similarly maintains a square roof, 10 by 10 meters in area. Sky House also follows traditional Japanese precedents—namely the eleventh-century square-plan Kasamori Temple. However, while both postwar houses maintain basic configurations of living, dining, and sleeping, Sky House asserts a strongly centrifugal character leading to the surrounding *engawa* balconies, and Umbrella House is stalwartly centripetal in its inward-looking character, akin to traditional teahouses. Moreover, Sky House is inherently designed to change configurations of living/dining/kitchen that abstract flexible living principles of traditional living on tatami, while Umbrella House literally maintains tatami living for sleeping, but is actually more fixed in its overall configuration of living/dining/kitchen.

9 Shinohara, "Umbrella House."

10 Shinohara, *Jūtaku ron.*

11 Fujimori Terunobu *TOTO Tsūshin*, no. 3 (1997); repri. in *Fujimori Terunobu no gen gendai jūtaku saiken* (Tokyo: TOTO shuppan, 2006).

12 Itō Toyoo worked for Kikutake from 1965 to 1969 and is also widely considered a spiritual follower of Shinohara.

13 Shinohara, "Umbrella House," [69]–[79].

14 Paul Valéry, quoted in "The Work of Art in the Age of Mechanical Reproduction," in Walter Benjamin. *Illuminations* (New York: Schocken Books, 1969), 217.

Shinohara and Kikutake's protégé Itō Toyoo synthesized these variations through successive designs of his White U House (1976) for his elder sister and the adjacent Silver Hut (1984) for himself.[12] The overall volume of the White U adheres to the basically square site, and the central earthen court directly expresses the notion of *doma.* For Itō's own home, he began with a square grid plan that evolved to become basically a nine-square plan with square bedroom volumes shifting out from this base. He maintained the openness of Kikutake through an open barrel vault "silver hut" structure, while maintaining the principles of Shinohara's plan geometry through the base for the home is using the *doma* floor as a platform for living with the outer square terrace abutting the L-shaped living / dining / kitchen volume.

Shinohara himself continued to embrace the square in many variations throughout his career. His masterwork House in White clearly maintains the square plan, with the center demarcated by the *tokobashira* column. While the roof structure is concealed by a flat white roof, he maintained the geometric rigor of the square all the way through the square gridded shoji frames. Shinohara further embraced the abstraction of square geometry in The Uncompleted House (1970), which maintains the square plan, further creates the square cubic volume in the center, and abandons the deep eaves typical of his earlier houses. He further embraced the three-dimensional cubic geometric form in Cubic Forest (1971) followed by a continuing lineage up to the V-shaped triangulation of square volumes in his Kumamoto-Kita Police Station (1990).

Following Shinohara's passing in 2006 the genealogy of the square continues in the twenty-first century through subsequent generations, particularly in the geometric rigor of Horibe Yasushi's square plan designs, such as House in Sumiyoshi (2015). This dwelling continues the tradition of the exposed umbrella roof on the second floor while also recalling dynamic square geometries seen in Louis Kahn's Fisher House (1967).

The variations on the square embodied in Shinohara's Umbrella House and subsequent iterations in his own work and that of many others affirm the "house as a work of art." This does not follow the notion of art as a divine original creation, but rather as a notion of geometric perfection in counterpoint to the vicissitudes of life. One constantly returns to fundamentals, but such perspectives may change over time and express the personality of the individual in a delicate tension between the universal and local, past and present, that continues to animate Shinohara's work. Again, as Shinohara noted, "We must not confine ourselves to the requirements of the individual residence, but attempt to develop principles of residential architecture that have wider social applications and implications."[13] "Art" is embodied here in its definition as the expression or application of human creative skill and imagination producing works to be appreciated primarily for their beauty or emotional power. The square, embodied in Shinohara's work in its variations and reproductions, indeed attest to its wider impact in the modern era and also recall the words of French poet Paul Valéry: "We must expect great innovations to transform the entire technique of the arts, thereby affecting artistic invention itself and perhaps even bringing about an amazing change in our very notion of art."[14]

Itō Toyoo, White U, Nakano Ward, Tokyo, 1976. Photo by Taki Kōji, courtesy of Toyo Ito & Associates

Shinohara Kazuo, Umbrella House, Nerima Ward, Tokyo, 1962, view from *hiroma* looking toward Japanese room. Photo by Murai Osamu

UMBRELLA HOUSE, 1961
Nerima Ward, Tokyo

With the completion of Umbrella House Shinohara pronounced, “A house is a work of art.” As a critique of Metabolism’s purported functionalism and rationalism, Umbrella House possesses all the hallmarks of the First Style, featuring disciplined use of geometry and abstraction while maintaining a dialogue with Japanese architectural patrimony, particularly that of *minka* commoner houses. With a footprint of 7 by 7 meters, the minuscule house also asserts the luxury of expansive living, or “superfluous space,” through the radical simplification of dwelling functions, to achieve the corollary effect of “insufficient space.” A main post slightly offset from the center anchors the square plan, while the four major components of the dwelling unit—living room (*hiroma*), eat-in kitchen, bathroom, and sleeping quarters—are arranged in a pinwheel fashion rotating around it. The conspicuous web of ceiling rafters and the main post allude to oil-paper umbrellas (*karakasa*) and are subsumed as a key visual cue in the imagination of premodern craft and visual culture.

Photos by
Murai Osamu (MO)

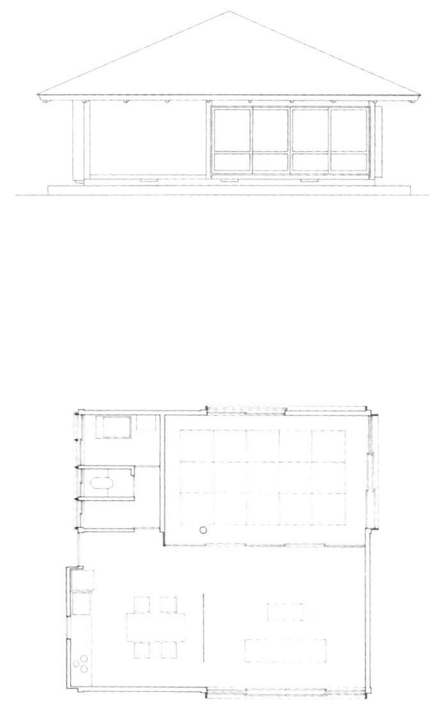

1:200

O

MO

Section drawing, 1960.

View from Japanese room looking toward *hiroma.*

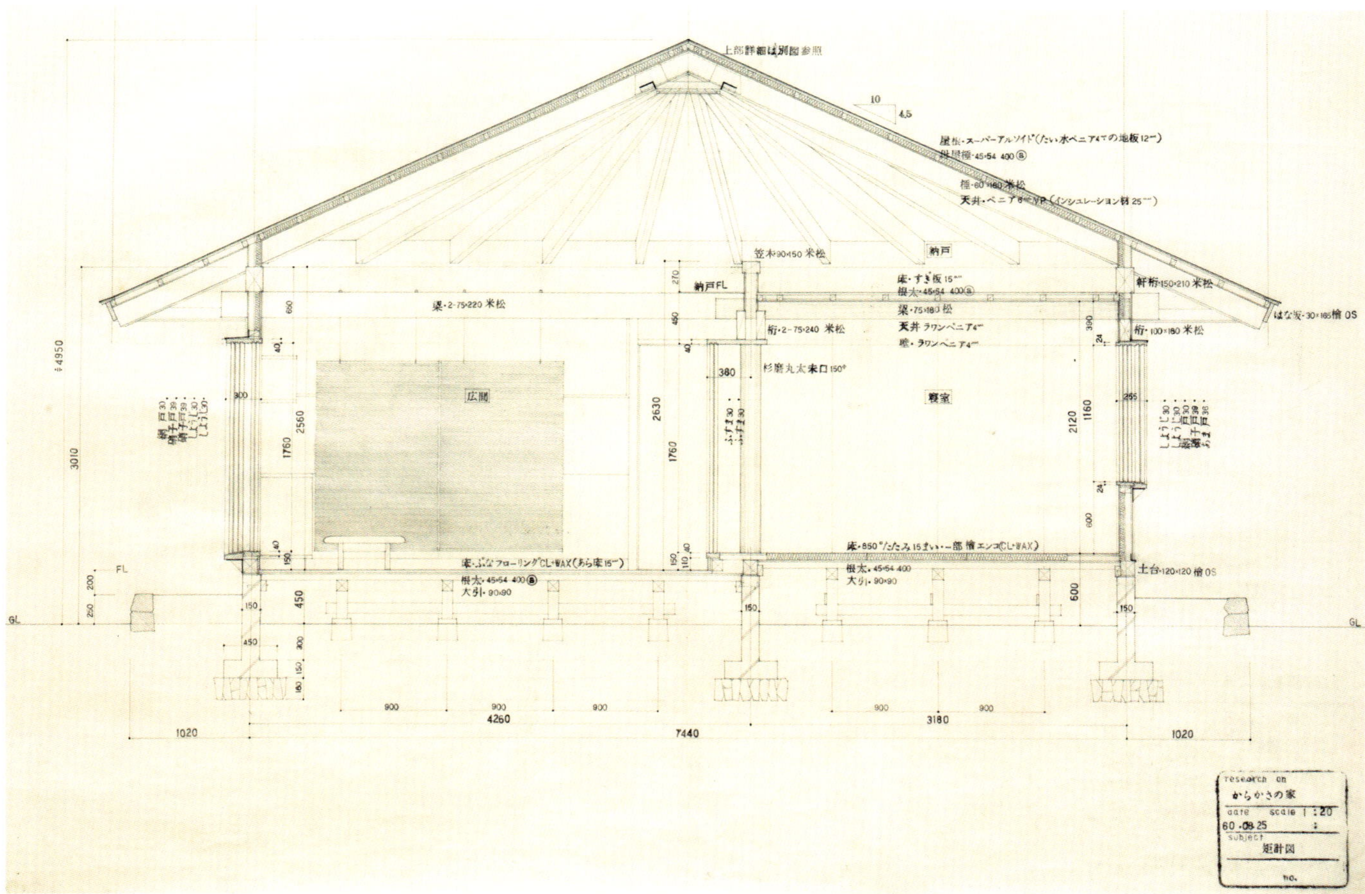

Umbrella House during construction. Photos by the client, Kawai Shōzō, courtesy of Kawai Emi

35. 12. 18.
南面の柱を建てているところ. 棟上げは12.24に行った.
35. 12. 30.
左端が棟領. 12.31に仕事納めで帰郷する由。正月は5日から作業開始

HOUSE WITH AN EARTHEN FLOOR, 1963
Miyota, Nagano Prefecture

Shinohara's first house in the countryside, this mountain retreat for photographer Ōtsuji Kiyoshi manifests most vividly Shinohara's analogy of *minka* farmhouses as mushrooms that sprout from the ground. Divided into four quadrants, the square plan is a rigorous study in spatial divisions. Half of the floor plan, the *doma,* maintains an earthen finish, which consists of a stable mixture of clay and lime. The square building is covered by a slightly convex, *mukuri* roof that stands out remarkably in its mountainous setting. The door on the northern, earthen-floored side of the house opens to a vista of Mount Asama. In the opposite direction from the raised, tatami rooms are the Yatsugatake Mountains. Expansive openings on the two opposing sides allow this natural landscape to appear as if flowing through the building, foreshadowing some of the more radical works of the Third Style.

Photos by
Ōtsuji Kiyoshi (ŌK) and Koyama Takashi (KT)

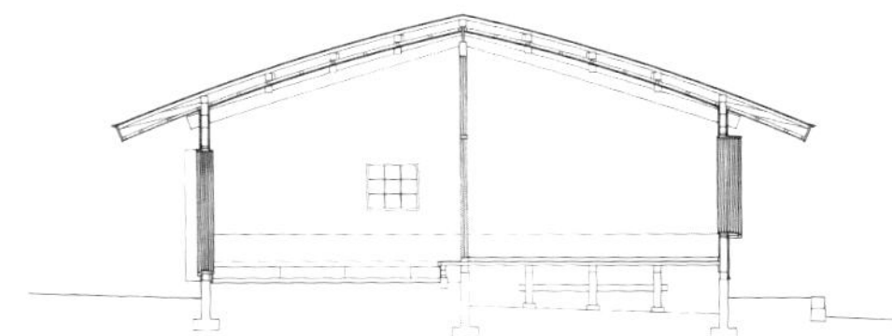

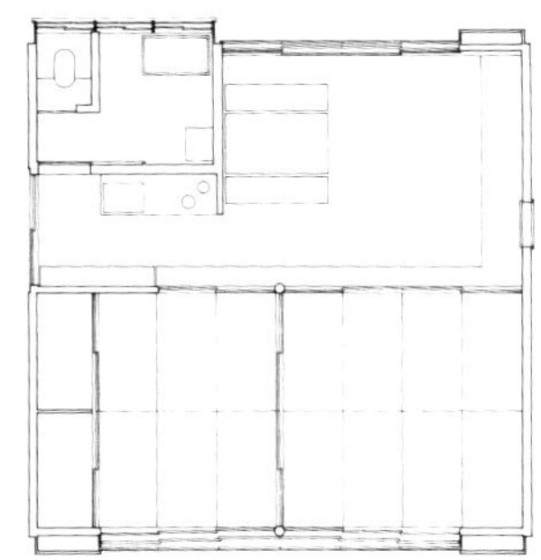

1:200

North elevation.

Doma.

View from Japanese room looking toward *doma.*

West elevation.

ŌK

KT

KT

HOUSE IN WHITE, 1966
Suginami Ward, Tokyo

House in White encapsulates the rhetorical pursuit of abstraction, largeness, and timelessness that dominated Shinohara's polemics in the 1960s. Twice the size of Umbrella House (1961) and designed as a counterpoint to House of Earth (1966), the plan here is a 10-by-10-meter square, anchored in the center by a main post made of polished cedar, situated in splendid isolation and piercing through the pristine ceiling and floor. Shinohara especially noted the rarefied origins of this piece of lumber from Kyoto's Kitayama area. The pyramidal roof, with its geometry accentuated by deep protruding eaves, is conspicuous on its tiled exterior, yet completely disguised inside by a gypsum-covered false ceiling, resulting in a pure cubic space. Though the house is both structurally and symbolically a timber-frame building suggestive of Japanese residential tradition, construction and ornamental details and proportional measurements have been erased in favor of geometric purity. House in White is a folly of the unexpected, spectacularly successful in its mediation of tradition and modernity while betraying Shinohara's underlying desire for the uncanny.

Photos by
Murai Osamu (MO), Murasawa Fumio for Shōkokusha (MF), and Ueda Hiroshi (UH)

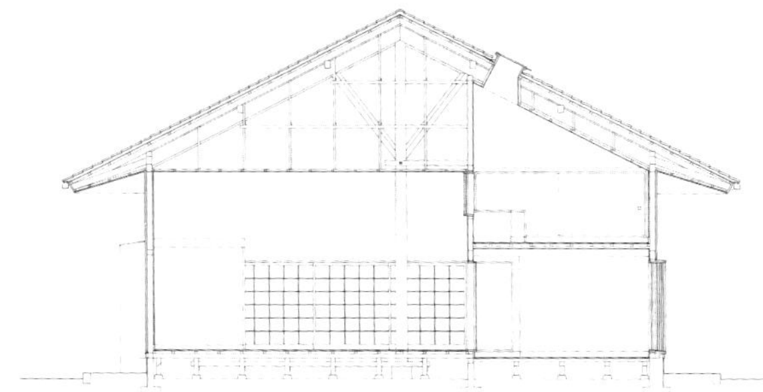

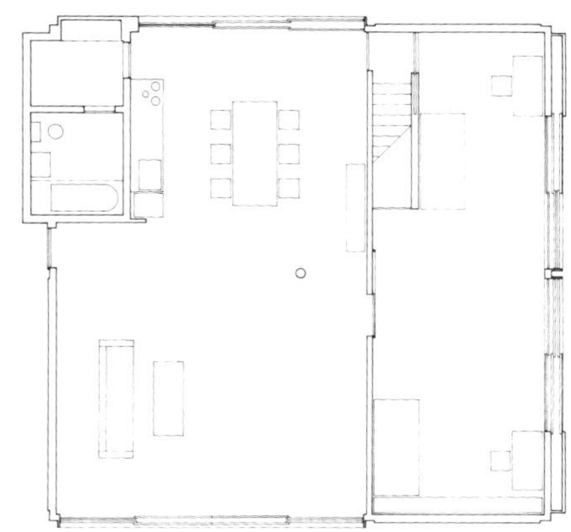

1:200

Hiroma.

Upper-floor bedroom.

The house and its neighborhood (after its relocation in 2008 to its present location).

Pillar in *hiroma.*

MF

UH

MF

HOUSE OF EARTH, 1966
Nerima Ward, Tokyo

House of Earth is the culmination of Shinohara's pursuit of the earth's creative and emotive powers. In 1964, at the exhibition he shared with artist Asakura Setsu, Shinohara put forth a conceptual project called House of Earth—Space in Black (*daichi no ie—kuro no kūkan*). The entire complex of 100 square meters is buried underground, represented as a figure-ground diagram of four dispersed quarters interconnected by narrow corridors. For Shinohara, the darkness of the underground symbolizes one's desires, anxieties, and feeling of alienation. Presented here is the realized version of House of Earth, which was designed in parallel with House in White (1966), and Shinohara indeed considered calling the subterranean dwelling House in Black instead to underscore their complementarity. Notably, the house's two levels are not stacked, but rather offset to occupy the full width of the site, thus forming a stronger descending procession. The rich colors of the upper level, its irregular quadrilateral plan, and a swooping roof, folded along an oblique ridge, all work together to reinforce the drama of this emotive journey.

Photos by
Murai Osamu (MO) and Murasawa Fumio for Shōkokusha (MF)

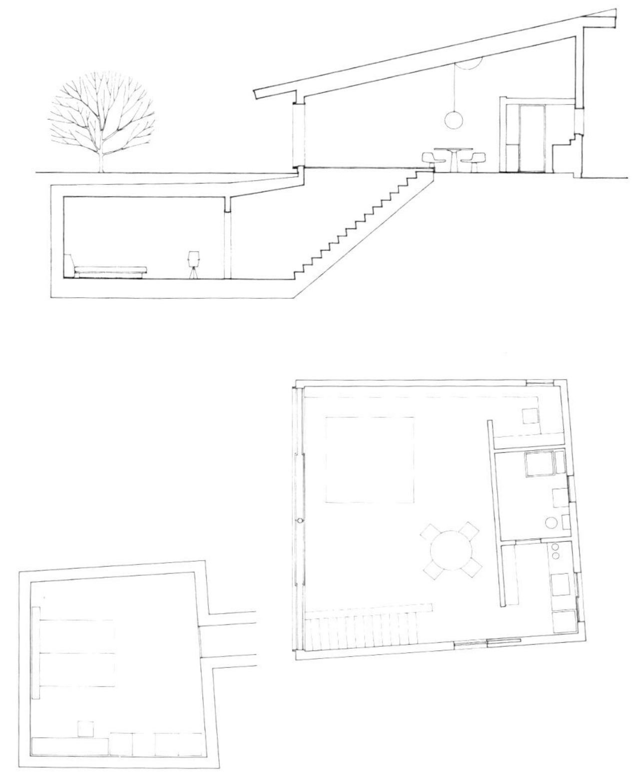

1:200

Doma living room, ground floor.
Mushroom dining table and chairs
set designed by Shinohara Kazuo.

MF

MF

Staircase to underground-floor bedroom.

Raised square platform in *doma*.

South elevation.

MF

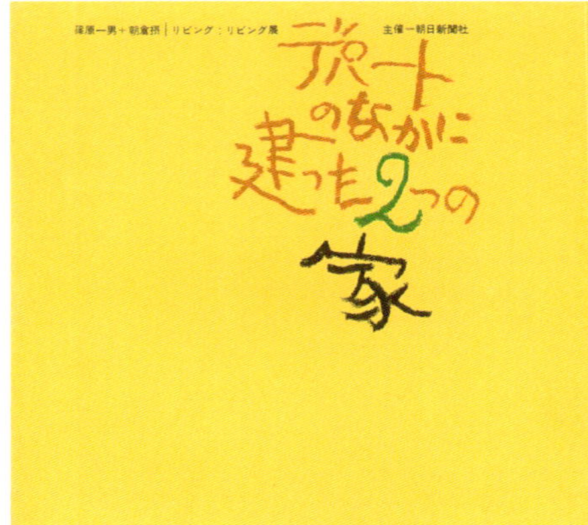

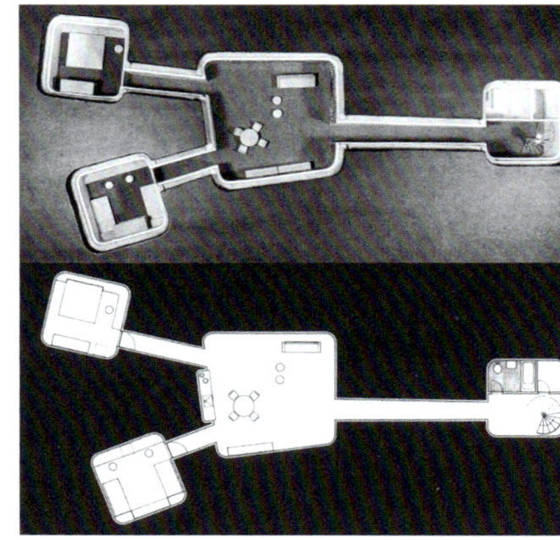

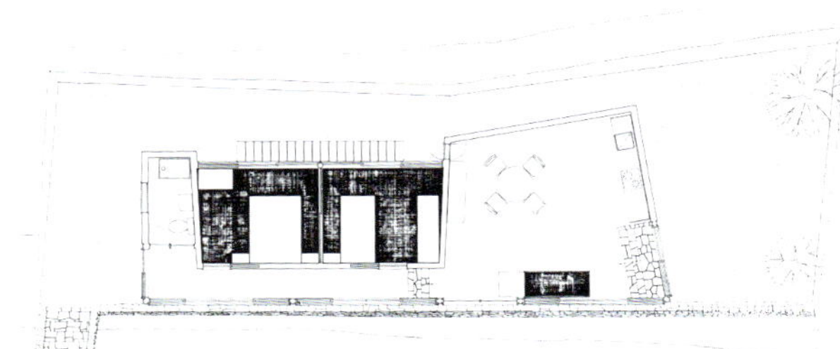

Awazu Kiyoshi, cover design, exhibition catalogue for *Shinohara Kazuo & Asakura Setsu: Two Houses inside a Department Store* (Odakyū Department Store, 1964). Courtesy of Odakyū Department Store, Tokyo

Shinohara Kazuo, House of Earth—Space in Black, 1964, unbuilt.

Shinohara Kazuo, D-1 Square House as installed in *Shinohara & Asakura* exhibition, 1964. Television and stereo console, system kitchen, and appliances by Shinohara Kazuo and Yaō Electronics; dining table and chairs by Kenmochi Isamu; lighting works by Tada Minami.

Shinohara Kazuo, M-Space House, 1964, unbuilt, north and south elevations.

Shinohara Kazuo, D-2 Earthen Floor House as installed at *Shinohara & Asakura* exhibition, 1964. System kitchen and appliances by Shinohara Kazuo and Yaō Electronics; Mushroom dining table and chairs set by Shinohara Kazuo; wall art by Asakura Setsu; lighting works by Tada Minami.

M-Space House, plan.

Shinohara Kazuo & Asakura Setsu Exhibition

Editor's Note

Just a few months before the 1964 Summer Olympics in Tokyo, the city's Odakyū Department Store hosted an exhibition featuring works by Shinohara Kazuo and painter and stage set designer Asakura Setsu.[1] Instigated by Kuwasawa Yōko, founder of the Bauhaus-inspired eponymous school of design, an affiliation shared by many of Shinohara's friends in the arts, the presentation was a *Gesamtkunstwerk* of living. Shinohara was responsible for the overall exhibition design and the architectural exhibits, while Asakura created artworks on *fusuma* panels, wallpapers, curtain dividers, and ceilings. Awazu Kiyoshi did the graphic design, Takemitsu Toru composed the music, Tada Minami designed the lighting works, and Tanikawa Shuntarō and Awazu collaborated on two poegrams as wall art. All these collaborators were leading figures of the 1960s Japanese avant-garde.

In the compact confines of a department store's gallery—a legacy of Belle Époque department stores that remains alive and well in Japan today—Shinohara designed two full-scale mock-ups of houses. Titled SF Originals '64: D-1 Square House and D-2 Earthen Floor House (also referred to as Prototypes 1 & 2), they were essays on the respective themes of division and connection. Two further conceptual projects, M-Space House and House of Earth—Space in Black (*daichi no ie—kuro no kūkan*), were presented as drawings and 1:50 models. A fifth project, the schematic design for a house for Asakura, Shinohara's co-exhibitor, was also on view.

The two Prototypical houses were conceived as limited-edition multiples (suggested runs of twenty and five, respectively), as Shinohara's answer to industrialized housing. He took particular care to work with Yaō, an electric appliance maker now under Fujitsū, to explore the potential for design in modern industrial processes. This collaboration resulted in an integrated television and stereo console and a system kitchen with two variations, both featuring black refrigerators that they also designed. Dubbed "Kitchen with Four Corners," the unit at Prototype 1 reconfigured the conventional kitchen-dining setup by intruding into the center of the living space, in a manner akin to modern kitchen islands. Shinohara further created the Mushroom dining table and chair ensemble for Prototype 2, in a nod to his analogy of *minka* commoner houses as fungi.[2] The more conceptual M-Space House appears to share Prototype 2's arrangement of main living spaces along a *doma* (earthen floored) linear corridor, but the "M" here stands for Möbius, referring to a continuous surface in mathematics with only one side and one boundary curve. As a smooth loop that returns in inversion, the Möbius strip's typology opens an entirely new realm to the theme of spatial connection. The subtle contour of the corresponding roof form anticipates the diagonally folded roof later seen in House of Earth (1966). House of Earth—Space in Black, the second conceptual project, pushed the limits of spatial division to their extreme. Various living spaces are placed in discrete compartments buried underground, separated by the dense, dark earth between them.

Shinohara Kazuo & Asakura Setsu: Two Houses inside a Department Store
Odakyū Department Store, Tokyo
April 3 to April 8, 1964

1 Shinohara's architectural projects are covered most extensively in the May 1964 issue of *Kenchiku* and May and June issues of *Kindai kenchiku*. For a discussion in English, see Okuyama Shin-ichi, "Meaning of the Archetypal House Project: Division, Non-division, and Connection," in *Shinohara Kazuo: Jūtaku zumen*, ed. Ishidō Takeshi et al. (Tokyo: Shōkokusha, 2008), 134–35.

2 Shinohara Kazuo, *Jūtaku kenchiku* (Residential architecture) (Tokyo: Kinokuniya shoten, 1964), 50–52. As Shinohara's first major theoretical publication, this book appeared just weeks before the exhibition's opening and can be understood as a complementary manifesto.

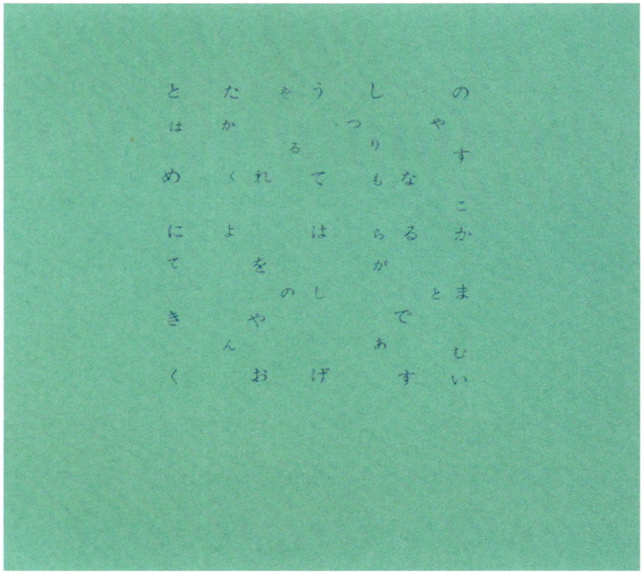

Tanikawa Shuntarō and Awazu Kiyoshi, Poegrams, for the exhibition *Shinohara Kazuo & Asakura Setsu: Two Houses inside a Department Store* (Odakyū Department Store, 1964). Courtesy of Odakyū Department Store, Tokyo.

What Is Design?

A Roundtable

Participants:
Shinohara Kazuo, architect
Tanikawa Shuntarō, poet, client of Tanikawa Houses, 1958 and 1974
Asakura Setsu, painter, client of Asakura House, 1966
Mitani Isamu, businessman, client of House in Komae, 1960
Hanyū Michio, painter and roundtable session director

This roundtable was part of a series of six such events convened by Shinohara Kazuo and published in the magazine *Bijutsu jyānaru* (Art journal) in 1960–61. The painter Asakura Setsu, poet Tanikawa Shuntarō, industrial designer Mukai Shūtarō, and graphic designers Awazu Kiyoshi and Sugiura Kōhei were recurring participants in this series. Session 5, which featured contributions from three guests who had (or would soon have) their houses designed by Shinohara is translated here into English. Explanatory notes have been added to this translation, below.

HOUSE IN KOMAE

SHINOHARA KAZUO The first discussion will be on architecture, and my works, with focus on the house for Mr. Mitani here, offered up on the altar of criticism. According to a review by a certain architect, this space is slightly too "moody." Certainly, I could have created a more taut space. I admit the way plywood and other materials come together and the general effect of the colors make the space atmospheric. We were in a hurry, the plywood and other materials were not as I had conceived them, and we ended up with these colors…

ASAKURA SETSU I don't know much about architecture, but does the ceiling have to be tilted for reasons of structural mechanics?

SHINOHARA You can tell from looking at this structural drawing… the pitch of the roof on the outside was necessary for reasons of structural mechanics. However, greater freedom was possible in the space inside. There was just one visual problem I wanted to express on the inside, the distinctive space existing outside.

ASAKURA I am of the opposite opinion. I think it would have been better had the pitch of the roof been expressed more powerfully inside.

SHINOHARA I don't like making the ceiling horizontal; it feels rather artificial, as if things have been tidied up. My intention had more to do with function and structure—to expose and make clear the structure of the roof on the inside. One other thing, with a horizontal ceiling, the life lived underneath it would no longer have been this sort of life. What is here now is a space that has been ordered and made abstract; the elements of life have been pared down to a bare minimum. In fact I wanted an even simpler expression. I wanted the direct expression of structural equilibrium, with rafters extended radially from the center of the ceiling. Had that been the case, the resulting interior as well as the life lived here would have been a bit more intense.

HANYŪ MICHIO With respect to the interior, the articles of furniture by Mr. Matsumura Katsuo[1] are all simple and succinct, but the refrigerator seems incongruous. What is your feeling about that?

SHINOHARA The design of the refrigerator. I am not sure I would go so far as to change that. Some conflicts do arise between the things we architects create and industrial products. That is to be expected. Only, I do question the way television sets are designed.

TANIKAWA Devices that have been made to seem rustic or folksy are contrived and not truly simple. Trying to make a concrete bridge look like a wooden bridge is offensive. I want a machine to be like a machine as much as possible.

SHINOHARA Right. The methods of approach are completely different. The problem is one of simply subdividing a large Japanese space of this kind. Elements such as a *karakasa* paper umbrella appeared, and the space gradually became traditional. *Minka* [close to the ground living] and *takayuka* [raised-floor living] emerged simultaneously.

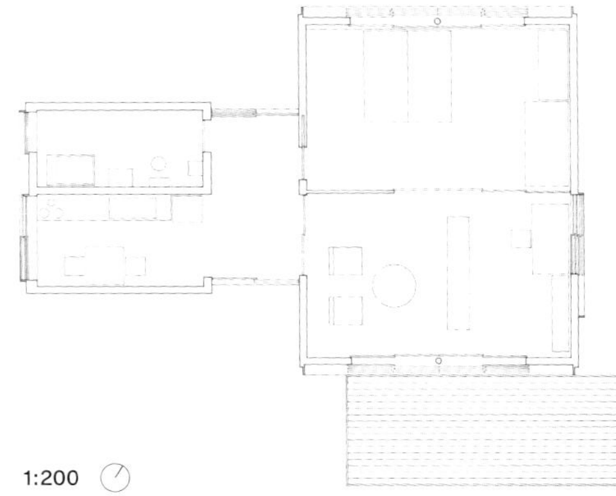

1:200

TANIKAWA Why was the plan subdivided? It seems to go beyond matters of function and point to some inner struggle. It indicates the direction in which you are heading. Isn't that so?

ASAKURA What are your thoughts, Mr. Shinohara, on tradition?

SHINOHARA There has always been a deep relationship between architecture, especially houses, and human history, and the issue of Japanese tradition has to be considered in that context. Therefore, I don't approach the question in a European way. To take an example, rectangles can have many different proportions, and logic dictates which one I choose to use. The square, however, is unique, and my choice of the square is more impulsive.

TANIKAWA Your architecture is conceptual—a better word might be ideational. In some ways, you are designing a house to express the fundamental idea of "dwelling."

ASAKURA Looking at photographs and drawings, I have the feeling that your aim is to achieve a kind of empty space. For example, when you compare a European sculpture and a Japanese figure of Buddha, the European sculpture is based on a perception of space as something that is full, but I think an Asura figure is a sculpture created in an empty space. In paintings, too, I think there is a great difference in consciousness of space between Japan and other countries.

TANIKAWA I don't much understand what empty space means, but Mr. Shinohara's is certainly an abstract space. You don't think about space in the context of everyday life. The idea comes first, and I think that is the correct approach. But you painted the east and west walls in two different colors—that was a mistake. You were compromising.

SHINOHARA This may sound like I'm making excuses, but I did consider various measures such as leaving the plywood of the wall as it was, and exposing the ceiling structure.

ASAKURA There is no texture. Even with this Japanese paper, *washi*. I think it would have made a big difference had you used 3-by-6-*shaku* (93.9 by 184.8 centimeters) sheets or 7-by-9-*shaku* (212 by 273 centimeters) sheets. Then the surface would have been bigger and suggested a single block, even from a distance.

SHINOHARA Ready-made *washi* were available in only three colors, and this length was pretty much what they had in stock. We were out of time. It wasn't a compromise, but it couldn't be helped. I knew that an impression of strength could not be created with the weakness of plywood on the gently sloping ceiling.... When it comes time to repaper it, I intend to consider the matter in earnest.

TANIKAWA Couldn't you have left it unfinished and entrusted the occupant to finish it?

SHINOHARA Color photographs needed to be taken [laughter].

TANIKAWA You were corrupted by commercialism [laughter].

ASAKURA Then, the bolts on the columns and beams are exposed, which is all well and good, but they might be mistaken for knotholes [laughter]. Thicker bolts would have been desirable. But for that, the columns are too slender.

SHINOHARA What I was doing here was trying to create a flexible space in which one can stand or sit. In that I think I succeeded. However, all the materials

Shinohara Kazuo, Tanikawa House, Suginami Ward, Tokyo, 1958, south elevation and view from south room looking to the north. Photos by Saeki Yoshikatsu

are wrong. I wanted the bolts themselves, and of course the columns too, to be thicker, but to a certain extent it is not quite what I had in mind, visually.

ASAKURA I suppose the construction cost and time available are decisive factors in architecture.

SHINOHARA I used 4-millimeter-thick plywood practically everywhere, with the idea that the interior finish would be redone later. Here, too, the thickness impacts materiality. I wanted to use 6-millimeter-thick plywood. Instead of lauan, I wanted something Japanese such as *tamo* or *shioji*. And the fact that I used *washi* to cover the plywood has been questioned, but for one thing, Mr. Sugiura suggested that I use something grainy, and Mr. Matsumura Katsuo also said, in connection with arranging the furniture, that he wanted something grainy. So that is how *washi* came to be used to provide a texture. I asked Mr. Sugiura for help with the interior, but that didn't work out. However, one thing I have hopes for, with respect to graphic design, is that there are in graphic design things in the manner of [Ogata] Kōrin.[2] I wonder if they might be used like a pattern in architecture. That is, I am wondering if collaboration with a broad range of designers, not just furniture designers, but photographers like Mr. Nara Gen'ichi and graphic designers like Mr. Sugiura, might be possible. Not murals but more basic things like colors and patterns.

TANIKAWA In principle, your approach is correct, but I don't think it is applicable to small houses.

If there were a work by Kōrin always in the same place in a house of 18 *tsubo* (60 square meters), you would be so overwhelmed, you wouldn't be able to relax. Though it might be interesting to design a room using such a pattern.... That might work in a child's bedroom, though you would want to change the way things are arranged inside it constantly.

ASAKURA I am opposed to using it in a child's bedroom! It would play havoc with the child's imagination [laughter].

TANIKAWA Then, why not leave it to the child? Let the child scribble, though children never draw where you want them to draw [laughter].

LIVING IN A WORK BY SHINOHARA

TANIKAWA The question is not criticism by someone who is looking from outside, such as Ms. Asakura, but whether the people living in houses designed by Mr. Shinohara are satisfied or not.

SHINOHARA I quite understand the things about which people are dissatisfied, such as the bedroom being on a lower floor...

MITANI ISAMU I am not at all dissatisfied.

TANIKAWA I wonder about how architectural critics walk around the building on the outside and say this or that about the mood. Is that approach really correct? There are things that can only be understood by living there. My father rather enjoys showing off my house to guests. He says openly that it is a house to be shown [laughter]. I imagine that is both an insult and a point of pride to Mr. Shinohara. There are two meanings to architecture. Architecture as a "monument" and as a "place to live in"... though I think both are necessary.

SHINOHARA I quite understand the idea of completely satisfying the requirements of a "dwelling." However, for me, there is something I need to do even more, something that takes precedence. But I am thinking about bridging the gap between those two positions a step at a time. However, most people think a house is comfortable if it allows them to live as they always have, and that is not the best house.

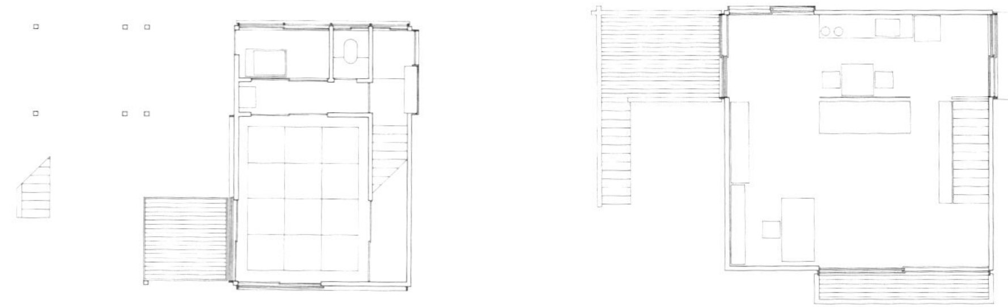

1:200

TANIKAWA To meet as much as possible the demands of the people who are to live in a house is, in a sense, to compromise and accommodate the laziness of users. Human desire being insatiable, no house will fully satisfy them. Satisfying demands through the development of technology is one approach, but if anything, Mr. Shinohara's position is to protest that.

This is a problem not just of architecture. It is a problem of the way humans think about families. For example, it might be convenient if two people thought of marriage in a completely functional way and lived together accordingly [laughter], but I think that would be wrong. Marriage is a basic form of human life, and I think that if possible it should have a religious dimension. I think the same can be said of a house for a family. I would not want a house to be simply functional. I want a house that suggests an image of life.

SHINOHARA In the house for Mr. Tanikawa, I designed a large space with trusses. It isn't easy to create an archetype, but that is what I want to continue to do. However, the works I have published up to now have also been designed with the idea of realizing spaces that people can depend on in everyday life in some way; I haven't been going out of my way to design something that is awful [laughter].

MITANI I have always been interested in architecture. When I see the sensei taking great pains to get things right, I'm glad I asked him to design the house. It feels as if the scales have fallen from my eyes; I have become a complete believer. This is just the opinion of an average, lower-middle-class individual, but if I had chosen to live in an ordinary house, I think I would now be leading an unreflective, complacent way of life.

SHINOHARA A fine client [laughter]. Designing anything less than a good building under these conditions would be inexcusable [laughter].

TANIKAWA The relationship between the client and the architect is extremely important. One-way communication is no good, and simply satisfying the demands of the client is laziness on the part of both the architect and the client.

SHINOHARA A sense of purpose with respect to houses has been lost to people today, ourselves included. After the war, the "living room/kitchen" was an ingenious melding of technology and purpose, and persuasion of the client went hand in hand with improvement in lifestyle. For example, the idea of equality between husband and wife and respect for the independence of children were directly reflected in the plans of houses, and architects no doubt felt their lives had a definite purpose. Today everyone knows these things, and people are free to do whatever they like. They can all buy the same ready-made items. It is no longer clear what constitutes a good house. In places such as the United States the sense of purpose with respect to life itself is already being lost. My work resists that development. A way of understanding what human life is about is expressed in the form of houses. When that is suddenly constructed on a site, the house, suggesting an image of how a husband and wife might live, is different in form from the expression of convenience the general public seeks to achieve. This is also true of the house for Mr. Tanikawa. For anyone with a commonsensical point of view, it has major defects. There is another aspect to what I am doing. With a site of 18 *tsubo* (60 square meters), under present circumstances, the plan is apt to be much the same no matter who does the design. In times like these, I want to design using a method that is exclusively my own.

TANIKAWA I understand that for you architecture takes center stage, but from the point of view of a more logical theory, as a more primary issue, shouldn't marriage take center stage . . .

SHINOHARA Up to now, I have kept that hidden. I have revealed on the surface only the shapes and spatial organizations that exist in Japanese tradition;

Shinohara Kazuo, House in Komae, Tokyo, 1960, north elevation and upper-floor *hiroma*. Photos by Saeki Yoshikatsu

I have not pushed to the forefront the issue of what human life is about. What Mr. Tanikawa said just now is that architects ought to have a clear sense of purpose, isn't that right? Tell me, how does one develop a sense of purpose today in poetry or painting?

TANIKAWA For me, it's simple—to encourage everyone to live in a house designed by Mr. Shinohara [laughter]. To live inside an ideal thing... however, in reality my awareness has not changed even after I began living in a house designed by Mr. Shinohara. I place marriage and family at the center of human life. My thinking revolves around that; the question is how to make the most of that in what I write. If anything, that can conflict with poetry, and my protest becomes poetry. The more established marriage becomes, the less one is able to live freely; one gradually loses vitality. The richer one's family life, the less one is able to write poetry. There are also those who feel that is an outdated idea, and that the happier one is, the more one is able to write poetry. However, life is more difficult to live with a happy family than one might suppose. One cannot write poetry if one is not dissatisfied.

SHINOHARA There is no "home" in Japan. There is no middle-class image of ordinary, everyday happiness, though there may be something like mood for the American middle class.

TANIKAWA People yearn for things such as the dining-kitchen[3] and the home bar.

SHINOHARA It all appears in reduced form. Priority is given to far less important things.

THE FUTURE IMAGE OF THE FAMILY

ASAKURA What I think about my house is that I want the house to change in several ways. I live on a hill now, and I have had such a wish even before I was conscious of it. I like looking up from below, or looking down on my own house from the very top of the hill. Or the gradual change in perspective as I walk up or down the hill. When I am inside the house, I change my view from room to room or to the garden. I hate the feeling that we are just a family, isolated from society. I want people to visit and to have the feeling that it is their house as well.

TANIKAWA You are a bohemian [laughter]...

ASAKURA There is a connection to the way I paint. I don't shut myself up and engage in a monologue as I paint.

TANIKAWA I can understand that. I don't believe in talking to myself as I work either. However, as much as I like to connect with people outside the house, I also like to protect my privacy.

SHINOHARA I think having a place that is quiet, even though it is in the middle of a house in a built-up area—a place that, once you enter it, is your own—is important.

ASAKURA But can you have privacy of family?

SHINOHARA You have to have it, don't you? For the unit called marriage.

ASAKURA Is that related to the house?

SHINOHARA It is closely related. My idea of a family is one in which members do not go their separate ways. It is a group consisting of a couple and their children. I want to give priority to protection of privacy for the family as a whole.

TANIKAWA To put it more directly, Mr. Shinohara is antipathetic to the development of a mass society—to the stereotyping of humanity. Ms. Asakura is not. She sees the entire world in the same way.

ASAKURA It is my job to make that the starting point.

SHINOHARA One other thing, there is the problem of the safety of the family. Especially in an age in which people are mistrustful of society, having everyone live together will be a difficult thing to achieve. That is why one shuts one's family up.

ASAKURA That is where the gap between the two of us lies. I am not confident I could offer an effective argument against fear and mistrust. But I do want to build a society whose principle is respect for the individual, based not on some facile humanism but on the creation of many opportunities for people to come into contact with one another.

TANIKAWA I don't understand that. I'm not saying everything starts with a husband and a wife out of belief in the Japanese family system, but I believe it takes a man and a woman to make a unit. I think it is a question of whether one has been happily married or not.

ASAKURA According to the report made by Mr. Ōe Kenzaburō upon returning from China, he had the impression that China is quite free. Mr. Kaikō [Ken] said much the same thing. My feeling on hearing such talk is that in China the ideal human seems to have been reduced to and considered in the context of the individual.

TANIKAWA It was probably because they could go as a group, that they felt solidarity with China [laughter]. They probably felt there were in all likelihood plenty of people like themselves. Conversely, there are similarities to the United States. No one minds squatting in toilets without doors. There is hope in China too, but there is also a level of anxiety, the feeling that we may not be able to survive.

SHINOHARA In Mr. Tanikawa's case, there is rich soil for poetry within the family, but the tendency in Ms. Asakura's paintings is in the direction of a mass society. Isn't that the difference between the two of you?

ASAKURA As I said earlier, I can't draw paintings while engaged in a monologue. Issues having to do with other people are important. I am able to draw paintings because there are others.

TANIKAWA When you put it that way, we are back to being the same.

SHINOHARA You two fight in the same place, but the foundations are different.

ASAKURA In my case, my biggest fault is that because of how my parents brought me up, I have always felt that men and women are the same, in sensibility and everything else. I have never been self-conscious about meeting a man.

TANIKAWA That is true. You think of men and women abstractly, as human beings.

SHINOHARA As objects [laughter].

TANIKAWA It is humanism. But if humanism means putting humans at the center of things, then I'm not human. But doesn't Ms. Asakura's theory become excessive? For example, it becomes a bit too much with children. If your husband is a human being, then a child you have with your husband becomes the child of a human. It is a bit creepy. Don't you ever feel that your child is different from all other children, that he or she is special?

ASAKURA Basically, I think my own child is lovely, but that doesn't prevent me from thinking of other children as my own. You would have to give it a great deal of thought if you had to design a house for a person like that, wouldn't you?

SHINOHARA Yes. In any case, that is an important problem. The basis of creative ideas.

ASAKURA For architecture and for art.

SHINOHARA The same applies for architecture in general, but to focus—let's think about the design of houses. It is clear that advances in houses depend a great deal on advances in technology, but as I said at the outset, that is not the sole factor in play. The fact that an advance in technology does not produce an equivalent advance in houses is the source of a major problem, where a connection can be found to other genres of art. What we have talked endlessly about, the human problem—where that connection exists. How we perceive humans, how we perceive family. To put it plainly, that perception or worldview has been the driving force in the history of human dwellings. Technology has been the means to an end. There are many problems arising from the excessive stereotyping of houses today, but that is accounted for by the loss of a sense of purpose in life. If we delve deeper into that problem, we end up confronting that fundamental problem discussed earlier. That is why I believe this should and must determine the nature of houses. How we perceive the family is indeed how we plan the house.

Translated by Watanabe Hiroshi

1 Matsumura Katsuo (1923–1991) is a furniture designer who collaborated with Shinohara on several houses in the late 1950s. Influenced by Charlotte Perriand's 1941 exhibition *Selection, Tradition, Creation* held in Tokyo, Matsumura was one of the pioneers of modern furniture design in Japan.

2 Ogata Kōrin (1658–1716) was a Japanese painter and designer of the early modern period and later identified as one of the key figures of Rinpa, an artistic style named after him. Often assuming decorative art formats such as screens, fans, and lacquerware boxes, Rinpa-style work is often characterized by its flattened pictorial plane, abstract and rhythmic composition, and vivid contrasting colors.

3 Dining-kitchen emerged in modern apartment design in postwar Japan, as a combined dining room and kitchen into a single space. It is typically equipped with a modern system kitchen.

Shinohara Kazuo's books of architectural theory: *Jūtaku kenchiku* (Residential architecture) (Tokyo: Kinokuniya shoten, 1964); *Jūtaku ron* (Residential theory) (Tokyo: Kamila shuppankai, 1970); *Zoku jūtaku ron* (Later residential theory) (Tokyo: Kajima shuppankai 1975); and *Chō-taisū shūgo tosh he* (Toward a super-big numbers set city) (Tokyo: A.D.A. EDITA, 2001).

The Meaning of Writing: Agitation and Pronouncement

Okuyama Shin-ichi

1 Shinohara Kazuo, *Jūtaku ron* (Residential theory) (Tokyo: Kajima shuppankai, 1970), 229.

2 Okuyama Shin-ichi, ed., *Afuorizumu, Shinohara Kazuo kūkan gensetsu* (Tokyo: Kajima shuppankai, 2004).

"I have kept thinking about the diverse problems of persons and space that are born out of or around the task of building houses; I have recorded these thoughts as far as I could, with my conclusions appearing regularly in journals of the Architectural Institute of Japan (AIJ) and various architectural magazines. For me this writing exacts the same travail as making architecture, and although the number of these commentaries was no greater than the number of houses that I designed, traces of this central and daunting task remain in each and every article. Not only does there remain the memory of the forbidding task of writing itself, also included is the recollection of the unflinching stance I evolved, which seems almost reckless when I think of it today: striking out against the ideas and the trend of the Japanese architectural mainstream in those days, thus putting everything including my own modest residential works at risk....However immature the results, my feelings at that moment and the situation surrounding me at the time are, in like measure, clearly achieved by those remarks."

—Shinohara Kazuo, from postscript to *Jūtaku ron,* 1970[1]

1 APHORISMS

In spring 2004 I completed a book titled *Aphorisms: Shinohara Kazuo's Spatial Discourse*,[2] in which I collaborated with Shinohara himself. The book appeared toward the end of his life but its beginnings go back to about three years earlier. The initial meeting with Shinohara and an editor from Kajima Publishing, one of Japan's most active publishers of architectural books and materials, took place in autumn 2001. It was held, as was Shinohara's habit at the time, at a café on a street corner of the stylish neighborhood of Jiyūgaoka—just one stop away from the Tokyo Institute of Technology (Tokyo Tech), from which both of us graduated and where we had always taught, as I continue to do today. Several months before, Shinohara had entrusted me with a quantity of drawings and related materials, on the occasion of his move from Jiyūgaoka, where he had lived for a few years after closing his studio at the university, to nearby Yokohama, where he remained until the end of his life. I became the custodian of a number of magazines and books in which his works and articles appeared. Our joint aim was to compile a book of his writings, which no doubt related to my years of work researching the writings of a number of contemporary Japanese architects.

After our first meeting with the publisher, and without having finalized what direction the work was to take, I began an attentive perusal of the mass of articles written by Shinohara over the past half century. My work had only just started. Until then, I had read his articles numerous times, but this was my first attempt at looking through all of them methodically, in chronological order, including the scholarly reports he contributed to the AIJ's journal. Since everything seemed in one way or another bound to a meaningful corpus, the work of highlighting the most consequential phrases and parts and looking for a narrative to connect such fragments was fraught with difficulty. Days passed as if I were continuously scooping up handfuls of fine-grained sand. The work continued in this manner for a good while, until after several months of effort there shone a gleam of hope.

3 Shinohara Kazuo, "Jūtaku wa geijutsu de aru," *Shinkenchiku* vol. 37, no. 5 (May 1962): 77–78.

Shinohara had for long expressed himself in two quite distinct manners. One was descriptive and tended to summarize his clear conception of architecture in strong condensed phrases. This may be called aphoristic, as typified in his celebrated essay "A House Is a Work of Art,"[3] a clear and recurring notion impossible to construct from any purely deductive standpoint. The other mode is found in his observation of the changing societal conditions in Japan, as these had evolved during his career, even if in his own mind Shinohara was all the while free of and essentially unhampered by these trends. The former manner we shall call "form and logic (*katachi to ronri*)," while referring to the latter as "gaze and circumstance (*shisen to jōkyō*)." Shinohara's words generated an abundance of meanings due to the implicit interconnections between both patterns. It was not difficult to see how well "form and logic" fit the image of the sturdily independent architect that by now Shinohara had made proudly his own. However, in those days the prescience of his unflinchingly analytic grasp of the contradictions of Japanese postwar civil society, embodied in his observations of the "gaze and circumstance" species of commentary, had still to be fully absorbed and taken seriously.

2 META-ARCHITECTURAL LANGUAGE

Shinohara Kazuo was an architect, who above all dedicated himself throughout his long career to expressing ideas in words and setting these willy-nilly before the public. This ambition and the reflex it engendered continued until just before his death. The most notable Japanese architect who similarly took to the pulpit was Isozaki Arata, a peer, interlocutor, and sometime rival six years Shinohara's junior. Before Shinohara and Isozaki, the main emphasis of an architect's own writing had been placed on explaining a given work, revealing the overriding logic of a design approach, or hammering home a single selfsame architectural concept. By contrast, over the last decades of the twentieth century, Shinohara and Isozaki put into play a newly created meta-architectural language, one in which words themselves could function at the same level as actual works of architecture. Nonetheless, there were great differences between these two protagonists.

Considered as a whole, Isozaki's polemical mode tends to isolate social issues from basic conditions of architectural design, devising a social raison d'être for architecture. While no one doubted the originality of his perspective, by the mid-1980s the architect's thoughts had gravitated to pairing "nation" and architecture. Given Isozaki's insistence on establishing architectural design within a master framework of hierarchical and socially planned spaces, architecture and the city were to evolve in parallel with the opposing extremes of citizen (*ningen*) and nation (*kokka*). More simply, his ideas conform to a postmodern version of the teachings of his mentor Tange Kenzō, who had pioneered the convergence of architectural design with urbanism in Japan. In the opposed manner, Shinohara directed his efforts to a determination of the meaning of architectural form and space in accordance with the uniquely ideal posture of the architect. Shinohara's provocative observations on the state of Japanese society were enunciated such that any consequences turned only upon himself and his inimitable individual works, which were never destined to materialize in the construction of a social space. Furthermore, Shinohara was not concerned with presenting himself as a cultured intellectual (*bunkajin*), a

Okuyama Shin-ichi, ed., *Aphorisms: Shinohara Kazuo's Spatial Discourse* (Kajima shuppankai, 2004).

practice many architects including Isozaki could not resist. This is well supported by the fact—possibly a surprising one—that the quantity of Shinohara's books is hardly large. Other than volumes that present his projects, he authored only four books (all in Japanese):

1 *Residential Architecture* (*Jūtaku kenchiku*)
(Kinoykuniya shoten, 1964)
2 *Residential Theory* (*Jūtaku ron*)
(Kajima shuppankai, 1970)
3 *Later Residential Theory* (*Zoku jūtaku ron*)
(Kajima shuppankai, 1975)
4 *Toward a Super-Big Numbers Set City*
(*Chō-taisū shūgo toshi he*) (A.D.A EDITA Tokyo, 2001)

Among these four, the second and third volumes, *Residential Theory* and *Later Residential Theory,* are both collections of previously published journal articles republished at Kajima's behest. Only the first and the fourth volumes were written new in their entirety. The first, *Residential Architecture,* is an elegant but audacious work based on research on the spatial composition of Japanese traditional architecture, carried out also toward his doctoral dissertation presented at Tokyo Tech in 1967. The fourth, *Toward a Super-Big Numbers Set City,* was a much later work dealing with the contemporary city, which had been a preoccupation of his throughout his life. The volume also contains a number of photographs taken by Shinohara himself, many of them during his journeys abroad.

All four books are engaging and appeal to a broad audience. *Residential Theory* has served as a required text for generations of Japanese architecture students over some thirty printings. These publications all are modest, lightly bound, accessible volumes. We may surmise that for Shinohara writing was scarcely focused on a goal of literary monumentality. In each phase of his long career, he found expression for his architectural ideas in words, and forthrightly published in the most widely read architectural magazines of the profession, recalling the practice of the hard sciences. Shinohara possessed a highly logical mind, which he employed to inquire into the mechanics of the world, with no greater aid than his pencil and paper; continual rounds of publication resulting in unrelenting study have the manner of scientific papers that stake out one's standing at academic conferences.

Shinohara's words hardly constitute the sort of definitive tome that might have introduced a comprehensive body of theory but instead reflect the competing influences of the ongoing architectural scene, both within and outside Japan, each correlated with the exciting new spaces being produced in his own work. Even more than a decade after his death, their influence shows no signs of abatement. The remainder of this short essay will examine the meaning of Shinohara's words in all their earnest, intermittent splendor.

3 ARCHITECTS AND WORDS

The task of architects is to design excellent buildings and offer them to society, impossible as it may be to escape completely the power of politics or the spell of capital. Insofar as this activity is widespread, no particular claim can be linked to the notion that representing ideas with words might be a primary duty. Nevertheless, based on two types of evidence, most well-known architects have indeed attempted at some point in their career to write down their thoughts.

3.1 Social Stance of the Architect

The dawn of our civilization was first revealed in language, and the diversity of languages deepened its modes and overall content. Language possesses not only such direct and denotative functions as spoken communication or writing, but also the inherent function connecting it directly to "thinking" by which *homo sapiens* were able to mature into present-day humans. The precise and effective command of words became a hallmark of leadership. Oratory as it developed in ancient Greece and Rome afforded a technique of public speaking that helped others to ascertain and mark out a potential leader's talents. Forged and applied extensively in the expanding domain of political practice, the complex evolution of rules of rhetoric as a mechanism producing and enforcing various meanings by words in combination was inherent in all such activity.

Though originally, language had to depend on sound itself for its every meaning, its more complex significance, transitioned to the book with its permanent materialization and access, followed the invention of a written language. The book signified a reification of human intelligence and became an emblem of social standing for its author. Vitruvius shines brightly as a founder of contemporary architecture, even after two millennia, because he is the author of the oldest extant book of architecture. By acknowledging the architect's role in society, the architectural book became an expression of ambition, and still the book is one of the motives that induces architects to spin the two different wheels of design practice and written work beyond their original task of producing good buildings.

3.2 The Concept of Architecture

Architecture is principally, in its aspect as *utilitas,* the material basis for production of the spaces, forms, and places that give support to our life, which is why the design professional is accorded a place to not only oversee design techniques but also to articulate a structural system, select materials, and oversee every aspect of execution. Yet architecture is the full complement of all these material tasks, and at the same time an abstract concept that plays an essential part in the spiritual aspect of our civilization. Human dwellings have a grand variety of aspects that do not focus on any final figure of completion, by contrast with other living creatures' nests and burrows, which long ago seemingly reached a completed form corresponding to each species and its environment. Otherwise it would be impossible to explain the order of a building construction system consisting of foundation, base, columns, and beams laid up over these, as well as a roof over that, which has so often been used as an analogy for the nonmaterial things produced by human activities, such as the edifice of language or the social edifice itself, to note only two commonplace phrases.

Architecture possesses all the familiar material aspects, yet the term has taken root in our daily life as an abstract concept. Superficially, the aspect of materiality in space appears to hold advantage, but all materials are destined to decay and eventually give way. Even if complete collapse can be forestalled or avoided, a certain transfiguration seems inevitable as time proceeds. Compared with that, the concept of architecture exhibits its own undeniable stability, standing as it does beyond the reach of age.

Taking the broadest overview, the architect's mindset insists that their work should not remain only within the material realm but that it also include what we know as the concept of architecture. In particular, this attitude has proven a remarkable feature of the European intellectual world with its philosophical background dependent on the speculative interplay between material and concept since the time of the ancient Greeks. In medical science, the surgeon with the skills to eliminate serious diseases or conditions holds a higher status in our times, but prior to the modern era, the physician who prescribed medicine for everyday complaints enjoyed an incomparably higher social position than the surgeon. The latter merely provided direct hands-on treatment to their patients. Theory holds priority over practice in all the useful sciences concerned with daily life. In the West, theory in all matters, especially the guise in which words can clearly stipulate any situation, was superior to praxis. Emblematic of one's reputation in society, an analogous social grounding likewise promotes the full circle of influence that the concept of architecture has long offered architects for the legitimization of their production and the recording of architectural theory.

3.3 The Architectural Treatise

An architectural treatise deals principally with what architecture is believed to be, and those tasks specifically allocated to architects. Whether the topic focuses on style, form, or technology, such discourse will inevitably encompass some systematization of the concept of "architecture," which must then be logically articulated. Since the prime aim of such writing is to embody a systematization, architects tend to direct all their energies to writing a peerless and unique volume or an ordered series of several such books, published as a single voluminous work. Beginning with Vitruvius's *De architectura* of the late first century BCE and passing by way of Andrea Palladio's *I quattro libri dell'architettura* (1570), or in the East, Li Jie's *Yingzao fashi* issued in various editions from 1103 CE onward, history is witness to the fact that certain architects have exerted themselves toward the systematization of the concept of "architecture" to a degree equivalent to if not higher than the actual making of architecture.

Half a century ago a work titled *What Can Be Achieved by Architecture?*,[4] written by the then still young Japanese architect Hara Hiroshi, expressed a notion ostensibly antithetical to this dominant tendency. Almost entirely skirting the significance of realized buildings as architecture, Hara shifted his premise to study what might result from architecture regarded exclusively as a medium of expression and treated as an intercessor between the concept of "architecture" and practical design activities. But as the attempt remained highly generalized, Hara's text nonetheless pursued that royal road toward a purported conceptual essence of architecture. In short, all the architectural treatises written by architects—despite variations of focus—tend to exhibit a remarkable consistency in their varied attempts to set forth a grand architectural concept.

4 Hara Hiroshi, *Kenchiku ni nani ga kanō ka?: kenchiku to ningen to* (Tokyo: Gakugei shorin, 1967).

4 WRITING IN THE FIRST PERSON ON PROSPECTS FOR SOCIETY

One of the most salient features of Shinohara Kazuo's writing is his insistence on maintaining a first-person voice. Surveying the architectural field in its broadest aspect was seemingly a matter of little concern at the time his first architectural texts were being produced. To use a metaphor from photography, modernist architectural theory had made every effort to capture the concept of "architecture" by allowing for the greater depth of field made possible by new wide-angle lenses. Shinohara, conversely, approached specific topics by means of a super-close-up lens to compress distance, and then having captured a detailed view, he immediately took in the whole of architecture by abruptly zooming out. Characteristically, his discourse would launch from within a thicket of highly personalized views usually in stark opposition to those tenets loudly professed by the Japanese architectural world in those early postwar days, thus setting the observations and inspiration of a single individual architect, Shinohara Kazuo, as his chosen point of departure. In this way, intentionally bypassing purportedly consensual feelings of the profession, he laid emphasis from first to last upon the sensitivity of a single individual, namely himself. Writing in the first-person became for him the most natural style of articulating his views.

Normally such a mode of writing would be ill-adapted to voicing anything beyond a shrill antithesis to the current of the times, but Shinohara's words were equipped with such originality that they did not easily lose their initial force, even after the opposition had begun to recede into platitudes. His statements were most often triggered by a specifically formulated objection to perceived trends, but for the most part they also posed deeper issues attacking the very roots of what were then the accepted norms of architectural culture.

4.1 "A House Is a Work of Art" and "Inscribe Eternity in Space"

At the beginning of the 1960s the entire Japanese nation seemed caught up in a building construction boom aimed at the Olympic Games to be hosted in Tokyo in 1964. Some of the works from this period are certainly masterpieces and indeed have been handed down to posterity, but on the whole the cultural value of building was not of great emphasis during this period, and the overall social production of architecture remained deep in the thrall of the postwar wave of conspicuous consumption and commercialization. One can easily imagine how little value the broader society would place on the work of an architect, who pours heart and soul into the design of a small house—with its space for just a single family. Shinohara believed, if his activities were to be recognized as having some legitimate value, private house design would have to move to the field of art (*geijitsu*)—which by this time denoted the whole of the cultural and creative sphere, including painting, sculpture, literature, and so on. In hopes of such a transformation, he launched his aphorism: "A house is a work of art" in 1962, and the phrase soon became a byword for his beliefs.

Japan in the 1960s was quickly taken over by the Metabolist movement, which successfully mobilized media channels and gained recognition internationally. Shinohara pointedly refused to accept Metabolism's architectural theme of

5 Shinohara Kazuo, "Jūtaku ron," *Shinkenchiku* vol. 42, no. 7 (July 1967): 133–40.

prefabricated and flexible systems. He also rejected the notion that such forms would somehow be transmogrified as time passed. Instead, Shinohara proclaimed the aphoristic refrain: "Inscribe eternity in space"[5] as counterevidence to the now uncertain and relative assessment—if not the absolute abandonment of any old-fashioned values as "beauty."

In 1966 his House in White, an icon with contemporary meaning, saw completion and publication. This work exposed the strongest possibility that indeed "a house is a work of art" and resoundingly supported Shinohara's pronounced intention to "inscribe eternity in space." Both phrases can probably be intuited as antiestablishment invocations, with Shinohara himself regarded as having turned his back on the advantageous boom times of 1960s Japan. The prescience of such aphorisms began little by little to be acknowledged in the 1970s, as Japanese society started to rethink the unqualified view of historical progress that had reigned since the early postwar period.

4.2 Wartime Experience in the Shadow of the Nation

Shinohara's words at all times pronounced a discerning evaluative tendency as well as a challenge to a new generation, which now stood outside the times with its all-too-shortsighted historical perspective. Without actually saying so, as Isozaki was so often to do, Shinohara seemed to refer to that place where the mass of human society had transitioned with suspicious haste, an impulse probably connected to the lingering shadow of the wartime experience of his youth.

Just before the conclusion of World War II, while still a mathematics undergraduate, Shinohara had been dispatched to the Japanese-occupied Korean peninsula with a cohort of students departing for the front. Fortunately, they were demobilized after only a few weeks of basic training, but the dilapidated condition of continental North Asia and the futile deaths of his fellow countrymen must have impacted the heart of a sensitive and youthful Shinohara, with his ever-keen spirit of observation. Gathering from his later behavior, it seems that his disposition was not always sunny, but he made it a principle to fix his eyes on a brighter future instead of abandoning himself to bewailing disastrous circumstances of the present. If there were ever to be a brighter future for Japan, he must have cherished the hope that an age in which individual pleasures would once again take precedence might soon begin to materialize under the new postwar order guided by capitalism.

Though the social situation of 1960s Japan was certainly renewed and reactivated by national projects such as the Tokyo Olympics (1964) and Expo '70 in Osaka, individuals as yet received little enough encouragement beyond this invigorating umbrella of national endeavor. Most leading architects were engaged in projects, sometimes large but often small, that were initiated in this climate of the rehabilitated nation. With such an atmosphere instilled in part by a new architecture, it might still be believed that Shinohara, too, had a prospect that the fulfillment of individual pleasure and desire would eventually obtain, once the renewed framework of freewheeling Japanese capitalism had moved from its initial production phase to one of consumption.

6 Shinohara Kazuo, "Jūtaku ron," *Shinkenchiku* vol. 35, no. 4 (April 1960): 91–100.

Though Isozaki Arata was not mobilized to the front, being six years younger than Shinohara, the trauma of war and recovery was shared by all. In Isozaki's case, however, as he was born in western Japan, the urban spectacle reduced to ashes had registered less surely in his mind, and it was only much later that he introduced the image of the city of Hiroshima in ruins as the recognizably archetypal scene (*genfūkei*) for his ingenious "future" city conceit. It seems that he must also have pursued the grail of individual pleasure, but he never attained the tone of theoretical optimism sustained by Shinohara's self-induced positive outlook. Perhaps this difference was related to Isozaki's affiliation with the University of Tokyo, with its continuing tradition of a former imperial university and a locus of government prestige.

5 OPTIMISTIC GAZE

Shinohara was a continual observer of the contemporary architectural scene, always casting a hopeful and optimistic gaze at the general progress of Japanese society. Since he never ceased to love and respect the past traditions of Japanese architecture, it might appear strange at first glance that he also persisted in maintaining a strongly optimistic view of the future. From the earliest days when he had tackled Japanese tradition head-on, he had never regarded it as a refuge because he assumed traditional materials and building elements only as points of departure, directly so in the beguiling works of the First Style. But he never ceased to advocate the latest mechanisms and construction procedures for any technological aspect of a building, such as the underlying structural system or other equipment if these could be explored within the limits of a given construction budget.

This decisive personal attitude is summarized in a famous aphorism enunciated in those days when Shinohara had only just commenced his design activities amid a burning passion to investigate and somehow reconfigure Japanese traditional architecture: "Tradition offers us a starting point for creation but can never yield an ultimate point of return."[6]

While the combined impulse to revere a historical past whilst dreaming of a better future is essential to human nature, each of us is nonetheless limited to a particular present. Perhaps most are simply afraid to veer too far from received opinion? Any scientist would readily predict radical improvements in science and technology as a way of portraying a strongly held belief in future society. The optimistic targets set forth in science fiction are indispensable, and as for the technical aspects of their work, architects likewise construct such futuristic images. This is how Metabolism came to be deeply embedded in the collective memory of the profession as the only postwar Japanese architectural movement with a worldwide reputation. Already, the Archigrams in faraway London had fascinated large numbers with their splendid drawings of an imaginative accelerating high-tech environment, more or less without concern for feasibility. By contrast, the imputed scale and the exoticism of Metabolism rendered it less fantastic—perhaps more realizable. But it is at the nexus of a practical and detailed working out of such optimistic imaginings as realized architectural expressions, albeit at a modest scale, that the uniqueness of Shinohara's message situates itself.

7 Shinohara Kazuo, "Jūtaku sekkei no shutaisei," *Kenchiku*, no. 44 (April 1964): 52–55.

5.1 "Create a Fictive Space with Beauty"

Only the actual existence of architecture as built can be said to introduce real works to society. Once a building designed by an architect is realized and recognized as worthy of further analysis and investigation, information will be conveyed to those concerned within the architectural field via publication. At the same time, the work will be assessed by the community of its users. Colleagues will undertake site visits in order to experience the building's spaces as constructed, which generates a real but invisible dialogue, albeit proliferating via hearsay or the internet. Following the widespread use of photography to report on and document buildings, two different sets of spaces have come into being—namely those appearing on the printed (later digital) page and those that are the product of a haptic experience.

In the case of private houses, they are rarely made accessible in any way to those outside the profession, or over time to anyone at all outside the circle of family and friends of a client or subsequent proprietor. Therefore most architects who design private houses make a considered effort to ensure that sufficient information about the house and its spaces appears in the media from the outset. Nor is effort spared to promote visitation by the professional community, by prevailing upon the good will of the owner.

The youthful Shinohara found himself in the same position as most other architects. However, as his work had early on received public attention for the uniqueness of his spatial compositions and the phenomenal beauty of his work as photographed, he was at the same time teased about the lack of any human feeling in his carefully compiled media presentations, most often by colleagues claiming: "Shinohara abstracts not only space, but also human life." A veritable battle line was drawn, contending the photographed versus lived experience of Shinohara buildings—the way in which space-on-the-page in the most widely read magazines where his houses were now most frequently seen as over against the actual lived experience of a Shinohara dwelling.

Indeed, from the first, Shinohara himself contributed to the growing doubt about any such unification. This doubt took root first in his personal disbelief as to whether lived actuality need really be expressed in the professional media. He appeared convinced that the space-on-the-page as portrayed by the media had little if anything to do with actual space as built, let alone with the life of the client and their family. The latter in particular could well be neglected or obscured; in other words, it did not matter in the least if these two aspects of house design coexisted as entirely separate systems.

By extension, in order for the single-family dwelling (in which a private lived experience was notably closed off from societal concerns) to occupy a different existence, Shinohara was perfectly willing to countenance a sharp divide between residential and general, or public, architecture; he even believed that promoting the radical duality and separate coexistence of space-on-the-page and the space of actual experience could prove an effective strategy. Such judgment came down to the following aphorism: "Create a fictive space with beauty."[7]

8 Shinohara Kazuo, *Jūtaku kenchiku* (Residential architecure) (Tokyo: Kinokuniya shoten, 1964), 103.

9 Taniguchi Yoshirō, *Kiyoraka na ishō* (Asahi shimbunsha, 1948). Taniguchi Yoshirō began teaching at the Tokyo Institute of Technology in 1929, shortly after graduating from Tokyo Imperial University and when Tokyo Tech was elevated to university status. He was promoted to full professor in 1943 and retired in 1965.

Walter Benjamin's celebrated *The Work of Art in the Age of Mechanical Reproduction* (1935) had claimed photographic representation to be a new mechanism for the production of meaning, well beyond the naïve belief in photography as a substitute representation for an absent work of art that merely summoned up a printed view of the latter before our eyes. Marshall McLuhan's *Understanding Media: The Extensions of Man* (1964) and subsequent works proclaimed that the media itself generated messages whose significance went well beyond any literal connection between two different things. Though both these now well-known books were readily available, there was as yet no Japanese translation of either. While some Japanese intellectuals may have been aware in a practical sense that human perception was nowadays more influenced by media than by the actuality of things themselves, there was in Japan still a replete confidence in the reality of *architectural* expression. This was the context into which Shinohara's declaration of a so-called fictional interpretation of physical space was injected. Near-universal refusal of any such notion as an anti-architectural sacrilege was thus more or less inevitable, even if today when the internet has spread worldwide, nobody can doubt Shinohara's "fictionality" on its own evidence even without the pioneering theories of Benjamin and McLuhan.

5.2 Beauty of Chaos

In a chapter of Shinohara's first book, *Residential Architecture* of 1964, titled "A contemporary enormous village (*gendai no shūraku*)," he noted with reference to a particular Tokyo suburb "The expression of a contemporary commoner's residential area should not be one of harmonious beauty, but rather a chaotic one."[8] Though the urban environment of Japan had in those days achieved a remarkably rapid postwar rehabilitation of sorts, it had not done so all of a piece. Instead the process went ahead via a near-random and continually repeated process of scrap-and-build. Therefore, whether in residential areas or city centers, there was no way that one might realistically anticipate any such thing as a disciplined or beautiful cityscape. That was exactly why most progressive Japanese architects regarded the urban context of those days as merely ugly, insisting all the while that a cityscape of European-style beauty in coherence should replace the present chaos as soon as possible.

In fact, Taniguchi Yoshirō, who served for many years as head of design in the architecture department of Tokyo Tech, had at the beginning of his book *Crystalline Design*,[9] published in 1948 just after the war's end, rendered the following criticism. Taniguchi claimed that the scenery beside almost any Japanese railway station with its clashing billboards huddled in total disorder represented a willed ugliness intended to pique consumer demand. His proffered solution was an exhortation to return to the pristine, or "crystalline," mind that the Japanese people had ostensibly possessed before the war. Taniguchi was to be sure an excellent architect of works exuded a harmonious esteem. Moreover, it is certain that Shinohara, too, entertained an irresistible yearning for the sincerity of Taniguchi's tranquil and pristine design ethic. With his own perspective on the ongoing rehabilitation of the Tokyo metropolis with his own eyes, Shinohara imagined the much maligned ugliness as morphing into beauty once urban conditions had reached a point of no return in the grip of on-

10 Shinohara, *Jūtaku kenchiku*, 184–85.

going grass-roots practices. Though like Taniguchi, Shinohara desired an absolute beauty—the "beauty of chaos" that Shinohara posited in those days was not uniquely idealistic. It designated, instead, a set of relative values that arose when most of society's members inevitably recognized it as a fact of life. He refers to it in just these terms in another vision of a remote future, pronounced toward the end of his *Residential Architecture:*

> My intention has been gropingly, and insofar as possible, to base a logic of design upon the very facts before my eyes, and I hoped to construct the "chaos" pertinent to my next step by taking up such facts as building blocks. The mother lode of art is said to be the chaos adrift within the human psyche. Once exorcised, our feelings and passions have no further need of art. Chaos places a human being in danger and engenders anxiety. Therefore, we must search to mitigate this anxiety by art. When the energy stored up within chaos rushes to a head and seeks a breakthrough, art will emerge.
>
> In articulating my current residential design theory, I have actually experienced a new "logic of chaos." I have suddenly and more than once passed through a state of inquiry obtained by the work of my hands via one sort of logical process, only to enter at once a fresh state of anxiety opaque to any such earlier process. That is why, in order to disperse such anxiety, I have to begin in a new way to design houses.[10]

In the 1980s, some twenty years later, the inspiration drawn from a certain "beauty of chaos" came to be regarded by the architect as the instance in which a vital logic had served to bind together his Fourth Style with his chaos of Tokyo theory. The case involved a snapshot taken by Shinohara in front of Shibuya Station and later used as the inspiration for a design studio at Yale University when he taught there as the first Eero Saarinen Visiting Professor in 1984. Ironically, at the beginning of the twenty-first century, this same "scramble" intersection in front of Shibuya Station has emerged as a top choice for selfie photos by tourists from abroad, in what is still a major urban subcenter undergoing rapid urban change. Though it had taken a full half-century—the better part of a human lifetime—Shinohara's insight into Tokyo's urban scene beginning from his observation of an ordinary residential suburb in 1964 had now become a byword for both the inhabitants of Tokyo and an international community of visitors, thus firmly achieving the rights of citizenship in urban theory, especially that of Tokyo.

5.3 Gaze upon a City

Since first putting on record his urban-related notion of the "beauty of chaos" in 1964, Shinohara continued to publish insights vis-à-vis the surrounding urban landscape, chiefly now in the important Japanese-language publication *Shinkenchiku,* for which *The Japan Architect* was for many years an English-language digest. Among these insights the following three articles are both representative and especially significant:

1 "Mathematical City" ("Sugaku-teki toshi"),
in "Kūkan no shiso to kōzō," *Shinkenchiku* (January 1967)
2 "Tentacle to Continuity" ("Renzoku to shokushu"),
in "Jūtaku ron," *Shinkenchiku* (February 1972)
3 "Irrational City" ("Higori toshi"), in "Higōri toshi to kūkan kikai," *Shinkenchiku* (March 1973)

There is insufficient space here to explain the content of each of these aphoristically based conceits, but the insistent emphasis pervading the series is the recognition of a metropolitan existence that extends well beyond any architect's designable target. Still, all things considered, why did Shinohara Kazuo, who had over the years identified private residential design as his principal field of activity, continue to concern himself with the city through the mid-1970s and long afterward?

Shinohara had taken notions of spatial composition as manifest throughout the history of Japanese traditional architecture as a starting point for his academic and practical research, having at the same time set the measurement and survey of traditional Japanese villages as the research goal for his laboratory from as early as 1966. This round of surveys shifted gradually afterward in the direction of a broader study of urban spatial structures, notably the form of Japanese castle towns of the Edo period; this research campaign was eventually brought full circle and terminated in 1977. We may assume that Shinohara's interests, having brought this theme to a conclusion, moved to a new phase for the next step of his research. When I later asked him about the intention of this shift, he gave the following, somewhat cryptic response:

One of my aims was to record exactly a new set of buildings in trying to determine the membership conditions of that set in itself, in order to obtain something on the order of a mathematical rule that could be generalized. That indeed was what I had been hoping for, but since I obtained no clear results, the issue has been hanging fire until now.

Considering that the above research projects postdate his "beauty of chaos" conclusion of 1964, Shinohara may have suspected the impossibility of analyzing the constantly changing present-day cityscape with any accuracy. In the case of those traditional townscapes condensed and frozen in time that he and his lab had examined, singular features such as the hypothesized and much discussed "division of space" or "frontality" (both induced from observation of surviving works of Japanese historical architecture) could easily be found and identified. Nevertheless, any serious extension of this methodology proved unrealizable. However difficult it may have been even to extract generalizable concepts from the limited conditions of traditional rural villages, Shinohara seemed set on the notion that in the living contemporary city—such as Tokyo, transfiguring itself day by day—there should be massive aggregate variables that would transcend the imaginative capabilities of a more conventional architect.

Shinohara, who had never until then been overseas, suddenly undertook several mostly solitary trips in the 1970s to observe foreign cities. It can readily be imagined that the serendipitous experiences of various scenes in strange overseas cities amplified his expectations. Acknowledging that the city could no longer be a target for architects as a mere accessory reference to their day-to-day design practice, Shinohara was most likely groping for some way of approaching the metropolis well beyond his now obsolete notion of seeking support for individual house design.

As a culmination of this thought process, Shinohara finally arrived at publication of his *Toward a Super-Big Numbers Set City* of 2001. He had by then reached his mid-seventies. The book again considers the potentiality of extracting design concepts from the unrivalled growth of Tokyo, while looking back at his earlier writings on urban topics and recent travels overseas. While the content of the book turns upon urban topics, it nonetheless draws a clear distinction from the thought processes engaged in by the usual sort of urban planner. In sum, the book confers a new way of looking at his previous work in single-house residential design, most of which belongs to an urban setting, while now freely admitting the city itself as *un*-designable—but in no way in terms of a discussion of form, making use rather of words and theory.

All this theoretical work by Shinohara began in 1964, and since that time thirty-seven years had passed. The two works newly written in their entirety, *Residential Architecture* and *Toward a Super-Big Numbers Set City,* both with residential design as their core theme, are thus linked by a single line of insight and inquiry into urban issues. The following phrase at the opening of *Toward a Super-Big Numbers Set City* suggests nothing less:

> This "city" of mine appears [inevitably] as along the line of a road. I have been walking lots of single roads.[11]

11 Shinohara, *Chō-taisū shūgo toshi he* (Toward a super-big numbers set city) (A.D.A. EDITA Tokyo, 2001), 8.

This self-reflexive process revealing the way in which one inspiration gives birth to the next, with a new subject arising in perspective at each turn, looks to be very like the history of the progress of Shinohara's method of designing houses as he had developed it through a succession of several self-designated styles. Whatever might happen, he had expressed his own ideas in words poured forth from his own physique in optimistic response to each successively perceived social context. These neat packets of words came to be designated as aphorisms, since they rarely flowed from established logical process or ratiocination.

6 TWO TYPES OF APHORISM

Earlier, I pointed out that two different aspects are to be found in Shinohara's writing, which we referred to as "form and logic," in characterization of his architectural ideas, and "gaze and circumstance," comprising mainly fragments of social observation. Throughout I have been at pains to stress how, with Shinohara, "gaze and circumstance" played an important backup role to his frequent flashes of "form and logic." In conclusion, let us now turn our attention to Shinohara's charming, if more than occasionally disarming, aphorisms as centered in the domain of "form and logic." It seems most likely that, for Shinohara, who had pursued a study of mathematics in his youth, this aphoristic formulation process bypassing as it does formal logic had functioned all along in a veiled role as theorem building in the near-mathematical process of propositional (or sentential) logic, which Shinohara used to aid, mature, and polish the practice of residential design.

Up to this point, I have attempted to interpret the meaning of Shinohara's aphorisms by citing several representative examples. In this way, it is easily suggested how such phrases as "A house is a work of art" or "Create a fictional space with beauty" might well offend the sensibilities of more traditional architects and at the same time stimulate the younger generations. By contrast, phrases and terms such as "Inscribe eternity in space," "progressive anarchy," and "savage machine"—all of which were used if not actually coined by Shinohara—can be regarded as loudly celebrating the forms and shapes of his own work. By focusing on both society and architecture, two different types of sayings, "agitation" and "pronouncement," colored and composed Shinohara's use of aphorism—both as explained earlier more or less in lieu of any stricter form of logic. In terms of chronology of the two types of aphorism, "agitation" was mostly limited to the 1960s, and appeared briefly again toward the very end of his life. "Pronouncement," however, remained a constant presence.

Usually a style of statement we might characterize as "agitation" would be exercised by an architect of reputation and achievement encouraging the younger generation by his record of performance, experience, and acquired social position. Yet the 1960s, when most of Shinohara's "agitation" formulae were issued and took hold, represents the period from Shinohara's mid-thirties to mid-forties. He had already wrestled with and completed his timeless House in White by 1966, but his position within Tokyo Tech was still that of an associate professor, and it was also still a period in which a lot of big-name architects, beginning with Shinohara's own mentor Seike Kiyoshi, were still in peak activity. Considering all these circumstances, it is less easy to understand where Shinohara's impulse toward "agitation" had arisen, or to what aim he pursued it. However noticeably self-absorbed in his professional persona, he unfailingly set great store by the common courtesies and protocols of polite Japanese society.

Ought we to imagine that Shinohara's invective was less directed at society or the architectural profession, than it was the performance of a sort of self-stimulus, fighting, in other words, with his back to the wall in a situation from which it would prove difficult or impossible to turn back? Consistent in body and spirit, Shinohara carried forth a strict and rigorous design ethic. Might more than one character have inhabited this relatively frail body? Shinohara-the-Architect, who had frantically come to grips with hitherto quite unknown spaces, coexisted with another, Shinohara-the-Author, who had continually encouraged the Architect by running alongside and admitting no letup in the latter's strict gaze; meanwhile both possessed and occupied a single body.

It bears repeating that the meaning of writing for him was not to leave a comprehensive treatise of architecture for posterity. He may instead have convinced himself that his design activities would have come to an end had he ever ceased to write. To use a military analogy, if residential design were the attack weapons for Shinohara, his writing played the role of a tailwind, constantly reinforcing with new creative energies from behind. He might also be understood as an actor in his own personal drama, navigating between total self-containment and a fear of negative reviews. Yet as already mentioned, Shinohara's net of aphoristic self-expression was constantly in play with his keen eye for the societal context of each period, begetting an intermixture of messages directed toward a perceived future society. Since these words of his were potentially composed by an alter ego, the two sorts of aphorism had given impetus to a dynamic mechanism that drove and intermittently expressed both Shinohara's thought and his creation.

7 OUR OWN TIMES

Our civilization has long been developing around a singular framework of thought. Even now as science and technology have spread over the world, diverse manifestations of the universal impulse we refer to collectively as World Religion are strongly rooted in the human community with little apparent hope of syncretism. In contrast, Japan has maintained and accepted several imported world religions that in the twenty-first century coexist separately without signs of mutual recognition, let alone interference, in an unholy if entirely workable alliance. We Japanese may seem ill-adapted to the construction of any universal system of belief. Yet numerous Japanese intellectuals have long embraced universal and rational systems of thought, such as have been cultivated in China and the West through their long histories.

Unlike other leading architects of his generation, Shinohara represented an intelligence emerging from a peculiar environment in Japan. Even while he wished for more people to appreciate his system of thought and its supporting theories, Shinohara never pretended that his methodology should encompass the totality of architecture. In relation to conditions that he had originally regarded as being confined to Japan, he hoped nevertheless for a more general, universal relevance—and to some extent he entertained the prospect of a broader acceptance of his ideas and inventions. Despite the harshness and disruption of his strongly voiced aphoristic approach, few concessions were made and little quarter given. Yet, surprisingly, Shinohara's activities received considerable support from the succeeding generation of Japanese architects and have aroused growing interest in different parts of the world.

In the intervening half-century, the goals of the architectural profession have been slowly realigning, always in parallel with social concerns. Can there be a thoroughly positive outcome from the massive international capital flows sensitizing the construction industry to environmental concerns at a global scale? Any such accommodation ought to lessen interest in Shinohara's historically more combative stance vis-à-vis the evolution of Japanese society occurring in the wake of the postwar economic miracle. Nevertheless, it seems that the seed of trying to live and practice like Shinohara has lain hidden inside the minds of architects seeking their breakthrough out of the impasse of the contemporary architectural scene. This seems to be why Shinohara's works have attracted new attention from a younger generation from abroad, despite how little is known or understood about the actual activities of his lifetime, even in our time in the ten or so years since the architect's death.

In the light of such far-ranging speculation, let us close by quoting a passage from the special article with which Shinohara ended his career as architectural polemicist. It

12 *Shinohara Kazuo,* "Katachi to kotoba no butai wo yokokitte," in Okuyama, *Afuorizumu,* 249–50.

was written as a coda for *Aphorisms: Shinohara Kazuo's Spatial Discourse,* the collected volume of writings produced close to the end of his life. Marking the end of his life's work in words and form, in one last stroke are inscribed Shinohara's twin lifelong intentional priorities: agitation and pronouncement. Such, then, was his final salvo:

> A set phrase from the past doesn't easily lead me to configure a new array of words, and is even less apt to inspire the creation of a new form. Nor is there any guarantee with the inverse path, that from forms toward words. Ideally, a compositional operation with words is like those competitive building games that make use of children's blocks, where there ought to be a clear link in both directions. Even so, at times I am able unexpectedly to extract some fragment of the next form. There have also been moments when a single form before my eyes was immediately able to trigger the next step by displacing a few deadlocked words.
>
> A sympathetic resonance could be cited between words and forms—like that between the movement of the chief puppeteer in a Japanese puppet show and those stage assistants (*kuroko*) traditionally dressed in black who are supposed to be invisible to the audience. This occurs in straining toward the moment of encounter when the next forms or new words will climax in a triumphant pose or figure-like tableau [*Mie wo kiru*]. For my part, I am forever piecing together the story of my next spatial discourse.
>
> At best, some sign of the next design phase—like a next archetypal space—will show itself but this is as yet more like a vague uneasiness. I happen to witness the flicker of its light and a human shadow.
>
> —Shinohara Kazuo, "Crossing a Stage Set in Form and Words." 2004[12]

Shinohara Kazuo in his laboratory at Tokyo Institute of Technology, ca. 1970. Photo by Taki Kōji

Shinohara Kazuo, South House in Hanayama, Kobe, Hyōgo Prefecture, 1968, view of hallway looking toward *hiroma.* Photo by Taki Kōji

Shinohara Kazuo, South House in Hanayama, Kobe, Hyōgo Prefecture, 1968, *hiroma.* Photo by Taki Kōji

Architectural Photography: Reading Taki Kōji

Ano Daici

TAKI'S *THE GEOMETRICAL IMAGINATION OF ARCHITECT SHINOHARA KAZUO*[1]

When I was attending university in the latter half of the 1990s students could still sense the lingering smell of the protest movement, and on the bookshelves of its photography club, mixed in with the technical photography manuals and old camera magazines, were monographs on Henri-Cartier Bresson, Ed van der Elsken, and Helmut Newton. So I think I came to know the name Taki Kōji from his work in *Provoke.* Influenced by Moriyama Daidō,[2] I shot the streets at night with high-ISO film and overstretching myself argued about "what that photograph means to you." Over and over I read the *Déjà-vu* special issue "*Provoke*'s Era"[3] and Nishii Kazuo's book *Why Still Now* Provoke*?* (1996).[4] But the connection to Taki's involvement with architecture came much later.

Provoke's inaugural issue was published in November 1968 by Nakahira Takuma, Takanashi Yutaka, Taki Kōji, and Okada Takahiko. The front cover was a photo of a woman's face by Taki. In the second issue Moriyama Daidō joined at Nakahira's behest, but with the third issue of August 1969 their activities came to an end. Then, these were reprinted in the collected volume *First, Throw Away the World of Apparent Realism.*[5] From the influence they had thereafter, it is better to call it a movement than an "activity."

Here I would like to read through these three short texts on photography and Taki's photographs published in *The Geometrical Imagination of Architect Shinohara Kazuo* (2007), while citing *Why Still Now* Provoke*?* on the state of photography at the same time.

> Yet for some reason I get asked to photograph by Shinohara-san. However, as the bitter result of the activities on photography like *Provoke* at the end of the 1960s, around the start of the 1970s I decided to stop taking photos, instead to limit myself to looking at photos and writing about them, so that he asked me was agonizing. I am not skilled in taking photographs, and I had gotten past thinking about the photographed world. In the end, unable to turn him down, I photographed things like Tanikawa House and House in Uehara. To photograph or not to photograph was my own problem, but there was no consideration about that. Why he had me take pictures, to this day I do not understand. Could it be that he did not understand photography?[6]

That he would "stop taking photos" was that he ceased photographing as a photographer, and even reprints in *Why Still Now* Provoke*?* were abandoned following Taki's wishes. Despite perceiving the photographs he took at that time as a "bitter result" to this extent, why did he continue photographing the works of several architects, beginning with Shinohara?

He abruptly concludes talking about photography: "Why he had me take pictures, to this day I do not understand. Could it be that he did not understand photography?" It is normal for an architect to hire a photographer in order to record and transmit a work of architecture as a photograph. However, because many of the photographs written (*ronji*) about by Taki were not of architecture or illustrations accompanying a text, and because questioning the representation of architecture through photography, naïve representation itself, is what

1 Taki Kōji, *Kenchikuka Shinohara Kazuo: kikagakuteki sōzōryoku* (Tokyo: Seidosha, 2007).

2 Moriyama Daidō (b. 1938) is a Japanese photographer widely recognized for exposing the underside of urban life. He is also most closely identified with *Provoke*, though his involvement only began with the second issue.

3 *Déjà-vu,* no. 14 "'Purovooku' no jidai," special issue titled "*Provoke*'s Era" (October 1993).

4 Nishii Kazuo, *Naze ima da* Purovooku *ka* (Tokyo: Seikyūsha, 1996).

5 Nakahira Takuma and Taki Kōji eds., *Mazu tashika-rashisa no sekai wo sutero: shashin to gengō no shisō* (Tokyo: Tahata shoten, 1970).

6 Taki Kōji, "Shinohara Kazuo wo omou: Sakamoto Kazunari ni yoru intavyuu," *Ka*, no. 31 (June 2007).

7 Taki Kōji, "Shashin ni nani ga kanō ka," *Shashin-ron shūsei* (Tokyo: Iwanami shoten, 2003). First published in *Mazu tashikarashisa no sekai wo sutero* (1970).

8 Taki Kōji, "Shashin 1," in *Shashin-ron shūsei*, 32.

9 This is the first of two volumes on Shinohara's houses published by Bijutsu shuppansha: *Shinohara Kazuo: 16 no jūtaku to kenchikuron* (Tokyo: Bijutsu shuppansha, 1971).

10 Murai Osamu (1928–2016) was one of the most important architectural photographers of postwar Japan and probably most recognized for his work on Tange Kenzō's Yoyogi National Gymnasiums (1964). Having photographed virtually all of Shinohara's houses from the First and Second Styles, Murai authored the definitive photos of Umbrella House and House in White featured in this volume.

many of his photographs started from in the first place, it is difficult to think that Taki took architectural photographs with this sort of goal. In all likelihood, it was not that he tried to represent Shinohara's architecture with photography, but that it was the praxis of "What is possible in photography": "Photography may be able to restore the direct connection between humans and the world by destroying the intercession of existing concepts, which may again awaken new words and thoughts."[7] To continue, from a two-part photograph, looking at the first part:

> Associating with Shinohara-san, I never imagined that [he] would ask me to take architectural photographs. I forgot how it came to be, but I recall that the first time he hired me to shoot was in 1968 of the South House in Hanayama. At the time I was in a teaching position at Wakō University, and since I had formed a group of rascals to publish the zine *Provoke*, I had no such idea to take pictures of prim houses. Yet somehow he convinced me, and I took them at any rate. After Hanayama South I ended up taking Suzushō House, Shino House, The Uncompleted House, Repeating Crevice, Tanikawa House, House in Uehara, and no matter how many shots I took maybe one would turn out alright. Surprisingly, each photo was valued by Shinohara-san. This was how the first part came to be.[8]

SOUTH HOUSE IN HANAYAMA, 1968 (HALLWAY)
A somewhat low perspective. Set on a tripod and raising the lens, shifting it slightly to the left to keep the composition balanced. Two polished logs immediately jump into sight, and the layering of the leaning chair also feels intentional. The same shot is also printed in *Shinohara Kazuo: 16 Houses,*[9] and in the complete works of Shinohara Kazuo from TOTO Publishing in 1996. Compared with how it is printed here, the contrast is higher but still within controlled tonality.

SOUTH HOUSE IN HANAYAMA (*HIROMA*)
The artificial lighting is stronger than natural light, dusk, and the eye level is rather low, although sufficient to see the top of the table. It appears that the camera was carefully positioned to reveal the overlap of the pendant light with the doorway to the left, from about the viewpoint of someone sitting in a chair. In *Shinohara Kazuo: 16 Houses,* a color photo apparently taken with 6-by-9 roll film with a technical camera, has a composition similar to this one. In these two photographs, the presence of chairs and vases, the positioning of lighting and the bull's-eye umbrella, and the direction the cup is facing are changed, and it's evident that each shot was taken with careful attention to detail. Perhaps converting color positive to monochrome, the tone of the second image differs from the first.

This South House in Hanayama is the first time Taki photographed a work by Shinohara. Compared with those by Murai Osamu,[10] there are no views taken at a distance and Taki's great photographic skills can be well understood. In contrast to Murai's high viewpoint and structural architectural photographs printed in *Shinkenchiku's* January 1969 issue and *SD's* January 1979 monographic issue, Taki's photos give a lyric impression and the vibrant sensation of the gaze of the photographer. This effect is particularly notable when comparing the cover photo and the second one on the interior page of

Shinohara Kazuo, Suzushō House, Hayama, Kanagawa Prefecture, 1968, *hiroma*. Photo by Taki Kōji

Shinohara Kazuo, Repeating Crevice, Ōta Ward, Tokyo, 1971, view from top landing of the first staircase looking toward second staircase. Photo by Taki Kōji

Shinkenchiku. From this contrast one understands that Taki's "skill"—"I am not skilled in taking photographs"—is not technical ability. The *Shinkenchiku* issue lists the building as completed in May 1968, which indicates that it was photographed around the time that *Provoke* began publication.

Shinkenchiku-sha[11] has its own photographers who take the photographs for publication, but how they came to hire independent photographers Taki and Murai is unclear. Even after this debut, in *Shinkenchiku,* Shinohara's works continued to be published with Taki's photos, and most of those photos were first published there, but now I would like to consider Shinohara's motives for selecting the photographs, focusing on specific photo collections as points of comparison.

SUZUSHŌ HOUSE, 1968

Photographed after the South House in Hanayama. Completed in March 1968, perhaps the photos were taken at a later point for some reason. An extraordinarily low point of view. An angle (with the camera) nearly directly on the floor. Seems taken with a single-lens reflex, a dense negative perhaps overdeveloped at a high temperature. The blown out (white) walls. The white of the spotted (= grainy) burned-in shōji screens. High key (lighting).

In *Shinohara Kazuo: 16 Houses,* another shot from the slightly higher perspective at eye level with the low tabletop is printed cropped on top and bottom in a double-page spread. The burned-in wall is gray and grainy. There is no teacup, but on the floor there is a cushion and to the left, a chair. The pendant's light falling on the carpet, avoiding the table, can be barely discerned. In comparison, the photographs in *The Geometrical Imagination*, completely differently from the South House in Hanayama, might be refusing to show the structure of the architecture.

REPEATING CREVICE, 1971

Handheld, looking down. The same development as Suzushō House. Taki's photos continue afterward to have more or less the same tone. The chair reflected in the glass is not noticeable at first; the high contrast makes the transparency of the glass stand out.

> Looking up the first staircase in the ruptured space, as if to repeat it, there is another staircase of exactly the same shape opposite the glass wall. This glass wall is the transparent border between two households.[12]

In *Shinohara Kazuo 2: 11 Houses* (1976), the contrast is still higher; even the legs of the chair seen reflected (in *The Geometrical Imagination*) have disappeared. Aside from this instance, the *11 Houses* monograph reproduces photographs looking up and down, but inserted in between is a photo by Yamada Shūji in a composition where they resonate with each other, which is worth seeing.

The house was completed in April 1971. The same year, 1971, Taki's review "The Fangless Youth" of the photo collection of Gochō Shigeo and Sekiguchi Masao *Hibi* was published in *SD's* June issue.[13] The snapshots taken by these two, both taught by Ōtsuji Kiyoshi[14] at Kuwasawa Design School, are seen as part of the movement that came to be called

11 Founded in 1925, Shinkenchiku-sha is Japan's leading publisher of architectural periodicals. Its titles include *Shinkenchiku*, which has remained Japan's most important trade journal for architecture since the end of World War II, *Jūtaku tokushū* (Housing special), and *The Japan Architect*. *A+U* is published by a sister company under the same umbrella.

12 *Shinohara Kazuo 2: 11 no jūtaku to kenchiku-ron* (Tokyo: Bijutsu shuppansha, 1976), 164. This is the second of two volumes on Shinohara's houses published by Bijutsu shuppansha.

13 Taki Kōji, "Kiba no nai wakamono-tachi," in *Hibi*, ed. Gochō Shigeo and Sekiguchi Masao (private edition, 1971).

14 Ōtsuji Kiyoshi was Shinohara's client for House with an Earthen Floor and House in Uehara.

15 Taki Kōji, "Kiba no nai wakai mono tachi," *SD*, no. 81 (June 1971): 117–19.

16 Shinohara, "Shashin kaisetsu," in *Shinohara Kazuo 2: 11 no jūtaku*, 167.

17 Ibid.

18 Shinohara, "Yasei," in ibid., 24–25.

"contemporary (*konpora*) photography." Even today the definition of "contemporary photography" is ambiguous, but as seen in the title of the *Hibi* (Days) collection, taking photos of the generally unassuming everyday landscape without using special techniques is something they have in common.

This practice is severely criticized by Taki: "Yet for creative work, the method, or in other words, aesthetics, is always a sort of trick. And this trick is supposed to be the mechanism that, from the existing world, allows a glimpse of the unknown world, only by taking to heart that this trick is ultimately a trick. This is not such a simple thing.... This is supposed to require picking out the voids and fissures in between everyday actions, not fixating one individual everyday action. They do not accept aesthetics as a trick, and their return to the safety of black-and-white representation is not a problem of aesthetics itself but nothing other than the conservatism of their ideology."[15] This opposition is precisely what Taki was practicing in his photography.

TANIKAWA HOUSE, 1974
Wide-angle lens, maybe 28 mm. A viewpoint as low as the bench seat. Of course, half of the image is the slope of the *doma* (earthen floor). It is certainly one of the themes of the architecture, but this sort of compositional thing appears as if discovered after the fact through the photograph.

In *Shinohara Kazuo 2: 11 Houses* a photograph with the point of view shifted to the right is used; its contrast is even higher, and the slope is blackened, burned in heavily. *SD's* 1979 monographic issue and the 1996 volume of complete works by TOTO Publishing feature a different photo that is very close in tone. Perhaps it could be said that the differences between these two photographs have not been given much attention, but this one photograph by Taki seems to be his most well-known. "The panorama 'summer space,' separated horizontally 9 meters in the front, 1.2-meter difference in elevation on the ground surface, 3.6-meter-long wooden ladder. This is a reconstruction of the ladder in the photograph of Cézanne's atelier. On the ground, grass is growing here and there."[16]

HOUSE IN UEHARA, 1976 (WEST ELEVATION)
The exterior night view that is also on the cover of Taki's *The Geometrical Imagination of Architect Shinohara Kazuo.* Photographed after it has gotten quite dark. Perhaps using a normal lens wide open, the bottom of the image looks out of focus. If the same negative was also used in *Shinohara Kazuo 2: 11 Houses,* the wall is crushed to black by increasing the contrast, and the sky was dodged to bring out gradation in the coarse grain. The last photo in the collection. A spread. In the parlance of the time, it would be *areboke* (grainy, blurred, and out of focus). "The street-side elevation on a spring night. The aluminum surface of the triangular windows glows in the light of the street lamps right in front. There is a public bath in the rear, and the smoke from its chimneys also adds to this landscape."[17]

HOUSE IN UEHARA (INTERIOR)
Maybe printed from a color original, like the second image in the South House in Hanayama. Reproduced in color in *Shinohara Kazuo 2: 11 Houses.* It is used in conjunction with the essay "Savagery."[18] If this is the same photo, it is boldly

Shinohara Kazuo, Tanikawa House, Naganohara, Gunma Prefecture, 1974, summer *hiroma.* Photo by Taki Kōji

Shinohara Kazuo, House in Uehara, Shibuya Ward, Tokyo, 1976, west elevation. Also cover of Taki Kōji's *The Geometrical Imagination of Architect Shinohara Kazuo* (2007). Photo by Taki Kōji

Shinohara Kazuo, House in Uehara, Shibuya Ward, Tokyo, 1976, interior view from kitchen looking toward entrance foyer and bedrooms. Photo by Taki Kōji

cropped down to about half of the original composition. Apparently a landscape format was changed to portrait. The cropping in this album is nice, but perhaps he wanted to destroy that orderly composition. An unfinished photograph indescribable in prose. In the monographic issue of *SD* (January 1979), there is a photo from a similar point of view by the photographer Hoashi Terutaka, discussed here below, which shows the door open to the interior room, revealing the architectural structure more clearly.[19]

As can be understood by reading Shinohara's commentary, it is very difficult to explain the photos. When putting that which is reproduced into words anew, the photograph itself collapses into a simple explanation of something ("a place where light converges at 45 degrees"), and it is not effective to add in that which is unseen (grass, streetlights, bath, which were not burned into the image). As such, photography's relationship with language is something complex, as it becomes consumed along with language as fashion.

> However, the mass commercialism of Discover Japan and From Gungho to Beautiful[20] beginning in 1970 take in *bure* [blur] and *boke* [out of focus] in an instant—the *Provoke* experiment before the "systematization of sensation" was stripped of its criticality [*mondai ishiki*] by being popularized as predominant evanescence and straight away swallowed up and discarded as technique.[21]

Japanese National Railways and Fuji Xerox each pursued massive advertising campaigns in projects led by Fujioka Wakao. The first poster for Discover Japan (October 1970) was a blurred photo, which became a big issue. The photographer was Iizuka Takeshi of Dentsū's photography division. According to Fujioka, Discover Japan was "discover myself," an imagined landscape made by anonymous photographers in order to inspire self-searching. This is the beginning of the age of *kansei,* or feeling. Moriyama is said to have fallen into a long slump in the period after *Farewell Photography,*[22] which lasted until *Light and Shadow,*[23] and Nakahira after collapsing in 1977 abstained from publication in magazines and monographs until *New Gaze.*[24]

Entering the 1970s, "grainy, blurred, and out of focus" became a fashion in the photography world. This style can also be seen in the photographs of Shinohara Kazuo's works. With the House in Uehara, the exterior photos by Hoashi Terutaka (who graduated from Kuwazawa Design School in 1966 and primarily worked in advertising photography) printed in *Shinohara Kazuo 2: 11 Houses* are quite similar in tone. At first glance seemingly by Taki, these images were printed together with his photos in the 1996 volume *Shinohara Kazuo* as well, with altered cropping. In addition, "grainy" prints from "extraordinarily low point of views" and such were numerous, and looking at the credits in these monographs is intriguing. As can be understood by comparing them, these photos can each likely said to be in service of the architecture. This is a definite distinction they have with Taki's photographs. When Taki confronted architecture with the camera, he aimed to pass beyond the prearranged framework of the architectural photograph, to find language there.

19 Shinohara, "Shashin," in ibid., 164.

20 *Mooretsu kara byuutifuru,* translated here as "From Gungho to Beautiful," was an advertising campaign launched in 1970 questioning the Japan's economic success as built upon tremendous environment costs and personal sacrifice. *Mooretsu* here stands for the gung-ho and go-getter culture of Japanese workers. The campaign was led by Fujioka Wakao of the Dentsū Corporation.

21 Nishii Kazuo, "'Capa no hakuchi' he tabidatsu no da," in *Naze imada "Provoke" ka*, 43.

22 Moriyama Daidō, *Shashin yo sayonara* (Tokyo: Shashin hyōronsha, 1972).

23 Moriyama Daidō, *Hikari to kage* (Tokyo: Tōjusha, 1982).

24 Nakahira Takuma, *Aratanaru gyōshi* (Tokyo: Shōbunsha, 1983).

25 Taki Kōji, "Shashin 2," in *Shashin-ron shūsei*," 138. All seven of these photographs, which depict The Uncompleted House, Shino House, Tanikawa House, House in Uehara, and House in Ashitaka, appear in the project image folios of these houses in this volume—either replicating their original presentation or in a slight variation.

His statement that "he did not understand photography" might indicate his lack of understanding of their difference with that type of photography. Any photographer knows that to choose photographs and put them together as a collection is comparable to taking the photographs themselves. Even with the collections of Shinohara's works, how did Taki think about his own photos being used as illustrations? Taki's brusque, detached way of talking about photography was perhaps the expression of his irritation with the fact that Shinohara having chosen his photographs (and him as a photographer) resulted in his experiment with photography, architecture, and language being picked up as a style.

With this House in Uehara, Taki's photography of Shinohara's works ended. Even though he said that he "photographed reluctantly when asked," it is hard to imagine that there was not a clear reason why he put down his camera. The *Provoke* movement became trivialized and consumed by the problem of the "grainy, blurred, and out of focus" style, which seems to have led to Taki's experiment with photography and architecture, just as with Moriyama and Nakahira ceasing their creative activities, and likewise the "dissolution of criticality." In *The Geometrical Imagination*, an additional selection of seven photographs were later noted as a second part:

> This selection of photographs is a cross section that illustrates how difficult Shinohara-san's works were to photograph. It reminds me of the time when Shinohara-san was shifting from spaces that are "visual" to spaces that are not. While taking photos of Shinohara-san's works, I felt spaces that could not be described through only visual means. I did not really care if I could not take very good shots. I reluctantly accepted to shoot for Shinohara-san, but in actuality I had sensed the essence of perception.[25]

"Sensed the essence of perception" refers to that which was not reproduced in the photographs; that said, there is a relationship between the photographs and the meaning of these words, indicating one answer to "what is possible in photography" with respect to architecture, however paradoxical. And the question remains, why does the architectural photographer photograph architecture?

This essay analyzes seven photos featured in Taki Kōji's book *Kenchikuka Shinohara Kazuo: Kikagaku no sōzōryoku* (The geometrical imagination of architect Shinohara Kazuo) (Tokyo: Seidosha, 2007). The reference images presented here are drawn from the Shinohara Kazuo Archive and may vary from those analyzed in the text in cropping, camera angles, composition, or texture due to differences in paper and printing. The Japanese-language version of this essay originally appeared in *Taki Kōji to kenchiku,* a special issue of *Kenchiku to nichijō* (2013).

Translated by Álex Bueno

Presenting the Second Style

Editor's Note

Toward the end of the 1960s Shinohara turned to a seemingly reductive, formalist approach to design. The rigorous geometry of Shinohara's Second Style emerged out of House of White's (1966) cubic interior, which reappears in the center of each of the four compositions selected here. At the same time he pursued the idea of fissure, splicing static volumes with movement and light. Shinohara's introductory texts to these projects suggest an ambivalence between the spiritual, emotive dimensions of space-making and a more stoic, syntax-driven approach. Sequencing of volumes in these interiors is choreographed with an almost baroque theatricality, as narrow double-height crevices give way to light-filled courtyards shimmering amid bronze-colored walls.

The image folios for Shinohara's Second Style houses of the early 1970s, The Uncompleted House, Shino House, and Repeating Crevice, presented here rely exclusively on the photographic work of the philosopher and critic Taki Kōji, which is also the topic of Ano Daici's essay in this volume. With few exceptions Shinohara's houses were given their public debut in the journal *Shinkenchiku,* Japan's premier trade journal of architecture. Known for its in-house team of highly skilled photographers, the journal would on occasion publish work by independent photographers such as Murai Osamu in the case of Umbrella House. Shinohara and chief editor Baba Shōzō's decision to use the grainy, 35 mm shots by Taki to show both The Uncompleted House and Shino House was without precedent and caused an uproar among their trusted photographers.

The first two houses of the Second Style appeared in the January 1971 issue of *Shinkenchiku.* As veteran editor Ishidō Takeshi recounts the story, the in-house photographers were rather flustered as they returned from their shoot, not quite able to grasp what these new works were supposed to mean.[1] After a considerable lapse Shinohara showed up at the editorial office, armed with two packets in his hands. One contained new photos by the usual independent photographer suspects, but these images were equally disengaged as those produced by the in-house team. Only then did Shinohara take out the contents from the second packet. These photos by Taki Kōji immediately conveyed Shinohara's desire for abstraction and sensorial stimulation.

Taki and Shinohara first met in 1964, after Taki reviewed the joint exhibition of works by Shinohara and artist Asakura Setsu.[2] The review appeared in the journal *Glass,* where Taki served as the editor and pushed an intense and multifaceted agenda that brought together design, art, film, photography, and architecture. Informed by structuralist thought from Europe, Taki, a few years younger than Shinohara, was one of the first to advance the concept of *kankyō,* or environment, as the conditions of a hegemonic framework under which a work of art is produced.[3] An interlocutor through both his critical writings and his creative collaborations with major figures in the field, Taki asserted an enduring influence on Japan's avant-garde.

1 Ishidō Takeshi, "Watashi no kono issaku," in "Taki Kōji to kenchiku" special issue, *Kenchiku to nichijō* (April 2013): 17–23.

2 Okuyama Shin-ichi, "Vital Encounter: Kazuo Shinohara and Philosopher Kōji Taki," *werk, bauen + wohnen* (December 2015): 28–31.

3 Taki Kōji, "Shashin to kankyō no shisō" (Thoughts on photography and environment), *Dezain hihyō,* no. 3 (June 1967): 29–33.

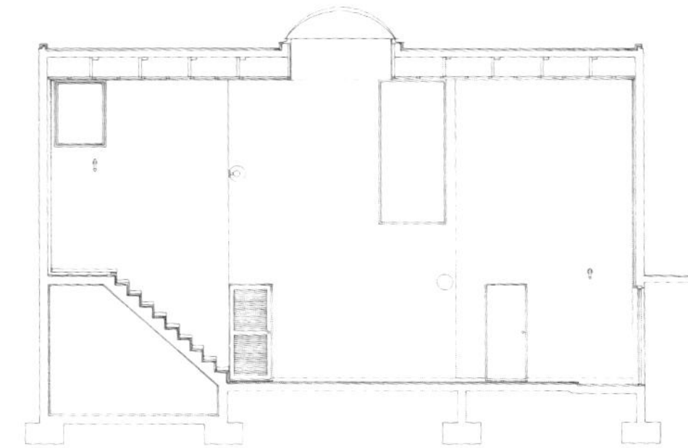

THE UNCOMPLETED HOUSE, 1970
Suginami Ward, Tokyo

Shinohara's first purely cubic work and based on a 10-by-10-meter plan, The Uncompleted House is defined by its towering void in the center, which he refers to as the main room (*hiroma*), even though it is superfluous in the conventional sense of function. Various parts of the house are arranged through multiple staircases such that adjacent rooms can be reached only by passing (or, detouring) through this emotive space. The strong axis through the center of the house creates a fissure and debilitates its seemingly Palladian serenity.

Photos by
Taki Kōji (TK)

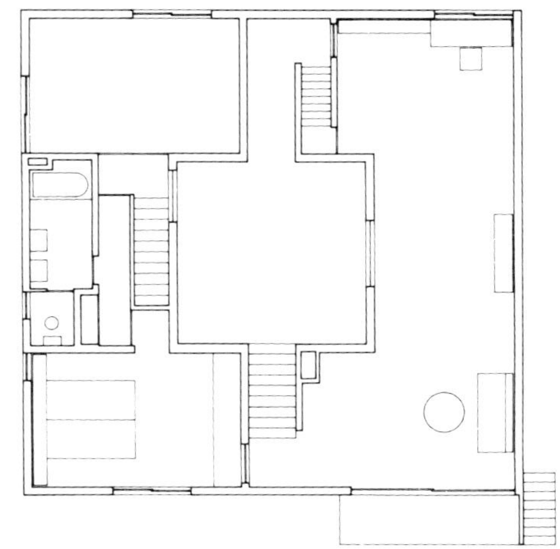

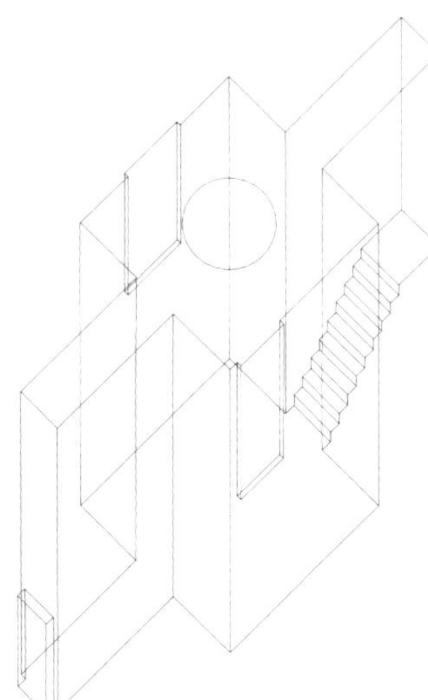

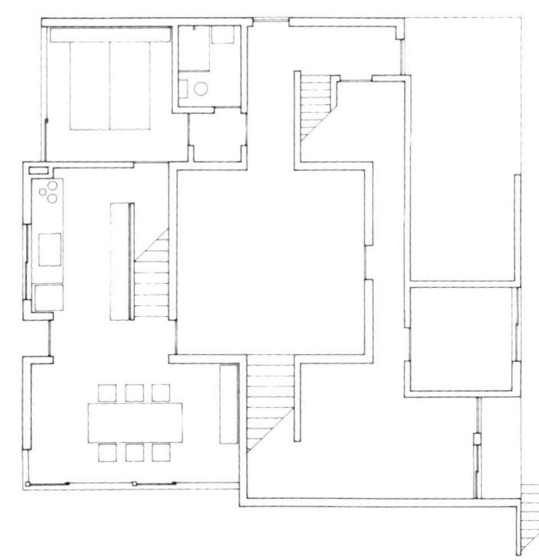

1:200

View from staircase lcoking toward *hiroma*.

Hiroma.

TK

TK

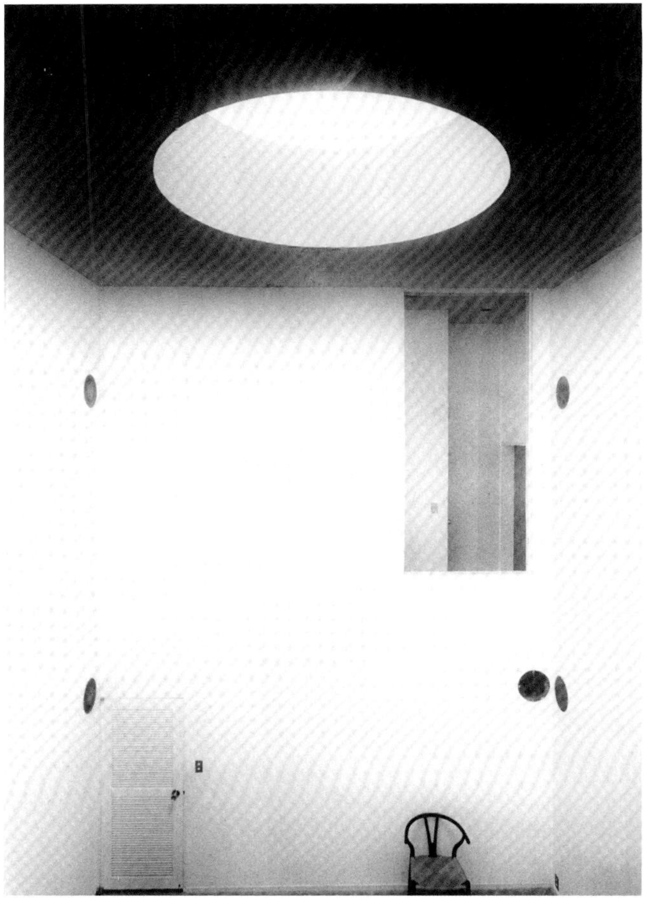

Southeast elevation.

View from *hiroma* looking toward entrance.

View from *hiroma* looking toward upper-floor living room.

TK

TK

TK

SHINO HOUSE, 1970
Nerima Ward, Tokyo

Designed in parallel with The Uncompleted House (1970) but built of wood, Shino House is bifurcated by a double-height corridor leading toward a cubic interior courtyard. Shinohara noted this space's spiritual, mystic quality, with its walls covered in bronze paper and shimmering in light coming from the sky. The house's various rooms are placed into two symmetrical wings. A pair of desks on the upper floor, one in the study and the other in the dressing room, look toward each other through the luminous void in the center.

Photos by
Taki Kōji (TK)

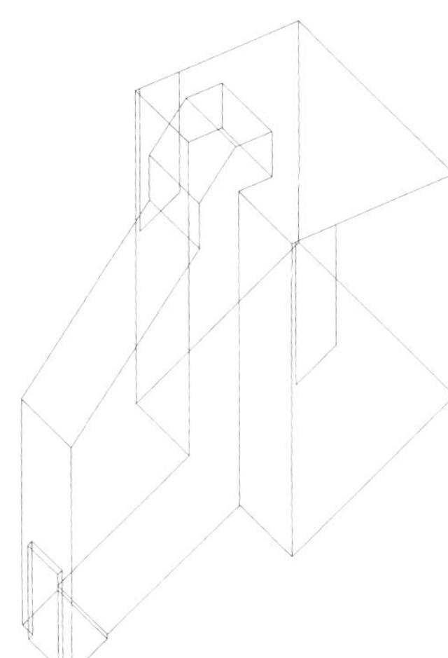

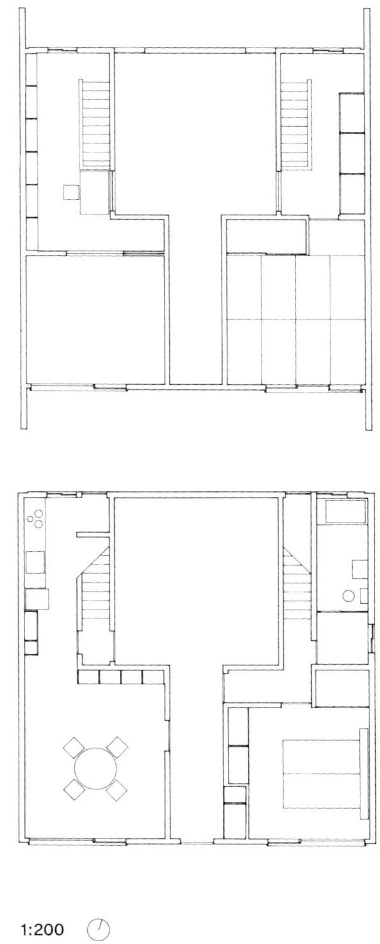

1:200

Hiroma.

View from living-dining room
looking toward upper-floor study.

TK

TK

Upper-floor study.

Living-dining room.

View from upper-floor dressing room looking through *hiroma* into upper-floor study.

South elevation.

TK

TK

TK

TK

REPEATING CREVICE, 1971
Ōta Ward, Tokyo

Configured as a spatial matrix for two generations of the same family—each with its own living and sleeping quarters—the house stacks the two generations vertically, on the two floors, and living and sleeping quarters are split horizontally between the two sides of the building. The fissure space through the center of the house both divides and connects. Two identical staircases, in the front and in the rear, tie everything together. The landing at the top of the first stairway has a view toward the second, and this sense of spatial continuity and threshold is reinforced by the almost-black color band in the ceiling, which in turn is punctured by skylights at each of the landings.

Photos by
Taki Kōji (TK)

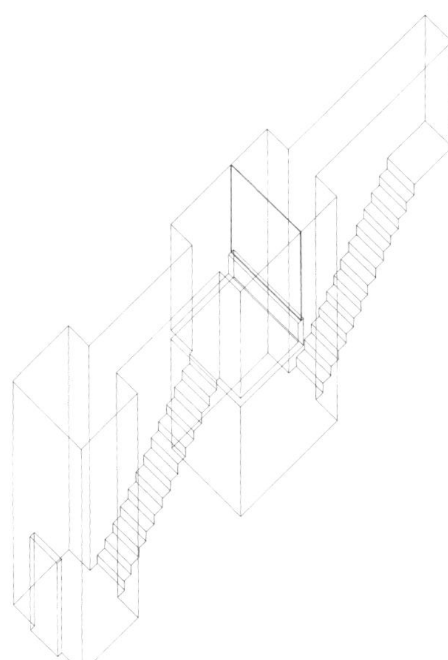

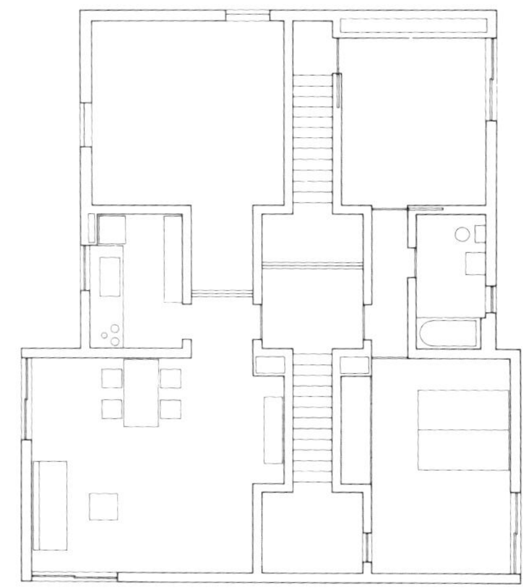

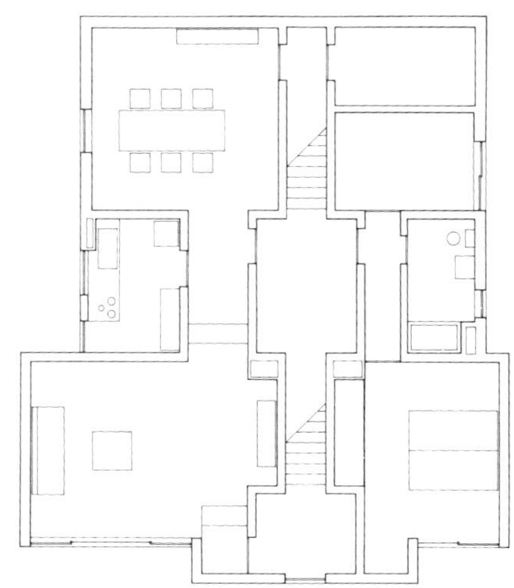

1:200

View from first staircase landing
looking toward second staircase.

TK

View from upper-floor living-dining room looking into lower-floor dining room.

First staircase with view of ceiling.

TK

TK

TK

SEA STAIRWAY, 1971
Nerima Ward, Tokyo

Painter Nomiyama Gyōji, the client, had in mind a one-room house like the studio he had in Paris, where he painted, slept, and ate in the same space. There is a grade change of a full storey in height from the front of the site to the rear, traversed by a long staircase. The main living space and studio were conceived as an atrium-like space in an earlier design, appended to this ascending promenade. Eventually configured as a shoebox, Sea Stairway employs details akin to those of House in White (1966) to conceal materiality and texture. The main space, encompassing the living area and studio and measuring 7.5 by 12.5 meters, is covered by a thin concrete slab without joists. Structural engineer Kimura Toshihiko reduced its maximum thickness to just 180 millimeters by a slightly convex profile in the roof slab to preempt any potential sagging.

Photos by
Murai Osamu (MO) and Okamoto Shigeo for Shōkokusha (OS)

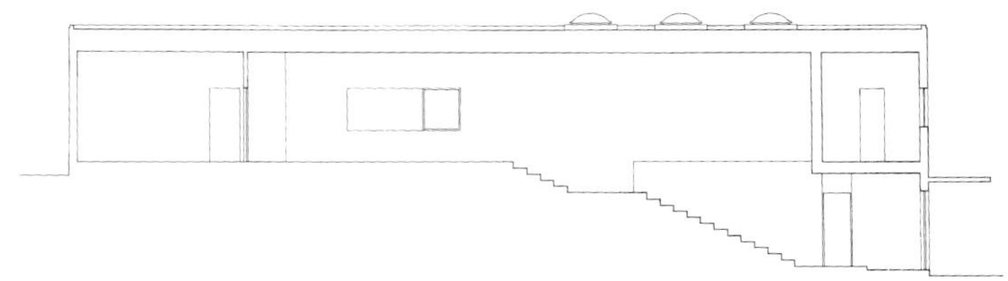

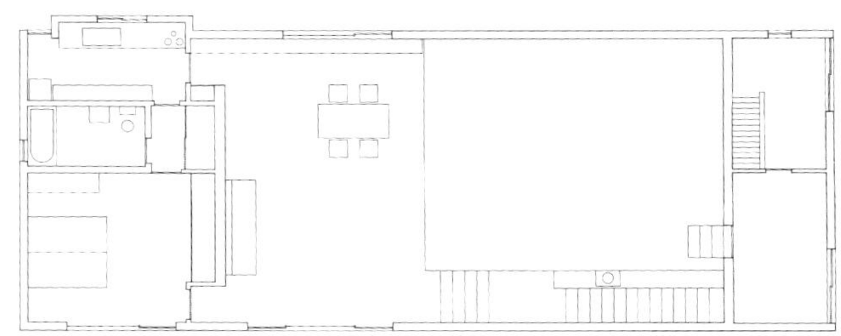

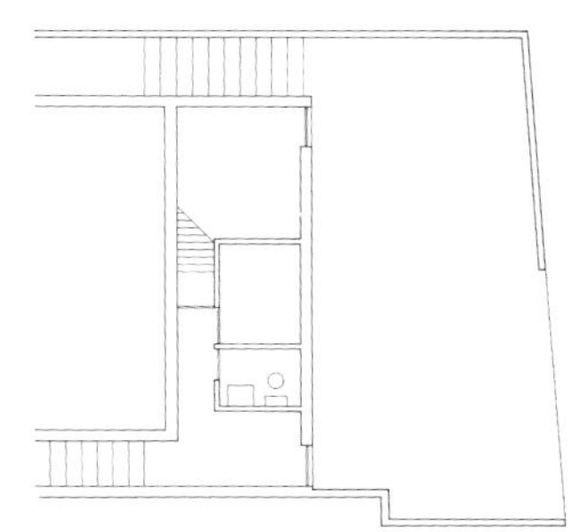

1:250

View from staircase looking toward living-dining space.

MO

View from living-dining space looking toward studio.

Staircase and door leading from studio to storage.

Studio.

MO

ɔs

os

Studio and living-dining space, Sea Stairway. Photo by Seng Kuan

"I would like him to learn how to live in this space that I made."

Interview with Nomiyama Gyōji

by Seng Kuan, Shiozaki Taishin, and Kobayashi Saeco

Painter Nomiyama Gyōji (b. 1920) lived in France from 1952 to 1964. He commissioned a house by Shinohara that came to be known as Sea Stairway (1971), in Nerima Ward, not from the center of Tokyo. This project was followed a few years later by a second commission in the seaside village of Itoshima, in Nomiyama's native Fukuoka Prefecture. Nomiyama continues to divide his time between these two houses, generally spending summer in Itoshima and winter in Tokyo.

1 SEPTEMBER 29, 2018, AT HOUSE IN ITOSHIMA

SENG KUAN Today we hope to better understand not only Shinohara Kazuo's works but also his relationships with clients. Because among Shinohara-sensei's clients were a number of artists like you, it seems important to understand how and why artists like you commissioned Shinohara-sensei to design houses and what sort of discussions you had together.

NOMIYAMA GYŌJI Shinohara-sensei was present when I received the Mainichi Art Award, and what he said then left an impression on me: "I had been doing residential designs, forty-six or forty-seven houses. Only a few are still living in the houses I designed, including Nomiyama-sensei[1] [laughter]." I lived in Paris for a time, in a house with only one room. Just the wet area was fixed, and the bed was wherever. Even coming back to Japan because I was by myself, I would have liked a similar one room. I spent some time with my younger sister and her family, but I could not stay with them for long, so I thought if I just found a piece of land somewhere, all I would need there is one room. I didn't particularly feel like asking an architect; I just wanted the space.

Then it happened that the husband of a female friend just a bit older than me, a professor at the University of Tokyo doing research on plants, had hired a certain architect to build their house. But then that professor had to go to the United States in the middle of it, and had to rely on a dependable architect to finish it.

My friend wanted to introduce me to Shinohara-sensei, telling me to have him build me my house. I refused but she insisted that no matter how simple the house I should hire an architect. So since it was only one room, and since Shinohara-sensei was stubborn, I had planned to ask him to introduce me to a student assistant. In the past, she had tried to introduce Shinohara-sensei to a neighbor who wanted a house built, but apparently he had refused. I was forty-five years old when I returned to Japan, now I am ninety-seven, so that was over fifty years ago.

SHIOZAKI TAISHIN The Nerima residence [Sea Stairway] was completed in 1971. You hired Shinohara-sensei for the Nerima house sometime after you returned to Japan.

NOMIYAMA Yes, I was a bit hesitant since I had not intended on asking him. So I met Shinohara-sensei since my friend had said I should have him introduce me to an apprentice assistant. I did not have any idea whether the house should be in concrete or wood; I just wanted a box. After saying he understood this, Shinohara-sensei remained silent. Then when my friend asked if he would introduce me to an apprentice assistant, he said no. Not knowing what to do, she asked why, to which he said that the request is too difficult, impossible for an assistant—I have to do it myself. She was confused, thinking that maybe that Shinohara-sensei could not let this one go because few clients would let him do as he pleased. After that, we met repeatedly but I never made Shinohara-sensei a concrete demand. I came to marry someone I met after returning to Japan but we lived separately, so the house would be for me to live in only at times. Because I had already lost my first wife in Paris, I had been single for ten years after that and had gotten used to living alone.

Just about half a year after I commissioned the house, there was a party for the completion of a house in Denen-chōfu for a client who worked for NHK [Japan Broadcasting Corporation], to which clients of Shinohara-sensei were

invited.[2] My house was not yet finished, in the middle of being constructed, so I was invited and went. The client greeted us saying that he was satisfied with Shinohara-sensei's great and careful work. Then Shinohara-sensei also greeted us, saying, "I do not design architecture for the benefit of the client. I would like him to learn how to live in this space that I made. It is something that he has to get used to. When he does, then he and the space will be one." My wife asked me laughingly if I was OK with this, being that we were having our house built by him.

After that, Shinohara-san called on me for a number of reasons but he never talked about the architecture. Often after his visits, I would not hear from him for a while, and after about a year had passed one day he called, saying that it was all over because he still did not know whether it would be allowed to have an atelier on that property. Nerima is not the suburbs, he said; it is a very halfway place [between the city and the suburbs], and he did not know what to do, that I should sell the plot and buy another one. So we went together looking for properties around Akasaka and such. However, it ended up that we did not find one, and he could not fulfill the commission. But a half year later, he came back saying he would do it after all, and another half year later he turned me down again.

I was living with my younger sister's family. My brother-in-law was the novelist Tanaka Komimasa, and at the time he suddenly got his break. They had two children, and my sister was getting hysterical having to take care of the children, her husband, and me, so I had to move out. Then Shinohara-san called saying that inspiration hit him. It had been about half a year since he had last turned me down. That time he brought a model and I listened to his explanation. I told him to go with it, but then a week later he told me he gave up on that one. When I asked him if it would take another half a year, he said, "No, a week" [laughter].

I understood that feeling well. Just like with painting, before doing a major work, the beginning is indecisive; this is wrong, that is wrong, but then at one point when it comes together, it changes completely and comes together all at once. I thought this was just like that.

SHIOZAKI TAISHIN I see; it's quite interesting. A conventional client doesn't understand that feeling. So was the proposal he came back with a week later completely different from the first one?

NOMIYAMA Yes, I thought he should spend time on it if he was able to.

The Nerima house was a kitchen and atelier in one room, and one day a publisher came for lunch, but I could not let him into the room, and my wife said that there should be a separate room for taking meals. When I told that to Shinohara-san, he said that the publisher won't come back for lunch [laughter]. On top of that, my wife had been saying that the design was done by someone who did not understand the kitchen, since the cabinet door bumped into the refrigerator. When my wife told Shinohara-san that she would ask Hasegawa Itsuko-san[3] to do the kitchen design, he got furious saying that only base animals worry about food [laughter]. It was nothing but arguments with my wife. In spite of that, Shinohara-san and I often went drinking in Ginza. Takahashi-san from BAU Construction,[4] the contractor for the house, also liked to drink, and he often joined us.

As for this house here, we spent over three years looking at sites in Fukuoka. This one was bad; that one was bad. He just would not commit. During that time, Shinohara-san turned me down, asking me to hire Isozaki [Arata]-san. My wife was running a bar, and Isozaki-san was apparently a customer there.

KUAN The two houses, one in Nerima and the other in Itoshima, how do you use them?

Nomiyama Gyōji at Sea Stairway, 2018. Photo by Seng Kuan

Studio, House in Itoshima. Photos by Seng Kuan

NOMIYAMA House in Itoshima we bought when a friend of my wife bought land for a villa. Maybe because he could not help getting involved when I took on a house, it came to be that Shinohara-san did it. Turning down commissions was probably a bad habit of his.

KUAN The idea of living in one room that you brought back from France became the strength of the space. Please forgive me for asking a rather private question, but how did you live in that one room?

NOMIYAMA How does someone live with their wife [laughter]? I have always been by myself so I do not understand how it is different. When the light coming in became bad I would go on walks for a change. I also write, and writing I do at night. During the day I paint and at night I write. In between I go out on walks. If I can help it, I do not want to paint with the lights on.

With the Nerima house too, Shinohara-san doubted whether it should really be one room. At first, his design had walls, and I wondered why he would not do what I had asked for. It only became a one-room space after he confirmed that I would be OK with no walls or partitions regardless of who came. When I said to him that he had thought hard about how to convince me, he thanked me for my cooperation.

Architecture is different from painting, though an [art], with painting one can say, if you don't like the painting, don't buy it, but architecture is difficult because it does not work like that.

KUAN The postwar was a period of intense changes for France and Tokyo. When you returned to Tokyo from France in 1964, how did you perceive the changes in Tokyo?

NOMIYAMA When I came back, Japan felt like a bizarre land. I went to Europe with the idea in my head that it was a land without humans living there. About oil painting, before the war [in Japan], there was not a single oil painting in the National Art Museum. Not one work by Cézanne. Only the Ōhara Art Museum [in Kurashiki, Okayama Prefecture] had a few oil paintings, so I went there many times. Because oil painting is a Western thing, I decided to study abroad because I had to see the real thing.

I did not even know whether female nudes by Matisse and others were paintings or sketches. So I thought I would go to a land that is not where humans lived. When I came back to Japan I felt it was a place without rules. How people walked and the cars ran around chaotically out of place made strong impressions. Billboards and trash cans were scattered all over.

In France, I just had to do as I had been taught. On the road, in the theater, at the movies, I was able to follow the rules, but in Japan I was terrified because it was not like that. After being back in Japan for about half a year, I was desperate to return to Paris. More than when I went to France, the difference was greater when I returned to Japan. Now would be the time to make architecture and draw up a contract.

Food is a strange thing. In Paris, I was fine when visitors came while I was eating. Even when the postman came, it would be, let's drink some wine. Not in Japan. I thought that in Japan changing shoes is a big difference. Even eating bread in the street, you can share your bread with someone who comes by, but not with rice. When a visitor comes while painting, Europeans can say, wait for a bit, and keep going, but the Japanese do not let anyone into the atelier.

I think that's why Shinohara-sensei brought all kinds of people to come see me.

KUAN Lastly, were there any changes made to this house after it was completed?

NOMIYAMA Only the heating and cooling equipment broke down, and a new pipe had to stick out on the exterior. I like [the house] so I have not changed it.

SHIOZAKI The outdoor corridor is now only the frame, but I read in something written by Shinohara-sensei saying that originally it was planned to be covered with translucent or opaque boards.

NOMIYAMA It seems that Shinohara-sensei was uncertain whether to form an arch in that part. We discussed it.

SHIOZAKI The island visible from the outdoor corridor is somewhat off-center, correct?

NOMIYAMA Shinohara-sensei himself came to see that the position of the island would be slightly to the left. After that he barely returned. The contractor was a man from Waseda [University], from what was still a new company. He lowered the price because he desperately wanted to work on a project with Shinohara-sensei. It was a price so low there was no profit. I went with him because he desperately wanted to do it, as long as I would publicize it for him. During construction, when Shinohara-sensei and Kimura-sensei[5] came, I took them to a French restaurant.

Shinohara-sensei was apparently pleased with the construction. It was planned to paint the exterior wall black, and I said I was not so gloomy but instead flirtatious out in the light. But, it was well built so it was left unpainted. That is what he said.

2 OCTOBER 14, 2018, AT SEA STAIRWAY, NERIMA WARD, TOKYO

SHIOZAKI Today I would like to ask you about yourself, Nomiyama-sensei. You have published many essays. Around when did you start writing? Was it from the time you were in France?

NOMIYAMA No, I was not writing [then], but I was friends with the culture editor of a newspaper in Fukuoka who asked me to write an essay. I refused, but he said he wanted writing from a painter. I told him it was impossible because I had a solo exhibition coming, but he said next year the show would be over. He was very persistent, and I ended up writing. He told me I should just write about what I did in a day.

SHIOZAKI The title of this book, *The Sky Above,* is really great. I get the sense that you are writing about things that cannot be seen with the eye. Your works are abstract paintings, but was the process of writing about meeting people different from painting things that cannot be seen?

NOMIYAMA They are not so much related. Students tell me that my writing is the same as how I talk. I often got asked to do book covers, and one publisher asked about famous people I have met. For Paris, Fujita Tsuguharu, among a few others, came up, so the essays turned into a book.

SHIOZAKI In another book, you wrote what we discussed last time about Shinohara-sensei. When architects build, they write about their buildings. Have you ever read the writings of Shinohara-sensei?

NOMIYAMA No, never. I do not know about other painters, but I have never written about my works. I have never thought about those on the other side looking at my paintings, that if I did this then my paintings would sell. Architects have all kinds of conditions, so they must have a lot to write about.

SHIOZAKI At the time, did Shinohara-sensei have the opportunity to see your paintings? Did you ever bring the work of Itoshima in the summer before you finished it?

Entrance, Sea Stairway. Photo by Seng Kuan

Nomiyama Gyōji at Sea Stairway, 2018. Photo by Seng Kuan

NOMIYAMA Shinohara-sensei never said a thing [about it]. But one day he asked if I could drop by his house, given that I was nearby. And he had one of my paintings. He said he was learning.

My works do not move around. If the atelier changes, it is different for me. Like the galleries say, the colors seem different. Writing, too, before I would write in the upper level. I could not keep writing what I left unfinished here.

SHIOZAKI I see. Your works and the place together form a set.

I understand that Shinohara-sensei would make sketches anywhere, like before going to sleep at his bedside. It seems he even sketched on hotel notepads.

NOMIYAMA For me as well, any paper will do.

KOBAYASHI SAECO Were the position and number of skylights in the atelier decided in consultation with Shnohara-sensei?

NOMIYAMA No, we did not discuss it at all. And Shinohara-sensei told me not to come during construction. Somewhat before my house was being built, apparently the owner of the house in Denen-chōfu often made up some excuse and went, but [Shinohara-sensei] said, "You really do not come." So after consulting, I saw it for the first time after it was completed.

KOBAYASHI So you confirmed the design with models, and then you just left it up to him?

NOMIYAMA No, the first proposal was a model, but there was no model for the revised proposal. Is it not at the university?

SHIOZAKI No, the model for Sea Stairway is no longer there.

NOMIYAMA Is that so? At the time I often went to the university. Tanikawa-san said that the house in Karuizawa [Tanikawa House, 1974] has no floor so I should tell him to build one. Tanikawa-san's house that was built before that had the front door in a strange place, but he would get upset and said, "This was no joke." After that, when I told Seike Kiyoshi-san that I had Shinohara-sensei build my house, he said [he was surprised] that I could live in it. But I like it [laughter].

KOBAYASHI What do you like most about this house?

NOMIYAMA Nothing in particular. If I ever have to put in railings here, I think I might go back to Fukuoka [laughter].

Translated by Álex Bueno

1 Both Nomiyama and Shinohara received the 38th Mainichi Art Award in 1996.

2 Completed a few months before Sea Stairway, Repeating Crevice is located in the Tokyo's suburb of Denen-chōfu, Ōta Ward.

3 Hasegawa Itsuko (b. 1941) was a member of Shinohara's lab at the Tokyo Institute of Technology from 1968 to 1979.

4 BAU Construction was responsible for many of Shinohara's houses from the Second and Third Styles.

5 Kimura Toshihiko (1926–2009) was one of Japan's most important and influential structural designers of the twentieth century. A graduate of the University of Tokyo, Kimura was trained in the office of Maekawa Kunio and established an independent practice in 1964. His list of collaborators is a veritable who's who of modern architecture in Japan: Maki Fumihiko, Shinohara Kazuo, Isozaki Arata, and Hara Hiroshi, among others.

HOUSE IN ITOSHIMA, 1976
Fukuoka Prefecture

Located on a cape in the westernmost part of Japan, House in Itoshima emphatically embraces its natural surroundings. Reminiscent of the configuration of Shino House (1970), the plan is divided between the residence wing and a studio wing. The house is situated at the head of a parabola-shaped valley, and its main axis forms the house's spine with the two wings flanking the sides. This axis extends out into the sea and frames a small island in the distance. Shinohara placed a series of three architectural moments along this axis: a semi-enclosed ceremonial entrance, a steel-frame footbridge, and a courtyard. Fine marble paving further lends spatial import to this procession. At the end of this sequence, a cubic courtyard is perfectly framed by only the sea in front and the sky above. The painting studio, with a strong sense of verticality and enclosed by fair-faced concrete walls, is radically different from that of the homogenous, abstract space at Sea Stairway (1971), which was designed five years prior for the same client.

Photos by
Arai Masao for Shinkenchiku-sha/DAAS (AM) and Ueda Hiroshi (UH)

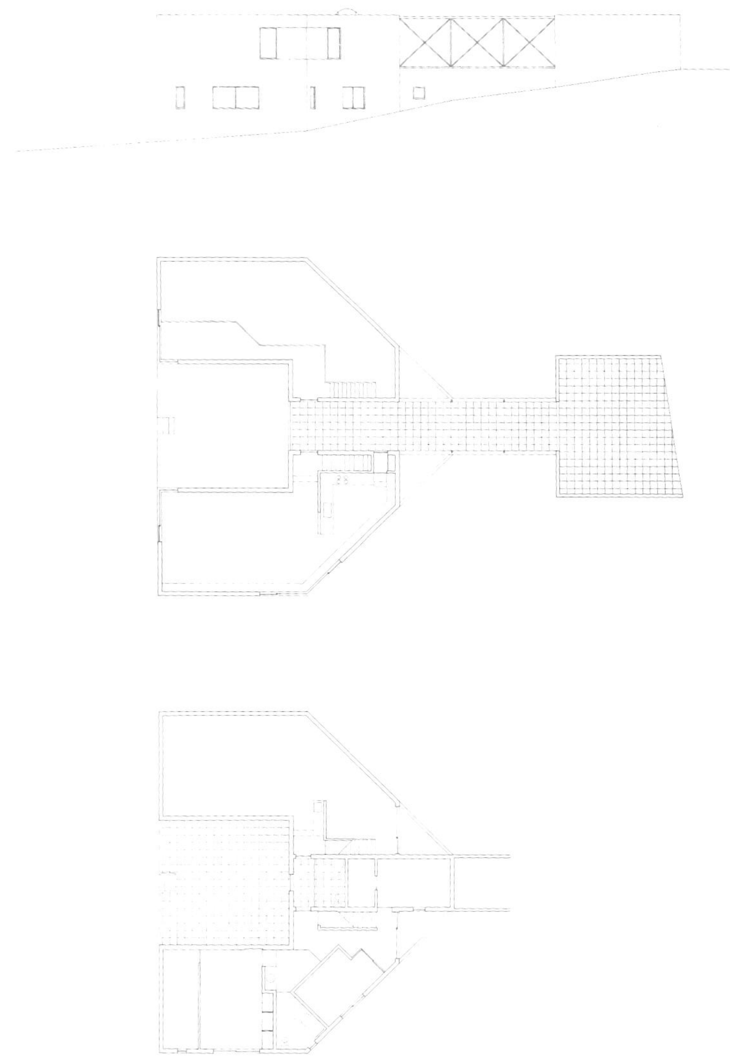

1:400

Courtyard.

AM

Bridge.

Studio, view toward entrance.

Studio, view from entrance.

UH

JH

AM

HOUSE IN KARUIZAWA, 1975
Nagano Prefecture

Situated on the main thoroughfare of the resort town of Karuizawa, this residence and studio have a bifurcated arrangement that allows for a courtyard or outdoor gallery between them. The plan of House in Karuizawa is otherwise dominated by three curves, each a quarter arc. Shinohara was interested in testing out the binary of convex and concave surfaces, and the courtyard also acts as a pathway, or "crevice," connecting the main road with the forested neighborhood on the other side. Curved walls, reinforced by inward sloping roofs, create a wave-like flow of spaces.

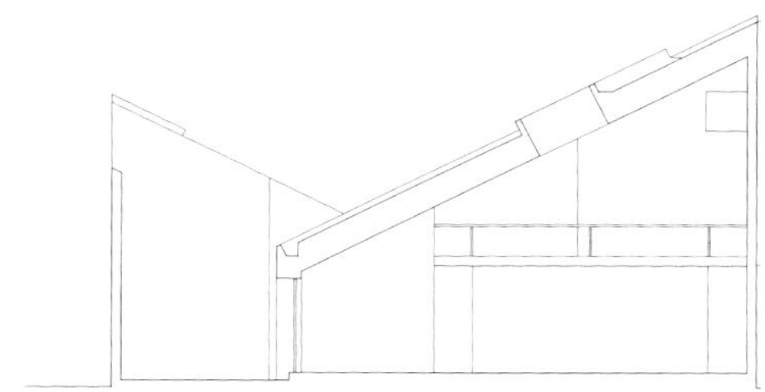

Photos by
Arai Masao for Shinkenchiku-sha / DAAS (AM)

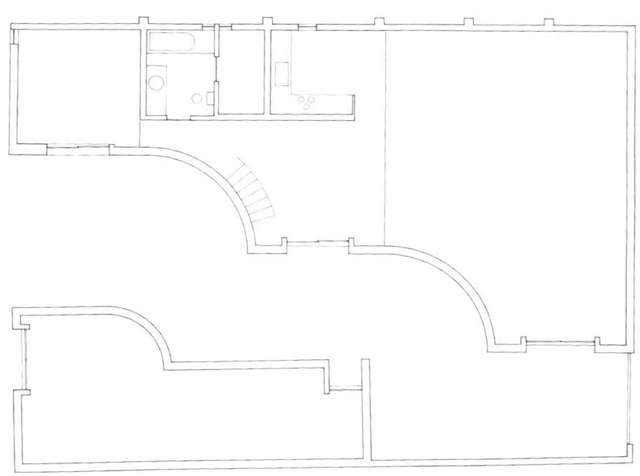

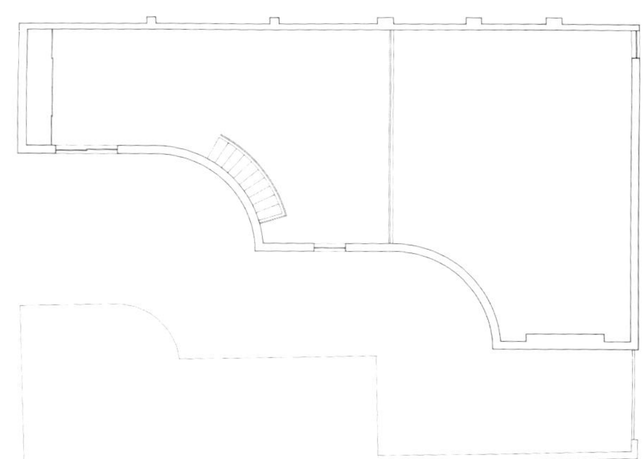

Studio.

1:250

M

Gallery.

Courtyard.

East elevation.

AM

AM

AM

Shinohara Kazuo, Fort d'Estrées,
Dakar, 1975.

"Translating" Shinohara: *Kunstform,* Style, and the Logic of *Aufhebung*

David B. Stewart

1 Ishidō Takeshi et al., eds., *Shinohara Kazuo: jūtaku zumen* (Tokyo: Shōkokusha, 2008).

My late colleague at the Tokyo Institute of Technology (Tokyo Tech) Shinohara Kazuo is well known today among Japanese architects for his wide-ranging written treatment of an array of architectural topics as well as some broader underlying urban issues. These concerns originally flow from a self-examination of his built oeuvre, and we may easily divide Shinohara's various manifestoes, articles, and book-length publications into three periods, each encompassing its distinctive formats and preoccupations. Our complementary forty-year teaching careers at Tokyo's national technical university overlapped for the space of a decade, from shortly after I first came to Japan in the mid-1970s. Afterward, he and I continued to meet more or less regularly, whether near the school or at his small Yokohama studio until Shinohara's activity began to slacken a few years before his death in 2006.

In July 1996, the volume *Shinohara Kazuo* had been issued by TOTO shuppan in Tokyo, comprising more than four hundred pages and a bibliography (thus amounting to a Complete Works). Posthumously, in January 2008, Shōkokusha published a much slighter book for students titled *Shinohara Kazuo: Houses and Drawings,*[1] which is a compendium of all the houses, without the public buildings. The former contains no text in English, and the latter an English translation of the brief "Fragments on Drawing" essay of 1973, along with translations of a few short project descriptions.

Many of his fellow architects viewed Shinohara as a difficult personality. This was hardly the case, despite his somewhat delicate constitution and several serious recurrent illnesses—health crises being thought of in Japan by some as a mark of artistic seriousness and integrity. Whatever the case, this architect possessed both these qualities in abundance. He did not brook random or uninformed criticism of his design output, which abounded in the celebrated "patient research" of Le Corbusier. However, Shinohara entertained different aims and ambitions from the Franco-Swiss architect, who built only a single building in Japan, the National Museum of Western Art at Ueno, completed in 1959 assisted by his Japanese disciples. In fact, from the very beginning of Shinohara Kazuo's architectural career he was greatly attracted to Ludwig Mies van der Rohe, whose works he knew only from books and magazines, travel abroad from Japan being almost impossible owing to monetary exchange control in the aftermath of World War II.

As is now well known, though far from thoroughly understood, Shinohara's oeuvre was divided into four self-designated styles, which he regarded as place markers of his progress toward an understanding of building construction but also its role in art and society. As the architectural profession is a young one in Japan, there are different modes of being an architect, and Shinohara first came to the field via an undergraduate formation and a brief period of teaching in mathematics—a highly unusual start for an architect. Although drafted into the wartime Japanese armed services, he never saw combat, and his training interval in Korea was never completed owing to the war's finish.

Instead, having majored in mathematics at a different college, Shinohara then retrained in architecture at the Tokyo Institute of Technology, where he graduated in 1953, becoming an instructor in the studio of Professor Seike Kiyoshi. Seven years Shinohara's senior, Seike unusually had studied at both Tokyo School of Fine Arts (now Tokyo University of the Arts) and Tokyo Tech, where he taught from 1946. In 1954, the same year that the ten-years-younger Maki Fumihiko received his master's degree from the Harvard Graduate School of Design, Seike first met the celebrated German architect Walter Gropius in Japan and shortly afterward traveled to the United States. Meanwhile, Shinohara, only three years older than Maki, did not travel abroad until two decades later—after which, and during the years of his Third Style, he came to be acquainted with younger architects such as Jean Nouvel and Rem Koolhaas and others who at the time were beginning to design buildings in Japan.

1 The young Shinohara was first, and rather unexpectedly, attracted by ancient Japanese tradition in monumental structures, especially in the Kyoto and Nara regions of western Japan. But to return to Shinohara's writing activity—his first published articles grew into a series of twelve discourses dealing with the "Methods [formerly, Characteristics] of Japanese Architecture" between 1957 and 1964.[2] Later writings from this early period gradually assumed the less controversial and more conventional aspect of research reports of the kind required in Japan to support academic advancement. He investigated and recorded "commoner housing" (*minka*) and village streetscape, as well as pursuing the history of early premodern town layout and its changes.

Increasingly, these successive serial installments included research and analysis employing measurement-taking and data-plotting, whether of agricultural villages or merchant housing in larger proto-modern towns dating to the Edo period (1603–1868). They were published in Japanese in two separate series under the auspices of the Architectural Institute of Japan (*Nihon kenchiku gakkai*) in 1966–68 and 1973–77, respectively. Regarded above all as a rite of passage, these exercises are little known beyond a narrowly academic audience, few of whose members now survive, but remain easily available in specialist libraries, now online. There were, on the other hand, in addition to these data-driven surveys (a research vehicle for which Tokyo Tech is still celebrated among other Japanese schools of architecture), the inevitable essay-like commentaries by Shinohara that commenced from 1954 on the occasion of the publication of his first work (House in Kugayama, remarkably picked up in Paris by *L'Architecture d'Aujourd'hui,* many years before I had joined its editorial staff).[3] These descriptions deal individually with successive works, but eventually seeded more extensive discourses exploring architectural theory and addressing Shinohara's aforementioned self-designated styles.

We shall return shortly to the fact that apart from his vernacular field studies, Shinohara personally chose several of the grander temples and *shoin* residential structures, dating from the Japanese medieval period of the pre-seventeenth century, in recognition of their out-and-out individualized achievements. In other words, he viewed them neither as exemplars of theory nor even as members of an architecturally significant set relating to a preemptive "Japanese conception of space." Nevertheless, one short English-language version was published under that very title in June 1964.[4] Its Japa-

2 The three essays were part of the series "*Nihon kenchiku no seikaku*" installment 1, "Kaihō-teki na kūkan to iu imi" (Meaning of open space); installment 2, "Kūkan no sōij-sei no haike" (The background to the analogousness of space); installment 3, "Hi-kaihō-teki na kūkan ni tsuite" (About non-open space), presented at meetings of the Architectural Institute of Japan in 1957–58.

3 Gohda Nobuo and Shinohara Kazuo, "Jeunes architectes en Japon," *Architecture d'Aujourd'hui* vol. 28 (September 1957).

4 Shinohara Kazuo, "Japanese Conception of Space," *The Japan Architect* (June 1964): 57

5 David B. Stewart, Okuyama Shin-ichi, Shiozaki Taishin, eds., *Kazuo Shinohara: Houses*, *2G*, no. 58/59 (2011): 242–45.

6 Shinohara Kazuo, *Jūtaku kenchiku* (Residential architecture) (Tokyo: Kinokuniya shoten, 1964). An English-language translation is forthcoming.

nese-language version, which originated in a book of the same date, has long since appeared in a revised translation.[5] However, even the more recent translation is much abbreviated and the actual title does not figure in the book.

Until 1964 there was indeed no book of any sort. This was *Residential Architecture* (*Jūtaku kenchiku*),[6] essentially a historical work looking to draw together the threads of Japanese tradition into a more or less coherent narrative. Publication of *Residential Architecture* precedes completion of the First Style, which was to be brought to a close by the justifiably celebrated House in White (1966). The book is of great importance in situating the initial works of this First Style, first of the self-designated place-marking modus operandi, which Shinohara undertook—albeit unknowingly at the time—with House in Kugayama.

House in Kugayama (1954) resulted from an in-studio competition and in some ways seems a near imitation at a far smaller scale of an unprecedented house Tange Kenzō designed and built for himself between 1951 and 1953 in Tokyo's western suburb of Seijō. The Tange house combined façade elements drawn from Mies's and Corb's modernism realized in a structural format of robust timber framing, which ultimately derives from the mid-seventeenth-century Katsura Imperial Villa. Steel would still have been difficult to come by and a concrete residence would at this period be virtually without precedent. But, above all, for a Japanese architect just starting his career, to qualify Shinohara's debut at Kugayama as a scaled-down "replica" is no putdown, since in Asia imitation was still regarded as the sincerest form of flattery. Moreover, Shinohara's source for Kugayama was later on freely pointed out by Shinohara as emulating a building under construction that he passed by almost daily. For both these houses, today we possess only photographs.

At the same time, there is no doubt that this nice emulation of a senior architect's work by a beginner is part and parcel of the more general postwar so-called Tradition Debate (*dentō ronsō*) here dealt with in Seng Kuan's detailed contribution to the present book. Yet this discursive and complex background element, germane to the evasive and rapid-fire evolution of Tange's mature idiom, amounts to something very different in the dozen years that passed within the gradual, self-searching formation of Shinohara's First Style between 1954 and 1966.

Shinohara was at first on the whole unacquainted with this "tradition," which in itself became an object of his Corb-like "patient research" in terms of its modes and forms as revealed to him one-by-one via historical example. Thus, for Shinohara, as he was wont frequently to reiterate, tradition was never a destination or "point of return," but uniquely a "point of departure" throughout the evolution of his First Style. This divergence is revealed in two separate instances. The first is a broad diversity among the earliest First Style works, in other words, those predating the 1960 Tokyo World Design Conference, the windfall event that precipitated the hasty invention of Metabolism among members of Tange's laboratory at the University of Tokyo. The second is the blunt omission of overt reference to Japan in the works of the short-lived Second Style after House in White of 1966.

I am unsure how early Shinohara began to feel coerced by the new economic climate of Japanese postwar recovery and to envision the private residence as a refuge from the inroads increasingly perpetrated by Japan Inc. against the domain of the individual in terms of personality and expression. Oddly, Metabolist enthusiasm in the little manifesto brochure published on the occasion of Japan's hosting of the Design Conference somehow put a stamp of vague optimism and good cheer on this mechanism, whilst purporting to rechannel the energies of the Japanese economic miracle toward a new megastructural world.

Increasingly, Shinohara's essays and public persona became connected with Metabolism's refutation. There is a dry if somewhat profuse formalism in his written language based above all upon an economy of repetition that is allowable in a language where virtually all sentences finish with the main verb. Yet the manifesto-like style is both atypical and idiosyncratic, nothing less than a recognizable idiolect. It must be this verbal style that people have at first found off-putting, particularly a majority unacquainted with the man himself. It is these “fighting words” that are most of all hard to translate, belonging as they do, now more than ever, to a time and a discourse that are decisively past.

In addition, we must recall that Tange, too shrewd to pose as anything other than a godfather figure to his students and others directly involved, was not himself a Metabolist. This was also in part because the young master found himself in Cambridge, Massachusetts, teaching studio at MIT in fall 1959. Shinohara's antipathy to the Metabolist movement pervaded the architectural press but never seems to have affected Shinohara's cordial relationship with the elder Tange—five years older than Seike Kiyoshi. In later years, both Tange and Shinohara maintained their own hauteur in these matters, and seem to have agreed to disagree. Or it seems more likely that any real competition between the two would have been out of the question, by virtue of Tange's fame and age.

2 The Second Style evolved directly from the verticality carried off—almost in spite of Shinohara's efforts—in the interior of House in White, a work completed in 1966. Its square shape and the pitch of its tiled roof are based on the remote if well-known model of Jōdo-dō of Jōdo-ji at Ono city in Hyōgo Prefecture (last decade of the twelfth century), a rare example of what is called the Great Buddha Style (with significant Chinese elements) as practiced by the Japanese builder-monk Chōgen. The complete unrelatedness of this prototype to any sort of residential design is remarkable. Although lit by shōji-screened sliding windows that might evoke Japanese living spaces but are common enough in religious architecture, the proportions of the oversize main room with its double-height ceiling as delineated by Shinohara are unorthodox. For they are unarticulated by the usual carpenter's moldings and other elements of wall design that would normally afford spatial orientation to a user or guest seated at floor level.

What we know today as the Second Style, but was not yet conceived of or named as such, moves toward an avowed reinterpretation of classical Western, early twentieth-century modernist “International Style” idiom. It was the briefest of all the four Shinohara styles, persisting only up until the House in

7 Shinohara Kazuo, "Da san no yōshiki," *Shinkenchiku* vol. 52, no. 1 (January 1977): 219–28. The English and Spanish translations appear in Stewart, Okuyama, and Shiozaki, *Shinohara Kazuo* (2011): 260–76.

Higashi-Tamagawa, completed in 1973. The latter constituted an epistemological rupture that occurred, coincidentally, shortly after its architect attained the rank of full professor at Tokyo Tech.

The texts that accompanied publication of the works of the First Style tend toward basic description and an emphasis on the metamorphosis and reassigned emotional significance of traditional elements such as the *doma*—that is to say the pounded earthen floor of the kitchen and other work spaces (derived from the old-time Japanese commoner's dwelling). His writings that relate to the Second Style retain Shinohara's unique emphasis on personal emotion as expressed in building but are now relegated to a less clearly symbolic and more abstract plane. This sea change represents the precipitous wave of abstraction that was attained for the first time in House in White, as if to banish any traditional element, even shōji, that might persist within a valedictory classicizing of the vernacular.

A major portion of Shinohara's Second Style works are of reinforced concrete often with recurrent stairs reminiscent of M. C. Escher prints that underpin a cyclical circulation pattern among "repeating crevices," all of which gravitate toward the hermeticism of a Chinese puzzle. While their "cubical" (or more frequently, rectilinear solid) exteriors Shinohara intended to recall the so-called International School of European-inspired modernism long ago invoked by the American critics Henry-Russell Hitchcock and Philip Johnson, at an exhibition at New York's Museum of Modern Art, his Second Style works are more interiorized, and their descriptive texts are more tight-lipped and less combative than their First Style predecessors. Assured but also even more self-reflexive one might say of them, almost to a fault.

3 The Third Style that commences—but always only in retrospect—with the completion of Tanikawa House in 1974 is far more inclusively circumstantial and situational and thus, by definition, more varied. Furthermore, this state of affairs was clearly reflected in the texts Shinohara issued one by one to accompany the initial publication of each. At that time, the unwritten rule was still that any Japanese building would first be published in Japan before exposure abroad. Shinohara's newfound freedom is admirably expressed in the article titled simply "The Third Style," which dates to the publication of House in Uehara in *Shinkenchiku* in January 1977.[7] And it is this long and eventful article to which I would like to devote a longer analysis here.

The text, cinematographic in terms of its vivid scenario of new discoveries in a faraway continent never before visited by the author, begins in Dakar, Senegal, whose half-imagined Frenchness was what first impressed and also disquieted Shinohara. Having arrived the previous night from Nouakchott in the Sahara Desert, long a fortified fishing village that in 1960 became the capital of the former French colony of Mauritania and still by the time of his visit contained fewer than 150,000 inhabitants, Shinohara was dazed when he awoke in the comparative urbanity of Dakar. Arriving at night, Shinohara recounts how he had first begun: "Mentally and almost without thinking... to construct an African city as a logical extension of those scenes [he] had already encountered." Yet tellingly he declares, "What I saw the next morning was...not the Africa I had imagined." We do not quite know what this might have been, although the text itself suggests a Dakar more radically deprived of European forms.

From Dakar, Shinohara had flown to Ouagaougou, then the capital of Upper Volta (today the country named Burkina Faso), established by the French in the early twentieth century and located once more on the southern edge of the Sahara Desert, yet nonetheless a city whose foundation predates that of Tokyo, as it was already an imperial capital in the fifteenth century. This town is home to a Grand Marché, one of the largest in West Africa, and the economy is based on trade, commercial activities, services, and industry. By the third quarter of the last century, its population had begun to double every ten years, although at the time of Shinohara's visit it still remained well under a million inhabitants. Shinohara took note of the residents' frank and open demeanor, which he found to be "even more than elsewhere" on the continent.

After strolling the town and briefly visiting the savanna, he traveled next to Abidjan, the economic capital of the Ivory Coast—today a city of five million and one of the largest in Africa. At the time of Shinohara's visit, the place was still a well-ordered, if large, modernist metropolis—a layout that in its plan surprised and even, he confesses, "bored" the architect, as he later on recounted his visit. So instead, he stuck to the crowded downtown alleyways that gave off a greater liveliness. This is what in Japanese may be called a "human smell," an expression that is in no way derogatory. As a Japanese, he would have been fascinated by the logistics of human movement in an alien social context, and above all in the everyday activities—what Americans quaintly refer to as "street life"—he would certainly have observed doings often moved from the darkness of house or shop into the light of day, afforded by a public thoroughfare or more intimate shared alleyway.

Shinohara next proceeded to Accra, the capital and most populous city of Ghana, today a city of three million. Yet another former fishing village, it had parts that recalled for him the old and crowded downtown center of Abidjan. Later, returning to Dakar, he undertook a detour via a small propeller aircraft to the seventeenth-century Ashanti capital of Kumasi 500 kilometers north of the equator, today a garden city of more than two million and hence also one of the most populous in Ghana. It produces gold ingots, hardwoods, and cocoa.

All this travel amounted essentially to a whirlwind tour of West African capitals. It was a journey made entirely without companions late in 1975 at a time when the working drawings for the small and severely radical House in Uehara were already complete. (The relation of the latter to then current French anthropological speculation is expertly examined by Tsukamoto Yoshiharu in his essay in this book.) At the time, for the Japanese civil servant that Shinohara was, Tokyo Tech required that he obtain an official government-sponsored invitation for each of the component visits. Yet this was not a research trip in the usual sense, such as the series of group-study visits organized at this same time by the ten-years-younger Japanese architect and associate professor at the University of Tokyo Hara Hiroshi, from 1972 to 1979, to study village morphology and settlement patterns in various areas of the world outside Japan.[8]

8 Documentation from these travels was published as Hara Hiroshi, *Shūraku he no tabi* (Tokyo: Iwanami shoten, 1987) and Hara Hiroshi, *Shūraku no oshie 100* (Tokyo: Shōkokusha, 1998).

9 The first part of Shinohara's essay "The Third Style" is titled "City of Naked Forms," containing his impressions from his trip to West Africa: Shinohara Kazuo, "The Third Style," in Stewart, Okuyama, and Shiozaki, *Shinohara Kazuo* (2011): 262.

By contrast, Shinohara's brief African sojourn was a more open-ended quest, namely a profound search for differences and first principles. As Shinohara concludes in the first part of his "Third Style" article, from which I have been quoting: "That most deeply characteristic of African spaces may never be an actual building or a streetscape, not even the ocean. Instead, it comprises the inhabitants themselves."[9] In broadly humanist terms, this is precisely what had been gathered and learned by Shinohara. In other words, especially within the freedom of an alien, unknown, and relatively untrammeled setting: people are more significant than the buildings they devise and put up—once the limits of a living vernacular have been crossed, then invaded by the nullity of ethnology and folklore.

Le Corbusier expressed this well in the context of his "Voyage to the East" sketchbooks of 1910–11, a period during which he debunked Berlin and Vienna as travesties of modern culture and turned to the classical and vernacular worlds of Greece, Turkey, and Eastern Europe. He, incidentally, detested "folklore," a term that has long been Gallicized and endowed with an extreme negative connotation, notably by the Left. While amused and beguiled by the historic architecture of Vienna in a postmodern world, Shinohara had stood out from among his colleagues as lauding the ad hoc and very human and rapid, helter-skelter reconstruction of Tokyo from its postwar ashes, an attitude from which his total opposition to Metabolism and Japan's economic miracle in general flowed. Africa, on the contrary, or at least West Africa and the cities that he visited there, was a moment of counterpoint and of the profoundest vision.

4 Notably, for me, Shinohara's trip to Africa occurs just three years after his initial trip outside Japan, which took place in autumn 1972 (including his visit to Vienna). Before reaching Europe he toured Morocco—in full realization, as he perceptively writes, that one day sub-Saharan Africa was bound to offer him an entire world of very different experience. Though Shinohara visited only a handful of the sixteen countries that make up the West African region of a vast continent still far from the Europe of half a century ago, he saw enough to realize how the old colonial styles of building remained completely ineffective in recomposing a "synchronic city." From an attempted interweaving of "diachronic spaces," as he characterizes the European city of the time, this nonfulfillment was abetted by an all-enveloping process of desiccation and erosion as witnessed by Shinohara in the yearly dry season of around mid-October in West Africa. Here was thus an urban typology of "naked [built] form" that he seems to have remarked on most pointedly in Ghana, whether at Kumasi or Accra. Such a space was "composed only of the traces of its humanity," which Shinohara undertook "the unusual step" of attempting to register via a "mobilization of [his] entire body," as he describes his spontaneous reaction at the moment of his visit. It needs to be recalled, in this context, that Japanese architecture is reckoned by the Japanese themselves as expressing neither overt movement nor time, a condition pointed out more than once by Shinohara in earlier writings.

5 Shinohara's visceral and kinetic reaction to the African city after arrival segues in the second section of the "Third Style" essay from observations of Africa itself to a slightly soberer exegesis of what he terms "A Dynamics of Ambivalence"

(the subtitle he gives to its second part). This flashback serves to introduce and then goes on to recap the formation of his personal architectural style up to the point of writing in 1977. From early in his career an ambivalent outlook on Shinohara's part drove his research as a counterpoint to the venerable tradition of Japanese building construction, with which he had been obsessively involved at least up to the completion of House in White in 1966. The strategy entered into his work as early as the competition for House in Kugayama, the very first small house project we've already discussed, whose planning stretched from 1952 to the building's completion in 1954.

For Shinohara, Japanese tradition is best encapsulated in the declaration: "Space has never existed in Japan, only void." This is a historically justified axiom whose proof we shall not go into. However, the leitmotif of ambivalence may likewise characterize any artist (Pablo Picasso is mentioned) or architect's relationship with his own previous working styles, and it was brought into play by Shinohara via the theme of an "anti-space." This term provokes a repeating dialectical propulsion toward and against an earlier perfection of style as the artist again and again embarks upon, charts, and traverses their career at any given phase. An anti-space, Shinohara reminds us, is "no mere exchange of one [earlier] style for another. It must sustain the very continuity it refutes (that style belonging hitherto to one particular architect), acknowledging the style to be peculiar to this architect, and to no other." Nor should it surprise that such a struggle is bound to climax in "a moment at which [such] transformation becomes virtual self-destruction"—even a "near all-out war" against the works of a prior manner or style. Its terminus ad quem was for Shinohara his House in White, that culminative work of his First Style and quite possibly the supreme pivotal point of his entire oeuvre.

The ambivalence finds its immediate resolution in the "cube" and "fissure" of Shinohara's brief Second Style, where as previously stated the cube in question more frequently approaches a rectangular solid. In any case, we are informed that the term "cube" is in fact a shorthand reference to International Modernism of the 1920s and 1930s, notably in Europe. Yet, that "modernism" also produced a handful of state-of-the-art examples in Japan toward the end of the same period, such as urban school buildings in reinforced concrete that are the equal of, say, Dutch sanatoria and factories, not to mention a respectable canon of residences by an earlier generation of Japanese architects. These projects derive ultimately from Le Corbusier and the Bauhaus. Shinohara refers intriguingly to his new Second Style as offering "a different co-efficient of ambivalence," adding that it may for the time being "replace the filter between things and myself." The text references, in particular, the initial work in Shinohara's new mode, the so-called The Uncompleted House (1970). It was indeed "uncompleted" and remains so today. The carefully chosen name is yet again a kind of shorthand, or aide-mémoire, principally for the architect himself.

Within this framework of a one-man, and hence correspondingly, "ambivalent," approach to the meaning of spaces, it's the suddenness of a stylistic about-face that in every case astonishes the observer—as it does the historian—and, more to the point, also if indeed we are to believe Shinohara Kazuo, takes the architect himself greatly by surprise. This time, in the transitional movement from Second to Third Style, it will be Tanikawa House (1974), whose "unified theme" of a main "simple, strong space" features a "misalignment of different aspects of naked forms" (namely a "sloping ground plan," and a "shelter built of a simple geometry") as its most representative feature.

Having tried to characterize the necessary and sufficient examples of Shinohara's continual, if temporally unpredictable, style-evolving process we may attempt to draw some conclusion from Shinohara's magisterial, if rambling, "Third Style" exegesis produced at the exact midpoint of his half-century design and writing career—just twenty-five years on from the architect's House at Kugayama, that early competition coincident with his being appointed a junior faculty member at Tokyo Tech.

6 The interpretation of this trajectory that I wish now to propose does seem far in terms of time or place from anything my colleague was himself likely to have focused on. Yet, like most Japanese architects coming of age professionally in the mayhem of reconstruction following the US Occupation, Shinohara was keenly aware of exercising a profession that had over time outgrown any real semblance of traditional Japanese building practice. He was also mindful of his starting point and aware above all of the great distance he had traveled to reach the House in Uehara. In his essay in this volume, our younger colleague Tsukamoto Yoshiharu—a student of Shinohara's student Sakamoto Kazunari—examines the theory and intentions manifest at House in Uehara: that virtual bombshell of a residential scheme completed late in the previous year and marked in January 1977 by the Third Style New Year's essay in *Shinkenchiku,* which we have been discussing.

With Shinohara now embarking upon his long-lived Third Style, the strategy proved so rich in thematic diversity that even at this early date he is driven to wonder aloud in the final paragraph of the essay whether "each and every such house [would] end up independent." What value ought we in retrospect to set upon this meditation on style in architectural historical terms? I propose briefly as a means of explication to move backward, or in Japanese art critical practice we might want to say sideways, to G. W. F. Hegel's *Lectures on Aesthetics* begun at Heidelberg as early as 1818 and then continued sporadically in Berlin from 1820 to 1829. Certainly Hegel possesses a history of reception in Japan, even if his doctrines were more far readily absorbed by the sciences than the arts. In Shinohara's writing there is little to suggest direct knowledge of or influence from Hegel. The possible exception occurs in the Third Style discourse, particularly his numerous and generalized references to "dialectic," but also sidelong glances at "negativity," plus a certain strategic concern broached toward the end of the Third Style piece for the Hegelian move beyond the "abstraction" of pure beauty toward the "concreteness" of a certain human beauty, as viewed within an untoward architectural context. At all events, for Hegel it is these two latter qualities that, when combined, form the *Mittelpunkt* of Art itself, or the beauty of the ideal.

Yet as I note below, it is Hegel's once-celebrated proposal of a trio of art historical categories, namely the three successive forms of art (*Kunstformen,* which for Hegel the very idea of art requires), that in a general sense may help us better understand and accept the near inevitability of Shinohara's method of self-periodization, given his stated goal of assigning a new artistic value to the individual private residence.

In its most sweeping terms, Shinohara's ambition encompasses Hegel's intent to undermine the conception of art as a mere object of sense and feeling, a route opened up in the West by Immanuel Kant, in favor of addressing Truth, that domain that Hegel, in his ever-Western orientation, sought to conjoin with art. Famously, this desire led Hegel to the notion of art in his own time as something already *past,* as being inadequate for the present-day needs of Spirit. It was not Shinohara's purpose to declaim the nature of art in its totality as something past. Rather, his concern was the essential "pastness" and, hence, the inadequacy in our own time, of the Japanese aesthetic tradition, namely in architecture—whether manifested as abstraction or concreteness. To establish this operative framework, Shinohara addressed head-on the final incapacity of a far from historically integrated or consistent local tradition to enable postwar Japanese society to represent itself to itself, the very task, according to Hegel, of all art.

Then, in medias res, Shinohara's "Third Style" essay jumps to the hypothesis that in a still developing country (such as, say, Ghana in the 1970s, even though it is perhaps less so today, and Japan, too, within recent memory), there was an analogy to be drawn. To make this idea stick for a Japanese readership there was no need to reference Japan's Meiji-period *giyōfū* style of building that had first imitated Western style architecture using native builders' techniques. In Accra a top-down imported colonial vernacular—today readable as little other than its own "naked" forms—nonetheless allows the city to represent itself to itself, according to Shinohara, is the ubiquitous presence and movement of the lithe bodies of inhabitants. For this we might even compare the *nishiki-e* prints of the later Edo period, in their depictions of the then upstart largest city in the world, where architecture appears but is of no concern, yet these pictures are full of clothed and all-but-naked individuals, until Meiji-style buildings first kick in during the third quarter of the nineteenth century and bodies, except for those shown in the Western-style clothing that very soon became de rigueur even for the imperial family, simultaneously fade from the scene.

Just how Japanese architecture in the person of Shinohara and all the variety of his yet to be declared Third Style might arrogate this modus operandi of African origin is less clear. I do understand and I even feel the images of sub-Saharan Africa evoked by Shinohara's close reading of its "naked" cityscapes in his amateur and often spoilt photographs (owing as often as not to choosing the wrong sort of film), and by contrast his insistence on the concrete traces of Africa's humanity. Yet how indeed did the architect intuit his own personal need to set out entirely alone for Africa in the first place?

7 To answer this question, if we ever can, one may return to Hegel's "forms of the beautiful" (or *Kunstformen*), whose progression was said by Hegel to be regulated by the fluctuating

relationship between the content of art—the Idea as Spirit—and its material and presentational mode. For Hegel, the first of these three forms is Symbolic Art, a kind of pre-art to be observed in many different historical cultures and based upon a comparatively abstract notion of Spirit, where *architecture* figures as the beginning of art. This, Hegel claims, "stands in the closest connection with religion" (*Aesthetics,* 1: 311), a perception that might go hand in hand with Shinohara's own first introduction to traditional Japanese structures; for Hegel, the earliest structures reconfigure nature by presenting for the first time a spiritual content that doesn't occur at all in natural things. Thus, the key term in Shinohara's First Style as designated in 1966, or in any case shortly after the completion of House in White, is likewise "symbol" or its adjective, "symbolic." And, like in traditional Japanese architecture, there is as yet no provision for enclosure of space. For Hegel, the breakup of the Symbolic form is the Greek temple as it was conceived to enclose the statue of the god, at which point it assumes a religious function external to its own purpose, structure, and fabric, initiating in this process a degradation and a pastness that leads to the reign of the next *Kunstform.*

Hegel's second *Kunstform* is a classical art, claimed to be embodied in its purest and archetypical manifestation no longer by the temple architecture of the Greeks, which remains an instance of Symbolic art, but instead by classical Greek drama and sculpture, which are no longer considered "pre-art" but as arts in their own right. This stipulation is regarded on Hegel's part as dictated by the identity of Greek religion, whose gods remain nonetheless immersed in Nature despite the perfection of their representation.

We may think of the ten houses belonging to Shinohara's brief Second Style, with their fissures and cubes carved for the most part out of faceless concrete, and thus monolithic at least in outward appearance, as retaining something of this earthbound paradox that Greek sculpture exhibited for Hegel. Unlikely as it may seem to a non-Japanese architect, these Second Style works all produced in little more than five years, were understood by Shinohara as emblematic of the celebrated "abstraction" of interwar European modernist architecture of the 1920s and 1930s. This was the intended contrast inherent to Shinohara's Second Style, which rejects all devices, proportions, and materiality of the Japanese tradition(s) upon which in one way or another each of the seventeen houses of the First Style firmly relies.

The third of the *Kunstformen* elaborated by Hegel expresses, as does the second, freedom of Spirit. However, in then modern-day (that is, Romantic) art one was now dealing with a new and historically unfamiliar inwardness. In practice it tended moreover beyond art itself—to religious faith and to philosophy. Ideal Romantic beauty is well able to depict suffering, as related to Christ's Passion, or the unbounded love that in Christian art is unfalteringly part and parcel of any depiction of the "Madonna and Child" theme. It may also represent secular virtues, such as bravery, that characterize the ideal of chivalry. Finally, represented in Hegel's Romantic art are to be found such aspects of Spirit as self-determination and firmness of purpose, which Hegel tends to illustrate by referring to Shakespearian paradigms as portrayed by that author's characters, who by this time were thoroughly familiar to German readers and theatergoers.

10 Shinohara Kazuo, "Mitsu no gen-kūkan," *Shinkenchiku* vol. 39, no. 4 (April 1964): 135–40.

11 G. W. F. Hegel, *Hegel's Aesthetics: Lectures on Art*, vols. 1 & 2, trans. T. M. Knox (New York: Oxford University Press, 1975).

12 Takeuchi Toshio published the Japanese translation of Hegel's *Completed Works: Aesthetics of Hegel* in nine volumes between 1956 and 1981: G. W. F. Hegel, *Heegeru zenshū: Bigaku* (Tokyo: Iwanami shoten, 1956–81).

Architecturally, Romantic art is best characterized by the exemplar of the Gothic cathedral in all its complexity and enclosure, as these qualities were expressed in the cathedral's upward soaring reach and a façade seemingly determined from within. In general, Hegel has little to say about secular buildings of any kind, and the human habitation in particular is consistently marginalized. Architecture for Hegel is an entirely transitional art across his entire discussion of the three art forms. Its practical nature as brute material transformed in the representation of Spirit is vouchsafed for Hegel via an unceasing process of escape from anything natural or mundane.

Paradoxically, Shinohara's frequently voiced belief in and his striving toward the domain of the private residence as something "eternal," in which there is also an aspect of the sublime, is cathedral-like. There is, for example, a strong hint of this sensibility in Shinohara's much cited appreciation of the client brief for the summer space of Tanikawa House, which in retrospect initiates his Third Style, namely, as a "church for a pantheist." This snippet has inevitably been quoted from the start wherever the house is discussed. It is of some interest that Hegel's stated view of the sublime portrays a denigration in his own mind of "excesses" in Asian art (whether Chinese or Islamic), which he found less developed in terms of his own teleology than the art of the West. The German philosopher considered essentially formless the intricacies of surface patterning that characterize such art, a mere species of "shock and awe" in the East's arsenal of means for engaging God by way of art. Meanwhile, Hegel does not himself refer or appeal to Japanese art, which would have been little known in Europe even at the time of his death. In Shinohara's early text titled "Three Primary Spaces,"[10] it is "ornamental space" that is pointed to by the author as the least significant of the three, thus by default ceding precedence in spatial terms to the other two: the functional and the Symbolic. Unfortunately, neither of these terms is any longer of much use to the Western theoretician, with the term "function" in its original German-language context having long ago been substituted for the original term from the turn of the century, a word that is closer in meaning to "aim." Symbolic is simply a wildcard, and we can do nothing but accept both of these from Shinohara as terms of art that in the Japanese postwar climate of discussion must have provided a useful contrast with Metabolism and other more or less spoon-fed theories of the time driven by expediency.

In addition to the foregoing comparison, it may be of interest to recall Hegel's elaborate engagement with Christian theology, as seen for example in his careful analysis of the pictorial side of Romantic art's mechanics of self-representation and the logic of *Aufhebung*. Incidentally, in English whilst a complete translation of the published notes of Hegel's *Lectures on Aesthetics* was appearing in four volumes during World War I in London, it was not until 1975 that a fully competent translation was made available by the Anglo-Scots philosopher T. M. Knox,[11] whereas the Japanese scholar Takeuchi Toshio began translating Hegel's complete *Aesthetics* series in 1956.[12] In other words, we can scarcely be dealing with any actual reading of the text until the Third Style of Shinohara was in full swing, despite ample acquaintance, discussion, and criticism of Hegelian philosophy in general at a far earlier date. In any case I do not intend this detour on translations as the point.

The point is that when we compare the varied contents of Romantic art in Hegel's formulation with the extreme diversity of the Third Style in Shinohara's, we encounter a secular teleology in the latter that is and has been all along since the work of the First Style, marshaled by the distinctive form of Hegelian dialectic. Hegelian dialectic is characteristically different in its terminology from that of Kant's Thesis-Antithesis-Synthesis model, rescued so to speak and expanded upon by Johann Gottlieb Fichte. Hegel, following up, most often prefers to use the triad of Abstract-Negative-Concrete, where the middle term "negative" is redolent of a methodological defect in the initial thesis, say, a superfluity of abstraction that could be improved upon, or eliminated, by a countermove of so-called *negative* (that is, experiential) trial and error. In Shinohara Kazuo's work, this negative value was supplied by an "anti-project" that he ran in parallel with the current architectural project that was the commission in hand. The anticipated goal was to attain a synthesis in the final work itself, ready to be presented to and then built for the client.

For Hegel, it was this final overcoming of the negative, or experiential, that led to the Absolute, and that in terms of his triad is therefore to be regarded as "concrete." This process of *Aufhebung* as overcoming limitations, but also more literally derived from the German equivalent of the phrasal verb "to pick up" (as when something may have fallen on the floor, according to the distinguished translator Walter Kaufmann) includes all the stages of logic leading up to it and may be sometimes described as the "unification of Truth through Reason." or seizing the wheat and leaving the chaff. This keeping what is of use in an idea or scheme, whilst eliminating and moving beyond its limitations, is what Shinohara attempted to do with Japanese tradition in his First Style, then accomplished less securely in his brief struggle to acknowledge and assimilate the Modern Movement, and finally made his own in the journey of the Third Style—taken, as he felt, to a new level in the three residential works of the Fourth. This strategy persisted as a working method in his public buildings that commenced toward the end of what had now become Shinohara's self-acknowledged Third Style, with the Japan Ukiyo-e Museum (1982). It continued as well in House in Yokohama (1984) that initiates the Fourth Style, which includes Tokyo Tech's Centennial Hall (1987). But that is another story more or less unfinished, as was Shinohara's incitation to the siren song of the ModernNext.

Shinohara Kazuo's
Travel Photos

Shinohara Kazuo's Travel Photos

Editor's Note

Shinohara Kazuo traveled abroad for the first time in fall 1972, after recovering from a major illness. The destinations of this first trip were Morocco and parts of Europe, and subsequent journeys included a more extensive trip through Europe in 1973, West Africa in 1975, France in 1979, and North and South America in 1984–85. Many of these excursions were accomplished alone.

Without pretending the slides he took on these trips were anything more than amateur snapshots, Shinohara engaged them in his polemical work on several occasions. The idea of traversing put forth in *Later Architectural Theory* (1975) was illustrated with such images.[1] "The Third Style," which served as his introductory text to House in Uehara (1976), was partly a travelogue of his trip through West Africa.[2] The "naked forms" he saw on this trip were made possible by an utter detachment through cultures and languages completely foreign to him. He saw shapes, shadows, colors, and movement freed from the encumbrances and distortions of a superstructure. He departed from Japan just as House in Uehara's design had been finalized, so the kernels of creative desires captured in these images were already present in his mind. The travels were another dimension of his critical engagement, allowing him to articulate his ideas through these moments of reality but in divergent contexts and scales.

Shinohara returned to these photos toward the end of his life. The book *Toward a Super-Big Numbers Set City* (2001), in which he situated his architectural career in the mathematical beauty of Tokyo's vastness and chaos, was illustrated with a large selection of these photos, albeit alongside a small handful of images of Tokyo. In 2004 the Center for Contemporary Art in Kita-Kyūshū organized an exhibition of Shinohara's travel photos titled *A Certain Point of View* (*aru shiten*). It was accompanied by an exquisite catalogue.

Most of Shinohara's travel photos were taken at eye level, as a series of raw encounters in his act of traversing. They form a series of frontal moments, on the perpendicular plane, as one moves through cities and landscape. Shinohara described the short, 80-meter walk from Komazawa University Station on the old Tamagawa streetcar line, located west of Shibuya, to the home he lived in as a child.[3] It was a series of three sharp turns, from the thoroughfare of Route 246 to the small lane where his house was located. The turn at each corner yielded a unique frame, but in their totality he saw the archetype of a village as naked reality.

1 Shinohara Kazuo, *Zoku kenchiku ron* (Tokyo: Kajima shuppankai, 1975).

2 Shinohara Kazuo, "Daisan no yōshiki," *Shinkenchiku* vol. 52, no. 1 (January 1977): 219–28.

3 Shinohara Kazuo, "Street with Human Shadows," in *Shinohara Kazuo: doori to hitokage*, trans. John Junkerman, exh. cat. (Kita-Kyūshū: Gendai bijutsu sentaa CCA Kita-Kyūshū, 2006), unpaginated.

Shinohara Kazuo's
Travel Photos

JOHN
IN

Shinohara Kazuo's
Travel Photos

Shinohara Kazuo's
Travel Photos

Shinohara Kazuo's
Travel Photos

FALAFEL
OPEN

Shinohara Kazuo's
Travel Photos

Shinohara Kazuo's
Travel Photos

Shinohara Kazuo's
Travel Photos

Shinohara Kazuo's
Travel Photos

Shinohara Kazuo's
Travel Photos

RUE
DU PORT

Shinohara Kazuo's
Travel Photos

SUDAMERICA
METRO

Shinohara Kazuo's
Travel Photos

Shinohara Kazuo's
Travel Photos

Shinohara Kazuo, Tanikawa House, Naganohara, Gunma Prefecture, 1974. Photos by Christian Kerez

"I had acquired a sculpture."

Interview with Tanikawa Shuntarō

by Christian Kerez

The celebrated Japanese lyric poet and writer Tanikawa Shuntarō (b. 1931) commissioned Shinohara Kazuo to design two houses. The first, in Tokyo's suburb in Suginami Ward and built in 1958, was one of Shinohara's earliest works. The well-known cabin in a highland resort area outside of Karuizawa, completed in 1974, inaugurated Shinohara's Third Style.

MAY 22, 2008, IN TOKYO

CHRISTIAN KEREZ When still a student I attended a lecture in Eindhoven [Netherlands] by Shinohara Kazuo with the title: "In Preparation for the Fourth Space."[1] That was more than twenty years ago, and ever since then I have been fascinated by his work. One of the houses I like best is Tanikawa House—the "mountain cabin" in Kita-Karuizawa, Naganohara (1974). I once said to a Japanese colleague that if I were offered the chance to see a house, this would be the one I would most like to visit. He replied that this was absolutely impossible. In Japan everybody, he said, had such respect for Tanikawa Shuntarō that no one would ever dream of asking whether it would be possible to see this house. And therefore I am extremely happy to be sitting here with you Mr. Tanikawa, and I'm curious to find out how you met Shinohara.

THE HOUSE IN SUGINAMI-TOKYO

TANIKAWA SHUNTARŌ As well as the mountain cabin, a few years earlier, in 1958, I had a small dwelling house in Tokyo's Suginami Ward built by Shinohara with my father's money. My father was friendly with the architect Taniguchi Yoshirō and initially wanted him to make the plans. Taniguchi was extremely well-known at the time and was actually too eminent to build a house for someone like me who was not even thirty years old. He therefore suggested Seike Kiyoshi, one of Shinohara's professors.[2] However he refused the commission and suggested his student. He said: "There's this interesting younger architect, Shinohara; he's the same generation as you."

When I then met Shinohara, he seemed to me like a philosopher. I was still young and it was my first time to build a house. I had no precise, detailed ideas but only a general abstract concept in my head of how a house for me should look—as a container for the spirit, so to speak. This very much reflected Shinohara's way of thinking. I wrote a kind of poem about how I imagined my house and he was very taken with this way of writing a brief.

KEREZ Would it be possible to read this poem? Was it ever published? What is the most important aspect of it, the mood?

TANIKAWA No, unfortunately it no longer exists. I can only vaguely remember what was in it: the house was to give the person living in it a kind of inner dwelling, a place of calm. Initially, it was conceived free of any practical considerations. At that time many young fellow poets believed that inhabiting a house, domesticity in the normal sense of the term, was not important. I was not that kind of vagabond poet; I wanted to embody a positive, constructive type and to protest against the dominant tendency. I therefore belonged to a minority that distanced itself from my generation. I wanted to have a real house where a family would feel well, a refuge where I could write my poems. In my concept the house was a workplace, a base, a kind of fortress in which I could lead my life and write my poems. The problem, however, was that I had just gotten married but my wife's ideas were not considered at all in this concept. My wife, it is true, did not have any particular demands, she was still very young and did not have a major part in formulating this domestic ideology and no great interest either, at least at first.

However, this is one of the main points of criticism of the houses built by Shinohara, including mine—that the opinion of the women and the functional aspects of living were not sufficiently considered. This was particularly criticized by women. And I have heard that several married couples who had a house built by Shinohara later split up [laughter].

But be that as it may, when I was shown Shinohara's plans for the house in Tokyo I was absolutely delighted by the simple forms. Then it was erected, built almost entirely by an old and experienced building contractor and carpenter.

[Looking at photographs in a book.] You can see the functional difficulties, for instance at the entrance—it was direct; there was nowhere to take off your shoes as one normally does in a Japanese house. On account of the many sliding paper doors there was also no private sphere, no separation in an acoustic sense—it was like a single space. I found that all very lovely, but I didn't consider the functional aspects. When the children were born we had an extension added a few years later, as the layout of the house was clearly not family-friendly. It just couldn't work. A student of Shinohara designed this extension—in the style of the Katsura Imperial Villa, he maintained.

KEREZ What about the furniture, was it also designed especially for this house? The way the house and furniture fit together seems very harmonious.

TANIKAWA Yes, there was this young furniture designer, Matsumura Katsuo.[3] The three of us designed the furniture especially for this house.

KEREZ I really like the fact that there are two such very different parts: a functional one and one to live in, divided precisely in the middle. The bedroom is just as important as the living room. This produces a very fundamental division—it is not a functionalist separation, it is really the division of the house at the center. In one of his aphorisms Shinohara says that if he had the chance to make a space he would make two spaces, one for the man and one for the woman. It remains a single space, but the division into two makes the large space more complex, more varied.

TANIKAWA Shinohara designed these two rooms in such a way that they could be used for both purposes, depending on the way you arranged the furniture—as free, available space. If I could live in the house today I would make better use of the space than I did when a young man. I would like to have kept the house. But when my son grew up he wanted to have his own house. We thought about whether we could transplant this building somewhere, but this would have been far more expensive than erecting a new building. And now nothing of it is left.

At the time [Suginami] was in one of the outer wards of Tokyo, and we had a relatively small parcel. With a little more room around it the house would have really been an ideal building, also seen from outside, from a somewhat greater distance—a really lovely house.

KEREZ The photographs of the houses particularly interest me; they seem to have been taken with great care—on the one hand everything appears a little casual, with the shadows, and yet at the same time they seem very consciously designed.

TANIKAWA Before his clients moved into a house he had designed, Shinohara took his favorite photographer with him and had him take photos according to precise instructions. It was his concept to make this photo documentation of the house at the start, entirely according to his ideas. Afterward he didn't care about how people used his houses.

KEREZ What about the execution of the architectural details—was that also a subject of discussion between client and architect, or did the client give the architect a free hand?

TANIKAWA Shinohara decided on everything himself. But during the construction he did not visit the site so often, I think. In fact he was essentially a mathematician, and he did not have an architect's license or diploma or something of that kind. In the concrete implementation of the project he remained in the background, and on this account his fees were also more reasonable than those of other architects. He got others to carry out the calculations for the construction plans.

KEREZ How did Shinohara illustrate his ideas and convey an impression of how the house would look when built? Did he have a model made, for instance?

TANIKAWA Yes, he had a model made, which he showed me. At this level, he conceived everything very precisely and in detail.

THE "MOUNTAIN CABIN" IN KITA-KARUIZAWA

KEREZ Let's now turn to the second house, the one in the mountains. How did that project run?

TANIKAWA My father had owned this site in the mountains of Gunma Prefecture in the district of Kita-Karuizawa for some time. Originally there were two buildings on the site: one that served as a workplace and another for the family. We spent the summer there every year. My father erected these buildings with a bank loan. And when I grew up and became independent, it was agreed that I could build a house there in accordance with my taste and at my own cost. I very consciously asked Mr. Shinohara again whether he would design this house for me.

Shinohara then got all the students in his studio to work on the design. Possibly it was also a project which, as professor, he assigned to his architecture students. Then I looked at all the plans they produced. The plan by Shinohara himself was better than all the others. I remember clearly that there was an entire series of plans.

This wasn't a dwelling house like in Tokyo, but a holiday house in which, however, it would be possible to live throughout the year. I had the vision of a more freely designed space. Shinohara took up this idea and gave it concrete form. My idea was first of all that we, my family and I, would spend time there both in summers and winters. As the plot was on a site once owned by the founder of Hōsei University, many others had built holiday houses there and formed a casual community of artists and professors. On this account I had a further idea of making a semipublic space that could be used for gatherings of poets, for example, as a literature house or for exhibitions. And so this large, free, multipurpose space was included in the design.

But unfortunately shortly after the completion of the house my mother became ill; she suffered from Alzheimer's and, as I had to help care for her, it turned out that I rarely lived in the house.

The floor without any boards is an earth floor with a slight incline—a most remarkable space. I had looked forward to using it for all kinds of things; for instance I intended to set up a stage in it. By the way, I remember another plan that also appealed to me: to define a large space by means of earth walls...

KEREZ Do you mean embankments?

TANIKAWA ... and then to build a house within this rectangle. I think the idea behind this concept came from African architecture with those round buildings. But it would have been too expensive.

KEREZ Did this architecture inspire you to write poems or texts?

TANIKAWA There is nothing that was directly inspired by it. But I do believe that Shinohara's designs for both the house in Tokyo and this house [in Kita-Karuizawa] influenced me considerably at a conceptual level. Shinohara was a man with really interesting ideas. Unfortunately there are no photos here of these. But through this really very narrow window, for instance, you see the ground outside directly; you look into the landscape. This is where I set myself up to work; it was my study. You look outside into the woods and toward a stream; I often worked there, wrote my poems there. The usual thing in this country is to make terraces and in this way to create a boundary to the surroundings. But Shinohara rejected this. His concept was that from inside, through the window, you should have an immediate, direct visual approach to the natural setting.

KEREZ There are a number of stories about your encounter with this house. May I ask you whether they are true or just rumor?

TANIKAWA Yes, please do.

KEREZ The first rumor we heard maintains that when you first visited the house you are supposed to have said: "The house that kills," as the impression made by this house was so extremely strong.

TANIKAWA [Laughter] No, that can't be right! Somebody must have made that up. That's inconceivable.

KEREZ So it is just a rumor! Another rumor says that during the first year, due to the dampness of the earth, individual pieces of plaster loosened themselves from the ceiling and fell down. Shinohara was very worried and wanted to have this repaired immediately but you, Mr. Tanikawa, are supposed to have said that this didn't worry you.

TANIKAWA No, that's not how it was [laughter]!

What is true is that it was so damp that mushrooms grew on the earth floor of the room and mold also formed. Therefore it was thought necessary to mount an air extraction unit on the ceiling. And I probably said: I would prefer to do without this, as the whole thing is so lovely and so successful. This natural floor is really good! As long as the house doesn't collapse I want to leave it the way it is, even if a few mushrooms grow there—I probably said something along those lines....

But something else that I said occurs to me. Nothing about the house that kills, that's certain, but something along the following lines: I haven't built a house; I've bought the large sculpture of a friend. That is to say, I regarded the house as a sculpture, whereas everybody said that I had built a house. But my own feeling was that I had acquired a sculpture from Shinohara.

KEREZ The house is in truly wonderful condition. The last time we visited it, in 2006, we were really impressed by the fact that in the interior the water basin and the tap are still at the same place as in the photographs. We heard that the house had been sold to a gallerist from Kyoto, but with the condition that he is not allowed to change anything. Is this right?

TANIKAWA Well, this man isn't from Kyoto; he's a gallery owner from Tokyo. He also has branch galleries in Paris and in New York—he's an old friend of my father's. That's whom I sold the house to.

KEREZ But with the condition that he is not allowed to change anything?

TANIKAWA No, without any conditions. But this Mr. Yoshii, the owner of the Yoshii Gallery, is an art connoisseur and collector who has numerous friends who are artists.

But do you know the story of this ladder? It is a reproduction of an object from Cézanne's studio. I didn't make any conditions but the present owner, this gallerist Mr. Yoshii Chōzō, bought the house as a kind of art object. He probably only goes there rarely. Whatever the case, it's his idea to leave the house the way it is.

Mr. Yoshii is known for the fact that he was a friend of Georges Rouault and that he brought many works by Rouault to Japan. He has, by the way, founded a museum for the writers' group Shirakaba-ha [White Birth Society], from the first half of the twentieth century: the Kiyoharu Shirakaba Museum in Yamanashi Prefecture.

KEREZ But the idea of placing a ladder there, that was your idea?

TANIKAWA As far as I remember we worked that out together. Shinohara had brought some photos with him... but you can't use the ladder—it's far too dangerous to climb.

KEREZ And the water basin with this tap?

TANIKAWA I bought that myself and had it mounted. Shinohara was amazed about this when the photos were being taken but he had no objections. That is Mexican folk art. Also the furniture... all the furniture that exists there was designed especially for this house by a designer called Ōhashi Teruaki[4] (if I remember the pronunciation of his first name correctly). He has since died, but he was a very well-known furniture designer.

KEREZ I was really impressed by this house; for me it is one of the finest houses that I know.

TANIKAWA Really? Yes, I also think it is lovely. It was once used for the cover page of a foreign architecture magazine, in winter, with snow. I really liked that.

By the way, the house has a silvery metallic roof. It reflects through the entire valley. A house belonging to the son of a former prime minister, a well-known English studies scholar and critic, stood not far away. He never complained, but I had the feeling that this strongly reflective roof was something of an imposition on him. His name was Yoshida Ken'ichi, a famous man and one who enjoyed a drink. Once I took a bottle of whiskey with me and went to apologize for the fact that I had built such a shiny roof [laughter].

KEREZ I find the way the house withdraws most impressive, as it doesn't have a real front and the entire roof surface is closed. It conveys something very secretive but also something very great, almost monumental, which creates an interesting tension. What I find especially beautiful is this double division: on the one hand this huge space, whose function one does not completely grasp, and beside it the rooms that one can describe as functional, which are small and compact and arranged on one side.

TANIKAWA There is a further remarkable detail: the little houses built by my father would have been too cold in winter. But I wanted to use the new house in winter also and to lay underfloor heating, at least in these small functional rooms. But at that time underfloor heating was practically unavailable in Japan. The construction company then installed floor heating, probably from Sweden or Denmark, which was actually intended for road surfaces. It was then so hot that you couldn't sit on the floor [laughter].

KEREZ For most architects a dwelling house is a functionalist instrument, whereas in his writings Shinohara emphasized that a house is art. Perhaps in this context it was necessary for the client to be an artist in order to create a house that is so very much like a work of art?

TANIKAWA What particularly impresses and amazes me about Shinohara is his enormous stylistic development, the way he was able to change. At the very start he built simple houses in a style based on Japanese tradition, later purely avant-garde concrete buildings—an unbelievable development!

[Mr. Tanikawa knocks over his drink, spilling it on the book, which he attempts to dry.]

KEREZ Ah, that doesn't matter at all … it will recall this conversation … [laughter] as a result the book has increased in value! I would be delighted if you would sign it, on this page …

TANIKAWA Incidentally, a poet friend of mine also had a house designed by Shinohara [House on a Curved Road (1978)]. This poet, Suzuki Shirōyasu, wrote a very different kind of poetry to mine, more experimental, avant-garde texts, and his house is accordingly very different.

KEREZ [Takes the book with the signature.] Now it is really something valuable. Before it was just an object, but now it has acquired a significance …

TANIKAWA I really liked Shinohara, although he was a difficult character.

KEREZ In what sense difficult?

TANIKAWA Well, how should I put it? He was a rather "cool" person. He was somewhat older than me, and if I made a joke of some kind he didn't like that. Clearly fun was not his thing. But I really regarded him very highly, and I am very happy that after his death somebody is so interested in these houses.

KEREZ That's very interesting. The first time I met Shinohara he said that he could not understand why I was interested in his work—he said that I made things that are far harder and more severe than what he does. He said he worked with far softer means.

TANIKAWA Did he never build abroad?

KEREZ No, at a very late stage in his career he took part in competitions, as Rem Koolhaas invited him to Europe. But he was deeply disappointed that nothing ever came of these projects. One last question: A period of almost twenty years lies between your first house and the second one. Did you remain friends in the intervening period, did you stay in contact?

TANIKAWA No, I had practically no personal contact with him throughout all those years. All that occurs to me is a short contribution that I wrote about an architecture book by him.

KEREZ Thank you very much for taking the time for this conversation.

This conversation with the writer resulted from an introduction provided by Eduard Klopfenstein, Professor Emeritus of Japanese Studies at the Institute of Asian and Oriental Studies, University of Zurich. Having previously translated Tanikawa's lyric poetry, Klopfenstein also helped facilitate this conversation by translating between Japanese and German.

Translated from German to English by Roderick O'Donovan
Edited and organized by Florian Sauter and Savvas Ciriacidis

1 Published as Shinohara Kazuo, "A Program for the 'Fourth Space,'" *The Japan Architect* (September 1986): 28–35.

2 Taniguchi Yoshirō (1904–1979) began teaching at the Tokyo Institute of Technology (Tokyo Tech) in 1929 and rose to prominence in the 1930s as one of Japan's leading modernist architects. In the late 1950s Taniguchi was involved in such projects as the Crown Prince's Palace and a memorial for former prime minister Hara Takashi. Seike Kiyoshi (1918–2005) was a more junior faculty member whose laboratory counted Shinohara among its members.

3 Matsumura Katsuo (1923–1991) was a furniture designer who collaborated with Shinohara on several houses in the late 1950s. Influenced by Charlotte Perriand's 1941 exhibition *Selection, Tradition, Creation* held in Tokyo, Matsumura was one of the pioneers of modern furniture design in Japan.

4 Ōhashi Teruaki (1938–1992) was a member of Shinohara's laboratory at Tokyo Tech in 1962–69 and designed the furniture in several of his houses, including House in White (1966). Ōhashi established his own furniture design firm in 1972 and collaborated with Sakamoto Kazunari and Itō Toyoo, among others.

TANIKAWA HOUSE, 1974
Naganohara, Gunma Prefecture

"Winter house, or pioneer cabin (house)
Summer space or church for a pantheist (need not be a house)"

Located in the outskirts of the highland resort town of Karuizawa, this house served as the retreat of poet Tanikawa Shuntarō. Shinohara responded to the client's cryptic program brief, excerpted above, which was not only styled as a poem laid out on a sheet of manuscript paper but also subverted many basic tenets of residential architecture. The house sits on a sloping site, and in the large "summer space" the ground is left unaltered and bare, without a finished, horizontal floor. Equally significant are the dramatic 45-degree diagonals that define the roof and the column struts inside. It is an encounter between nature and artifice, the darkness and softness of the earth against the rigid geometries of reason. Inside the house, the inclined ground is deeply unsettling, forcing constantly traversing lines of movement in an effort to resolve the inherent tension.

Photos by
Ueda Hiroshi (UH), Taki Kōji (TK),
and Arai Masao for Shinkenchiku-sha / DAAS (AM)

North elevation.

JH

Shinohara Kazuo, sketch of an early design, ca. 1972: a wooden cabin next to a rectangular enclosure, which is surrounded by freestanding reinforced concrete walls, with no roof.

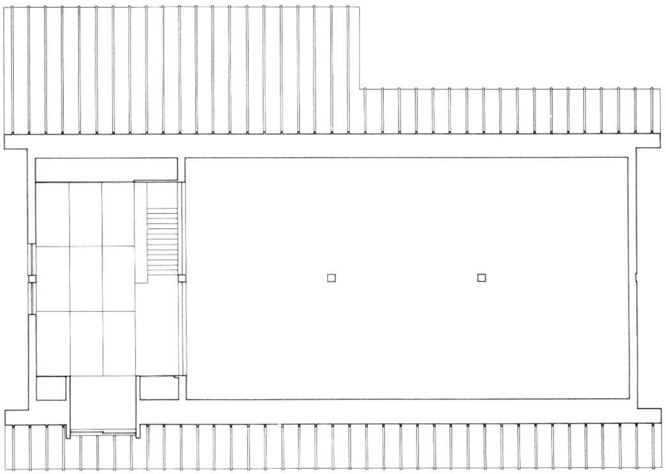

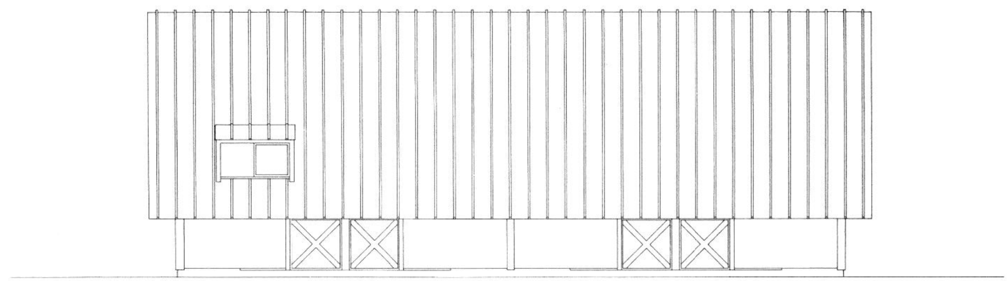

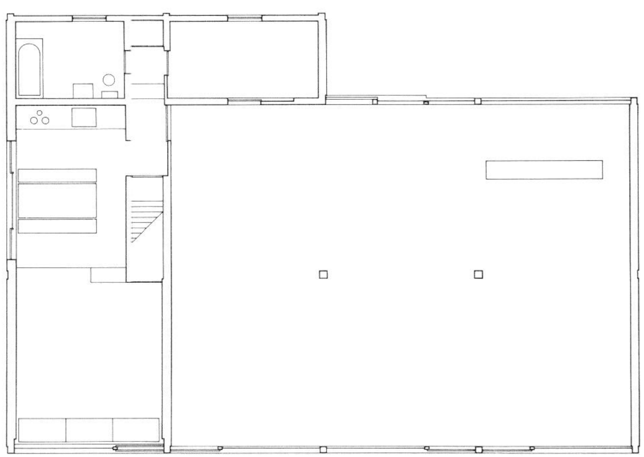

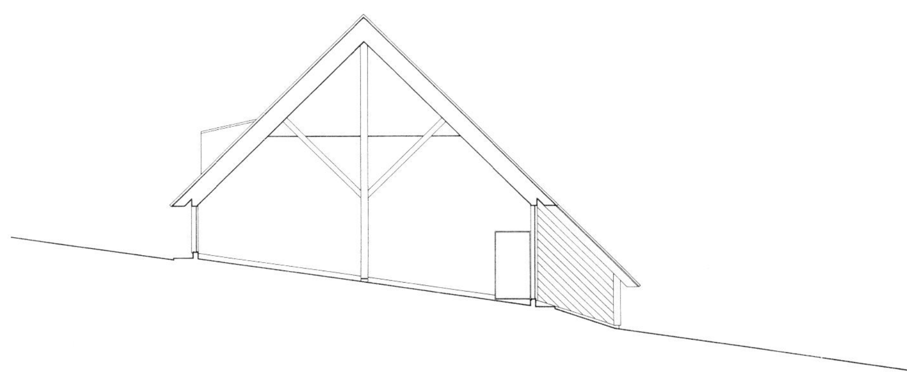

1:200

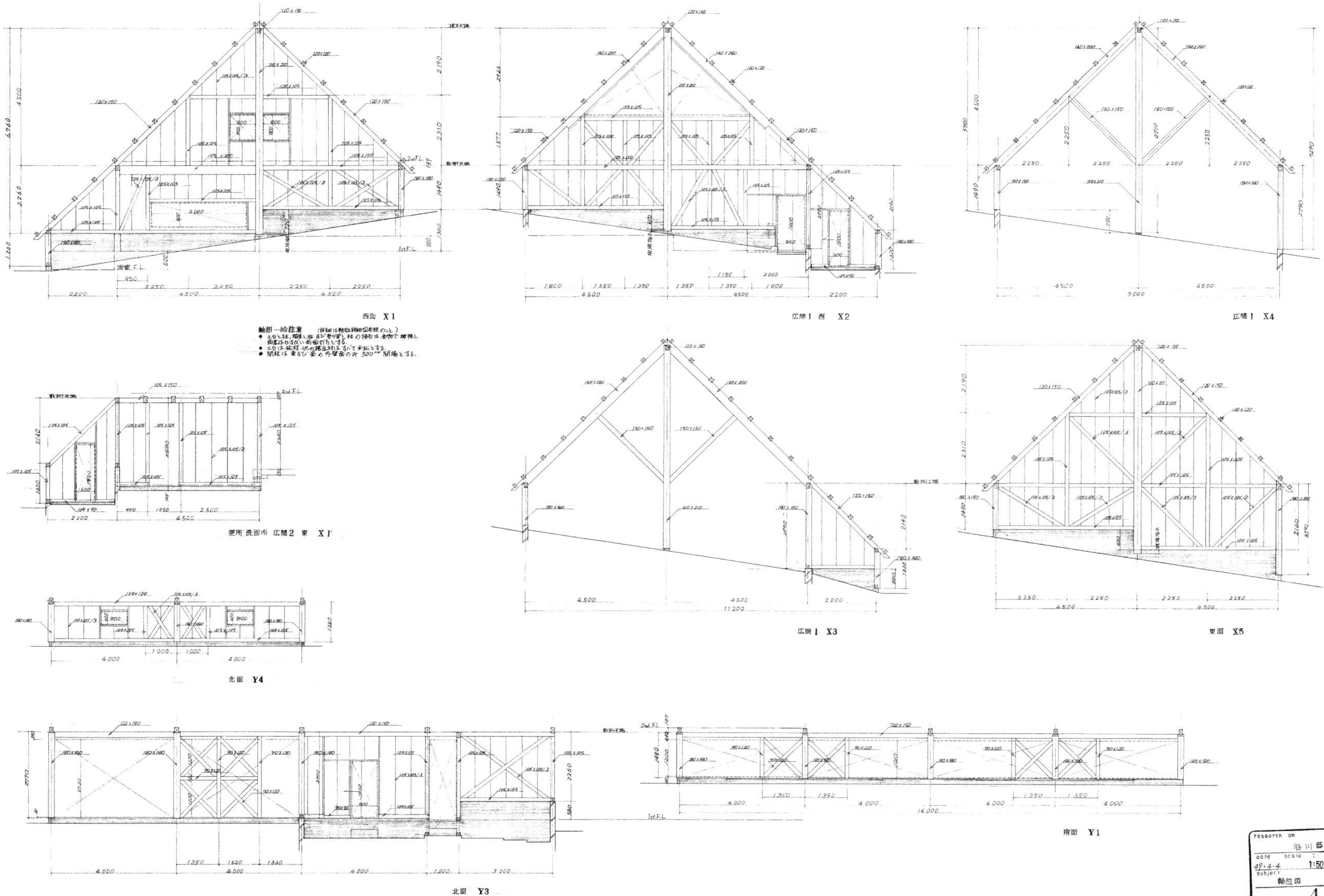
西面 X1
広間1 西 X2
広間1 X4
便所 洗面所 広間2 東 X1'
広間1 X3
東面 X5
北面 Y4
北面 Y3
南面 Y1
research on 谷川邸
date 49·4·4
scale 1:50
subject 軸組図
no. 4

TK

Framing drawings.

Summer *hiroma.*

Summer *hiroma*.

UH

East wall.

Summer *hiroma*, view looking south.

TK

AM

In winter.

TK

TK

Cleared lot after the original wooden house was demolished. Photo by Ōtsuji Kiyoshi

"I sometimes think how living in this house is not a simple matter."

Interview with Ōtsuji Seiko and Ōtsuji Tetsuo

by Hosaka Kenjirō

Photographer Ōtsuji Kiyoshi (1923–2001) and his wife Ōtsuji Seiko commissioned two projects from Shinohara Kazuo, first the country house, House with an Earthen Floor (1963), then House in Uehara (1976) almost twenty years later. This interview mainly addresses House in Uehara.

MAY 14, 2017, AT HOUSE IN UEHARA

HOSAKA KENJIRŌ How did Shinohara Kazuo come to design this house?

ŌTSUJI SEIKO Kuwasawa Design School[1] had just started their evening program, I believe. My husband and Mr. Ishimoto [Yasuhiro][2] were invited to teach. And because Ishimoto and Shinohara were friends, Mr. Shinohara also came. They were invited to a lecture by Mr. Ishimoto, people in that circle, including Ōtsuji Kiyoshi. Shinohara Kazuo was also part of it. My husband felt, as they smoked and talked, that Mr. Shinohara was clearly an impressive person.

HOSAKA What kind of discussions did you have regarding the design of the house?

ŌTSUJI He asked me, "Do you have any requests?" I said not really. As long as it gives us shelter. Even though my major was something like home economics, I didn't have a single request about making the kitchen in a certain way, or about the storage of dishes and other things.

HOSAKA What about your husband Otsūji Kiyoshi?

ŌTSUJI My husband had the whole first floor to himself, which made him more than happy. There were these bookshelves. Later [pointing to table before her], this was pushed up against the wall with empty space around it, which he really liked. We ate upstairs and slept, at the beginning, in the room in back. Mr. Shinohara didn't give us our own bedroom.

HOSAKA What was the story behind the third floor coming about in a very late stage?

ŌTSUJI Until very late in the design process, my husband failed to mention we had a son. Mr. Shinohara was surprised, "Oh, there's another person?" So he simply put another floor on top. My husband had only spoken about his mother living with us. Mr. Shinohara was a man of few words, and my husband wasn't much of a talker, either. I guess communication wasn't great.

HOSAKA What was your impression of Shinohara Kazuo?

ŌTSUJI He was very feminine. With a refined voice. A kind of "Is that so?" style of talking. I'm more of a low-city [*shitamachi*] person. I found it very hard to converse with him, so I let my husband do the talking. I almost never saw him smiling when he spoke with Mr. Shinohara. In some ways, it seemed the house was completed without speaking a word.

HOSAKA What was it like after it was completed?

ŌTSUJI There was much coming and going of my husband's students and the like, which was okay as long as we had a big table. It was more like a meeting place than our own living room.

HOSAKA Weren't you bothered by the diagonal columns?

ŌTSUJI Not at all. The children would lean, climb, and slide on them.

HOSAKA What is your favorite place?

ŌTSUJI It would have to be the second-floor living room. That chair. You can see the sky from there, through the triangular window. You could see birds fly

down and alight in our trees. And you could see pretty far away. Things like airplanes flying. It's actually nice to have it open all the way to the top. That's because there are no eaves there. When I had nothing to do, I would sit in the corner and just stare out. My husband too. That's what we'd do.

HOSAKA How has it been living here for forty years?

ŌTSUJI I'm truly grateful for this house. After my husband passed away, I lived here for a while with one other person, my daughter. When she got married and left, I lived alone. Then my eldest son returned and I was moved down here. Everything from here to over there, and from over there, was left by my husband.

I kept planning to go through everything, but I never got around to do it. I'm living here, and so more things have accumulated. When I'm gone, I guess someone else will move down here.

INTERVIEW CONTINUES WITH THE SON, ŌTSUJI TETSUO

HOSAKA What did you think of the house when it was completed in 1976?

ŌTSUJI TETSUO I was sixteen, a freshman or sophomore in high school, so I wasn't aware of how great a building this was, or maybe I didn't have much interest. I did feel it was different from the norm, from my friends' houses and the house we had lived in till then. I did feel that it was a really different kind of house.

What I was most happy about was I had this big room all to myself, much larger than what I had before. I was only interested in my own room at the time. When the house was first completed, people would come and talk about the diagonal columns, but I only saw them as room dividers. When people see the diagonals, they often say, "A lot of heads get bumped there, right?" But till now there hasn't been a single bumped head.

HOSAKA What are the characteristics of the third-floor room that was yours?

ŌTSUJI The windows are round. With square windows, you feel a lot is cut off. But with round windows, I would lie on my bed and feel as if I could see everything.

HOSAKA Shinohara Kazuo also designed the vacation house called "House with an Earthen Floor," which your father built before this one. Did you become aware that it was done by the same architect?

ŌTSUJI Of course. When this house was completed, I found out it was the same architect. Mention "a house by Shinohara" and everyone says tiny toilet and bathroom, narrow kitchen, and no storage space.

That was also the case with House with an Earthen Floor. I believed that's why he was able to design expansive living spaces. It was what he prioritized in a building; that was the big thing that they had in common.

HOSAKA The space in the house is well used.

ŌTSUJI Storage is really a problem. There is no space specifically for storing things. So it was up to us to figure out how to create storage within the open spaces. It wasn't enough just to lay things out. As a family, we had to have considerable abilities for putting things away.

Before I came, these shelves weren't here, neither of them. It makes me wonder how my parents made do living under basically the same conditions that exist today. They must have been really good at hiding furnishings like these.

First-floor studio. Photo by Ōtsuji Kiyoshi

Second-floor foyer. Photos by Ōtsuji Kiyoshi

It seems some visitors even referred to the way the overflow of household things was scattered as one of the good things about this house. I sometimes think how living in this house is not a simple matter.

HOSAKA What did you feel when you left to live in another place?

ŌTSUJI I left when I was thirty, when I had gotten married and rented a condominium in Kawasaki. It was a conventional place, but my impression was that the walls were heavily layered with various materials. The space here is empty, naked. There was an airiness to it. Life is simple and comfortable. In the case of the building I moved into, the floor area might have been the same as here, but it had a kind of oppressiveness about it.

HOSAKA Are there any plans to rebuild the house?

ŌTSUJI Absolutely none. We have no plan to rebuild. With such a house, a house with strong character, once you get used to it, that character becomes an integral part of the house that you accept and can live with. There's no way to replicate that character in any other form. I'm very happy with it and don't feel anything else is necessary.

HOSAKA What do you think about the house's exterior appearance?

ŌTSUJI Thinking about it again, I feel the exterior is more modest with respect to the interior, which is relatively active. You can see that in these diagonal columns. But there is no such activeness on the outside. It's just an assembly of simple building blocks.

Although the exterior doesn't convey a strong impression, the form itself is quite impressive. But compared with the inside where living occurs, I feel on the outside, it's a box with a relatively subdued appearance.

This interview is the transcript of the film *House in Uehara*, produced on the occasion of the exhibition *The Japanese House: Architecture and Life after 1945* at the National Museum of Modern Art, Tokyo.

Translated by Norman Chan

1 In 1954 Kuwasawa Yōko founded Kuwasawa Design School as a specialized design school strongly influenced by the Bauhaus movement. Later she also founded Tokyo Zōkei University. With the connection probably first made by Seike Kiyoshi, Shinohara's mentor and a key contributor to Kuwasawa School's founding, Shinohara and members of his lab maintained close ties with both institutions. Several of Shinohara's clients were instructors at Kuwasawa School, such as Asakura Setsu, Yamashiro Ryūichi, and Ōtsuji Kiyoshi.

2 Ishimoto Yasuhiro (1921–2012) was a Japanese American photographer renowned for his work on Katsura Villa. He was born in San Francisco and studied at the Chicago Institute of Design (later Institute of Design of the Illinois Institute of Technology) in 1948–52. He took up long-term residence in Japan in 1961 and soon began teaching at Kuwasawa Design School.

HOUSE IN UEHARA, 1976
Shibuya Ward, Tokyo

A commanding yet jarring forest of vertical and diagonal columns provides the structural frame to this residence/studio, located in a dense urban neighborhood. The main volume is enveloped by a fragile shell: a thin roof slab above and peripheral walls rising directly from ground to ceiling—in a single pour of concrete. Two asymmetrical rows of columns respond to the need to cantilever over the carport. While the framed structure of this house may resemble certain *minka* motifs—with the clear contrast between frame and fill showcased prominently on the front elevation—the girthy concrete of the structural members creates a debilitating interior. In a tour de force of detailing, the pristine ceiling and floor contrast with the violent intrusion of diagonal columns and column heads, making for awkward interior partitions and circulation. The last-minute addition of a rooftop living space for the clients' son, accomplished with a semicylinder formed by corrugated steel, necessitates a new circulation order and underscores the jungle-like spatial experience both inside and out.

Photos by
Taki Kōji (TK), Hoashi Terutaka (HT),
and Matsuoka Mitsuo for Shinkenchiku-sha/DAAS (MM)

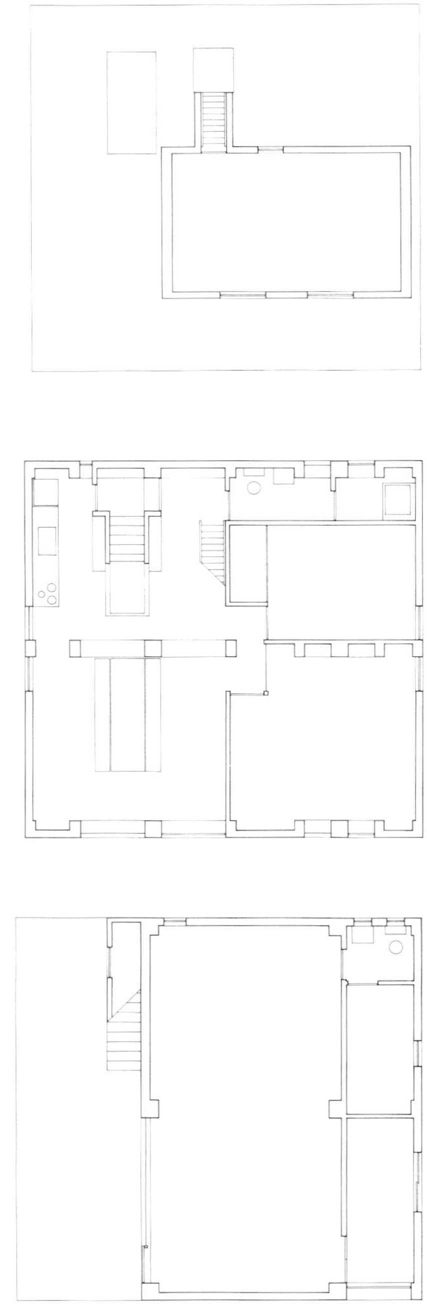

1:200

Wall in second-floor smaller bedroom.

Third-floor bedroom.

TK

HT

West elevation.

First- and second-floor interior space before the floor slab was fully extended in construction.

Second-floor foyer, with view looking into the two bedrooms.

HT

MM

HT

Interior space during construction, with space above carport and opening for entrance staircase in foreground.

Section drawing, 1975.

TK

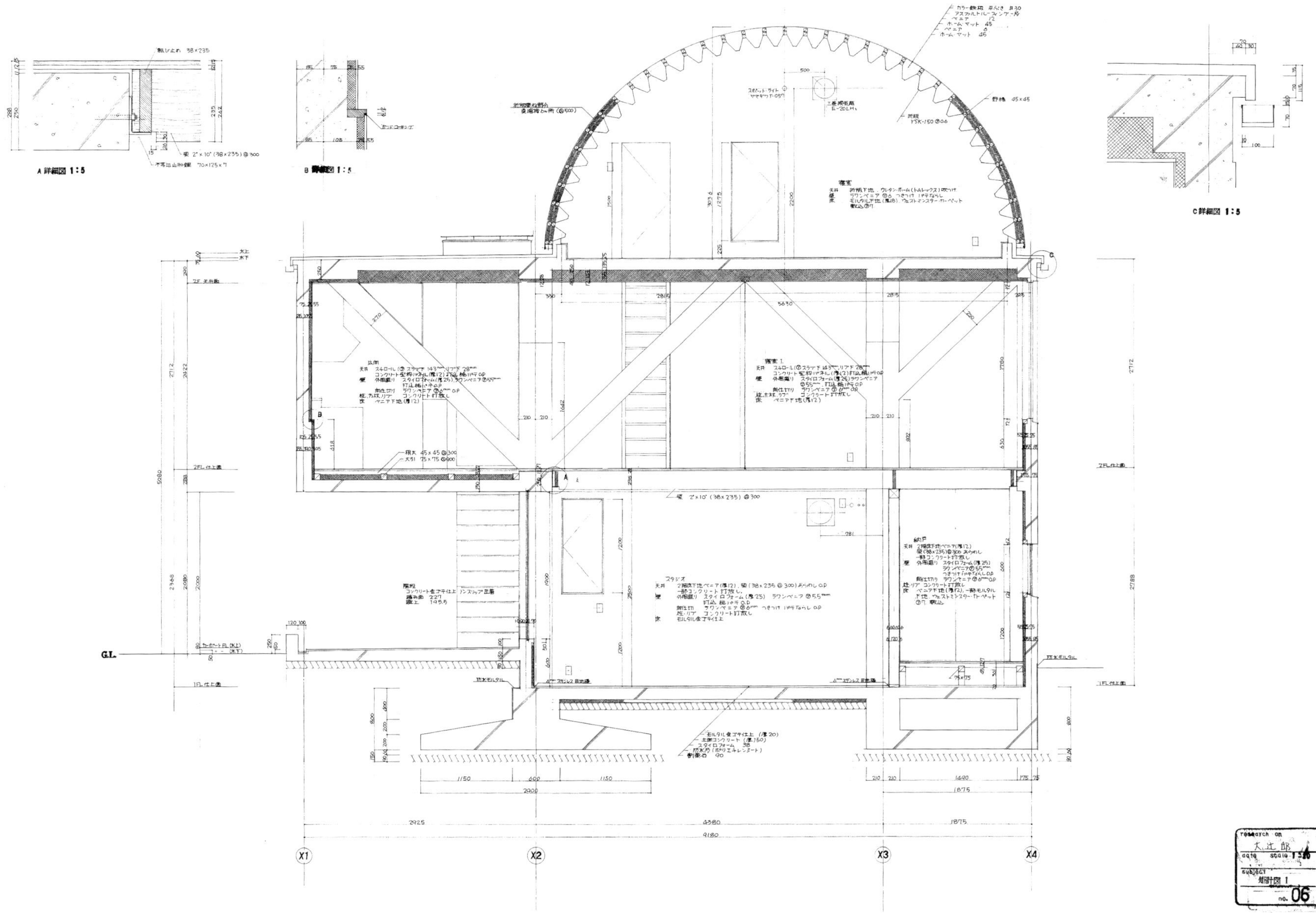

TK

Carport, entrance to first-floor studio, and staircase to upper-floor residence.

TK

TK

TK

Second floor, view looking into large bedroom.

Second floor with living-dining space in foreground and view looking into kitchen.

Two open windows.

TK

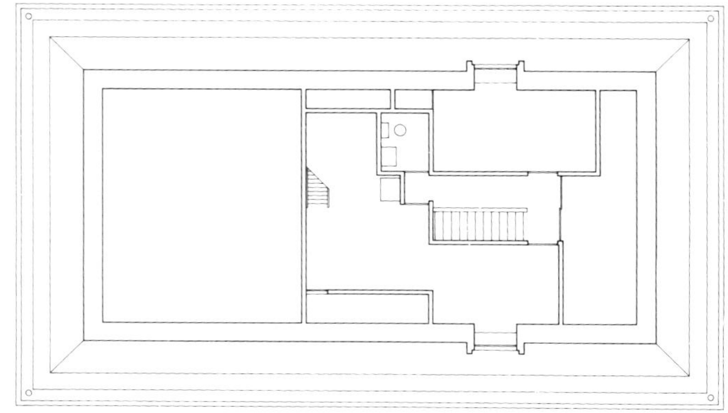

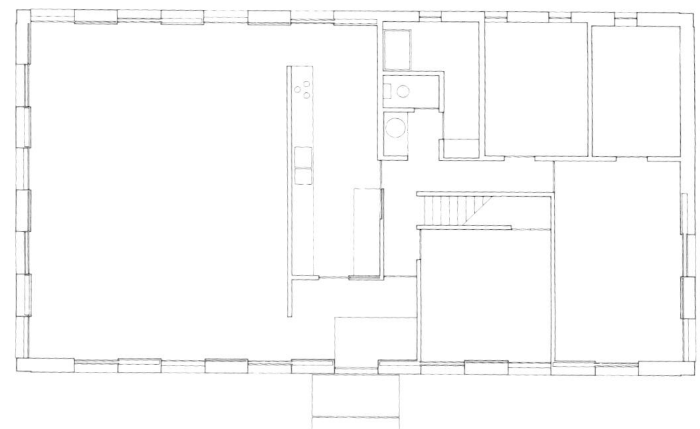

1:200

HOUSE IN ASHITAKA, 1977
Numazu, Shizuoka Prefecture

This house at the foot of Mount Fuji is defined by a cavernous space where the omnipresence of the concrete envelope actually obviates the feeling of structure. Just like Tanikawa House, House in Ashitaka has an enormous hip roof set at 45-degree inclines that climbs more than 6 meters in height. At the ground level, where the walls are plumb, a strict rhythm of 1.1-meter-wide intervals alternates between wall panels and windows. The same binary scheme is repeated in the apertures, which alternate between fixed and operable windows. This crenellating pattern of concrete wall panels around the house provides sufficient shear reinforcement to support the large concrete roof, which behaves as a shell to make possible the unimpeded void underneath. The private quarters inside the house, distributed on two levels, in fact belong to a freestanding timber-frame structure independent of the concrete envelope. Shinohara evokes Stonehenge in describing the alternating wall panels, and from the side the 45-degree concrete roof resembles a pyramid.

Photos by
Ōhashi Tomio (ŌT) and Taki Kōji (TK)

South elevation.

ŌT

TK

ŌT

Interior before construction
of timber-frame structure
for residential components.

Hiroma.

Hiroma.

ŌT

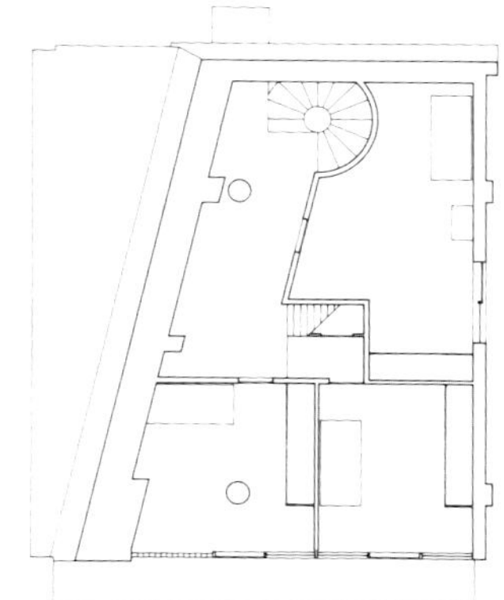

HOUSE UNDER HIGH-VOLTAGE LINES, 1981
Setagaya Ward, Tokyo

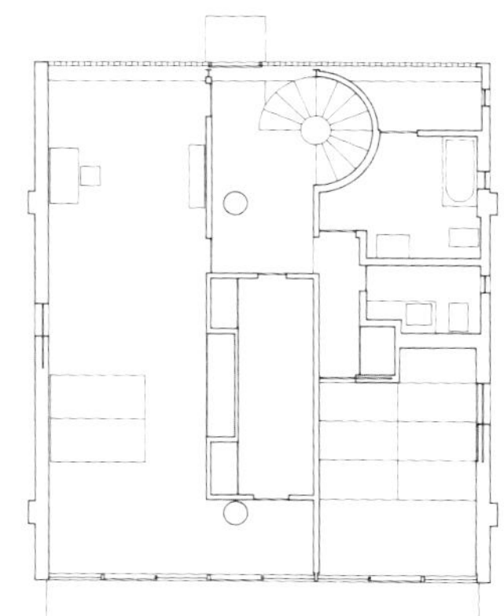

Located in a leafy residential neighborhood but with a high-voltage line hanging above the site, this house is Shinohara's *sachlich* matter-of-fact approach to give form that expresses the confrontation between the forces of the city and the private space of individuals. By code there needs to be a clearance around the power lines, resulting in two transparent tubes or cylindrical voids in the sky, yet the client asked to maximize the building envelope. The building's structure rests on two main pillars, but here the theme of fragmentation is achieved through a cascading sequence of circular forms in descending sizes—from the two giant tubes in the air, to the two round pillars in the middle of the house, to the scalloped floor slabs, and finally the circular eyes in the glass blocks. Liberal use of vivid Corbusian colors further reduces the building to its parts.

Photos by
Ōhashi Tomio (ŌT) and Arai Masao for Shinkenchiku-sha / DAAS (AM)

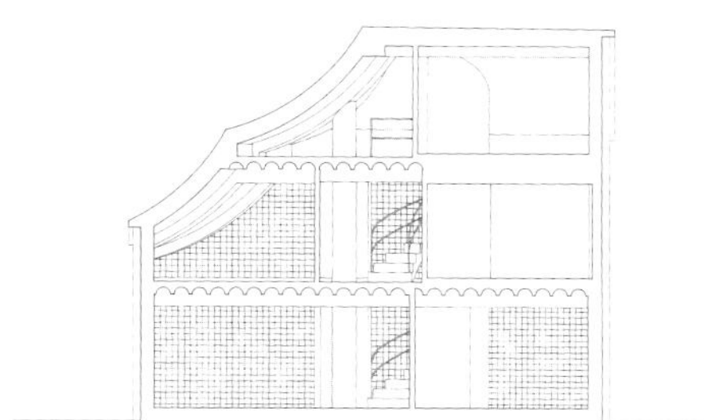

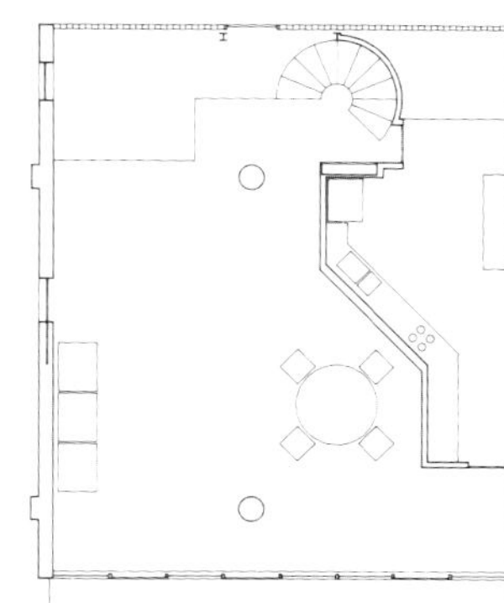

1:250

Roof under high-voltage power lines.

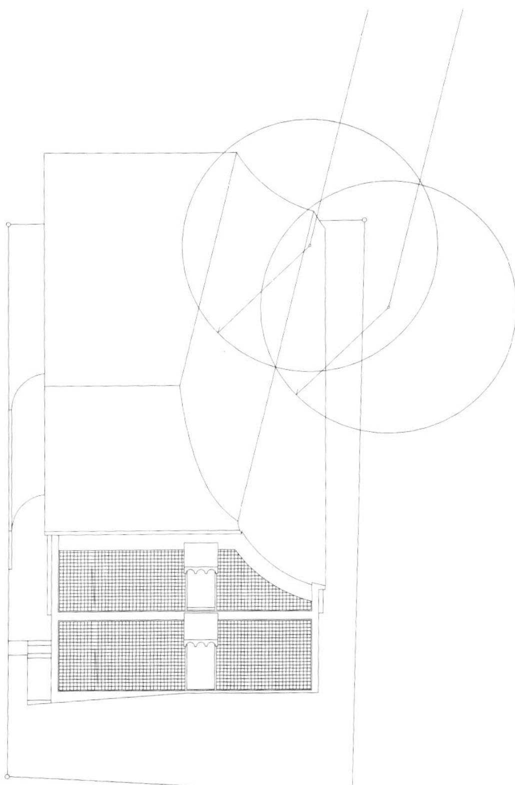

ŌT

Second-floor bedroom.

South elevation.

Shinohara Kazuo, sketches of north elevation.

ŌT

Shibuya Crossing, ca. 1979.
Photo by Shinohara Kazuo

ModernNext

Shinohara Kazuo

1 On the occasion of Shinohara's first solo exhibition held in 1979–80 at the Société des architectes diplômés par le gouvernement (SADG) in Paris, which has since been renamed the Société française d'architectes.

1 TWO PROLOGUES

Projecting a photograph of the congestion in front of Tokyo's Shibuya Station at the end of 1979, I felt the shock and interest of the audience in the small hall at the Centre Georges Pompidou [Paris] with a perceptible note of derision. The topic of my lecture[1] was the concept of my residential works and its changes in expressive method over time. My first nonresidential work directly confronting the city had been Centennial Hall at Tokyo Institute of Technology (1987), so I wasn't yet able [in the lecture] to deal with urban theory directly. All the same, while my concepts of the city and the house do not completely overlap, they do complement one another, and I have always thought of these two enveloping concepts as expressing my spaces. I spoke about the spectacle produced by the flood of disordered forms, colors, and materials around Shibuya Station. If, indeed, the Japanese are unlikely to build a city in any other way, we must surely accept this as a neighborhood representing the Tokyo of today. As a Japanese architect, then, I thought we ought to aim at a realistic urban theory. Not least, I added in support of this proposal the fact that I myself enjoy this district. At that point and for the first time ever, I pronounced the word "anarchy," saying that from the area around Shibuya Station I'd extracted a concrete (*gutai*) concept for today's urban theory, which I named "progressive anarchy." Judging from the audience's reaction and my host's comment that "anarchy" possesses great significance, "anarchy" thus achieved the right of citizenship in the domain of urban theories.

A short party chat with some architecture faculty members at the Technical University of Vienna in the spring of 1984 revealed the following: two architects acquainted with the recent cityscape of Tokyo declared that "Tokyo is a city (*toshi*), but Vienna is a town (*mura*)," to which I replied, "For some time now, the Japanese have thought of Tokyo as the largest town in the world." This exchange occasioned pleasant laughter. From the window of the hall, Viennese music was being played, marvelously extending the Karlsplatz streetscape. Along with visions of Paris, a typically beautiful modern European city that the majority of Japanese adore, I was overwhelmed each day by the weight of the beauty of Vienna, where I had been staying as a visiting professor for less than two months. Its street façades, amazingly preserving their styles of Gothic and Baroque, display substantial thickness. The outline of each building is clear-cut, without ambiguity. To me, the entire city seemed like a museum. That the great value Vienna holds on the world stage will be perpetuated is indisputable, but from the perspective presented by Tokyo as an image of the city of the near future, the buildings of Vienna appear fixed in time at the end of the nineteenth century. Perhaps it is best described as a "beautiful town" enveloped in peaceful harmony.

2 CHAOS AND TRADITION

THE FUTURE OF STATIC TRADITION

Japanese architecture possesses the lineage of Buddhist temples imported from China in antiquity, as well as a lineage of residential architecture—including palaces and commoners' dwellings—that more or less took its style from Japan's medieval period (*chūsei,* 1185–1600) onward. The latter residential typology is today seen as characteristic of Japanese culture. Quite apart from architecture, each of the cultures of tea, Noh, and ikebana, all similarly characteristic of Japanese culture, established its own style during the medieval period. Their materials and structure are emblematic of simplicity, and they share a static "beauty." As such, this beauty offers a distinctive presence among world cultures, and fortuitously also allowed for a certain harmony with the fundamental conditions of contemporary society. Notably, also the traditional structure of Japanese architecture seemed by chance to resemble the state first achieved in Europe by Western modernism, such as the approach taken by Ludwig Mies van der Rohe. I believe this accidental resemblance between the simple structure of the wooden post-and-beam frame and the dominant modernist strategy favored by industrial society at that time, greatly influenced the capacity of Japanese architecture in its ability to catch up with developments in global architecture over a short period during the 1950s following World War II.

It is hard for those who visit Japan today to discover that static structure in the city. Even in unchanging cities like Kyoto that did not suffer wartime bombing and are often said to have preserved their old form, it is a fact that only a handful of beautiful *machiya* (merchant row houses) remain. In Tokyo, there are barely any left.

SHIFTING FROM THE EARLY-MODERN CASTLE TOWN EDO
The way Tokyo was first constructed, still during the medieval period (known as Edo until 1868), was to take advantage of its natural topography. Rather than what might really be called a castle stood an austere, fortification-like wooden building at its center, around which were clustered meager single-storied houses (*minka*). Subsequently, the lineage of Tokugawa shōguns, who were responsible for Japan's early modern feudal system, relocated there, and Edo came to be the capital of the entire country. Its center was the rebuilt Edo Castle, and the periphery remained as it had been when the castle grounds first became the site of the Imperial Palace 120 years ago. Reflecting a class system, the warrior caste closely surrounded the castle, while housing for the laboring masses spread out from the periphery of the city. Presently, the area within the rail loop called the Yamanote Line exactly corresponds to the original Edo layout. The basic shape of the streets on its map more or less remain in Tokyo today. Of course, railroads, and then following World War II, highways, were elevated above the surface. Roads have generally been widened, and toll-road bypasses made their appearance. But the inner outline of Tokyo retains the form of the early modern city.

In Edo-period *ukiyo-e* woodblock the main avenue frequently appears at the center of the neighborhoods of ordinary townsfolk. This image may be exaggerated, as it often depicts *machiya* at a grand scale. However, in general these were more like crude wooden shacks. In the period beginning in 1868 known as the Meiji era, there was a determined break with the feudal system destined to implement a European style of modern society. Along the main streets of Tokyo, European-style reinforced concrete buildings little by little replaced the former one- and two-storey wood-frame buildings—the latter in general having had a shop below with a residence on the upper floor. Within these enormous, village-like agglomerations were built, for instance, offices and banks imitating European Renaissance styles. Following World War II, buildings seeking

"Tokyo as Castle Town." Image courtesy of NTT/Hakuhōdō

2 Editor's note: Japan's city planning and building code promulgated in 1919 limited the height of all buildings to 100 feet, or approximately 31 meters. This rule was relaxed beginning in 1963.

to reproduce a modernism imported via the United States increased. Until the end of World War II, 31 meters was the greatest height attained.[2] But after the war, owing to technological advances, high-rise structures surpassing 100 meters began to be built—despite ours being an earthquake-prone nation. And across the whole city, traditional neighborhoods came to mix randomly with such new buildings, even while retaining the outline of the proto-modern feudal city. Thus, came to be born the "enormous village" (*kyōdai na sonraku*) that was Tokyo.

In a number of downtown neighborhoods, following Japan's socioeconomic growth, vigorous commercial competition took hold. Ginza, Shinjuku, Shibuya, Ikebukuro, Akasaka, Roppongi, Harajuku, and still other districts came to life with an influx of people seeking to follow the latest trends. The randomness of the buildings lining their streets finally exceeded a certain level. One instance of this is the cityscape surrounding Shibuya Station, which is chaos, materialized.

SYNCHRONIC CITY:
THE MEETING OF DIFFERING SYSTEMS

I've already suggested that a number of matters having to do with tradition in Japanese architecture, for example, its stasis, simplicity, the standardization of timber components and tatami sizes, and so forth, are preserved in certain features of residential spatial practice. In some few "fragmented" (*danpenteki*) areas of Kyoto are graceful *machiya* that preserve their old style. By the same token, if in certain areas or along certain roads Tokyo had welcomed architecture making use of new technologies, while at the same time striving to retain the forms of its older *machiya*, it could have become a distinctively beautiful city. When preparing this text, I found by chance a landscape image of Tokyo in a full-page newspaper advertisement. It portrays a modern version of the "castle town" with Edo Castle still at its center and has the excitement of a relative proportional balance between tradition and a contemporary design technology. In actual fact, such *machiya* simply do not exist in sufficient numbers.

On a trip to South America in the fall of 1984, I was in São Paulo for two weeks, where I often walked its vibrant built-up districts. When I first went out along Avenida Paulista, I was shocked to experience the superb perspective of modernist buildings packed along both sides. I felt that perhaps Ville Radieuse of Le Corbusier's dreams—that concept expressed in his plan for Paris—had been realized. Of course, the basic modern norm cohered into a single system, and the diverse collection of various forms on Avenida Paulista are different, but it is nevertheless a splendid modernist city. In New York, the perspective of Manhattan's Avenue of the Americas, though quickly traversed and realized only along one side of the street as a series of nearly uniform high-rise office buildings, had interested me two or three years earlier. Now inside of me, one more "Modern City" was added by São Paulo. In addition, it was more interesting to me that these modern districts were linked to the context of older neighborhoods with entirely different cultural contexts.

In the roads intersecting Avenida Paulista, there remains a heterogeneous streetscape that embodies the historical background of a former Portuguese colony. That clear "gap"

(*dansō*) makes these areas appealing. It is similar to the interesting combination of the modernist "forest" of high-rise buildings with Edo-period Japanese-style "fields" in that "fictive" Tokyo landscape I'd found in the newspaper advertisement. The contrast of the "march" of modernism along one straight avenue, as figure against the "ground" of a latticed fabric of the Portuguese vernacular, was seductive.

On my very first trip abroad in 1972 my encounter with the "culture of heterogeneity" found in European urban areas was what chiefly grasped my attention. For example, in Granada, Spain, and Casablanca, Morocco, I found aspects of European tradition and Islamic culture everywhere I went, and I realized that it's this collection of gaps that makes such cities appealing. An idea of the "synchronic city" took shape within me from this time onward. The medieval Italian hill towns are beautiful, but they're suspended in time. This becomes evident wherever no "discrepancy" or "gap" exists that might have incited a dynamic "movement" among their features.

In counterexamples of this nature, synchronic encounters set against the background of a deep history may create a "bundle of relationships" with clear differences among their elements. The beautiful older cities of Europe generally display this kind of context. But Tokyo—that is, the Tokyo of today—is different.

3 CHAOS AS A KEY CONCEPT

1960: THE "BEAUTY" OF CHAOS

In the mid-1950s, when I started out as an architect, my works were without exception residential—something that I like to view as experimental housing. I was first drawn to architecture in general by a strong sympathy with the tradition of Japanese architecture. Aiming to understand the essential system that functions at the core of traditional structures, over the decade and a half until the end of the 1960s I continued in a dialogue with these simple and unchanging structures. A self-completing structure scarcely depends on any continuity with another. For instance, in House in White (1966), not one but several, even many, solutions are possible, but none is essential to the space itself. The European and Middle Eastern custom of housing different families between shared or party walls did not exist in Japan. Of course, after World War II, the apartment-block typology became common, but that is a different problem.

In theory, in the contemporary enormous village (*gendai no shūraku*), the possibility that everything will converge in a single order does not exist, and above all not in Japan. Around 1960, optimistic Japanese architects placing their faith in technology drew up urban schemes, one after the other. Japanese modernism was approaching its peak. Pursuing my own one-by-one residential design practice, I knew instinctively that the cities dreamt up by these modernists could never be realized.

Fifteen years after its military defeat, Japan in 1960 was beginning its rapid ascent toward a renewed industrial society. Modernism fantasized a future based on engineering technology with the ideology of the industrial society as supreme; "beautifully cohered" cities were laid out because such a city must "logically" come to be. However, I predicted that given

Avenue of the Americas (Sixth Avenue), New York City. Photo by Shinohara Kazuo

the character of contemporary Japanese society, for example, the fact that there were few—if any—conditions to enforce coherence (*tōitsusei*), "logically" Japan's "radiant city" would not be built. In addition, I felt that no condition other than "chaos" could be expected from the commercial buildings rising in grand disorder in Tokyo's several downtown areas. Still more so, because such "chaotic" districts were assuredly the "contemporary form" elected by the Japanese themselves, I also believed that Japanese urban theory could only be realized by allowing the city to be "positioned" (*ricchiten*) in such a mode. I clearly stated that "Japan's future cities, neighborhoods, and streets could not express anything other than a 'beauty of chaos.'"[3] My prediction about Japanese cities has been proven after twenty years. Now, in the last year or two, many have begun to talk about the "fun" being inherent in Tokyo. In other words, there is currently a delight in Tokyo's landscape of chaos, or in activities enabled by such a landscape, completely unrelated as it is to the well-ordered streetscape and planned-city aesthetic anticipated by modernism.

THE MATHEMATICAL CITY, THE IRRATIONAL CITY, AND PROGRESSIVE ANARCHY

In response to the Japanese modernism of the 1960s that fantasized about huge reinforced-concrete infrastructure built in the form of urban megastructures, I proposed that "urban structure must by nature entail an extreme abstract system; it would be a set of mathematical functions tending toward infinity; that is, the structure of "urban functional space" (functional in the mathematical sense, *toshi kansū kūkan*) itself must determine the form of the city."[4] This set of "infinity" functions, which includes time as a principal factor, expresses the truism that "chaos" will to some degree effect a presence. Using "mathematics" metaphorically, I was thus able to demonstrate how a process of "simple plastic modeling is incapable of denoting the structure of the contemporary city."[5] Entering the 1980s, "chaos" and "fluctuation" began to be introduced as significant terms, from new areas of fields such as physics, chemistry, and biology. When we attempt to understand the city as a living entity, static equilibrium can never be its structure. The city must be dealt with as a kinetic mechanism capable of generating chaos in its wake.

I have explained that what I term the "city of irrationalism" is a city in which "discrepancy" or "gap" is exposed between elements that may be grasped via their cultural particularities or background—be they buildings or streets. Here the most important point is the mechanism giving rise to some appealing activity, when the "difference" between elements is unique, clear, and forceful. This city of irrationalism as I defined it included a critique of all lack of concern for the world of meaning such as derives from the interest of Japanese formalist modernism in mere quantitative measuring functions. Irrational space is, of course, more generally synonymous with a space of meaning. The richness of a city arises through exceeding the measure of any rational relationships among elements. I've never been a member of any Japanese modernist movement, but in 1980, by which time it seemed modernism in Japan had been nearly erased, I nonetheless included the phrase "praise for the spirit of the 1920s" in the description of one of my projects.[6]

3 Shinohara Kazuo, *Jūtaku kenchiku* (Residential architecture) (Tokyo: Kinokuniya shoten, 1964).

4 Shinohara Kazuo, "Sugaku-teki toshi," in "Kūkan no shiso to kōzō," *Shinkenchiku* vol. 42, no. 1 (January 1967): 115–18.

5 Shinohara Kazuo, "Higōri toshi to kūkan kikai," *Shinkenchiku* vol. 50, no. 3 (March 1975): 151–62.

6 Shinohara Kazuo, "The Context of Pleasure," *The Japan Architect* (September 1986): 22–24.

7 Shinohara Kazuo, "Le Plaisir et son Contexte La Chaise, ou la métaphore du plaisir," *Techniques et architecture,* no. 2–3 (1986): 162–63.

CUTTING THROUGH THE SURFACE OF THE "EMPIRE OF SIGNS"

Advertising without restriction of shape, color, or material covers much of the surface of all the buildings of Japanese cities. Once this chaos exceeds a certain level, visual activity arises. There is no response to the traditional structure of the old Japan. Because contemporary Japanese society is economically prosperous, any urban place is now safe. People in their choice of clothes follow the latest world fashions. The bizarre space that requires no particular reference to any country in the world or to any Japanese historical period generates a bizarre liveliness. I referred to this as "the pleasure of the subconscious."[7]

Because Japan may be called a bureaucratic state, building standards are fastidiously obeyed. Anti-seismic supervision—since earthquakes are frequent—is regularly carried out. Unruly conditions seen in countries that have reached an economic standstill do not for the most part exist in Japan. Yet in the small-scale eking out of architectural space that results from some of the highest land values in the world, there nonetheless exists a poverty of a different kind. Owing to the *wabi, sabi* aesthetic of the tea room, which took hold after the medieval period in Japan, and its conceptual resonance that seems to form a pair with a reduced lifestyle maintained within a small space, we Japanese live at a point just before falling into such poverty. Even those Japanese best skilled at conforming with a willed minimal existence, however, possess little awareness of the city beyond their homes. Because architectural restrictions related to form, color, or material don't exist in Japan, an extreme "chaos" is nurtured. That structural battle between order and disorder is bound to be the expression of the Japanese city.

TWO-DIMENSIONAL INSTALLATION

A two-dimensional surface chaos then rules Japanese cities. If this situation were to be eliminated, these cities would devolve into an agglomeration of random quantities of utterly mundane one- or two-storey timber-framed houses, together with three-storey or utterly characterless box-shaped concrete structures—not at all the neatly drawn residences foregrounded in newspaper advertisements. Such is more or less the same ordinary, everyday urban landscape visible throughout the small shopping streets situated near most any commuter railway station beyond Tokyo's central area.

This same two-dimensionality can be said to be characteristic of the entire spatial consciousness of Japanese culture. Even in clearly three-dimensional arrangements such as ikebana, one's conscious focus is a composition as viewed from the front. In the case of architecture, while there can be no space without a third dimension, the Japanese consciousness is always fixed along the sight line from the front for each and every wall plane. For my doctoral thesis I undertook an analysis of the spatial composition of Japanese architecture, in which one of the topics was an approach labeled "frontality" (*shōmensei*). Representing the tradition of Japanese architecture, the structure of the one small space of the tea room is the prototypical example. Every wall plane is an independent element, each with its independent design—window(s), *fusuma* panels, the selection of its wall material. This masterly discreteness (*risansei*) has been equivalated (*dōichishi*) with the spirit of tea. While the etiquette of tea retains strict rules, the ideology behind the tea room structure encompasses a subtle ungrammatical coexistence of control according to a strong order and as much randomness as can be tolerated.

The two-dimensional installations that tend to cover the surfaces of those buildings located in Tokyo's multiple commercial subcenters focus on their lightness and liveliness of appeal. The Japan that has been termed [by Roland Barthes] an *Empire of Signs* is structured according to a visual chaos that extends to everything—form, shape, material, or illumination. Of course, the diversity of "meaning" and so to speak nonnationality of the arrangement of these elements also support this empire. Yet the very surface-ness of Japan's architecture makes the "empire" thin and light in the extreme.

4 HIGH TECHNOLOGY AND CHAOS

THE ENORMOUS VILLAGE AND ELECTRONICS

Our contemporary age is said to be shifting toward a highly informatic society. Japan is at the cutting edge of one aspect of this technology, especially as regards electronics and miniature devices. The urban theory of 1920s modernism anticipated the arrival of present-day industrial society and multiplied its architectural images. Japan had attained a high degree of industrialization, but its cities hadn't the foundation or traditions to extend such a system. As the Japanese became aware of highly informatics-driven society having overtaken conventionally modern industrialized society, Japanese cities, and notably Tokyo with its confusion of random elements, began to commit to electronic systems as they were at the time.

Heavy industrial facilities manifested clear formal characteristics, such as those of immense bridges or ocean liners. However, a supercomputer, as opposed to earlier mainframes, can be contained in a small box. Electronics has migrated to banal containers, and from there into the bags and pockets of the many individuals that walk the city center. All are carrying small, inexpensive yet powerful electronic products, but the mechanism itself is restricted to a simplified and nearly invisible black box.

The role of today's everyday high technology affecting Tokyo's centers is a new necessary condition for urban theory. When the chaos of the city produces a bustling activity, this confusion of components in its exterior surfaces nevertheless retains a two-dimensional quality.

The ability of the city to respond to a diversity of random desires becomes the essence of the urban mechanism. In several areas of Tokyo, a new type of urban form may be expressed within this sort of context, while the capacity for super-technology and the chaos among the collective state of its elements need not contradict each other. Along Japan's so-called Tōkaidō linear city extending continuously from Tokyo to the Osaka area, which was of course generated by the naturally occurring sprawl of each city, inside a high-speed super express that accomplishes the journey in some three hours, it's not uncommon to hear the train conductor apologize for "the inconvenience of arriving three minutes late at Osaka."

8 Shinohara Kazuo, "Kenchiku he," *Shinkenchiku* vol. 56, no. 9 (September 1981): 28–35. English and French versions published in *The Japan Architect* (September 1981) and *L'Architecture d'Aujourd' hui* (April 1983), respectively.

THE ZERO-DEGREE MACHINE
A PROGRESSIVE ANARCHY EMERGES TOGETHER WITH HIGH TECHNOLOGY.

My article "Towards Architecture" features a dual topic: progressive anarchy as a concern of urban structure and my "zero-degree machine" as an issue of architectural structure.[8] However, since I can now consider architecture and the city simultaneously, chaos and the machine substitute for one other, so that the "urban machine" and the "chaos of architecture" rise together.

With reference to photographs showing the shoddy aluminum-foil finish covering the legs of the US Apollo 11 lunar spacecraft and a head-on view of the US Navy Tomcat F-14 fighter plane, I examined the relationship between their terrifying capabilities and the visual idiosyncrasies of their respective containers. In certain parts of these machines, their essential functionality is maximally realized, and, through the *sachlich* (matter-of-fact) joining of their parts, the functionality of the whole machine is maximally achieved. Today's machines are no longer expected to exhibit a visual unity like the streamlined imagery of the 1920s, as exemplified by the ocean liner. The new machine can thus be called a "zero-degree machine." Neither parts nor whole can express a meaning appealing to sentiment. In other words, present-day systems of incoherent (*hi-tōitsuteki*) form are those that embody both randomness and chaos. However, the formal "gap" between the parts, or the formal "gap" between the parts and the whole, endow the machine with dynamism. Into this, people read meanings that hadn't existed till now. This process shares a commonality with the chaos of the city that has no rules or intention toward holistic unity, rendering a possibility of deciphering "new meanings" that were formerly nonexistent. Chaos, in this sense, functions as a key concept not only for buildings but also for the city—at the same time, demonstrating that machines may also function as a concept for both architecture and urbanism. When people cross neighborhoods, like Tokyo's Shibuya, which arose out of the joining of infinite urban parts as fragments, they decipher all kinds of unexpected, multifarious meanings. In other words, because this neighborhood will generate diverse new meanings, the city becomes one large space machine.

In their own right, internal mechanisms of high technology have far exceeded the level at which they could be used as metaphors for architecture or the city. The essential problem of the Apollo spaceship landing craft is not resolved in a sphere of understanding through any contrast between its functionality and the shoddiness of the aluminum foil covering its legs. This form-and-function are realized through the cooperation of a colossal super-technology with electronics as its base. However, I am certain that the elements of the movement and the basic concept of technology as a whole are manifested, even in fragmentary details, such as the issues cited here.

The new architecture and the city share chaos and machine as key concepts.

F-14A Tomcat aircraft from Fighter Squadron 102, over the aircraft carrier USS *America*.

Buzz Aldrin removing the passive seismometer from the Apollo 11 Lunar Module, July 21, 1969.

AN URBAN MACHINE PLAN

A university's main gate faces toward the entirely average, small shopping street around its railway station, located some ten minutes by train from Tokyo's main Yamanote loop line. Centennial Hall will function as a technology museum displaying hardware items on a lower level, as a space of exchange providing for software information—science and technology—in meeting rooms above, and on the highest floor a restaurant and bar, also a place of information exchange. This "machine floating in the air" was tentatively selected from a number of image proposals. It amounts to an image of a cylindrical volume, its metallic surface floating horizontally. Starting from basic practical requirements, a complex outline of interpenetrating cubes and semicircular end planes was fixed [the cylinder above having been halved]. The built-up cubical shapes respond to the configuration of the site, changing to flat surfaces projecting from the combination of two unequal rectangles in plan [joined by lines drawn to form a trapezoidal mid-space]. The walls on the northeast and south function like a mooring mechanism for a flying object. Acting as a beam, the 11-meter-diameter semicircular end planes create a "bridge" 33 meters in span. On the other hand, the flat wall surfaces composed out of cubes join with the semicylindrical planes to form a single volume, and so its enveloping wall planes cannot be calculated separately. The structural engineer arrived at equations with 530 nodes and 3,200 unknowns, which presented an unusually complex structural analysis.[9]

Once the overall structure had been nearly fixed, I bent the axis of the horizontal semicylindrical plane in the middle, for the eastern axis to face precisely the corner of the entrance from the railway station, a 30-meter distance from the main gate of the university, and the western axis to pierce the center of a roundabout then at the center of the university campus. I proposed the former as symbolic of the surrounding neighborhood and the latter as symbolic of the university campus itself. At this point, a strong randomness was introduced. The composite cube in the main part of the building below and the horizontally spanning semicylindrical planes are based on differing structural contexts. Added to these, the black COR-TEN steel–pipe structure dumbwaiter—to service the restaurant on the top floor—the lightweight curved and sloping entrance canopy, racks suspended on the west for independent air-conditioning systems on each floor—the function of each, realized to the maximum, intentionally determined their form and they were all matter-of-factly joined. Between these discrete parts, and in between the parts and the whole, arose a multifarious bundle of random relationships. There was no meaning of coherence attributed beforehand—no commemorative monumentality. But, instead, unanticipated and diverse meanings—emerging between people and the overall space—were facilitated.[10]

In the design process for a number of projects before Centennial Hall, I'd variously experimented with discreteness, gap, fragmentation, and *sachlich* matter-of-fact juncture. In the wall structure for the Japan Ukiyo-e Museum (1982), I created one of its main themes out of a structure formed by scattered two-dimensional shapes.[11] Its two visible elevations were composed of six 8-meter square units, three to a side. I followed a rule of making the geometric shapes by connecting a corner and a midpoint of each square as simply as possible

9 Editor's note: The structural engineer was Kimura Toshihiko, one of the most important engineers of the postwar period and a close collaborator of many of the leading architects of postwar Japan. Virtually all of Shinohara's works from the Second Style onward, with the exception of timber-frame structures, were collaborations with Kimura.

10 Shinohara Kazuo, "Chaos and Machine," *The Japan Architect* (May 1988): 25–32. French version published as "Ville, Chaos, Activités," in *Cahiers du CCI*, no. 5 (June 1988).

11 Shinohara, "Kenchiku he."

12 Shinohara Kazuo, "A Program for the 'Fourth Space,'" *The Japan Architect* (September 1986): 28–35. French version in *L'Architecture d'Aujourd'hui* (October 1988).

without giving rise to any singular harmony of structural elements. This gave form to a "figure and ground" of glass and reinforced-concrete walls, the latter of course constituting the principal structure with its anti-seismic potential. Yet, logically, the glass and concrete elements are set up as interchangeable.

In House in Yokohama (1984), the expressive concept emerged together with that of the memorial building of a university [Centennial Hall].[12] Of course, since scale and function differ greatly, no actual methodology is shared. However, from the point of the direct representation of my thinking about architecture and the city, their concepts are simultaneous to each other. Objectively [in *sachlich* fashion], by joining these three-dimensional spatial elements with primary geometrical shapes, I hoped for the creation of some new meaning. On the other hand, even in the two-dimensional figures, such as windows and doors, I used discrete forms. The interior and exterior interact through these unusual forms. At such time as an individual traverses the aforementioned bundle of relationships created among fragmented elements, random noise accompanied by new meanings arises. The term random noise is here intended as synonymous with spatial activity. Recalling that the famous phrase "a house is a machine for living" springs from an entirely different background, this small House in Yokohama "landed" in the bushes as an isolated "space machine."

5 EPILOGUE

When Centennial Hall was completed and its overall form appeared to loom over the street, a popular tabloid reported that children had been joyfully screaming "Gundam," the robot hero of a science fiction animated film. In the children's eyes, the building appeared to be an "*objet*," but one capable of movement just like a living being. I found this very interesting.

Every system must include "fluctuation" (*yuragi*)—an expression of chaos. It is said that in newer areas of such fields as biology and physics, phenomena incorporating chaos are being actively investigated. In the same newspaper that printed the illustration of an imaginary Tokyo neighborhood already referred to, there was a short article one day around that time reporting that "an organization had been formed to promote the practical use of 'fuzzy logic' in computer systems able to deal with human-like 'ambiguity.'" Chaos and randomness are far from useless to many systems. For a long time they have been considered something to be eliminated, but on the contrary the notion of dealing with such phenomena as mechanisms to stimulate a systemic vitality is rapidly gaining great strength. I read the comment of one biologist who said that, even in computers, any leap in performance would be difficult without the ability to accommodate random noise. To be sure, within any business or other type of organization, it is living beings, that is to say humans, who make its essence a "living" state. When aiming to approach any living system, especially one that is composed of humans, chaos and random noise count as essential elements.

House in Yokohama, computer rendering.

The "beauty of chaos" I first predicted in 1960 has come to join up with this sort of activity in science and technology. So at this point, I welcome the very enjoyable "Gundam" episode, taking the building as resembling a robot hero, a life form in the space of science fiction, made by arranging everyday spatial parts, which for me always comprise primary geometric shapes.

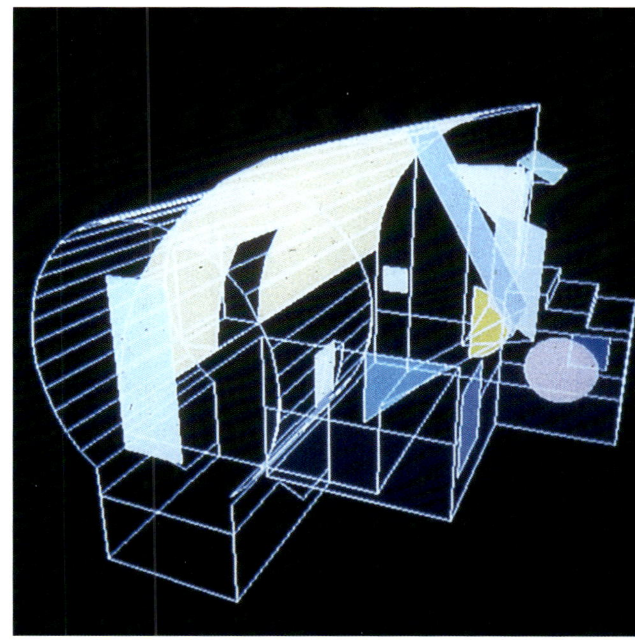

My concept of progressive anarchy as essential to lending the city a vitality like that of a living system was an intuition. I have no interest whatever in any unconditionally disorderly landscape, which can always be discounted as a mere social phenomenon. The anarchy and random noise I'm expecting to discover provide a new vitality for architecture and the city—my personal interest would entail a mechanism of an "order" pertaining to a level different from before.

Now we are entering the ModernNext.

This essay was originally published as "ModanNekusuto he no messēji: toshi, kaosu, kassei," in *Kenchiku bunka*, no. 504 (October 1988): 30–39.

Translated by Álex Bueno

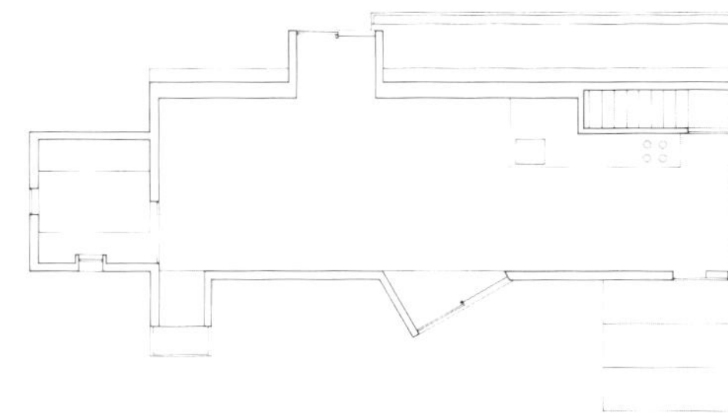

HOUSE IN YOKOHAMA, 1984
Kanagawa Prefecture

A variety of expressive devices—from geometric volumes and abstruse shapes, to vivid colors inside and reflective aluminum panels outside—are assembled into this highly sensuous house in the suburbs. The house is an analogue of the modern Japanese city, where discrete components standing on their own terms are conjoined into a machine. Situated next to a conventional wood-frame house repainted in black and used as his atelier, Shinohara's domicile for his post–Tokyo Tech life is described as a spatial mechanism that projects a series of "random noise," that conjures up new vitality. On one end of the building is a cylindrical projection that contains a tea room, and on the other end, rotated 90 degrees, is a semi-submerged cubic tatami space.

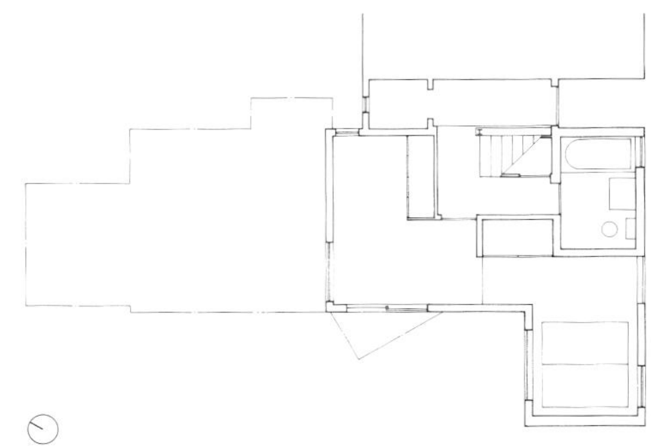

Photos by
Hoashi Terutaka (HT), Arai Masao for Shinkenchiku-sha / DAAS (AM), Ōhashi Tomio (ŌT), and Justin Knight (JK)

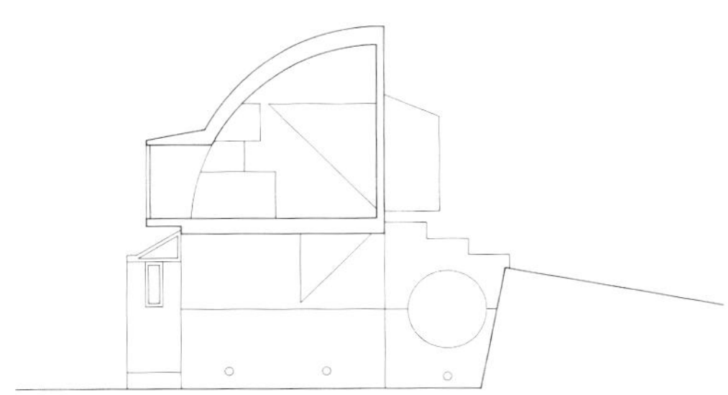

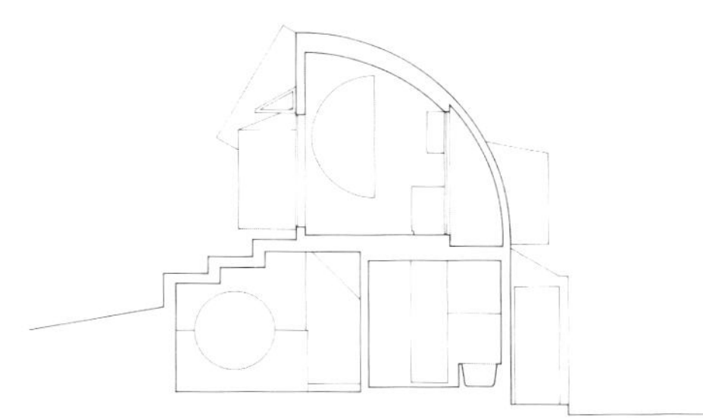

View looking east.

1:200

HT

Lower-floor bedroom.

Lower-floor bedroom.

View from upper-floor living space looking toward storage.

Upper-floor living space.

AM

ŌT

HT

HT

JK

JK

South elevation, model of House in Yokohama and renovated wooden house where Shinohara Atelier was located.

West elevation, model view.

Shinohara Kazuo, sketches.

5/30

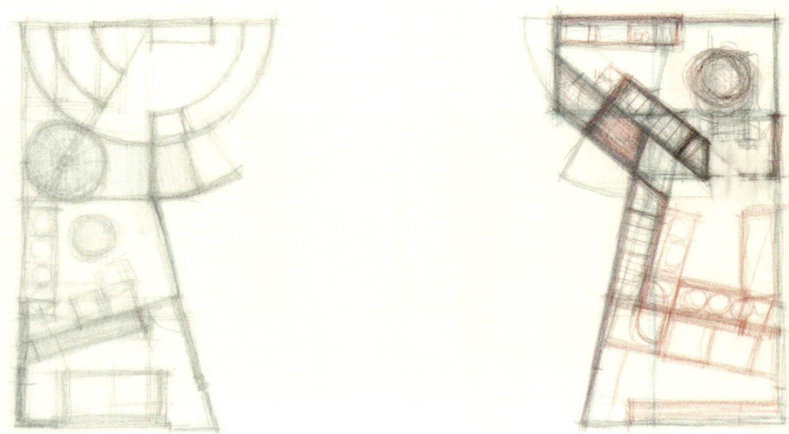

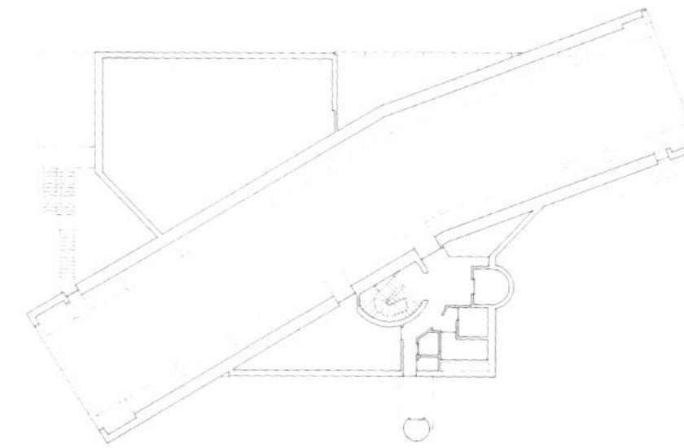

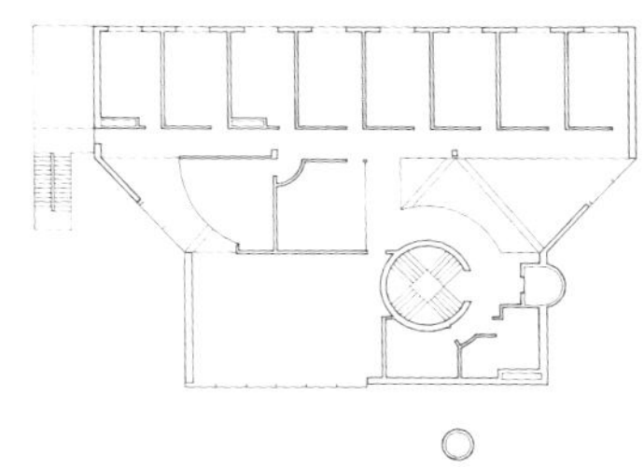

CENTENNIAL HALL AT TOKYO INSTITUTE OF TECHNOLOGY, 1987
Meguro Ward, Tokyo

In the 1980s Shinohara came to embrace more overtly the generative potential of urban chaos, a point he first noted in the 1960s. Located on the threshold between the campus of the Tokyo Institute of Technology and the generic suburb outside, Centennial Hall towers over Tokyo's messy urbanity as a "zero-degree machine," unmediated in its power and logic as a fighter jet. The challenging site has a highly irregular geometry in plan, squeezed into a residual plot adjacent to a busy suburban rail junction, and is surrounded by a dense yet low-lying neighborhood typical of boom communities of postwar Tokyo. Shinohara's imposing design both responds to and rises above this urban chaos. The complex infrastructure of the city appears to have infiltrated into the double-height hall in the lower part of the building. On top is a long half-cylindrical feature that juts out from the main volume, piercing into the horizon in two directions.

Photos by
Iwan Baan (IB), Arai Masao for Shinkenchiku-sha / DAAS (AM),
Ōhashi Tomio (ŌT), and Christian Kerez (CK)

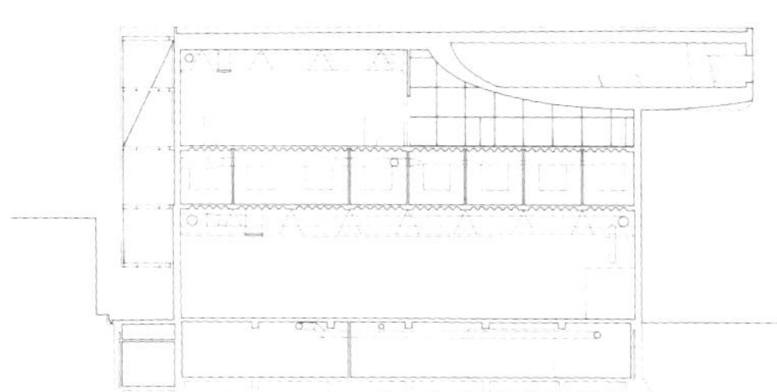

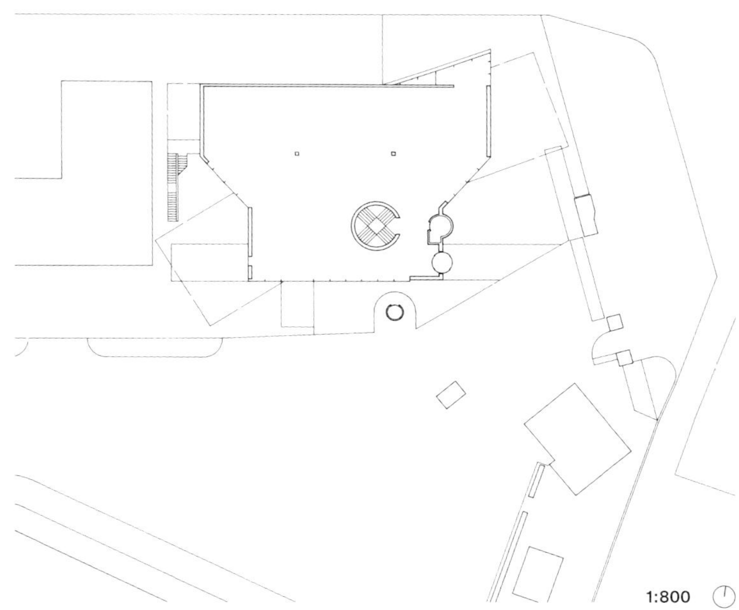

1:800

East end of Centennial Hall and main gate of Tokyo Institute of Technology.

構内禁煙
ドクターズ
キャリア
フォーラム
(DCF)
12/8(火)
ZEON
CCC
NEC
駐車禁止
車両入退構時間
東京工業大学
Tokyu Store

IB

AM

AM

First-floor multipurpose hall.

Third-floor lounge.

Fourth-floor restaurant and lounge.

ŌT

CK

ŌT

At night.

View from Ōokayama Station, an interchange between two local commuter rail lines.

Shinohara Kazuo, sketch of elevation.

Clay study models.

Shinohara Kazuo, sketch of plan.

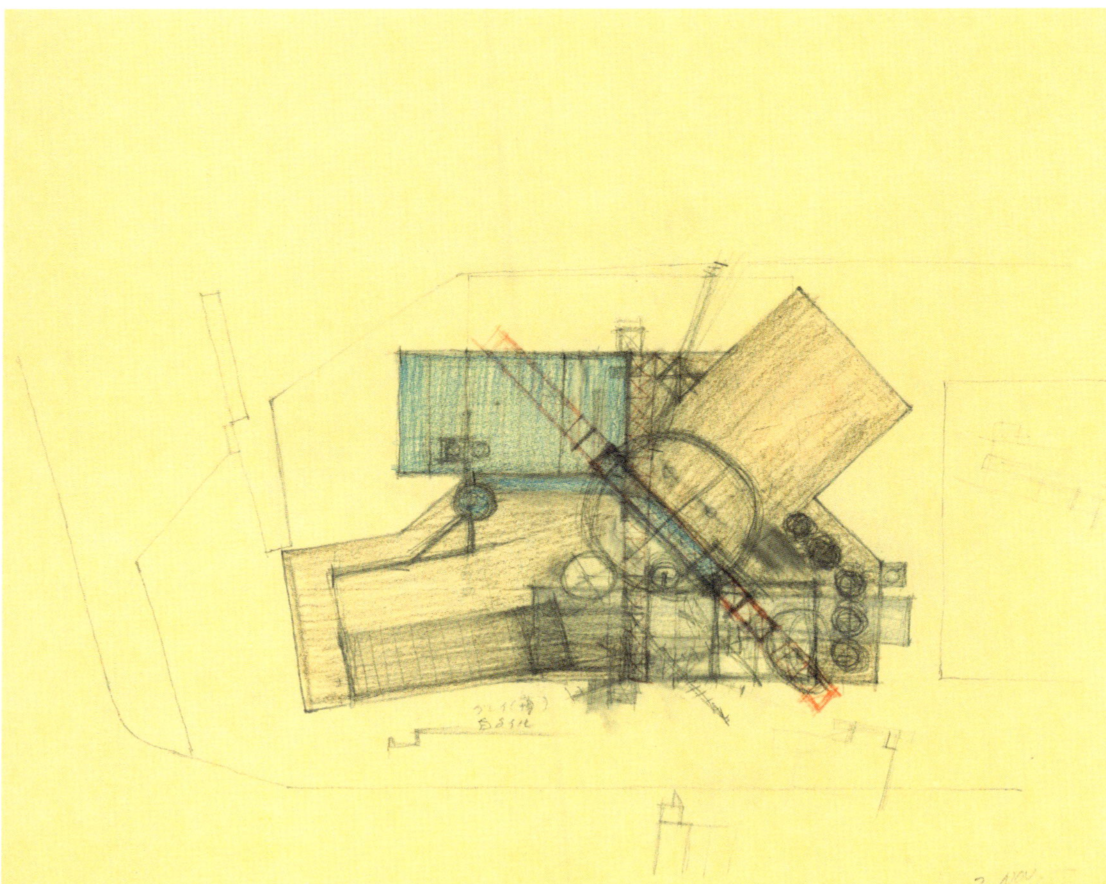

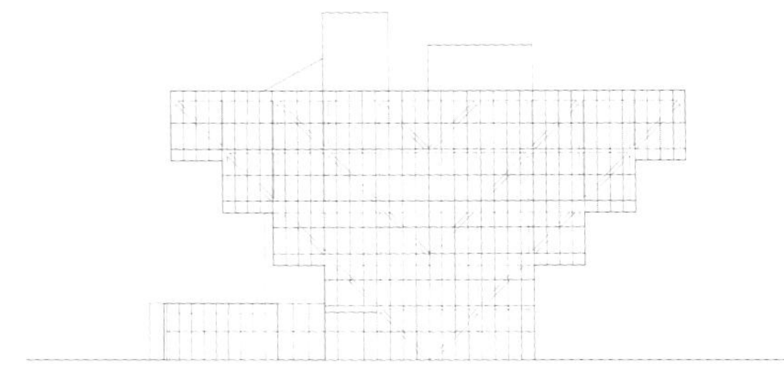

KUMAMOTO-KITA POLICE STATION, 1990
Kumamoto Prefecture

This monumental police station is a vessel for its functions. Shinohara carefully distributes various uses, those having to do with everyday lives of citizens versus others that deal with crime, corresponding to urban conditions of this elongated site. With its inverted ziggurat form, the main elevation does not intend to express police authority, but rather to give the "appearance of a gently floating sense of speed and to allow it to confront the street." Along the long, northern edge the building assumes a more relaxed, humorous form, with an undulating wall along the street and a cylindrical tube toward the top of the building that conceals the air-conditioning units.

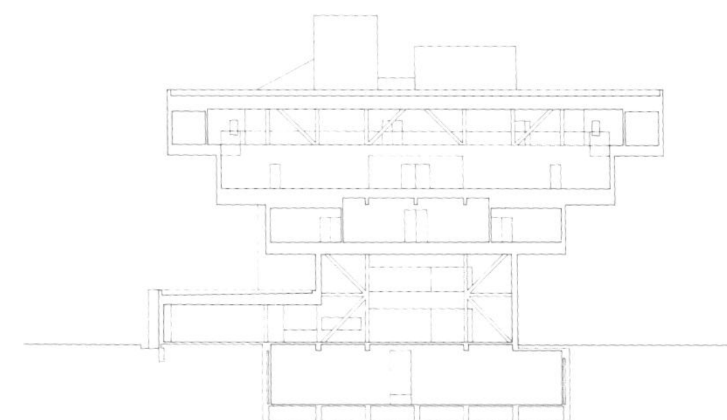

Photos by
Ōhashi Tomio (ŌT)

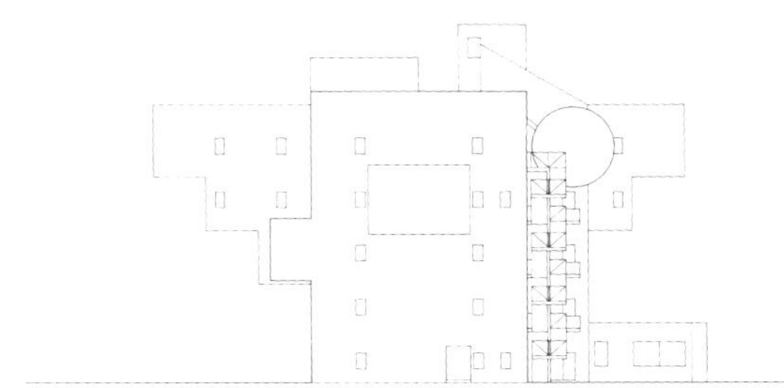

1:800

West elevation.

ÖT

North side.

Shinohara Kazuo, sketch.

View from the east along the north side.

ŌT

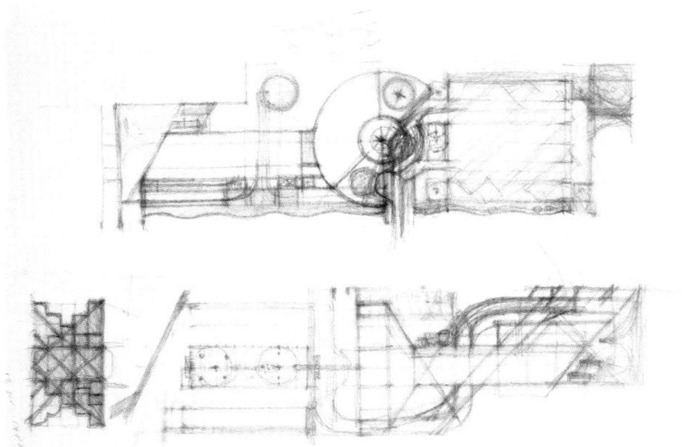

ŌT

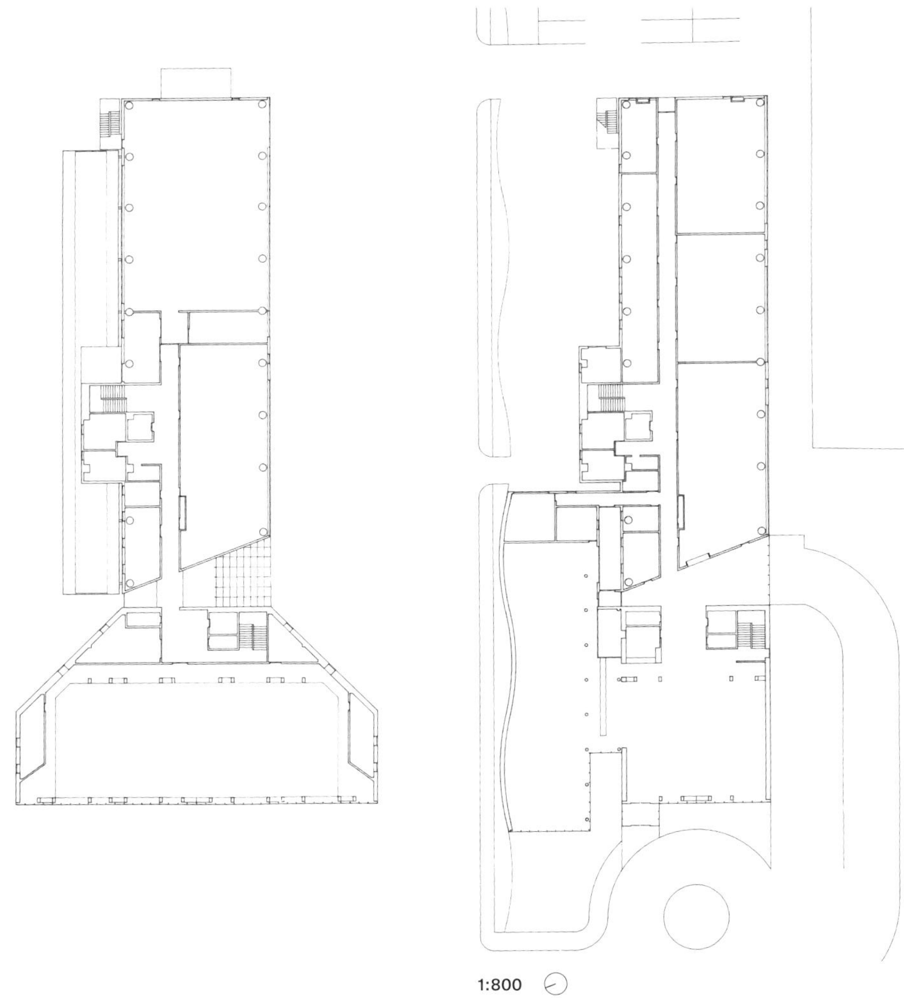

1:800

Dogon village of Banani, Bandiagara Escarpment, Mali, 1988. Photo by Tsukamoto Yoshiharu

Shinohara's Contrasts

Tsukamoto Yoshiharu

"A HOUSE IS A WORK OF ART."

Shinohara Kazuo was an architect that developed his well-honed aesthetic and architectural theory as a cultural criticism on both housing and urban theory through his residential designs. With a series of architectural works and their corresponding manifesto-like texts, he situated his works as developments in his "style," each based on different principles. Yet Shinohara's "era of styles" is marked by various factors such as the economy, the political system, technology, and living, which are not generally thought to be developed by individuals. What is the Shinohara style? This essay will follow Shinohara's styles and examine some common methodologies within their development.

One encountered works by Shinohara, who continued his creative practice with a focus on the house, through magazines. Simultaneously announcing the beginning of a new series and the end of the previous one, he asserted stylistic renewals most effectively in the medium of the architectural magazine. His multiple series of houses and manifestos had a strong influence, continually attracting the interest of many readers. From the 1960s to the 1990s there were many magazines that specialized in architecture, but the one that Shinohara trusted most was *Shinkenchiku,* where his teacher Seike Kiyoshi had once served as editor. Since its founding in the 1920s, *Shinkenchiku* has been devoted to the publication of newly completed architectural works, without pushing the critical agendas of the editors or the practice of special issues. Often issues that presented new government buildings and public museums would also include houses. Yet in 1986, when the *Shinkenchiku jūtaku tokushū* (*Shinkenchiku* residential special issue) spun off into its own monthly title, it featured House in Yokohama by Shinohara Kazuo on its inaugural cover. Shinohara did not welcome this publication split, however. Lesser in both scale and accessibility compared to public architecture and office buildings, houses should still be on the same battlefield as public buildings, challenging them and vice versa. Shinohara told me this when I was a student.

Written twenty years earlier, "A house is a work of art"[1] became one of Shinohara's famous aphorisms. In the background was Japan's regained momentum from the postwar recovery, evident in the turn toward industrialization, scale expansion, and mass organization in the production of architecture in Japan. He soberly observed how a broad social mandate became a prerequisite in the mainstream architectural world, through the building of public facilities in the realization of democracy and houses in the rationalized supply of housing. In this new reality he strove for the recognition that the production of a single house was an artistic practice. Yet there he did not sink into negativity, instead situating residential design as a critique of civilization that "participated in the creation of culture directly dealing with humans (*ningen*) themselves." In "identifying that we are independent of the processes of social production," he inspired us architects involved in residential design—"*freedom* will arise before us." This sense of criticality resonates far, even with the Arts and Crafts movement in which William Morris and others resisted the usurping of *pleasure* from work by industrialization in London at the end of the nineteenth century.

1 Shinohara Kazuo, "Jūtaku wa geijutsu de aru" (A house is a work of art), *Shinkenchiku* vol. 37, no. 5 (May 1962): 77–78.

2 In English the essay appears as Tange Kenzō, "Tradition and Creation in Japanese Architecture," in *Katsura: Tradition and Creation in Japanese Architecture*, ed. Tange Kenzō (New Haven, CT: Yale University Press, 1960), 14–36.

THE TRADITION DEBATE

When Shinohara debuted as an architect in 1954, there was a rising debate in the architecture world, instigated by *Shinkenchiku's* editor Kawazoe Noboru, over tradition. At the time Japan had just regained its independence with the Treaty of San Francisco coming into effect, and reestablishing identity was a big issue. Tracing back the origins of Japan, it is impossible to avoid the differences between the Jōmon period from around 14,000 BCE to the tenth century BCE and the Yayoi period from around the fourth century BCE to the third century CE. The former is a hunting-and-gathering society, and the latter is an agricultural society since the introduction of rice cultivation from the continent; the aesthetic difference between the roughness and forcefulness of the Jōmon and the refinement and gentleness of the Yayoi seen in unearthed pottery and remains had been held in contrast. All that has been confirmed from ruins, however, is that there were pit dwellings in the Jōmon and raised-floor granaries in the Yayoi; the reconstruction of architectural characteristics is something that has been imagined from genealogical investigations of architecture in later periods. The pit dwelling came to be seen as the origins of the *doma,* or earth-floored spaces, at the entrance of *minka* rural commoner houses, and the raised-floor granary evolved into the *shinden*-style residences of the Heian-period aristocracy. This typological framework established the parallel axioms of Jōmon—pit dwelling—*doma* and Yoyoi—raised-floor granary—*shinden.* In this debate over tradition, often with a binary view—Jōmon or Yayoi—Tange Kenzō understood the fundamental principle of the creation of culture in Japan as the conflict between Jōmon, the populist (*minshūteki*), which might be called the manifestation of the people's expressive will, and Yayoi, the dynastic, which might be called the appearance of an awareness of stylistic tradition, and he put great value on Katsura Villa as the convergence of the two lineages.[2] However, his works at that time—Hiroshima Peace Memorial Museum (1952), Tange residence in Seijō (1953), Tokyo Metropolitan Government Building (1957), and Kagawa Prefectural Government Building (1958)—are dominated by structures with raised floors and orthogonal lines, which he was able to call an exemplary interpretation of *shinden* style in the language of modernism. Why did Tange's creative work tend toward the Yayoi? Tange's design theory took architectural practice as the synthesis that sublates the contradiction between the modernist concept of thesis symbolized by public facilities and the industrialized production style, and the antithesis of the experience of Japanese history. Additionally, Tange had a dialectical view of history, seeing that the oppositions between form and expressive will, also between the elites and the masses, are layered on top of the opposition between thesis and antithesis, and sublating at once the contradictions between them it is the synthesis that drives history and marks periods. But, as mentioned above with his valuation of Katsura, due to his conception of Japanese tradition in terms of thesis, antithesis, and synthesis, the Jōmon and Yayoi dialectic in the theorization of tradition theory became subsumed within the modern-Western and Japanese culture dialectic in the theorization of creative work. Namely, Tange's theory of tradition can be said to have internalized the gaze toward Western modernism.

Jikō-in, Yamato-Koriyama, Nara Prefecture, est. 1663. Photo by Seng Kuan

Totsukawa Village, Nara Prefecture. Photo by Shinohara Kazuo

Kusakabe House, Takayama, Gifu Prefecture. Photo by Shinohara Kazuo

Doma at Kusakabe House, Takayama, Gifu Prefecture. Photo by Shinohara Kazuo

THEORY OF JAPANESE TRADITION

Written about five years after this debate over tradition, Shinohara's "Theory of Japanese tradition" (*Nihon dentō ron,* 1960) takes up the representative Japanese architectural heritage, tracing even its social and technological background and pointing out the fact that there were many temporal errors in the contemporary assessments of tradition.[3] For instance, looking at the dark, bleak quality swept by wind and rain in Japanese *wabi, sabi,* or the unique post-and-beam structure anticipating Mondrian, he argued that these were not what was intended by those who established them, rather they stemmed from misunderstandings from the passage of time or contemporary trends. In this way, through the serialized sections on "the methods of Japanese architecture" in this essay on tradition, he shed light on the essential nature of Japanese architecture, while relativizing the impressionistic evaluations of their appearance.[4] The architectural works examined in "the methods" are broad ranging: Izumo Grand Shrine and Shōsō-in (I. "the ancient"); Kyōto Imperial Palace and its main hall Shishin-den (II. "on the raised-floor residence"); Golden Pavilion, Silver Pavilion, Katsura Villa and Jikō-in (III. "the logic of space"); the *minka* in Totsugawa, grand residences of Kamitokikuni, Shimotokikuni, and Kusakabe families, the pit dwelling, and the tea room (V. "in between aristocratic residences and *minka*" and VII. "the irrationality inside the dwelling"). Shinohara's discussion continues by combining a scientific perspective on architectural structure and how things should be, with a perspective on the society and culture that surround them, looking at religious belief and political power, *wabi, sabi,* living as part of nature, irrationality, and so forth. The strongest expression of this is thus on the *doma* of the *minka* in which commoners lived. With the *shinden* lineage at the opposite extreme, he made their contrasting natures clear. Notably, he aimed to understand dwelling and that which surrounds it, as his observations indicate his affinity toward the imagination of cultural anthropology and ethnography:

> Anyone who visits Katsura, pretending to be the aristocratic lord of the estate or someone invited by him, does not see it from the point of view of the attendants who work in the shadows. There is an alienation of perspective, and if viewed from that of the attendant, it would give a different impression. While aristocratic residences are sites to serve upper-class society, which holds power, *minka* are sites for production by commoners. Yet while the massive *doma* of the grand *minka* are sites for production, they are also spaces in which the wealth or political power of a family is revealed.
>
> Having a conceptualized ideology recognized and designed as architecture, aristocratic residences are easy to reproduce without selecting the site. In contrast, being shaped by their connection with daily life, *minka* do not have an ideology, and demonstrate the multifarious differences in locale. *Minka* are "mushrooms." That living sensation cannot be expected from aristocratic residences.
>
> *Minka* arise from the interconnections with the creation of contemporary dwelling under completely different social conditions. They are definitely a method for assembling a space for lively dwelling.

3 The essay was originally published in Japanese as "Residential Theory" ("Jūtakū ron") in the April 1960 issue of *Shinkenchiku*. The new title, "Theory of Japanese Tradition," was used when it was included in the volume of collected essays published as *Jūtaku ron* in 1970 by Kajima shuppankai.

4 These sections of the essay "A Theory of Japanese Tradition" roughly correspond to academic reports Shinohara published in journals of the Architectural Institute of Japan (*Nihon kenchiku gakkai*) in 1957–60.

If the aristocratic residence is an "open space," then *minka* can be contrasted as a "non-open space." They are not "closed spaces" in the sense of Western masonry construction.

These observations conclude in a discerning awareness: "The tradition of this country includes a great number of irrational elements, and even if it has a stagnant aspect, the idea that the creation of the dwelling must begin from that point is one method, an ideology." When seen from the present, the form of the dwelling born from a harsh environment and living at odds with it, the conservative dwelling shaped by this entirety, includes something that can only be called irrationality. However, if one can accept the parts as appropriate to the purposes of those involved, the dwelling can become a means of resistance against the fragmentation of people and society progressing due to the pursuit of contemporary rationality. "The architectural significance of the *minka* is especially in the lived interaction between the human and the dwelling." If "architecture" can be sought in the *minka,* an "architecture" claiming to reinterpret the *minka* must be horrifying.

Positing that the essential nature of Japanese architecture is in various types being created by layering the characters of aristocratic residences and *minka* upon the axis of "open space" and "non-open space" that arises from the contrast with the "closed space" of masonry construction, "Theory of Japanese tradition" does not traverse the contrasts between Western modernism and Japanese tradition or between Jōmon and Yayoi. Namely, by theorizing Japanese tradition without being aligned with Tange's dialectical rhetoric, was Shinohara criticizing the prior debate over tradition, and particularly Tange's dialectical view of history? Compositionally, this essay resembles Claude Lévi-Strauss's contemporary work *The Savage Mind,* which is a critique of the historicist materialism in Jean-Paul Sartre's existentialism.[5] It was a *structural historical* critique.[6] Rather than entering the debate in a timely fashion, he was taking a critical distance from it.

CONTRAST AND ALIGNMENT (MATRIX)

In Shinohara's "Theory of Japanese tradition," not only are the abstract "open" and "non-open" spaces contrasted, but their surroundings are as well. Along with being open, the Katsura Villa is for the upper class, for power, for serving them; along with being non-open, the *minka-doma* is for commoners, for daily life, for production. While it may be somewhat rash, coalescing the commoners, daily life, and production into the "black" of the *doma* covered in smoke and soot, and the upper class, power, and servitude into the "white" of the *hinoki* (Japanese cypress) construction, the discussion until this point can be organized by combining the two contrasts of open and non-open, white and black, to form a two-by-two matrix (Table 1).

	Open	Non-Open
White	Katsura Villa *(shinden)*	
Black		*minka (doma)*

Table 1.1: The First Style: Confronting Japanese traditions

The lineage of *shinden* such as the Katsura Villa is situated as open and white; the lineage of the *minka* and *doma* is situated as non-open and black. Yet the spaces for open and black, and

5 The French original *La Pensée sauvage* was published in 1962. The Japanese translation appeared in 1976, the same year as the House in Uehara: *Yasei no shikō*, trans. Ōhashi Yasuo (Tokyo: Misuzu shobo, 1976).

6 Nakazawa Shinichi, *Rebi-Sutoroosu, yasei no shikō* (Tokyo: NHK shuppan, 2016).

7 As Shinohara states, "My own cubic form appears first as the image of the total outline or profile. When several floor levels are necessary, the floor is treated as being in the same class with the wall surfaces used to partition off the elements of the floor plan. The theme is the expression of the cube not as a process, but as an existence. My cube is not, therefore, the same as that arrived at through purely logical considerations." See Shinohara Kazuo, "Machine and Savagery," trans. Charles S. Terry, in *Shinohara Kazuo 2: 11 no jūtaku to jūtakuron* (Tokyo: Bijutsu shuppankai, 1976), 29.

non-open and white are blank, because there do not seem to be any examples of them. Conversely, if something fits, even something made today, it could be the creation of Japanese tradition at the level of the *minka* or Katsura Villa. Namely, this matrix problematizes the structure that separates aristocratic residences and the *minka-doma* while bringing them closer to each other. For instance, Shinohara states that "the tea room was intentionally pursuing a non-open space." From this claim one can imagine the tea room not as something of the past but as something that is continually generated. Examining Shinohara's work here, the raised-floor-style House in Kugayama could be said to have been his pursuit of the open and white, while the *minka*-like House with an Earthen Floor (1963) and the subterranean House of Earth—Space in Black (1964) reflect his pursuit of the non-open and black. So what about House in White (1966)? In this house, the square plan covered by a pyramidal roof is divided asymmetrically in a 2-to-1 ratio, and the space comprising two-thirds of the ground level with a wooden floor is topped with a 3.7-meter-high ceiling, painted in white along with the walls. But looking at photographs of the interior reveals the windows have shōji screens that shine dimly white; lacking an *engawa,* or veranda, this space cannot be called open. The isolated central column and kitchen also recall *doma.* Yet the stove (*kamado*) is replaced with a gas range, and the room does not become blackened with soot. That is, House in White fits into the empty non-open and white square in the matrix of Japanese traditions.

	Open	Non-Open
White	Katsura Villa *(shinden)*	House in White
Black		*minka-doma*

Table 1. 2: The First Style: Confronting Japanese traditions

The matrix of the aristocratic residence and *minka-doma* seen among Shinohara's work demonstrate that "Japanese tradition" is not singular, but open to possibilities, and includes unexamined possibilities suggested by the empty slot in the matrix. Following this matrix, it is possible for contemporary creative work to be in dialogue with ancient architecture, vernacular architecture, and architectural works of the past, and for a young architect like Shinohara to have attempted "his own" style. The discovery of this synchronous and structuralist matrix may be his First Style, "Confronting Japanese Traditions."

CUBE AND FISSURE

Shinohara dubbed the large white space in House in White "my cube." This definition of cube differs from that of the West in which masonry walls surround and connect with each other, in that it is abstracted inside the whole of beams, columns, and roof articulated with walls and partitions.[7] Accepting the opposed spatial natures of Japan and the West, European modernism comes into Shinohara's creative field by sharing the phenomenon of the cube. Japanese society was at the peak of the High-Growth Era boosted by the Tokyo Olympics and Osaka Expo, and this momentum manifested itself in Metabolism, which did not understand the city as the basis of permanence. This architectural ideology, which originated in Japan, saw the city as the basis of incessant regeneration.

Rather than comparing the culture of adaptable wooden architecture and the state of Japanese cities, un-unified through economic growth and the recoveries from earthquake and war, as inferior to the superior lithic culture and historic cities of the West, Metabolism tried to reinterpret these perceived shortcomings as a superior modifiability aimed toward the future. Its most symbolic model was the replaceable capsules that interact with the individual linked to the semipermanent tower-like core that interacts with urban infrastructure; the contrast between permanence and transience layered onto the contrast between part and whole, architectural space from the scale of the individual to the megalomaniac scale of the city, was emphasized as a unified vision. This was the Japanese version of Ville Radieuse applying European modernism to the opportunity for growth in the Japanese economy. In contrast to this view, arguing that from early on the contemporary Japanese city could not become that radiant city, Shinohara's investigations were directed toward the fundamentals in order to definitively distance Japan from the modernism of the West. Seeking an antithesis to the spatial principle in Japanese architecture of "division," his investigations in his Second Style, expressed as "interpathy (*kōkan*) with Western modernism," searched for a third option that was not the Western architectural principle of "connection." The beginnings of this were in North House in Hanayama (1965) and South House in Hanayama (1968), in their narrow spatial "fissures" trapped between two walls, which were extracted from the form of the corridor gardens (*tōriniwa*) of *machiya.* Instead of connecting cubes as units of space, volumes were organized as outer shells, divided by fissures in the interior, and fitted with facilities for daily life, which became Shinohara's method for ensuring coexistence of the cube and the fissure.

Understanding the fissure as that which presents itself in the contradiction between connection and division sounds like a dialectical move, but reading the contrast overlaid onto the contrast between connection and division—for instance, the dynamic movement of the cubes adjoining one to the next and expanding, to the static frontality of Japanese architecture, or the closed space of cubes evoking a sequential layout, to the open space not aiming to familiarize itself with the neighbor—changes one's impression (Table 2).

Japanese	Western
open	closed
static	dynamic
frontal	movement
division	connection
whole to parts	parts to whole

Table 2: The spatial principles of Japanese and Western architecture

Table 3 puts together two oppositions in a matrix, the opposition between open and closed at the top of Table 2 and the opposition between partition and connection at the bottom.

	Open, Static, Frontal	Closed, Dynamic, Movement
Division	Japanese traditional space (First Style)	cube and fissure (Second Style)
Connection	Western modernism	Western cube

Table 3: The Second Style: Interpathy with European modernism

This matrix situates the discussion up until this point. First, Japanese traditional space accounts for "division," "from whole to parts," "open," "static," and "frontality." His First Style, which includes House in White, belongs here. On the other hand, the cube of Western architecture accounts for "connection," "from parts to whole," "closed," "dynamic," and "movement." The villages and street spaces that Shinohara witnessed in Spainish and North African towns in 1972 belong to this box. Maintaining the functional structure made by the connection of cubes and having released itself from the closed cube through the introduction of concrete post-and-lintel construction, European modernism accounts for "connection," "from parts to whole," and "open." Le Corbusier's Maison Domino is here. The remaining blank slot, corresponding to "division," "from whole to parts," "closed," "dynamic," and "movement," becomes filled by the Second Style concept "cube and fissure." With two parallel walls that divide the ground plane and the floor that divides the remainder in cross-section, penetrating the center of the concrete shell that is the cube, The Uncompleted House (1970) belongs here. The traversing shown in the matrix from closed to open, from the cube of Western architecture to European modernism, and from Japanese tradition (First Style) to "cube and fissure" (Second Style), appears as if it is a mirror inversion of parallel dimensions. This framework is perhaps the core of the "interpathy with European modernism" in Shinohara's Second Style.

EQUIVALATING THE HOUSE WITH THE CITY

The fissured space without facilities for daily life carried a complex and ambiguous character, like the feeling of being outdoors despite being inside, like street spaces of the city intruded into the house. This character differs from straightforward inside and outside when making buildings; it is something that arises from an intervention into the extracted contrast between the house and the city as a principle of architectural space. With The Uncompleted House as a turning point, as if there had been some awakening, residential works that radicalized the contrast between inside and outside, came to vivify Japanese architecture journals. Seminal works of the next generation, such as White U by Itō Toyoo and Machiya in Daita by Sakamoto Kazunari, and Row House in Sumiyoshi by Andō Tadao were clustered in 1976 in particular. The spatial structure of these residences would not have emerged without traversing the formal imagination led by the contrast between inside and outside. Yet Shinohara, who was the pioneer of abstract spatial expression in the house, had not pursued "inside and outside." Focusing on the expression of interior space, he therein synthesized the whole (cube) and the parts (facilities for daily life) with the fissure. In Shinohara's lab at the Tokyo Institute of Technology research was conducted on villages and castle towns, under the communal hypothesis that the particularities of village structure (the whole) appeared in the relationship between the roads that traverse it (fissures) and the individual building (the parts). In the residential interior, the village and the castle town, the quantitative repetition of the parts and their arranged order were investigated. However, it does not mean these differences in scale are insignificant, nor does it signify that the quantitative space of unlimited expansion and sequentiality would lead to a coherent urban plan. Shinohara's "parts and the whole" was an attempt to point out that the same struc-

8 Kutsuki Yoshitsuna, "Arudo Fan Aiku no kenchiku shisō ni okeru 'tai-genshō' no gainen ni tsuite: Dogon shūraku ni kansuru ronkō wo toshite," (A study on the concept of "Twin Phenomena" in Aldo van Eyck's architectural thought: through his treatises on the Dogon villages), *Nihon kenchiku gakkai keikakukei ronbunshū* vol. 70, no. 596 (2005): 191–98.

ture was hidden in each residential interior, the village and 4the castle town. This effort makes possible the equivalation (*dōichishi*) of the house with the city.

Shinohara's structure and equivalation schema also appeared in the ideas of Aldo van Eyck, a member of Team 10, which led the 1959 meeting of the International Congresses for Modern Architecture (CIAM). This representative figure of Dutch structuralism demonstrated regret over modernism through his interest in architecture of primitive societies. Not content with merely reading field reports from traversing through the center of Africa by the likes of anthropologist Marcel Griaule in the early 1930s, he journeyed to the villages of the Dogon people in 1960. Provoked by Bernard Rudofsky's *Architecture Without Architects,* I too traveled as a student to West Africa when I was living in Paris, but my main destination was the Dogon villages. Griaule's *Dieu d'Eau,* which I read at the time, points out that the Dogon houses, villages, and even the earth in their creation myths are all modeled after the human body. From this view, Van Eyke deciphered the reciprocity from parts to whole and from whole to parts. At each step, while each is "a complete or separate entity," the world itself extends across their material embodiments of each step. Namely, integrity is implied by the parts. Van Eyke understood this as connecting with the equivalation of the house with the city. He also noted the fact that "twin" phenomena, such as up and down, twins, the two sexes, and heaven and earth, extend across the entirety of the Dogon cosmology at every stage: house, village, region, myth, and so forth. That at the Otterlo meeting Van Eyke supported a universal way of humanity common across differences in area, and period was linked to various contrary values, such as "part and whole, uniformity and diversity, inside and outside, open and closed, density and vacancy, permanence and change, individual and collective," namely that they are "twin phenomena" (at the time "dual phenomena"), and criticized that modern architecture and urban planning tear apart and pervert them into absolute (yet meaningless) halves.[8] Transcending region and academic field, the contemporary intellectual framework was being renewed.

THE SAVAGE MACHINE

What marks the end of Shinohara's Second Style, which set up the equivalation of the house with the city, with the contrast of "the parts and the whole," was House in Higashi-Tamagawa (1973). The fissure breaking up the symmetry of the arranged order creates a "street" inside the house in which the cubes compete. This spectacle exhibited a beauty and vitality similar to the streetscapes of cubes he witnessed in Spanish and North African towns. The space of this fissure can be described as the "exterior street spaces of the city intruding into the interior of the house," but it is through metaphorically understanding this case as the relationship between house and city as a contrast between inside and outside. However, this feeling of order is proximate both technologically and socially to the connections between cubes in the village of simpler times. For Shinohara, who had been stating that "the contemporary huge village (*gendai no shūraku*)" cannot express anything but the "beauty of chaos" since the 1960s, this view did not mean that the chaos of the city surrounding one had emerged in the house, or that the house and the city had been equivalated. Observing the changing

Dogon village of Banani, Bandiagara Escarpment, Mali. Photo by Tsukamoto Yoshiharu

A toguna, Mali. Photo by Tsukamoto Yoshiharu

glow of top lights inside the very space of the fissure, Shinohara drew out a contrast between certainty and uncertainty. Here, positing certainty as the system of architectural technology and uncertainty as the system of the things of the city and the surrounding environment, the collision between the two can in principle hold the same structure as the chaos of the contemporary city. Additionally, it seals the contrast between inside and outside into an easy metaphorical expression of the issue on family, community, and the relationship between house and city. Shinohara dubbing this concept the "savage machine" resonates with Gilles Deleuze's *"la machine littéraire"* in describing Marcel Proust's *In Search of Lost Time.*[9] What the "literary machine" makes clear is that, while in the traditional narrative the relation with language is governed by the narrative's meaning, the links with words in the novel, in which what will appear next is uncertain, do not necessarily have uniformity. Conversely, in an ordinary machine, the links between parts are governed by their contribution toward a purpose, and the possibility of any other links is suppressed.

Looking at Shinohara's Second Style from this perspective, strong coherence can certainly be discerned in the cube of the shell of the entire house, giving the space of the initial fissures strong symmetry, and so on. That which can critically surpass this Second Style is the "gaze toward the city" of the Third Style. Its methodology forms an opposition between the "certainty" of the materialistic system of architectural technology and the heterogeneous system of the things of the city that surround it, retaining the "gap" between them and joining it without mediation. The composition of Tanikawa House (1974) is an assemblage of "naked things," abruptly joining a geometric frame delineated by the 45-degree roof, vertical columns, and 45-degree supports, with the dirt incline, which lacks initially coherent meaning. Shinohara explains that when this space is freely traversed by someone, an interaction occurs, and diverse meanings are created that the architect did not arrange. At House in Uehara (1976), the concrete outer shell and the terminus of urban transportation that is the parking lot are bound together inside of the property, which is restricted in the dense residential district. The gap between the two appears on the second floor where the concrete braces supporting the cantilevering of the outer shell are scattered about. Moreover, after construction began a children's room was added to the program, resolved by annexing onto the roof a steel-frame vault space distinguished from the main structure; this addition amplified the gap such that Shinohara described it as "anarchic." In House in Ashitaka (1977), covered by a hipped roof made of folded concrete slabs, alternating shape-shifting light and shadow are projected onto the floor surface of the interior. House under High-Voltage Lines (1981) joins together the technological system of electrical transmission of two high-voltage power lines that traverse the sky above the property with the concrete post-and-lintel structure. Within the cylinders, hollowed out with the residual shell from the top by the invisible cylindrical pillars formed by the isolating distance from the high-voltage power lines, appear concrete beams warped into incongruous shapes. This deformation is not treated like a shell with the curvature upturned, intruding the interior, perhaps intending not to fit it into a recognizable category of concrete (such as the shell structure). Being a post-and-lintel frame that

9 Gilles Deleuze, *Marcel Proust et les signes* (Paris: Presses Universitaires de France, 1964).

		Uncertainty, Urban Things				
		Earth's Slope	Electricity Grid	Automobile	Sun	...
Certainty, Architectural Tectonics	Timber-frame, 45-degree roof	Tanikawa House				...
	Reinforced concrete, rigid-frame	House in Hanayama No. 4	House under High-Voltage Lines	House in Uehara		...
	Reinforced concrete, 45-degree roof				House in Ashitaka	...

Table 4:. The Third Style: Gaze toward the contemporary city

normally follows the geometry of orthogonal coordinates, the deformation appears in the spaces of the house as a clear gap (Table 4).

Shinohara's First and Second Styles situated Japanese traditional architecture and modernist architecture respectively within the matrix completed by multiple contrasting phenomena, and as if walking freely among them despite being off limits, reliving the principles of architecture and cities of the past, found blank spaces in the matrix, and turned them into creative points of departure. In contrast to this binary schema, in the Third Style, the opposition between the architectural system and that of urban things continually overlaps with the opposition between certainty and uncertainty. Because uncertainty is open to the constantly changing contemporary city, that contrast cannot lose its validity. For this reason, each work is unique, and Shinohara called each "a series of one." Until the Second Style, the environment surrounding the works had not been so actively contextualized. But Shinohara's joining of the house and the city does not signify the serialization of the house and city within the spatial equivalation made scalable by standardization. It is rather the joining of the differing systems, elements of the scalable city with the non-scalable and non-standardizable house.

CHAOS

Overly pursuing the determination of the origins of architecture, much architectural theory seeks a purified form, uncontaminated by the various things surrounding architecture. However, contrary to this pursuit, Shinohara's Third Style is an investigation of the hybridity of architecture that might awaken the extraordinary within the ordinary by being actively contaminated by the things of the city. This methodological restoration of contaminations that occur axiomatically is not a closed system; many possibilities are opened up, and one cannot traverse these possibilities. There are blanks still remaining in the matrix in Table 4, and though it is not as if there were significance in filling them, it does not necessarily mean that one will repeatedly encounter dramatic things that might increase its horizontal axis. Partially with an attitude of giving up on the initiative, how did Shinohara feel about this? Did he feel a freedom different from that he had gotten in his First and Second Styles?

10 English translation published as Shinohara Kazuo, "Towards Architecture," *The Japan Architect*, no. 293 (September 1981): 30–35.

The words "savage," "naked things," and "gap," which were repeated throughout the Third Style, followed his ruminations on the "machine." What Shinohara was pursuing was to allow for the emergence of a device that could read diverse meanings by giving a coupling mechanism to the compositional elements initially not made to sustain a purpose for transmission. The gap is a type of binding mechanism, and the collection of the naked things that support them becomes a production device, namely a machine.

In "Towards Architecture" of 1981, the American F-14 fighter jet is mentioned as a machine and its parts contrasted with the 1920s ocean liner, which is governed by its streamlined whole.[10] With the F-14, the parts maximize required functionality, and its materialistic joining maximizes the functionality of the machine as a whole. It is a "zero-degree machine" whose elements are connected to one another irrespective of aesthetic adjustments. This contrast is a position similar to Roland Barthes's literary criticism that situated Albert Camus's novels as the *"degré zéro de l'écriture"* with respect to the heavily ornamented écriture of existing literature beginning with classicism. Through this analogies of the F-14 and the ocean liner to architecture, Shinohara is invoking Le Corbusier's Ville Radieuse and juxtaposing it with Shibuya Scramble Crossing of 1980. By doing so, in contrast to the unitary order of modern urban planning that forces the parts to serve toward coherence as a whole, this logic revealed the contemporary city in which appears the incoherence of the series of its parts, the "beauty of chaos" of Tokyo. In fact, while paying respect to Le Corbusier's machine of the 1920s, architecture and urban traversing, Shinohara dared to take on the machine, architecture, and urban traversing in the Tokyo of 1980. This is the Fourth Style, "ModernNext."

On the one hand, if the binding mechanism of the 1920s is a coherence converging into a singular value, the binding mechanism of the 1980s becomes a discrete, incoherent *gap.* On the other hand, the fact that through the Second Style the house and city could be equivalated, and through the Third Style the house (architecture) and machine could be equivalated has already been established. "Since I can now consider architecture and the city simultaneously, and chaos and the machine are interchangeable, it follows that 'urban machine' and 'architectural chaos' are also established" ("ModernNext" 1988, translation of full text published in this volume). The Fourth Style equivalates the machine, architecture, and the city under the commonality of the joining of the parts. With this as a horizontal axis, a matrix can be made with the contrast between coherence and incoherence on the vertical axis, to form Table 5, which plots the examples given until this point.

	Connection of Parts		
	Machine	*Architecture*	*City*
Contraction, Coherence	*Ocean liner*	*Modern architecture*	*Ville Radieuse*
Discrete, Incoherence	*F-14 fighter jet "zero-degree machine"*	*Centennial Hall at Tokyo Tech*	*Shibuya, "Beauty of Chaos"*

Table 5: The Fourth Style: ModernNext

The question is whether something fits into the blank intersection of "incoherence" and "architecture." The Third Style discussed above created a *gap* by actively being contaminated by the things of the city. In contrast, in the Fourth Style, the *gap* was formalized as a binding mechanism with Shinohara's effort to establish it as a new principle for architecture. What created the opportunity for this was the "floating cylinder." It attempted to draw something from the sky and transformed ordinary elements into the unfamiliar, such as the walls and columns that connected it with the ground. The floating cylinder appeared in the House in Yokohama, Centennial Hall at Tokyo Institute of Technology, and Repeating Crevice Annex, and developed into forms detached from the ground in the Agadir Convention Center competition proposal, the Euralille hotel project, the Helsinki Museum of Contemporary Art competition proposal, and the Yokohama International Passenger Ship Terminal competition proposal. I recall the time I was shown the model for Agadir in Shinohara's atelier and was taken aback, having gotten the impression that it was not sitting on the ground line but on the skyline. What was this floating cylinder? Was it a reversal of the truth and falseness of the architectural limits around the high-voltage power lines in the Third Style? Perhaps it is the opposite of the *minka,* which Shinohara saw as mushrooms fruiting from fungal growth in the ground, but something that is articulated in the sky like imaginary numbers that exist only in the mind? Like the operation of complex numbers, real numbers, and imaginary numbers, the architectural form incorporating the impossible to intersect Shinohara called "progressive anarchy."

Shinohara's CONTRASTS

The foregoing is a review of Shinohara's contrasts developed along his changes in style. Shinohara dubbed his First Style "My Tradition," which, amid the discussion of Japanese identity coming to terms with modernity through the two contrasts of Western modernism/Japanese tradition and Jōmon/Yayoi (as if to hide in the Japanese traditional interior spaces), he extracted the two contrasts of *open/non-open* and *white/black*, and discovered uninvestigated territory within the Japanese architectural tradition. Amid the Metabolist discussion of the bright future made by technology and economic growth through the two contrasts that part/whole and *static/dynamic,* his Second Style extracted the two contrasts of open-frontality/closed-movement from the differences in the compositional principles of architecture between Japan and the West, situating Western modernism as a traversing inside those pairings, and ran his own modernism alongside it as a traversing that did not mix with it. Amid the discussion over securing residential space in response to the degradation of the residential environment, due to pollution and excessive construction from urbanization, through the contrast of inside/outside, his Third Style created various hybrids from the pairings of "certainty, architectural tectonics" and "uncertainty–urban things," focusing on the openness of meaning (wholeness) through the joining of its parts.

As the beauty of the chaos of Tokyo began to be accepted positively and the modernism that imagined from the *machine-à-habiter* to the agglomeration of them in the Ville Radieuse as a coherent order began to be questioned, the Fourth Style situated the traversal of the 1920s and of contemporary Tokyo,

11 Shinohara Kazuo, "Kūkan no shisō to kōzō: toshiron to jūtakuron no aida ni," *Shinkenchiku* vol. 42, no. 1 (January 1967): 115–18.

which equivalated machine, architecture, and city as a joining of parts with the contrast coherence/incoherence.

Developed through renewals of style, Shinohara's contrasts were selected to close off contrasts that would lead to the understanding of common things and ideas in society. Being the root of language for discussing architecture and the city, the parts/whole and inside/outside contrasts were particularly rigorous. As for *parts/whole,* the ideas that try to designate the parts and the whole to the same phase as pure addition were suppressed. In understanding the city from the house without any discontinuity one must conceive quantifiable space cohered by standardization as something that can be rearranged in any which way, like understanding from the individual to the state within a uniform space. Shinohara criticized this conception and formulated the parts and the whole as independent phases, the joining of which would be a collision.

With respect to inside/outside, the ideas that try to connect inside and outside within the same phase were suppressed. Where thresholds were subdivided, stratified, and ambiguated, such as in the case of the "outside of the inside" or "inside of the outside," this contrast thoroughly delineated the restoration of the coherence of inside and outside, and conversely, where they were being enforced, it delineated the assurance of the certainty of the inside through isolation from the uncertainty of the outside. Each is a clear expression of an attitude against the contradictions created by modern society; while greatly familiar with sociological themes such as family, community, ethnicity, and gender, Shinohara did not align himself with them. In the contrast interior/exterior, the unconscious center of balance was placed within that which architectural design can directly have a hand in, controlled by a one-point-perspective line of sight aimed from the inside outward. This is because "the array of innumerable mathematical functions of the city" cannot be comprehended without avoiding that.[11]

Shinohara's styles can be called matrices of architectural expression set within the relations between architecture of the past and the present state of the city, or explorations of unexamined areas therein, or even traversals thereof. He arrived at a structure that could equivalate machine, architecture, and city, by first forming a structure confronting Japanese traditional architecture, next adding to that a structure interpathetic with the principles of Western architecture, and finally traversing a structure actively incorporating the collisions between the things of the city that compose contemporary society. By gradually layering mathematical functions, toward understanding complexity as complexity, he continually rearranged these structures. Some might say that it would have been practically impossible and meaningless to have followed his footsteps toward the fifth style that he had predicted. However, now as the social system is wavering from its fundamental premises due to the new climate and the COVID-19 pandemic, criticizing the rhetoric to which the social system conforms, Shinohara's styles, reverberating through his works and discourse, are being rediscovered and will surely inspire architectural practice hereafter.

Translated by Álex Bueno

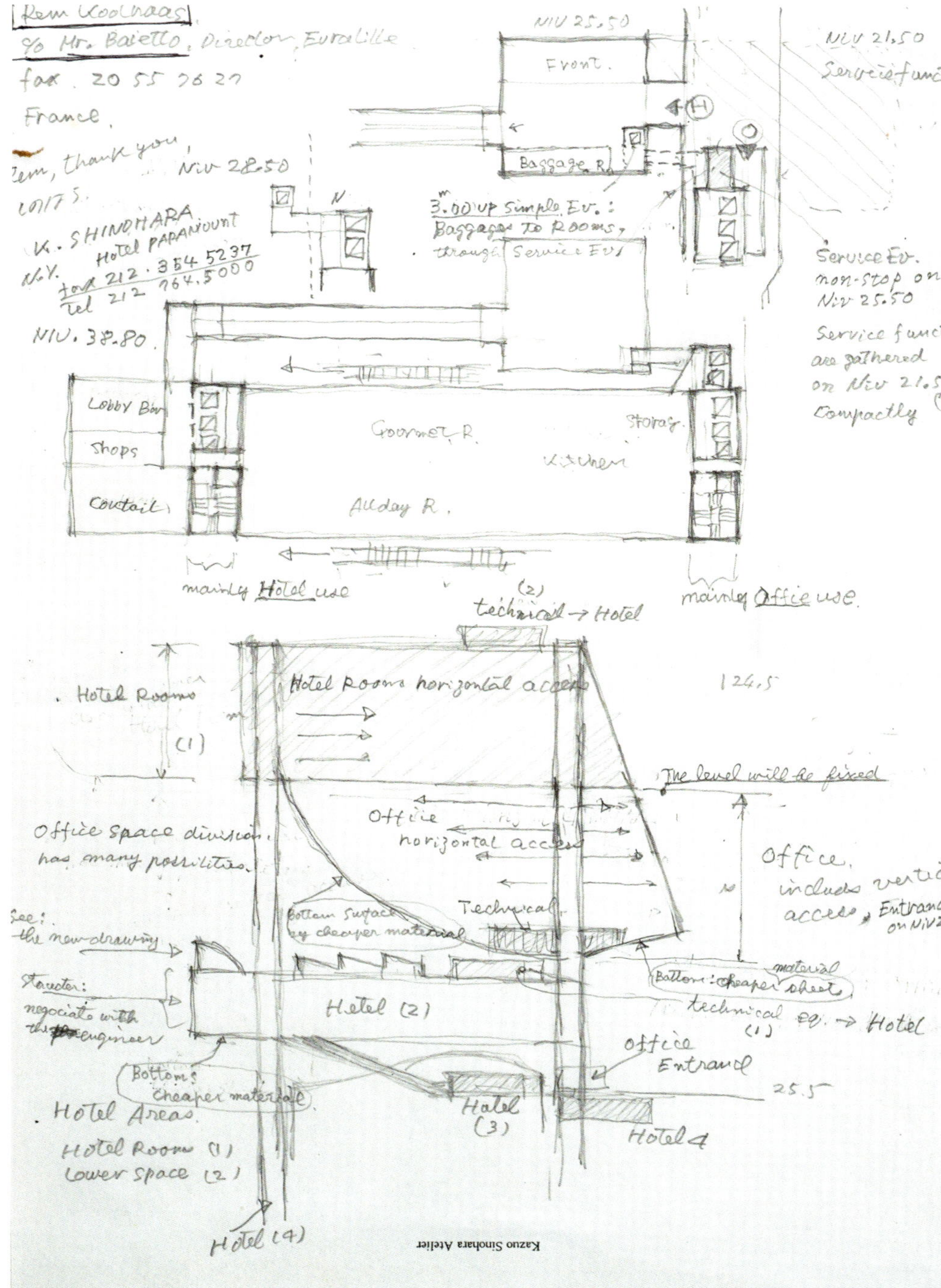

Shinohara Kazuo, memo to Rem Koolhaas on the second iteration of the Euralille hotel project, undated (ca. 1990).

"Beautiful architecture is smaller than you think and bigger than you expect at the same time."

Interview with Rem Koolhaas

by Seng Kuan

Begun in 1989, Euralille was a massive public works and urban programming project to reinvent Lille's railway station area, precipitated by a new high-speed rail system placing Lille at the crossroads between Belgium, Britain, and France. Led by Rem Koolhaas, the Office of Metropolitan Architecture (OMA) was commissioned with the master plan. In turn, OMA invited Shinohara Kazuo to design a hotel complex directly above the railway station.

By the late 1980s Lille was well on its way to postindustrial decline, and the matter-of-fact, *machine*-based location of the hotel site above the railway tracks must have appealed to Shinohara. For Koolhaas, the idea of the program had become abstract, decoupled from the site or city, but floating in a radically new geographic and cultural territory. The hotel project would have been an extraordinary opportunity to put to test Shinohara's confrontation between architecture and the city.

SEPTEMBER 28, 2019, IN TOKYO

SENG KUAN To get things started, let's go through some of the basics. For Shinohara the Euralille project started in '89–'90 and went on until '92. There were a couple of exhibitions in Paris, I think, related to it. One was *Architecture and Utopia*. When did you first meet Shinohara? What first brought you to Shinohara? What was the first building by Shinohara that you saw?

REM KOOLHAAS I came to Japan for the first time in 1987. At that same time, I met Itō Toyoo and went to play pachinko with him and won the bank. There was one building I really wanted to see and that was Centennial Hall. So on that same visit I went to see it. There is a chance that I met Shinohara on that trip, but I am not sure. After going back to Europe, I was already involved in the Euralille project, and I was profoundly moved by Centennial Hall because I thought it was the first of a new kind of building that dared to be completely arbitrary and that didn't need any kind of reasoning to establish itself. I thought that in that particular case it was also very compelling. So when I had an opportunity in Euralille to name architects for some of the major pieces of the overall competition, I contacted him. First, of course, I had to convince the French because he was not a familiar name. The client actually took my suggestion seriously and agreed that we should contact him. After we did that, I met him a number of times in Tokyo. He also came to France and I believe also to the Netherlands.

Then started a long process, which was complicated because the cost of the entire operation for us, but also for all the other architects who were participating, was very low. And that low budget was actually part of the entire argument because only if we could all collectively make sure that the investment was not outrageous would the overall project be able to impose its logic. It was very complex, doubly complex, because the conditions were technically complicated, the building had to be realized over a railway station, so there was a slight contradiction in that. But Shinohara really heroically wrestled with those issues and actually seemed to be extremely, almost, fanatical in trying to realize the building. That created a real intimacy between the two of us because I really tried to help him wherever I could. We mentioned engineers and I think that he worked with our engineers. We had two versions that we'd really loved and we'd thought should happen, but then in the end we could not make it work or the developer could not make it work, so the project was postponed. After the postponement there was a political shift, things changed, there was a new mayor... the support for the entire effort was diminishing, so that's how it happened. But in those periods, particularly in the periods in Tokyo, Shinohara took me to some of his buildings. The one I remember the most, the house in Tokyo, over a garage, with a big concrete...

KUAN House in Uehara, the forest of concrete columns.

KOOLHAAS Yes, there is a forest where a big concrete V runs through the living room.

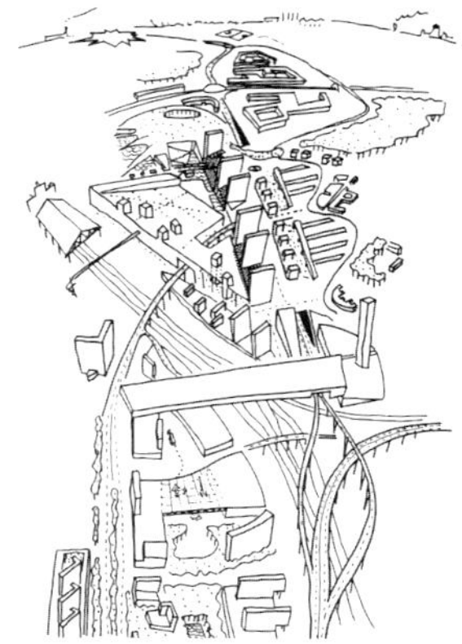

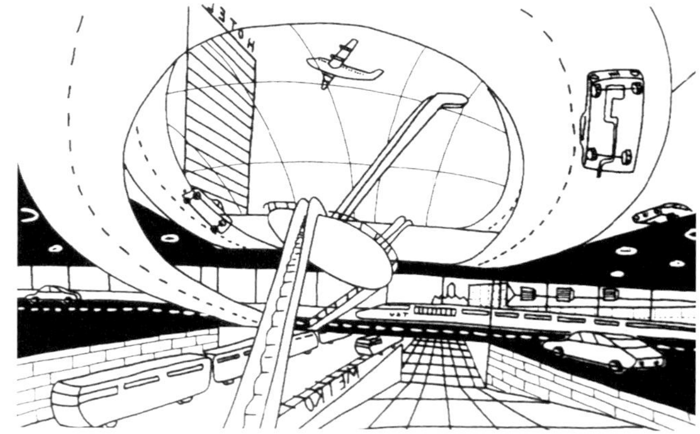

KUAN It was built originally as a forest and then the middle slab was inserted afterward as something hanging, so that verticality became emasculated.

KOOLHAAS I didn't realize that at the time, and this is the first time I have heard it. I was actually mystified, I never understood what happened because that building with forest was the opposite of what I saw. But in reality, what I saw was also extremely impressive, maybe even more so because there was this very oppressive ceiling, and the effort to keep this ceiling up with this massive V seemed to be completely mismatched. That was even more compelling because it was very clear that the couple that lived there, for a very long time, established a routine, where the man always passed the V on one side and the woman on the other side, it seemed as if their bodies were asymmetrical in the opposite direction because of that. It was also obvious that between Shinohara and them existed an exceptional relationship, an interesting one also to observe, how certain people can actually love, completely absorb the implications of a very strong architecture. Particularly in a private house, that is an exceptional thing.

I remember when he took me to Yokohama, to his house there. It was also very impressive. And a one-of-a-kind detail I remember from Shinohara, apart from his face, was his refined way of dressing, very colorful. He always had an amazing raincoat, corduroy pants, and shirts, and jacket. They were orange, pink, bottle green, and always intense colors. Somehow it was really exciting in itself to see somebody who was clothed outside the realm of architecture.

In retrospect, what strikes me most is that kind of arbitrariness—which I really admired in Centennial Hall because of the incredible conviction and the unbelievable scale of the entire project, it was not small and not big. I always think that beautiful architecture is smaller than you think and bigger than you expect at the same time.

KUAN That is a very poignant observation. I understand exactly what you mean.

KOOLHAAS If you look at that type of architecture, it is not big and therefore not monumental. If you look again now, those buildings were influenced and maybe to some extent triggered, but later became completely exacerbated by the market economy and by neoliberalism, a kind of star architecture. And so, what was initially deeply moving about the arbitrariness, twenty years later became almost obscene and almost disgusting in terms of generations that built one arbitrary or absurd thing after another. In that sense, if you look at the Euralille project, particularly the one that is in two parts, which I think is truly amazing, you notice that it has a power and a conviction that is totally missing from any of those architectures today.

KUAN Maybe this is a way to answer my next question. There appears to be some degree of contradiction in terms of context between Centennial Hall and your Euralille? Because Centennial Hall as an emblematic project of his Fourth Style of the idea of ModernNext, very much born out of his idea, of his reading of Tokyo as this massive chaotic city, but at the same time, of course, your Euralille is born of a master plan—your master plan—and it was driven so intensely by massive infrastructure, by this pretense of functionality, at the same time this issue of arbitrariness, and this, let's say, this medium scale, in-between scale of monumentality, maybe as a way to address this contradiction.

KOOLHAAS Well I don't think I could work on it, and particularly on that second version. Actually, the project was intended to be anti-contextual, in the sense that it really openly confronted two realities, and two scales, two mentalities and two worlds, it depended on its kind of beauty to embrace that openly. Nevertheless, it was seriously perceptive in terms of the other elements that were there. There was the park in front, there were also the remnants of a castle, or fortifications by Vauban,[1] and that was really very significant for him as he knew Vauban's work. I think that no architect's gut rhetoric in the last

Office for Metropolitan Architecture, Euralille Master Plan, 1989–94. Images courtesy of OMA

Albert Laprade, Cité Administrative (phase I), Lille, France, 1955. Photo by Velvet (Wikipedia Commons)

thirty years has been precise in terms of context, not a single architect who claims to be contextual has been contextual, and most of the architects who claim to be anti-contextual were maybe the best and most contextual, with perhaps most refined analyses of an existing situation. In other words, you can be anti-contextual and still analyze and comprehend the situation very well.

KUAN I can see what you mean.

KOOLHAAS And anti-contextual can also be a true incident. At the time, I was still planning to write a book about Tokyo, I was deeply influenced by this chaotic reading of Tokyo. In parallel, I became aware that it was not enough as a position, and that one had to think about it thoroughly. At some point—I talked about it maybe in *S,M,L,XL*— I thought that an architect, whether they want to or not, are doomed to adopt a position of planning even though it will be futile. That was an evolving situation I found. And in that sense, the figure of Shinohara and his writing was also important for me.

KUAN Maybe we can also talk a little about the thinness of Shinohara's hotel project at Euralille. The primary program is a hotel; it stretches over the railway tracks, so the thinness of the plan, the thinness of the building obviously is a clear response to this condition. But I have to wonder if it became a very deliberate stylized gesture to express something, that became a very powerful motif for him and for many other architects from Euralille going forward.

KOOLHAAS It had to do with the city, Lille is an interesting city because it had never been a luxurious city or rich city, so that meant that everything there had to have an inherent soberness; there were many prototypes of very thin buildings in the city. The Cité Administrative, which faces the Lille Grand Palais [now Zenith Arena],[2] was a beautiful building. Any architect who saw it was immediately struck because it's probably from the mid-twentieth century, a slab out of brick that had an incredible presence. The thinness there was really noticeable, and that was one of the elements that Shinohara also picked up. Of course, thinness is the essence of a slab, and so to some extent, because of the situation, the slab was the only option.

KUAN I see. Well, we covered a lot of ground very quickly. Thank you. Maybe we can talk a little bit about the context of Japanese architects in Europe in that moment, in the late 1980s. Many architects, like Andō [Tadao] and Itō [Toyoo] and certainly Isozaki [Arata] by that point, had established themselves outside of Japan, but that was primarily something that was happening in the United States through IAUS [Institute for Architecture and Urban Studies] and others. But Shinohara was somewhat of a unique figure. I think IAUS had recognized him; there was an exhibition and a catalogue from IAUS on Shinohara, but he became much more of a fixture in the European context in the late '80s than anywhere else, even Japan. So, I wonder if you could say something about his particular, if there is something to his architecture, to his personality, that made him, in a sense...

KOOLHAAS Suitable...

KUAN Yes, suitable for that environment.

KOOLHAAS I would say his architecture was the opposite of suitable; maybe that was intriguing in itself. It seemed deeply opaque and deeply incomprehensible and that was fascinating in his houses. I understood, also later, that what explains why the Japanese house is so amazing, is maybe one very simple thing, that all the furniture in a Japanese house is kind of childish, never designed as furniture and never really designed as a presence. If you look at the furniture of Sejima [Kazuyo] or Itō, it is always as if a child had drawn it, tripods never four legs.... If I imagine the same mentality in my houses they would also be kind of Japanese, because you never even see a table, or it's always purely architecture with a few dark presences that look almost like

children's drawings. The main way in which people can then look at Japanese architecture was through its mysterious quality, an inaccessible quality almost. And that was what was so heroic about Shinohara.... From that world of complete mystery, maybe mystification, in a European situation, which was really hardcore, a situation where the developer and money were almost the dominant actors, he was really able to do something really refined, without any preparation, and which nevertheless was different and very new for him.

KUAN There's one more project I wanted to show you; I don't know if I included the photograph. His very first competition abroad was for the DOM headquarters in Cologne in '81, and it struck me as something very reminiscent of Superstudio. It's like a suspension bridge with two piers and then this very large, hovering suspended horizontal slab, and everything is covered in mirrored glass. It reminded me of Superstudio, anyway. But I guess if you met him first in '85 or '87 that wouldn't have registered, but ...

KOOLHAAS When was he born?

KUAN 1925, so by '81 he would be 56.

KOOLHAAS So when I knew him he was 62 and I was 33. I was surprised from the very beginning that he didn't treat me as a junior, instead we were equal; he was always interested in having a conversation. I don't know what that could be based on, because I have no idea if he knew my book about New York.[3] But he probably knew that I was writing a book about cities and that he was influential with his idea of Tokyo....

I am wondering, in retrospect, whether that exposure to architecture in Japan, not only to Shinohara, but also to Isozaki, and Japanese dimensions, was not actually of critical influence in my own houses, nobody has ever made that connection. Because, during the same period I was working on the Villa Dall' Ava, it had been debated in French courts for several years, so it was half built and it was an amazing sort of concrete butterfly, so it stayed in that really brutal concrete aspect. I think that Shinohara and I went to see it together.

KUAN Shinohara showed a picture of Villa Dall'Ava in an essay he wrote in the early 1990s.[4]

KOOLHAAS In '87 I also met Taki [Kōji]; we became very close. He was exceptionally generous in spending time explaining a lot of conditions. That may have even been one of the reasons that I invited Shinohara. It could be, now that I think about it. Taki for me was a much better interpreter than anyone related to America.

KUAN But to expand beyond Shinohara and Lille to the broader context of Japanese activities in the late 1980s, when people like Sejima and Kuma were really starting to emerge, in this very late phase of the Japanese Bubble period. I think that's a critical moment. When this new generation engaged with the international scene, much more so than in Isozaki's time with IAUS and New York; it's a different level of engagement.

KOOLHAAS Do you agree that Centennial Hall was one of the first moments of that "arbitrariness," or were there earlier ones?

KUAN In the exhibition [at Harvard on Shinohara], I think we tried to make an argument that there is this, perhaps not arbitrariness, but this ambition to be confrontational, or at least to be controversial, from the very beginning, from the 1950s onward. But the urban context of Tokyo changed so dramatically in the late '70s, and these journeys to Africa and elsewhere ... and also readings of European critical theory in that period, I think gave him some justification, or the desire to impose this arbitrariness.

Office for Metropolitan Architecture, Villa dall'Ava, Paris, 1991. Photo by Hans Werlemann, © OMA

Shinohara Kazuo Atelier, second iteration of Euralille hotel project (ca. 1990), elevation drawing.

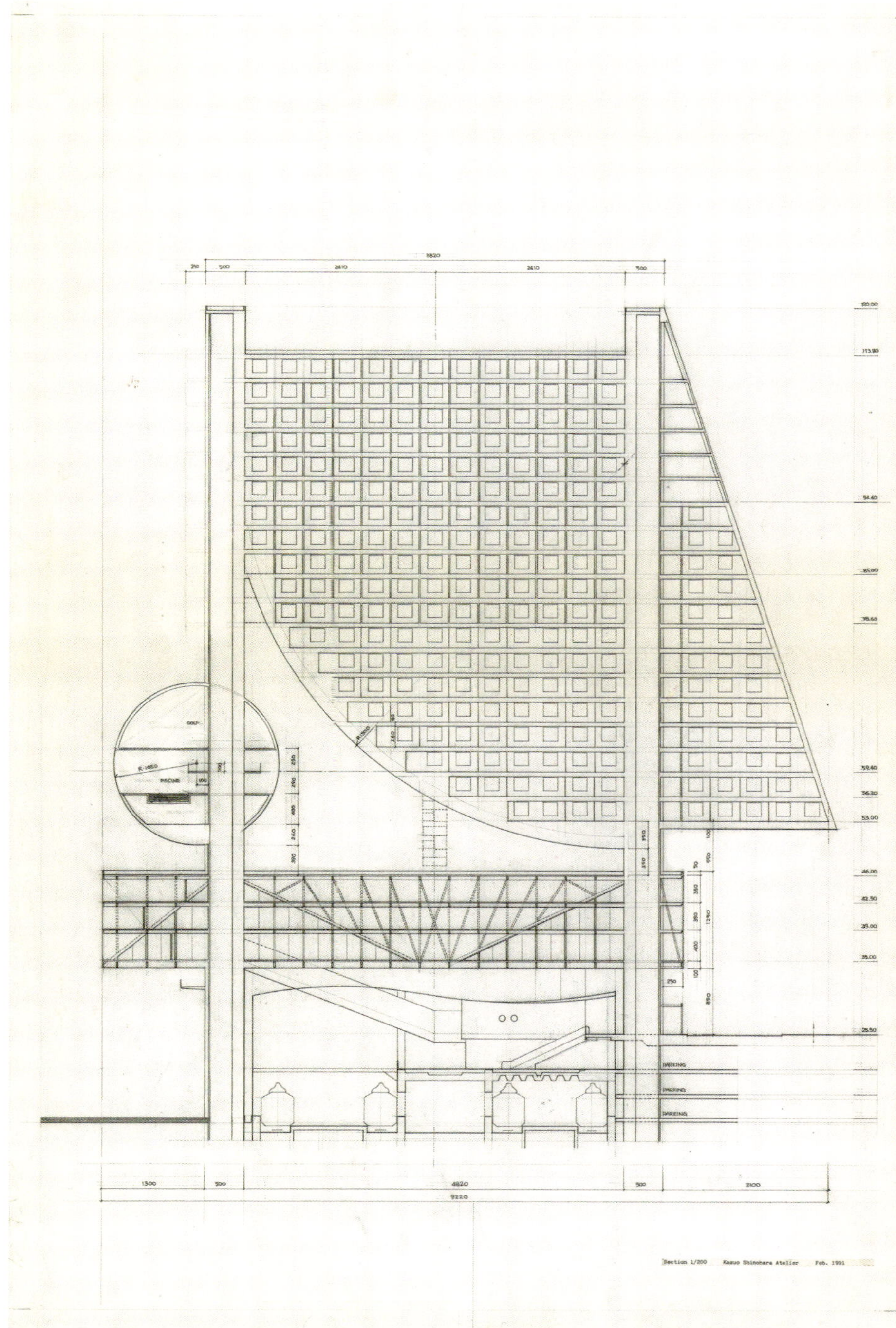

1 Sébastien Le Prestre de Vauban (1633–1707) was a Marshal of France under Louis XIV. One of the greatest military engineers in history, Vauban led numerous infrastructure and fortification projects, particularly in frontier locations, that helped define France as a modern state. The citadel of Lille is among the most significant and remains in active military use.

2 Cité Administrative is a high-rise complex designed by Albert Laprade and built in two phases, in 1951–55 and 1966–71.

3 Rem Koolhaas, *Delirious New York: A Retroactive Manifesto for Manhattan* (New York: Oxford University Press, 1978).

4 Shinohara Kazuo, "Modan shidō: yōshiki ga tsukurareru toki." *GA Japan,* no. 4 (Summer 1993): 112–19.

EURALILLE, 1990–92
Lille, France
unrealized

Shinohara was commissioned to design a hotel complex directly above the TGV railway station in Lille, as part of a master plan by the Office for Metropolitan Architecture and Rem Koolhaas to develop a new model of an urban hub at the crossroads of western Europe. For Koolhaas the Euralille project reflects a late modern condition where "programs have become abstract in the sense that they are no longer connected to a place or a city." Shinohara's main structure straddles the 45-meter-wide tracks of the railway, resulting in a thin building slab. The project went through two major redesigns, when other programs were added to and taken from the hotel complex. These programmatic adjustments are clearly legible on the building's façade, where the building's thinness flattens these spaces into primary geometries on a two-dimensional plane.

Photos by
Hoashi Terutaka (HT)

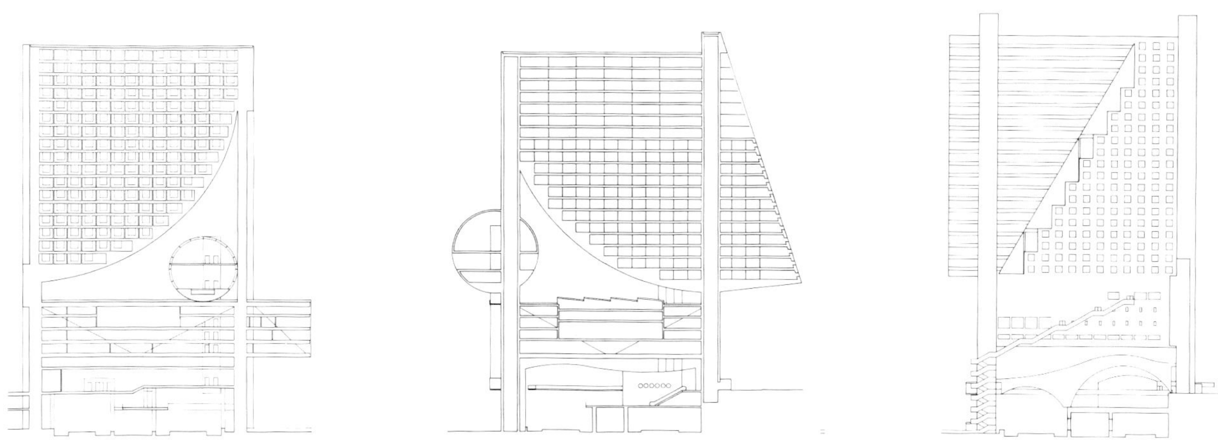

Elevation drawings of first, second, and third iterations.

Model view of second iteration.

1:2000

HT

Shinohara Kazuo, sketches of first iteration.

Model view of third iteration.

Model view of first iteration.

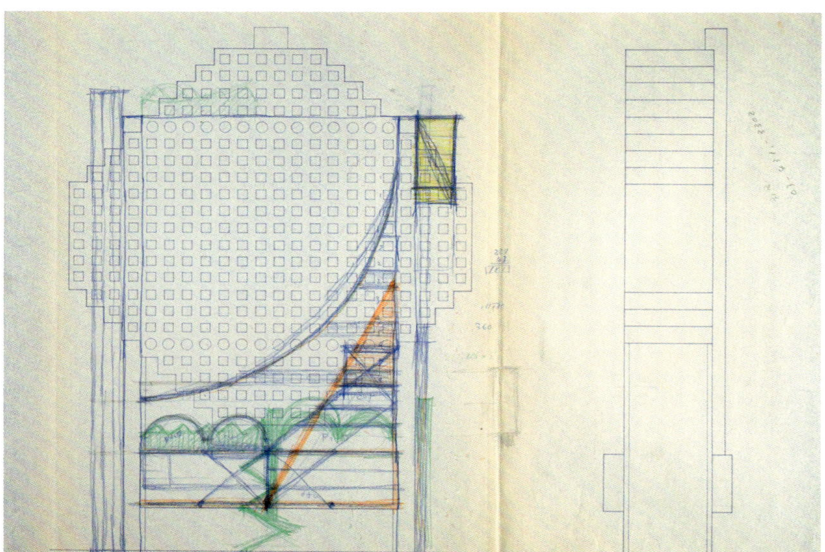

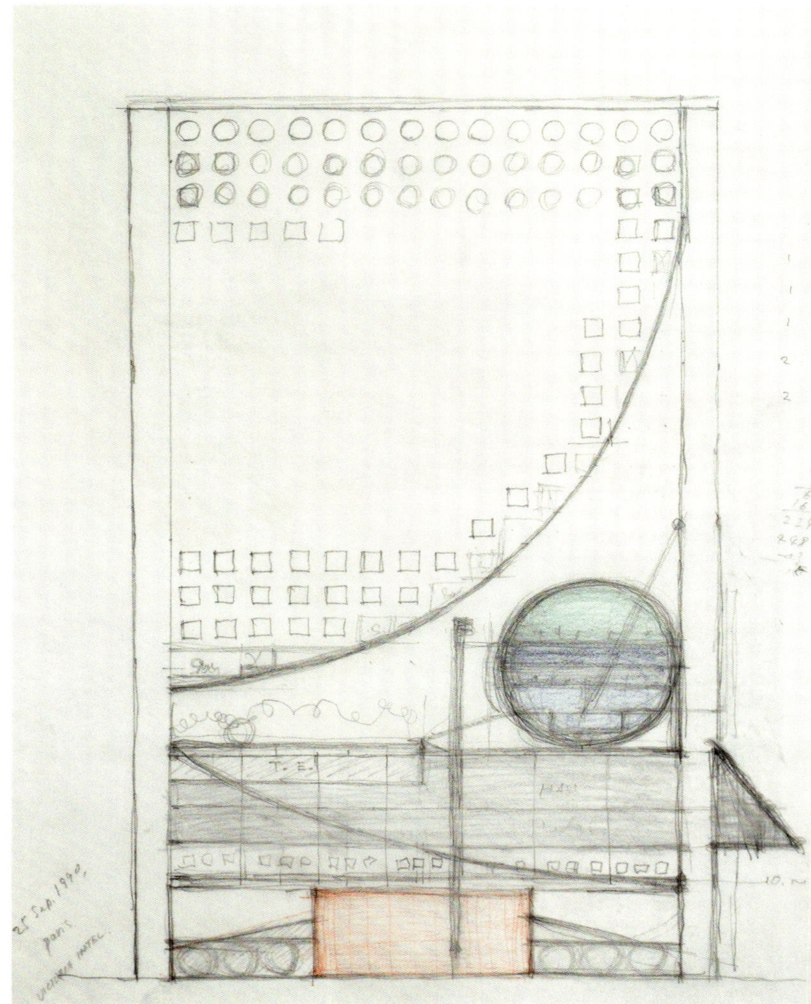

HT

HT

DOM HEADQUARTERS, 1980
Cologne, Germany
competition scheme, unbuilt

One of Shinohara's first forays into nonresidential architecture, and the first outside of Japan, this office building is covered in a shimmering glass surface that conveys the image of an object floating freely in air. A modular system based on cubic blocks that measure 8 by 8 by 8 meters, with two towers reaching 28 meters tall and a long horizontal volume extending 112 meters wide, belies the cable-stayed structural system underneath that achieves the large span. This scheme ran counter to the postmodern historicist fashion of its time, and in his submission Shinohara described it as "an ode to the youth spirit of modernism of the 1920s."

Photo by
Hoashi Terutaka (HT)

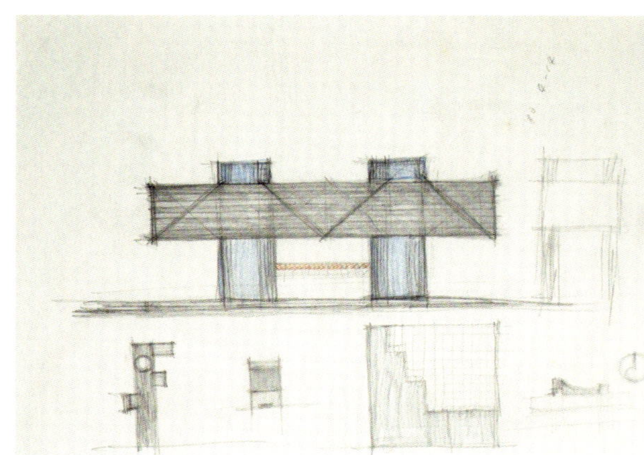

Shinohara Kazuo, sketches.

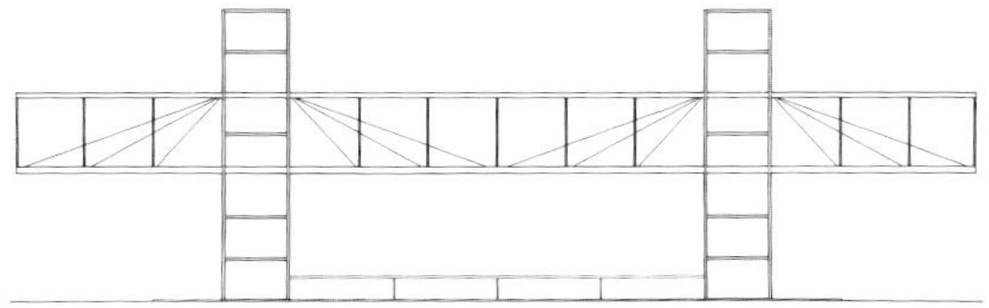

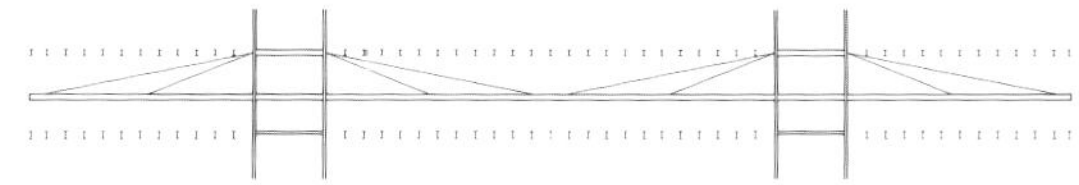

1:1600

Structural diagrams.

Model view.

HT

NO. 2 NATIONAL THEATER, 1986
Shibuya Ward, Tokyo
competition scheme, unbuilt

Shinohara called the scheme "urban machine." Complexities of the dramatic stage are taken as a metaphor for the myriad functions of the building—a machine where all the different roles are choreographed. The various parts of this spatial ensemble are laid out in a clear axial arrangement: large theaters on the north-south axis, and smaller ones and public gathering spaces in the shorter, east-west axis. Shinohara's idea of "the inorganic equipped with a sense of drama," explored here, would resurface at the Helsinki Museum of Contemporary Art (1993) and Yokohama International Port Terminal (1995) competition schemes.

Photos by
Shinohara Kazuo Atelier

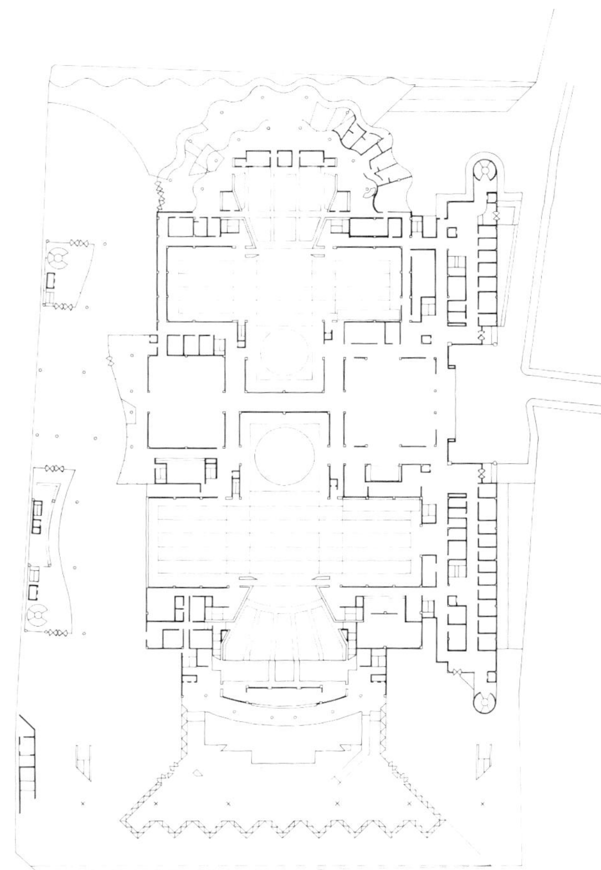

1:2000

Model views.

Shinohara Kazuo, sketches.

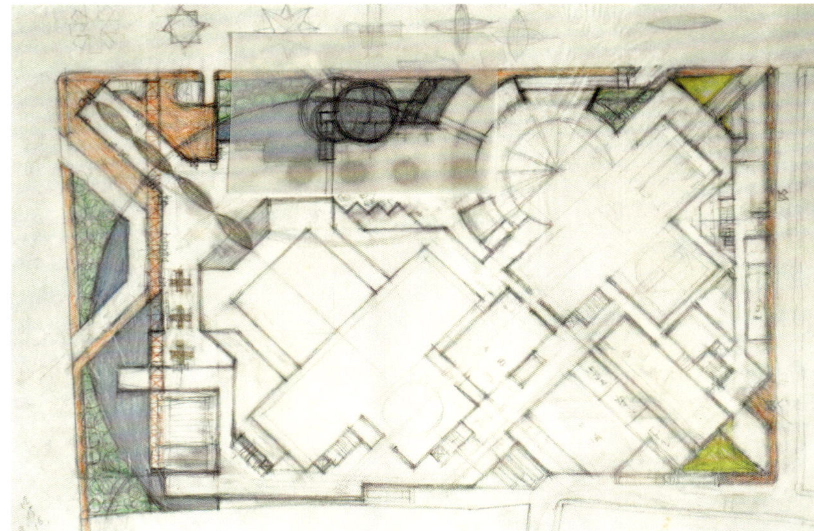

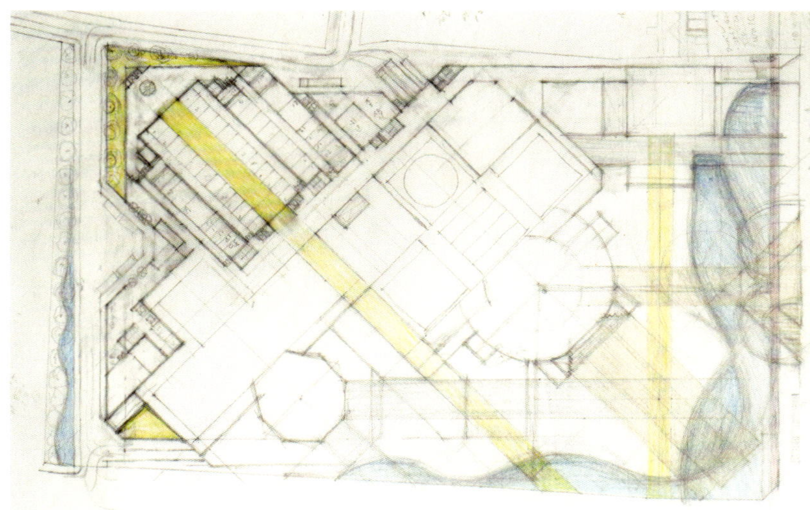

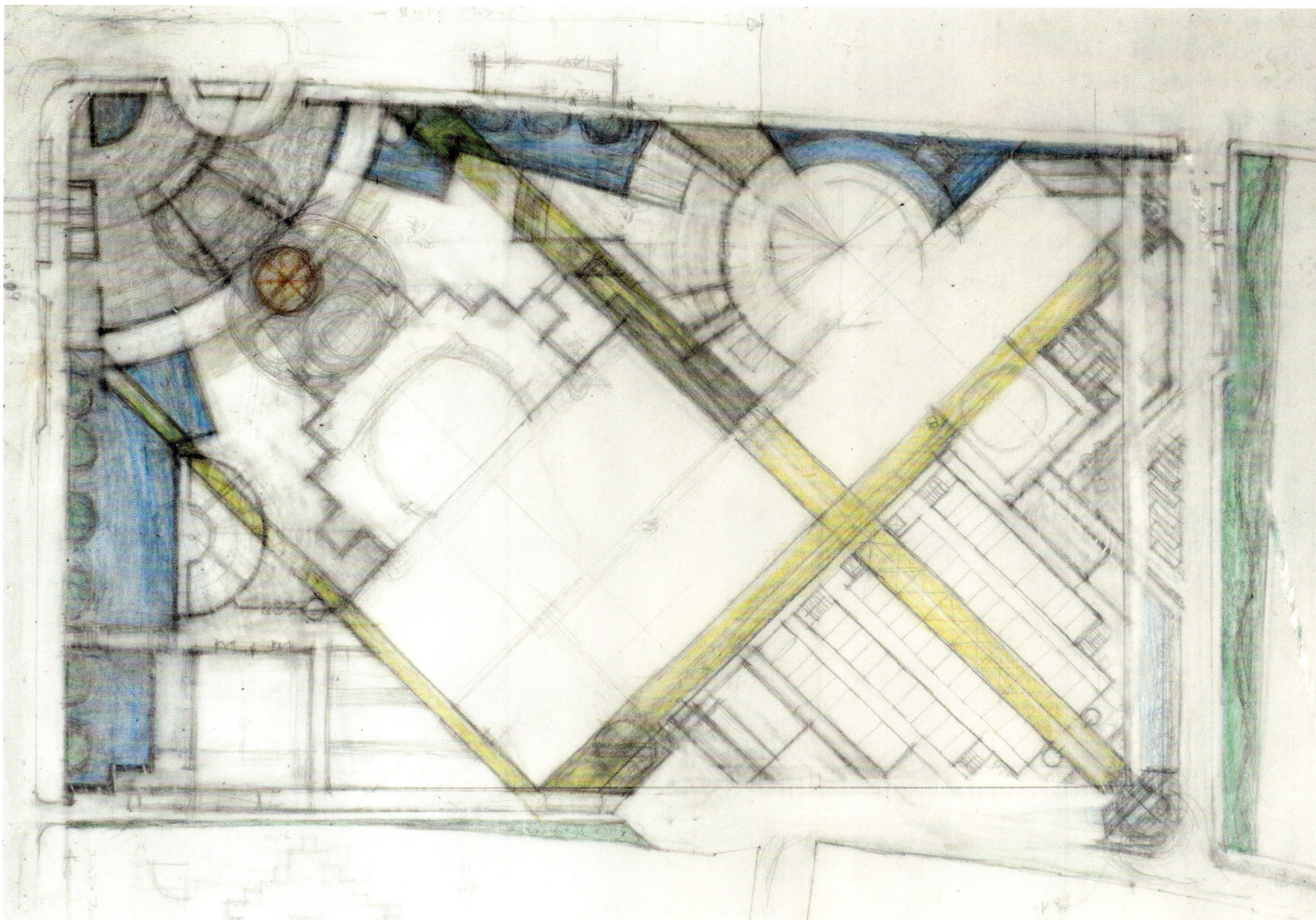

PARIS: CIRCUS ON SEINE, 1989
France
exhibition display

Presented at the exhibition *Paris: Architecture and Utopia,* held at the Pavillon de l'Arsenal in Paris, Shinohara's contribution was one of forty projects by various architects, each addressing one of three sites in Paris. Shinohara chose the Quai André-Citroën on the Seine's Left Bank. Bordering this long esplanade 600 meters wide and 40 meters deep is a mélange of industrial buildings and modernist housing blocks. The image of currents and waves in the river propelled Shinohara to break from primary geometries toward more composite forms. Most of the volumes are lifted into the air and rendered as machines. The globe-like hotel structure, 50 meters in diameter and containing a large void in the center, foreshadows several important proposals that soon followed.

Photo by
Hoashi Terutaka (HT)

Site plan.

Model view.

Shinohara Kazuo, sketch.

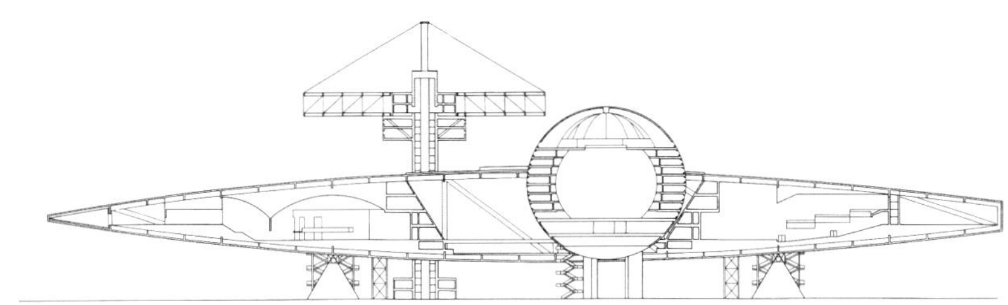

1:3000

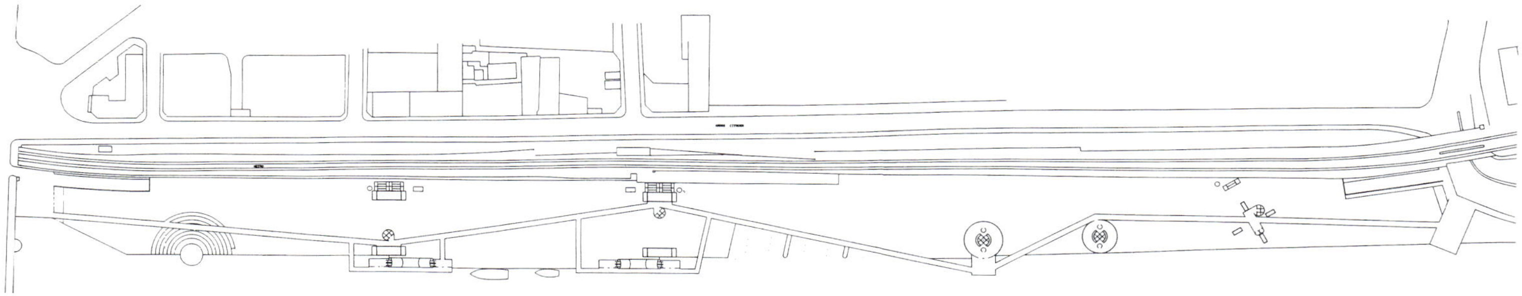

1:4000

HT

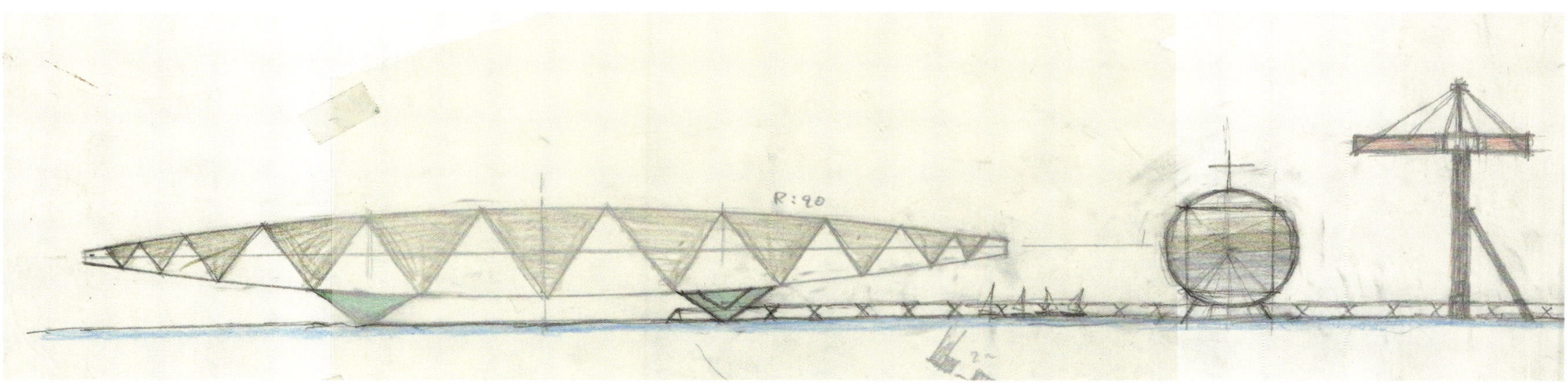

AGADIR CONVENTIONAL CENTER, 1990
Morocco
competition scheme, unbuilt

The idea of a "giant radiating *objet*" came from impressions of Casablanca's blue minarets from Shinohara's first overseas trip in 1972, as he crossed the Mediterranean Sea from Spain into North Africa. Here the russet sand dunes of Agadir are cast against the cobalt blue Atlantic. The unbalanced half-donut form, covered in metallic sheathing, hovers over the natural landscape and projects an uncanny but mesmerizing glow on the horizon, as if constantly in motion. Since the site is also in close proximity to a royal palace, no windows are found in the direction overlooking the palace. The complex program consists of a luxury hotel, convention center, and entertainment facilities.

Photo by
Hoashi Terutaka (HT)

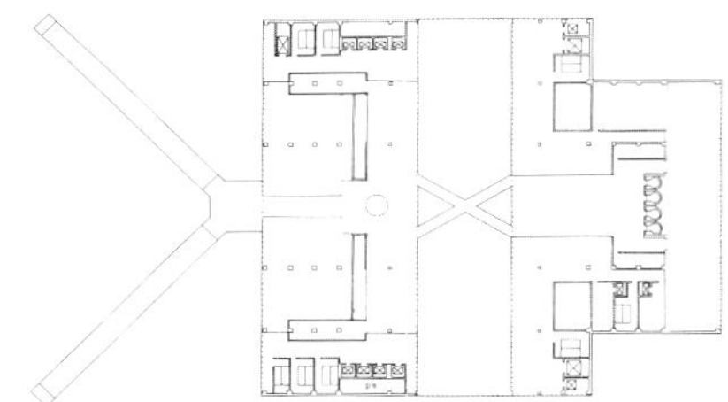

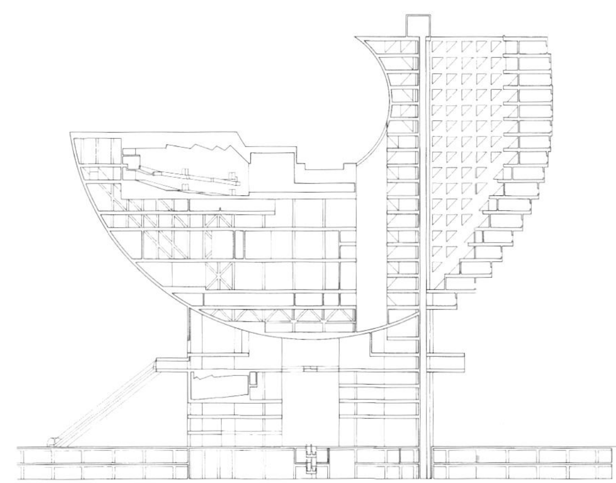

1:2500

Model view.

Shinohara Kazuo, sketches.

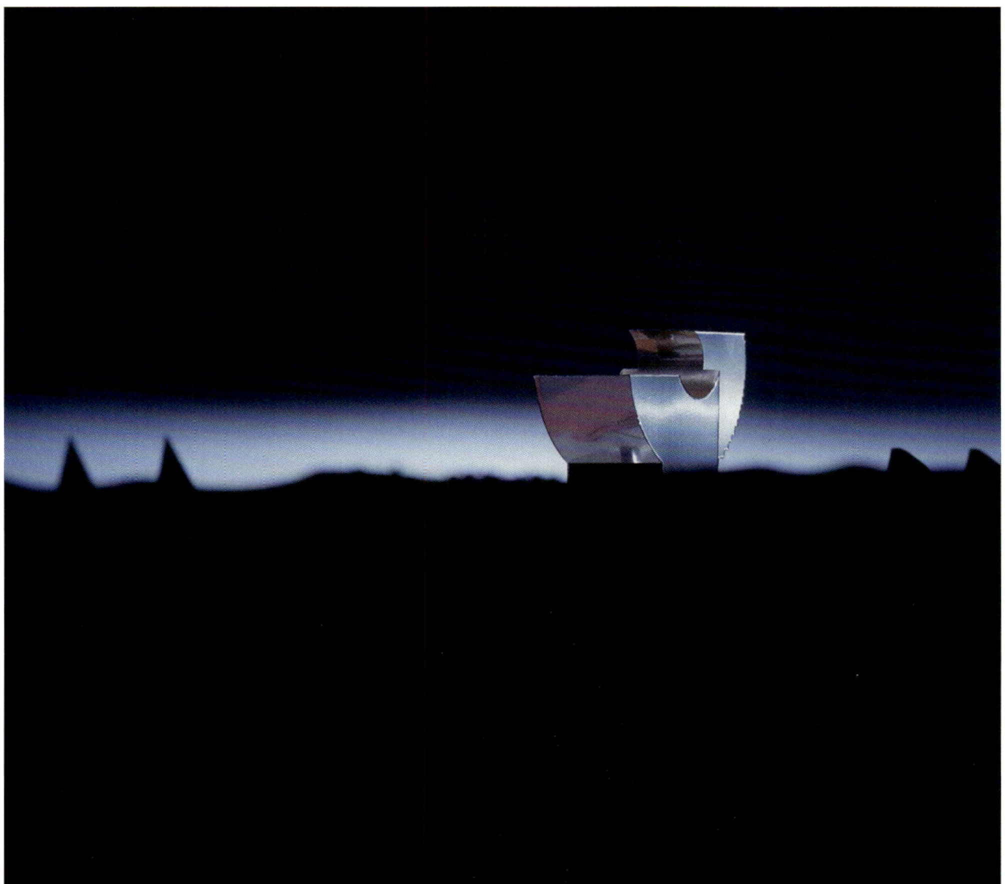

HT

REPEATING CREVICE, ANNEX BUILDING, 1991
Ōta Ward, Tokyo
unbuilt

Part of the same series as House in Yokohama (1984) and Centennial Hall (1987), this addition came twenty years after the original work of the Second Style. Referring to the strong cubic forms of Mediterranean hill towns, the question was how a cube would conjoin with adjacent units. Tilted slightly to the right, a strong cylindrical tube floats prominently and competes with the geometric clarity of the existing building. In the lower level, the curved underside of the tube above intrudes into the bedroom.

Photos by
Hoashi Terutaka (HT) and Justin Knight (JK)

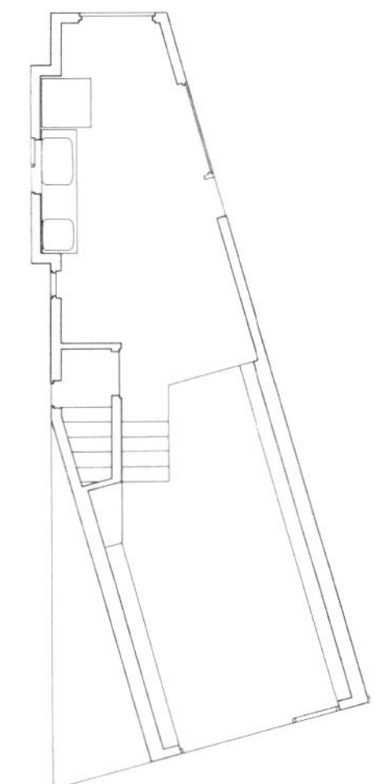

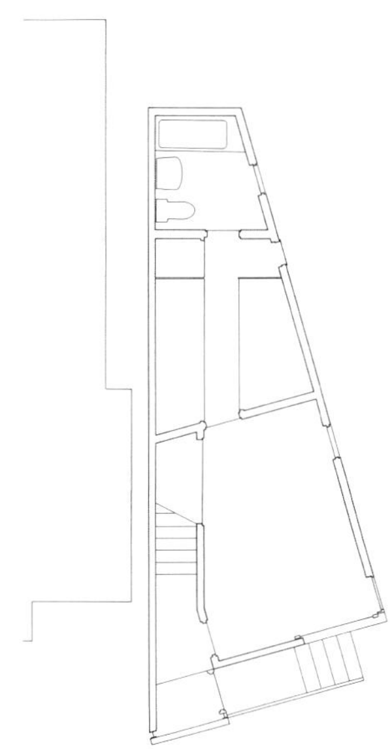

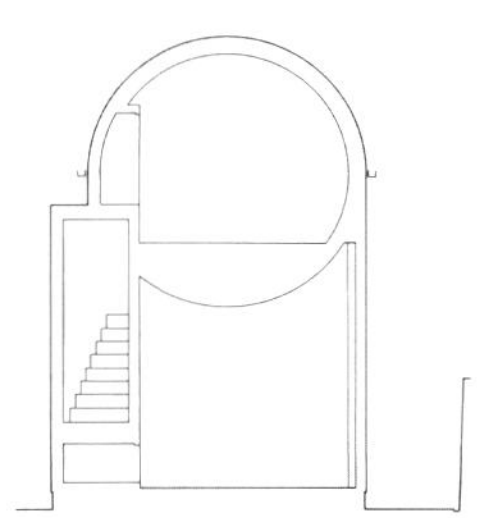

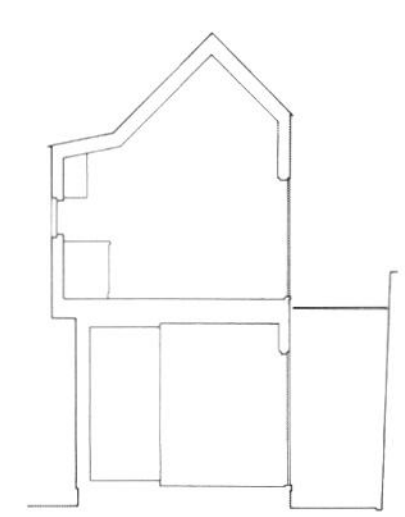

Model view.

1:200

HT

Model view of Repeating Crevice (1971) and proposal for the Annex.

Shinohara Kazuo, sketch.

Axonometric diagram.

Shinohara Kazuo, sketch.

JK

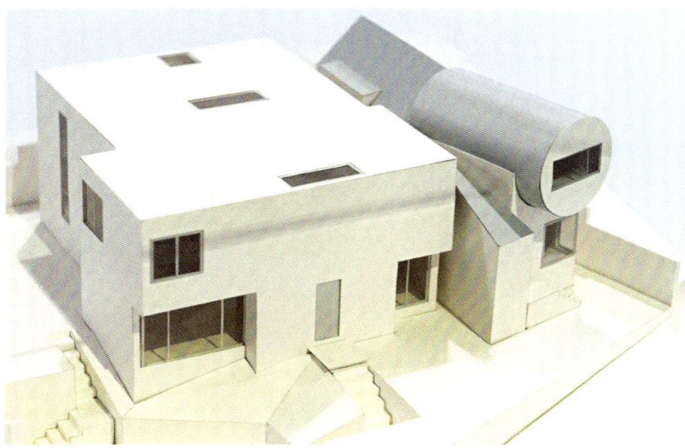

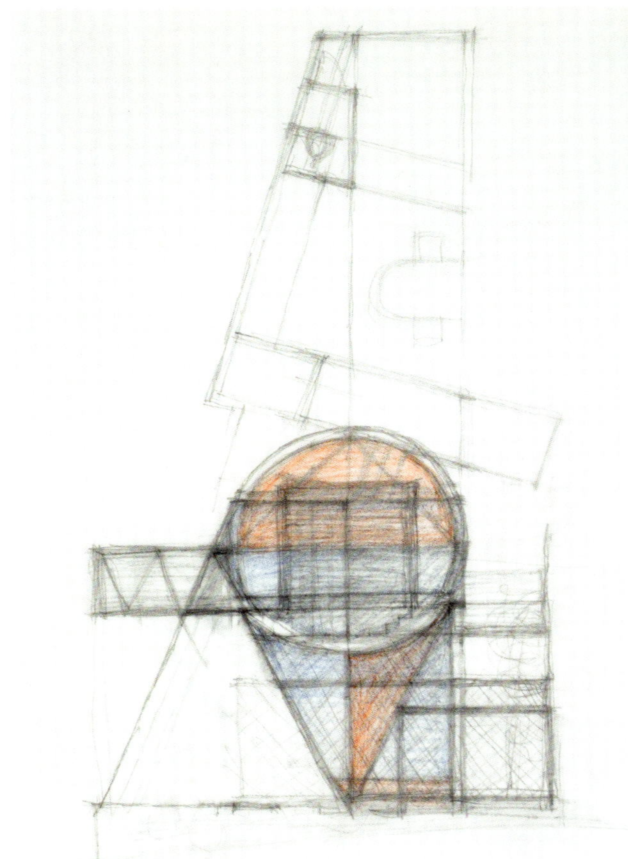

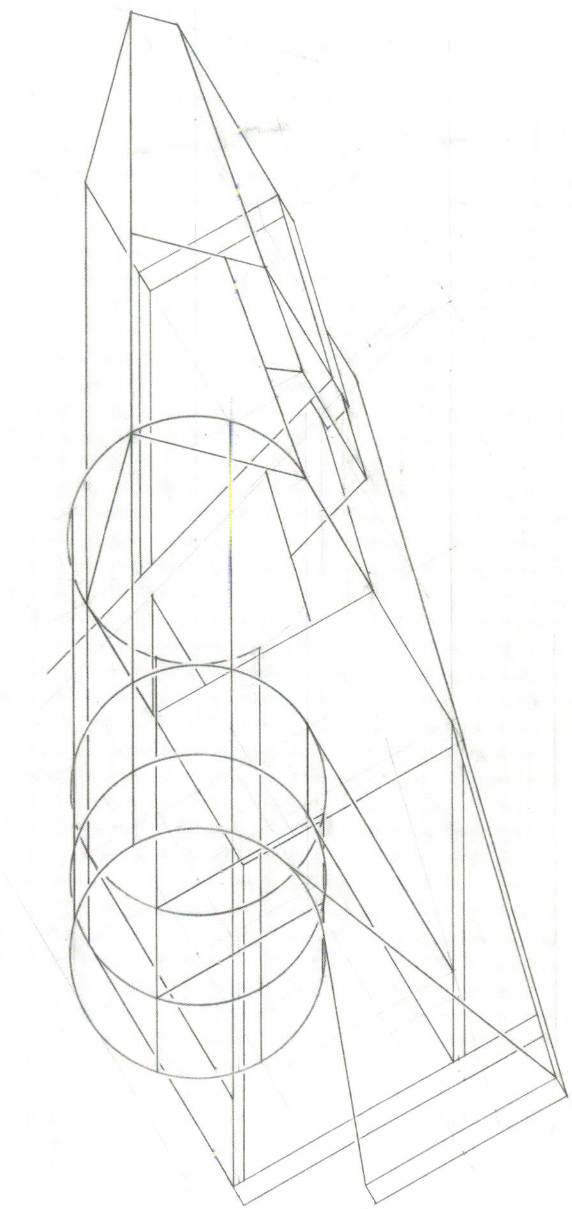

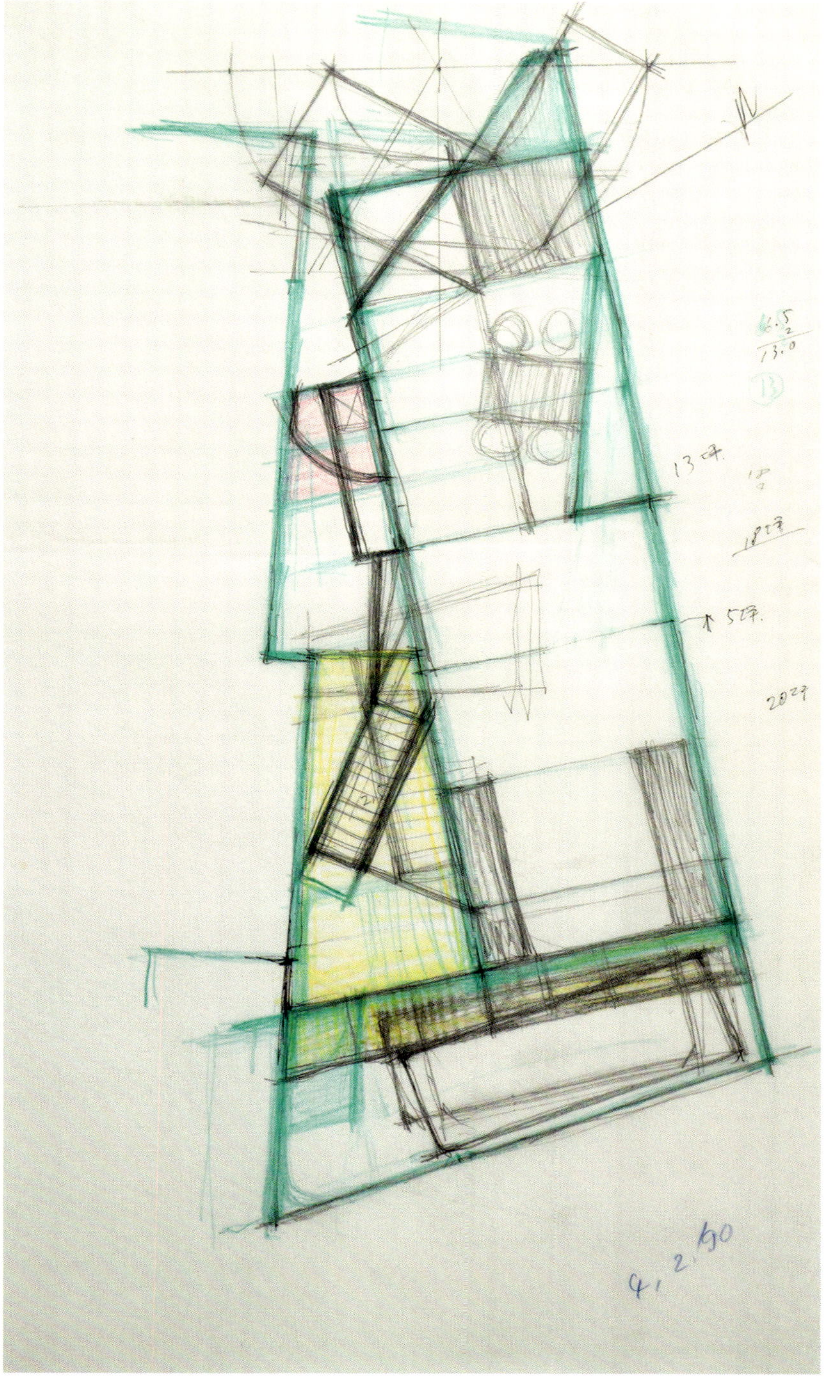

JAPAN UKIYO-E MUSEUM, EXTENSION BUILDING, 1992
Matsumoto, Nagano Prefecture
unbuilt

Commissioned ten years after the original Japan Ukiyo-e Museum in Matsumoto, also designed by Shinohara, this extension is polemicized as a veritable essay on "order" and "chaos." The basic composition is a series of primary geometries—triangles, squares, and cylinders—that give way to two prominent circular, conch-like elements with offset centers. The full circle, at 16 meters in diameter, contains the main gallery spaces, with three 300-millimeter-thick steel floor plates set at 4, 8, and 12 meters aboveground, respectively. These plates are overlapped by a larger semicircular disc, 22 meters in diameter, that extends the exhibition spaces in the upper levels.

Photo by
Justin Knight (JK)

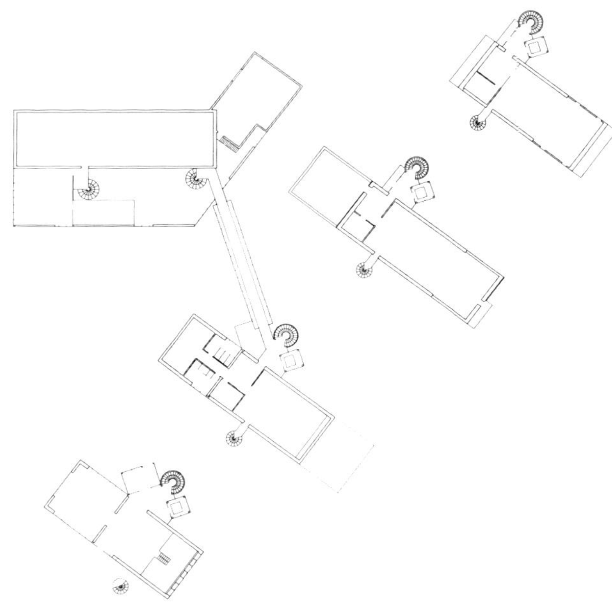

1:1000

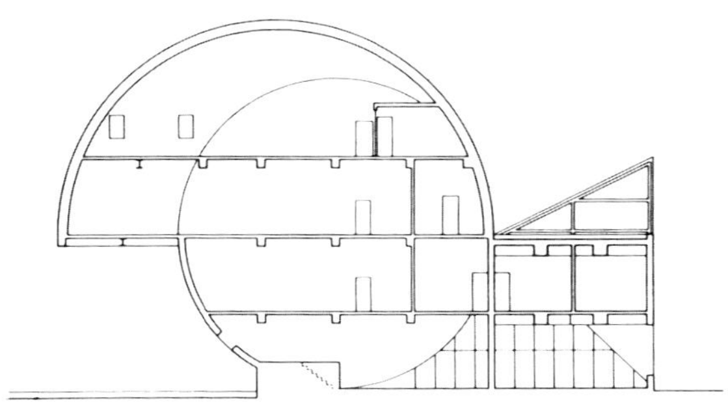

1:500

Shinohara Kazuo, sketches of Japan Ukiyo-e Museum, Matsumoto, Nagano Prefecture, 1982.

Shinohara Kazuo, sketches of Japan Ukiyo-e Museum's Extension project.

Model view, proposal for the Extension in foreground.

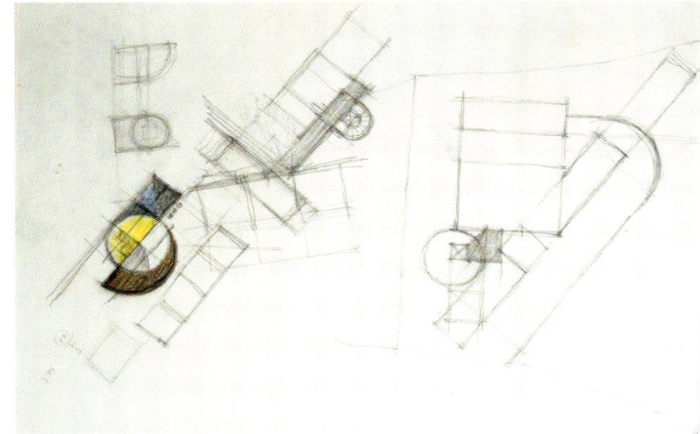

JK

HAMBURG URBAN VISION, 1993
Germany
exhibition display

Part of a forum to redevelop a 260-hectare area to the east of Hamburg's historic core, which was hastily rebuilt after World War II, the large site is crisscrossed by a branch of the Elbe River and three canals. Shinohara embraced the historical context of Hamburg's built form, especially *sachlich* matter-of-fact articulation of façades in the waterfront warehouses of the Speicherstadt and the iconic Chilehaus nearby. Tapering to the canal waterfront along the western edge of the site is a long linear office block. Its form may be interpreted as a horizontal extrusion of the thin slab that Shinohara explored at Euralille. This waterfront row is punctuated with a series of voids all in primary geometric forms, defining a "festival space." To the east are housing blocks arranged in striations at 100-meter intervals.

Photo by
Hoashi Terutaka (HT)

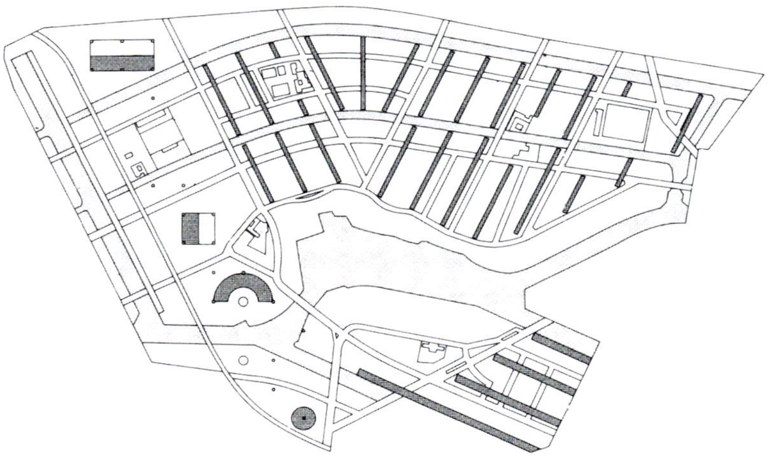

1:25000

Shinohara Kazuo, sketch of waterfront office and commercial block as "festival space."

Model view.

HT

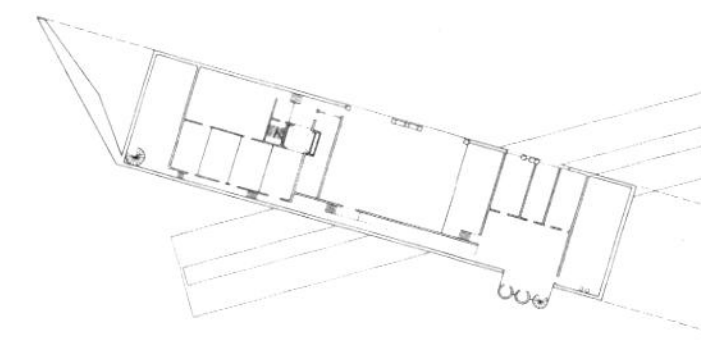

HELSINKI MUSEUM OF CONTEMPORARY ART, 1993
Finland
competition scheme, unbuilt

The site of this museum is strategically situated among some of Finland's most important architectural monuments: Parliament House, Alvar Aalto's Finlandia Hall, and Eliel Saarinen's Central Railway Station, all located off a scenic inlet in the Gulf of Finland. Responding to the powerful urban axes and view corridors of these structures, Shinohara's scheme intersects two enormous elements, each housing a gallery and suspended in midair. The upper gallery, spanning 110 meters in length, is hung off 40-meter-tall piers on two ends. The lower gallery, for exhibiting the permanent collection, is a cylinder 14 meters in diameter and 90 meters in length. While the scheme may appear as a sensible response to site context, Shinohara notes his yearning for "the inorganic equipped with a sense of drama."

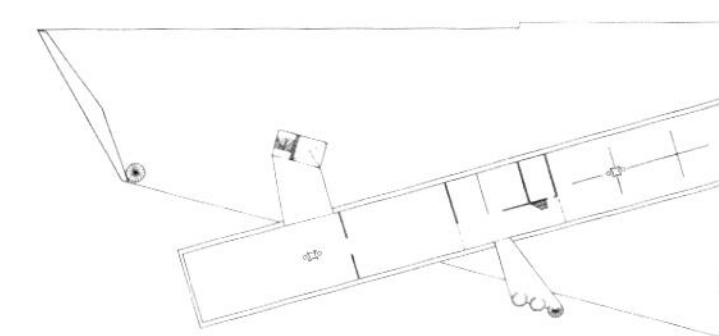

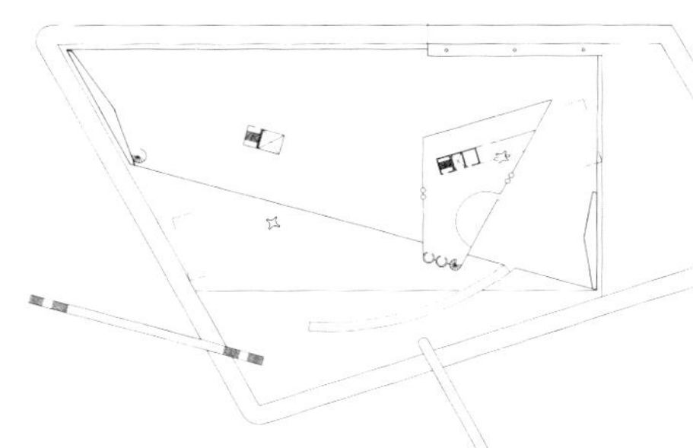

Photos by
Hoashi Terutaka (HT)

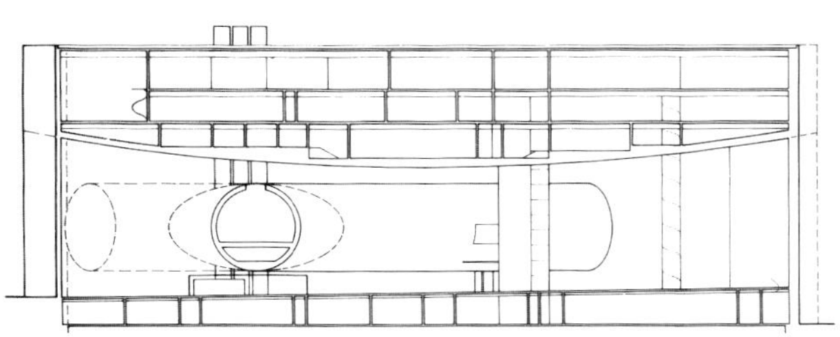

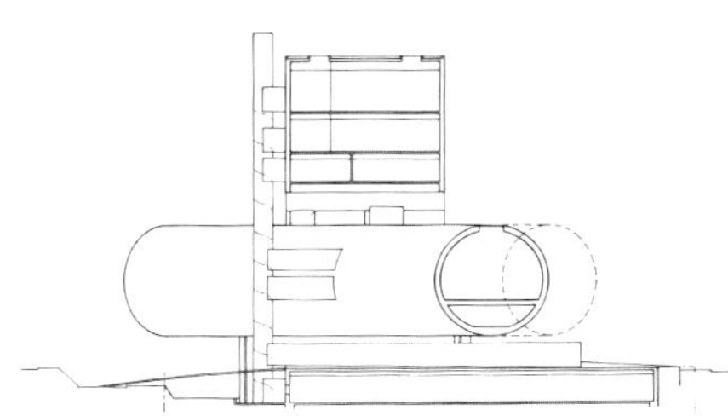

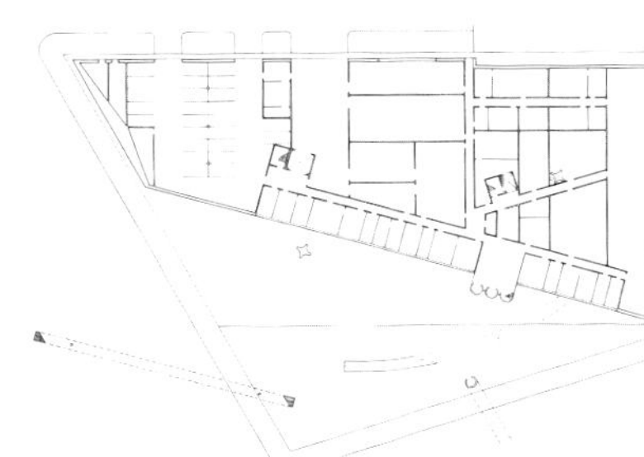

Model view.

1:2000

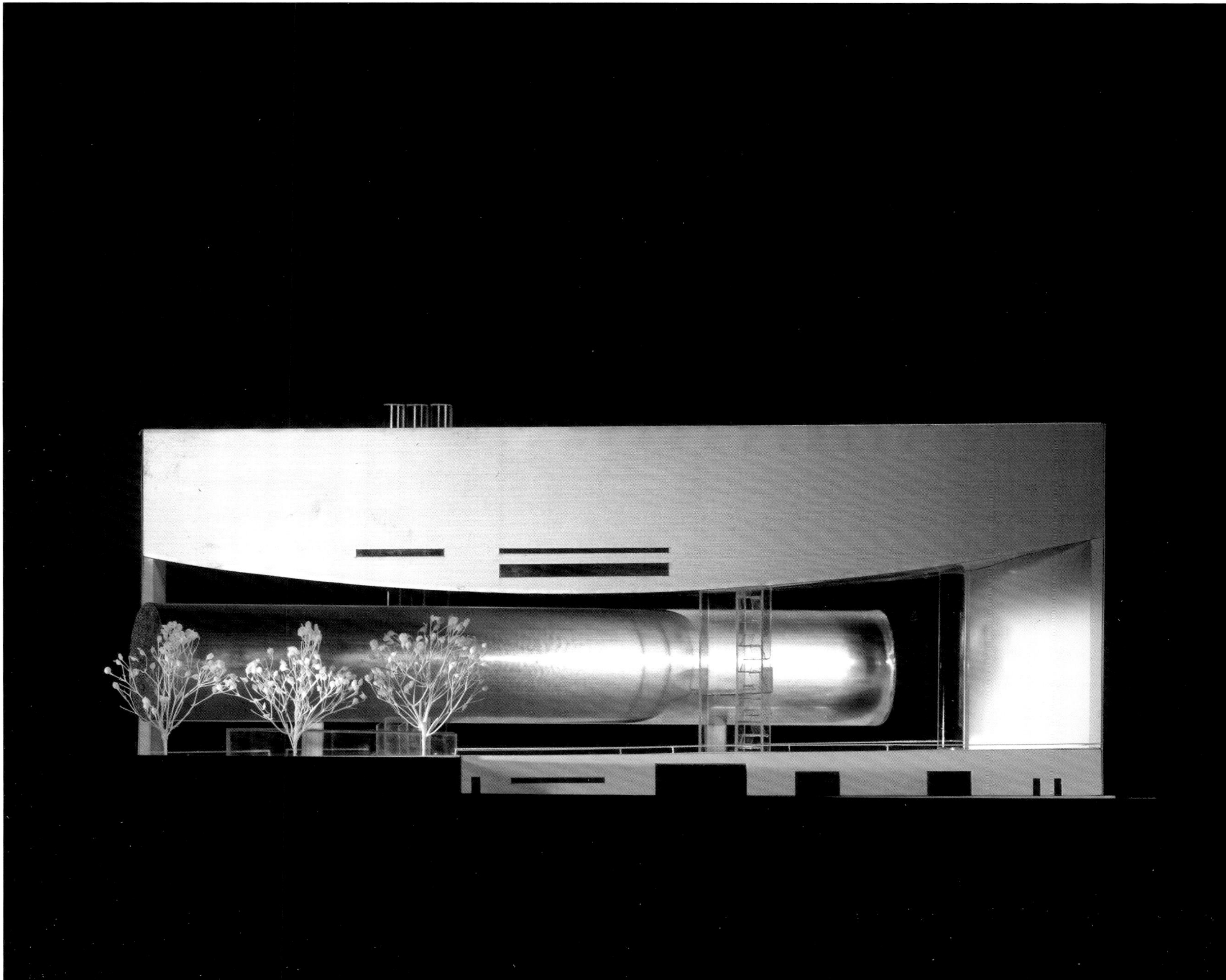

HT

Shinohara Kazuo, sketches.

Interior views of model, lower gallery for display of permanent collection.

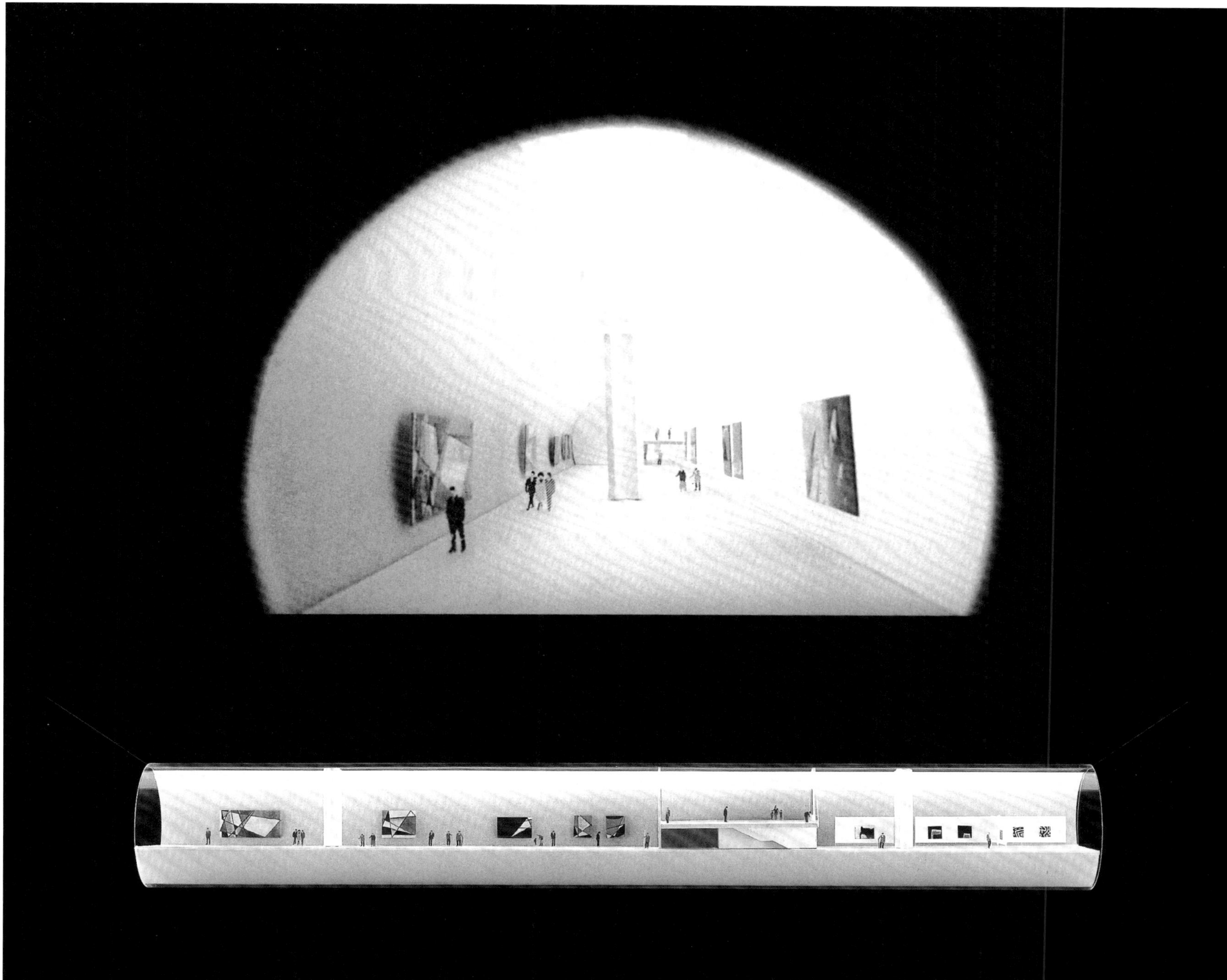

HT

YOKOHAMA INTERNATIONAL PORT TERMINAL, 1995
Kanagawa Prefecture, 1995
competition scheme, unbuilt

Covering a long pier projecting deep into Yokohama Bay, the port terminal building is conceived in terms of horizons and silhouettes, the first encounter by passengers sailing into the harbor at dawn with “Japanese form.” The symmetrical curvature on its side elevations peels away from the ground to an ethereal effect, while the elongated form consists of a series of distinct volumes and geometries that flow from one into another, mediating the complex functions of a port facility into a coherent whole. Cylindrical volumes projecting from the exterior further soften the contours of the buil-ding against the coastal silhouette. Moving onward from this series of institutional-scale projects, Shinohara began to imagine returning to minimal spaces as aesthetic and social resistance.

Photos by
Hoashi Terutaka (HT)

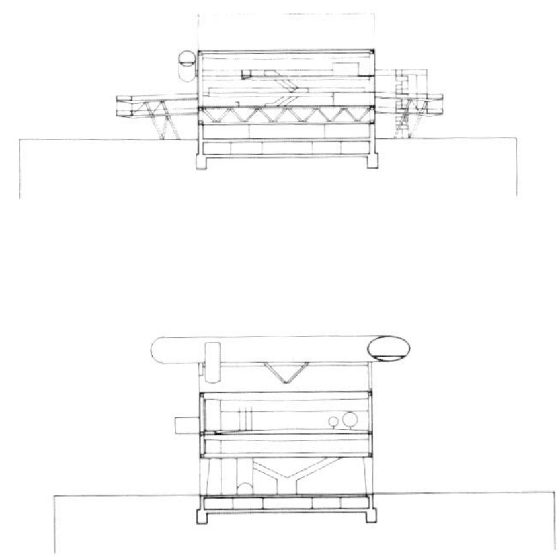

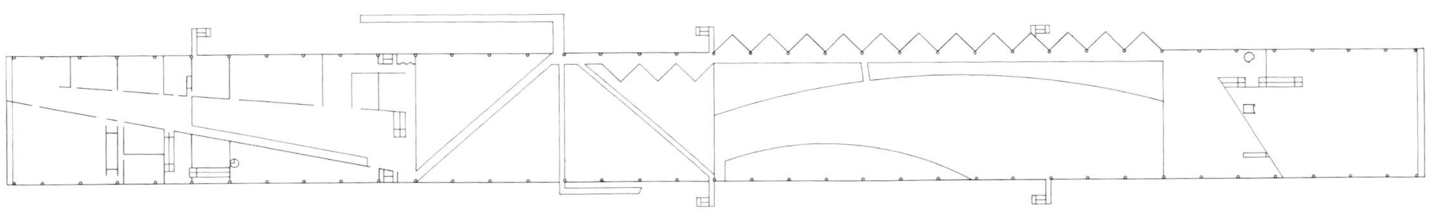

Model view.

1:2000

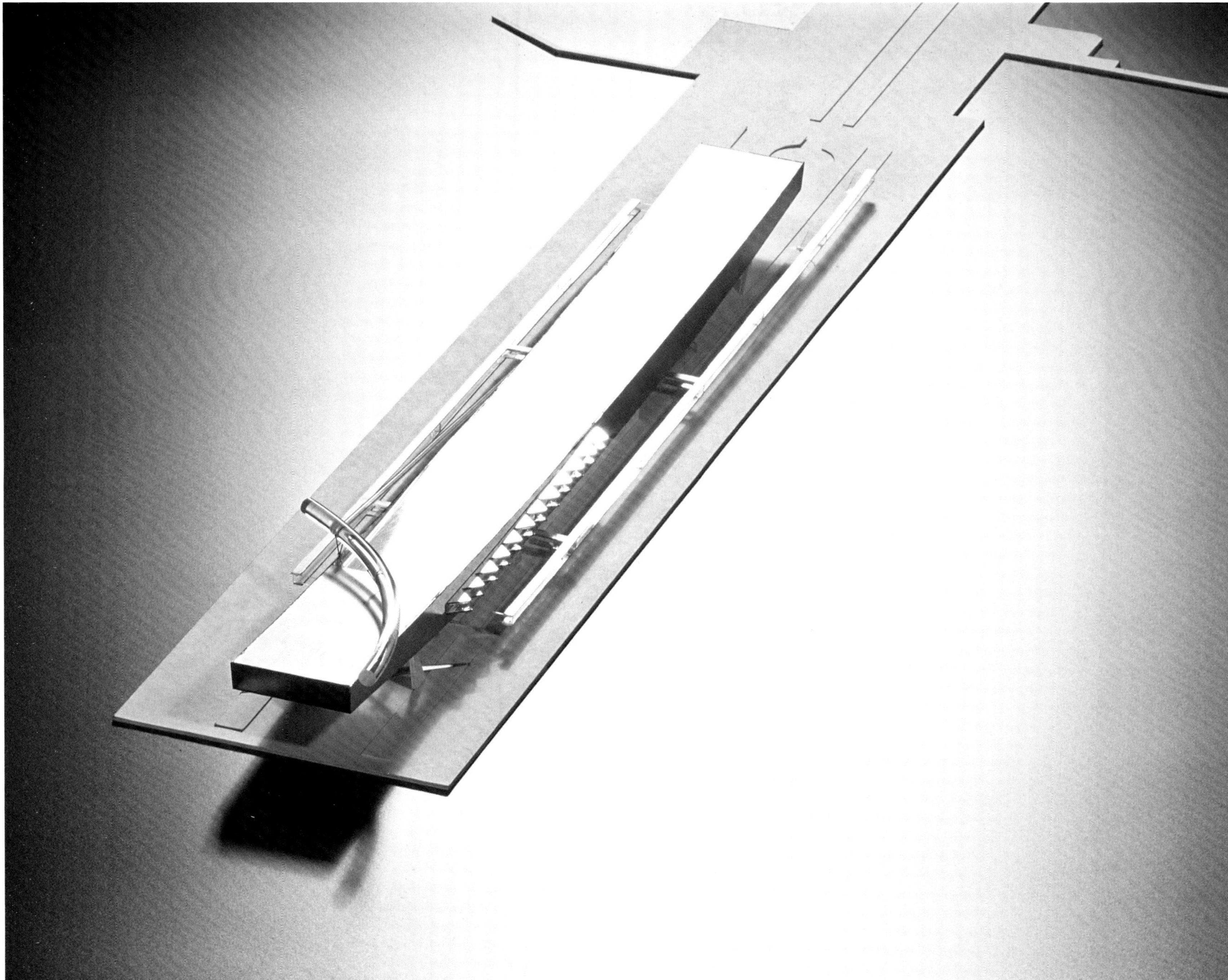

HT

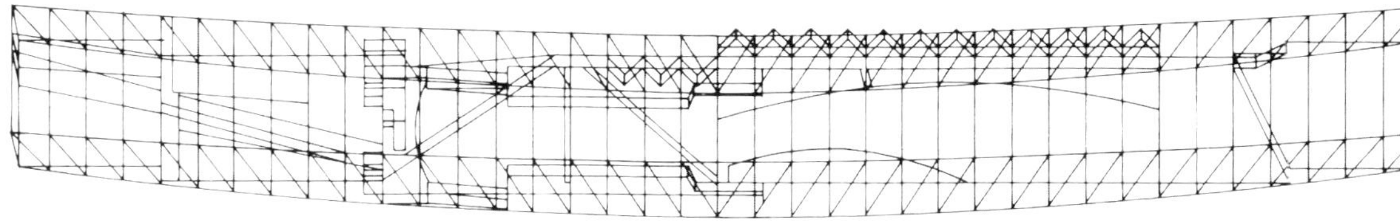

Structural diagram.

Model view.

Section drawing.

Shinohara Kazuo, sketches.

HT

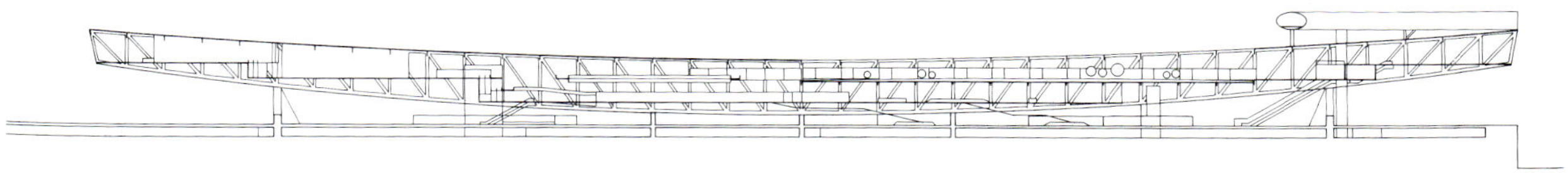

1:2500

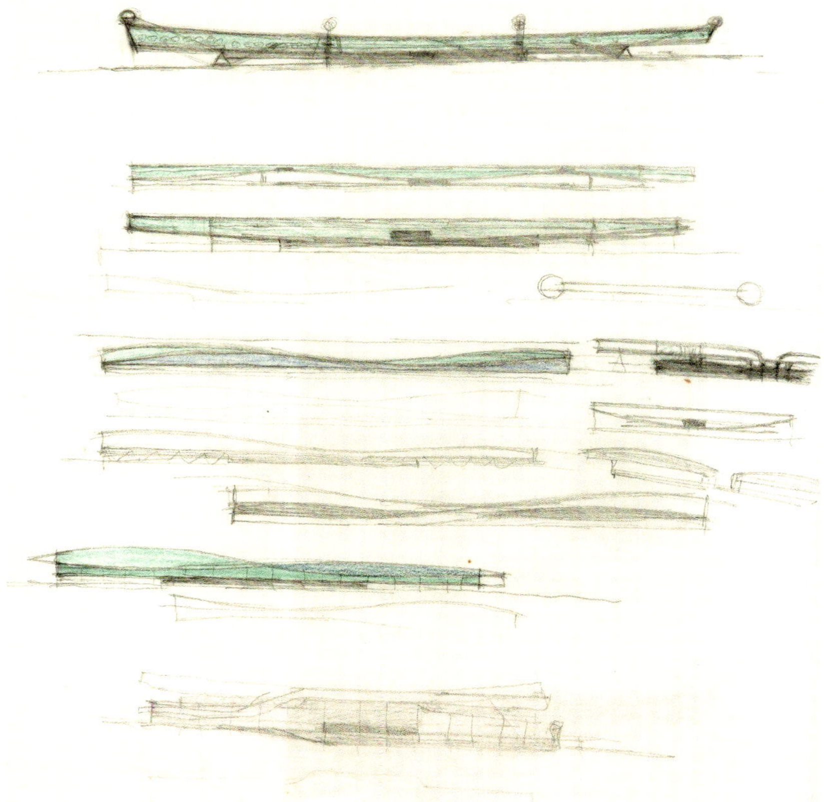

Shinohara Kazuo, House in Tateshina, designed 2001–06, unbuilt. Photo courtesy of Shinohara Kazuo Archive

Sloping Ground:
The Styles of Shinohara at Tanikawa House and House in Tateshina

Shiozaki Taishin

TWO TYPES OF SLOPING GROUND

Over the course of his architectural career, Shinohara Kazuo designed two residences that feature an earthen slope within an interior space. One is the mountainous retreat that was designed and built outside of the resort town of Karuizawa for the poet Tanikawa Shuntarō in 1974 (Tanikawa House). The other is a posthumous work that was never completed, known in full as Primary Geometry of the Tateshina Mountains (House in Tateshina).

Uncovering the links between these two residential projects reveals their pertinence to how Shinohara twice created an inexplicable situation involving an earthen slope within an interior space, while differences between the two projects demonstrate how Shinohara's works evolved as a continuous series.

EMBANKMENTS AND EARTHEN FLOORS

As a child I often played around the embankments near my house. Sometimes a big group of us would roll all around the embankments, while other days I would walk around them from morning until night, searching for and gazing at the bamboo shoots that spruce up resiliently on the edges of these banks. In Japanese, *dote* refers to the embankments that are built by piling up earth high along the side of a river or road. The place where I used to play was actually part of a small hill—and perhaps more accurately called a cliff. Nonetheless, we used to call this meeting place a *dote.* For kids who enjoyed playing with mud, the "d" sound of *dote* connoted a particular sensation of wetness, and clumpy mass of mud (*doro*). Living as we did in the artificial environment of a planned new town, I think we were also, at some subconscious level, seeking a sense of nature that could be found in the copiousness of this earth. Whatever the case, I doubt I was the only one who felt this way: for us earth was a material that resonated with the heart of a child. At the same time, it was a natural substance that was relatively accessible, in the context of a daily existence surrounded by humanmade objects.

Due to the custom of having *doma* (earthen floor) in Japan, it is popular to use earth as a material for floors (or walls). Shinohara, too, designed two residences early in his career that made ample use of these earthen floors—House with an Earthen Floor (1963) and House of Earth (1966). At these two houses, however, the floors are made of hardened and compacted blocks of earth. The fluffy earth, or black earth, in which weeds stubbornly try to grow, inevitably gives us the impression of a sort of primordial Mother Earth (*daichi*) that represents the origin of life. We are invariably put in mind not only of the gentleness of this Mother Earth, but also the awe-inspiring presence of a natural world that symbolizes the memory of the human race. In ancient times, a home was an enclosure that kept dangers at bay, a shelter that protected one's way of life from fearsome foreign enemies, the elements, and other natural forces. Just as the monsters that often appear in myths, legends, and fairy tales are metaphors for natural disasters, the nature found in the great outdoors is a potential threat to human life. The earth that has been brought into the interior, then, naturally makes us sensible to this ominousness that should not have been ushered indoors in the first place. When this earth takes the form of a sloping surface, we cannot help but become aware of a sort of intense

1 Shinohara Kazuo and Isozaki Arata, "Taidan, kenchiku ni tsuite," *Shinkenchiku* vol. 50, no. 10 (October 1975): 139–40.

confrontation between humans and nature. By smoothing over the earth and making it flat, we were able to turn the earth of Mother Nature into a floor for human habitation. When we stand on this sloping surface, we experience a tactile sense of the untouchability of this nature before we acquired it—the menacing threat of its vastness.

Shinohara incorporated this sort of sloping earth twice in his residential designs, with thirty years between them. He typically endeavored to make each project a one-off design—so what exactly was Shinohara's objective in bringing this sloping mound of earth into an interior after a long gap?

TANIKAWA HOUSE, 1974

Tanikawa House, located on a parcel of land surrounded by rich, verdant deciduous pine forest in the mountains of Karuizawa, was built as a retreat for the poet Tanikawa Shuntarō. Tanikawa had already commissioned Shinohara to design a residence for him (Tanikawa House, 1958), so this mountain retreat was the second house that the poet had asked Shinohara to design. This Tanikawa House, in Karuizawa, comprises a living space (*hiroma*) for the summer and another for the winter, as well as a small study alcove and a Japanese-style room on the second floor. Throughout the summer living space one finds the same sloping raw earth as outside the house, while the winter living room is equipped with the usual conveniences, including an adjoining kitchen. When Tanikawa commissioned this house, he sent Shinohara a note containing a poem written on a single sheet of manuscript paper, containing the two lines: "winter house or pioneer cabin (house)" and "summer space or church for a pantheist (need not be a house)." Accordingly, these two living spaces were designed to fulfill Tanikawa's requirements.

About thirty years after Tanikawa House was completed, I had the opportunity to visit. Standing in that space, I felt an intense discomfort that arose not because a long time had passed but because this was a space that had harbored this sense of unease all along, for thirty years without reprieve, ever since the building was completed. This sensation was different from the sense of fulfillment that elicits a kind of bodily dynamism in Shinohara's other residential projects. Isozaki Arata described a feeling that was likely similar to this one in a dialogue published in *Shinkenchiku* when Tanikawa House was first unveiled:

> Shinohara-san, I feel that you are becoming more and more conceptual, in fact...the conceptual aspect of your work has acquired a concreteness....
>
> A sloping surface identical to the terrain outside exists inside the house. It is not just the meaning that is different in terms of how one feels when standing outside, as opposed to when standing in the covered interior—it is the sensation that changes. An extremely unstable feeling emanates from this house once you are inside. It is an incredible feat that you could express this sensation in that form.[1]

Five beams span the 9-meter depth of the building. In this distance there is a height difference of 1.32 meters in the ground, which is equivalent to one unit of the windows with diagonal

Shinohara Kazuo, House with an Earthen Floor, Miyota, Nagano Prefecture, 1963. Photo by Koyama Takashi

Shinohara Kazuo, Tanikawa House, Naganohara, Gunma Prefecture, 1974. Photo by Taki Kōji

Interior, House in Tateshina, unbuilt. Photo courtesy of Shinohara Kazuo Archive

bracing (1.2 meters for glazing plus 12 centimeters for horizontal members in the frame). The gradient of the slope is approximately 1.5/10 (about 8.5 degrees). This is a gradient that one can experience in the context of a road or a natural slope, but it is slightly steep for a sloping floor in an indoor space. In all likelihood, it is an angle that would make one want to sit down, but the earth rebuffs the impulse. If I were still a child spending my days playing around the embankments, I would not have hesitated to sit down on the wet earth. But in the Tanikawa House I found myself frustrated by the sensation of not being able to find a fixed position, and profoundly uneasy. This feeling was encouraged by the presence of all these overlapping physical and geometrical objects: the vertical pillars; the angle braces at a 45-degree angle; the vast, sloping white ceiling at a 45-degree angle that extended at a right angle from those braces; and the light entering through the glass, which continued horizontally along the ground, just around eye level. But what exactly was it that Shinohara was trying to create from these overlapping elements?

In his comment quoted above, Isozaki offers a reading of how Shinohara produces a sense of spatial transformation by using the word "concreteness (*gutai*)." This term appears to be exceedingly accurate: Shinohara himself uses "concreteness" time and time again when explaining an entire series of works that take their starting point from this particular work:

> It has been my method to approach the concrete via the concept of naked things. This process is based on the elimination of the meaning of things, i.e., a process of *abstraction.* The concrete in my definition of savage space must emphasize its directness which needs no recourse to operation, or maneuvering. Because I understand that abstraction, or tendency to abstraction, is my most fundamental concept or method, I am not very clear about whether or not I shall ever experience an encounter with concrete objects.[2]

As I will outline later, Shinohara positioned his works as permutations of his own style, in accordance with how his thinking and philosophy evolved. Tanikawa House is an early instance of his Third Style. Shinohara had consistently advocated a movement toward abstraction through two styles: the First Style, which displayed a strong commitment to Japanese traditions by extracting the methods of division/connection and frontality, and the Second Style, which was based on creating a fissure-like space with a strong sense of verticality—a sort of inorganic, cubic shell. Shinohara's Third Style marked the first time that he had recorded in writing his intention to move toward the concrete. The spaces that emerged out of the relationships between concrete things—what Shinohara called "naked things"—stripped of all cultural meaning, as well as the gaps thus created, were the subject of these writings. Although I lay out in full detail the connotations of abundance and fertility that are called to mind by earth at the start of this essay, I immediately turn this argument on its head: He rejected all connotations of wetness in relation to the sloping earth that he brought upon himself.

> I attach no deep significance to the sloping surface of the floor. Here, the only things that have any sense of reality are the numbers that quantify the gradient of the slope,

2 Shinohara Kazuo, "Now and Function," *SD*, no. 172 (January 1979): 11–12. The original text was published bilingually in Japanese and English. The passage quoted here is as originally published.

3 Shinohara Kazuo, "Ragyō no kūkan wo ōdan suru toki, *Shinkenchiku* vol. 50, no. 10 (October 1975): 158–63. This is a new translation for this publication.

> and the differences in elevation. One slope among all the gentle undulations across the site enters into the house, and exits once again through the opposite side. That is all I intended. . . .
>
> I was unsure if it would be possible for the posts, walls, and braces to express only each of their respective functions—to accomplish such a natural and commonplace thing. If possible, I would want to go so far as to get rid of all of these elements pertaining to the spatial framework, as well as the various meanings that have been embedded in the entirety of the space itself.[3]

At this point, the sloping earth has no other significance for Shinohara other than the fact that it represents the gradient of the undulations across this particular site. Like the other elements of the space, it is one of many objects that are concrete (*gutaiteki*).

Incidentally, there are several objects that have been placed along this sloping surface of earth. A simple bench without a back has been placed next to the window, while a sink for wetting the ground and for washing is diametrically opposite. Also there by design is a ladder, which has become well known through the several photographs that deliberately depict it. There was a particular inspiration for this ladder, which narrows as you climb higher up: Shinohara designed it by tracing the form of the ladder in the atelier of the painter Paul Cézanne, based on a photograph. When painting still lifes, such as an assortment of apples, Cézanne would position apples he had drawn while seated in a chair alongside them on the same canvas as apples that he had drawn by climbing up the ladder and looking down on them. The impossible simultaneous existence of these perspectives gives this gathering of apples an uncanny sense of depth.

Shinohara brought the earthen slope inside the house. Stripped of all cultural significance, the bare earthen slope collides with primary geometrical angles shielding from above, with pillars and other elements that harbor no meaning other than what they are as objects; out of this a gap (*zure*) and a sensation of the uncanny emerge. This situation is akin to the urban relationship between ourselves and the concrete objects of a city that come into conflict with each other. It also bears some resemblance to the relationship between the reality of Cézanne's uneven, misshapen apples, and those of us who gaze upon them.

HOUSE IN TATESHINA, 2006

House in Tateshina is a small cabin, a posthumous work by Shinohara. From 2004 to 2006 I assisted Shinohara on the design of this cabin while pursuing my doctoral work. Shinohara had already closed down his studio, and had no staff working for him; in addition to writing, he spent his days in his Yokohama home making repeated sketches by himself. The design was more or less complete when I became involved, and the period over which this house was designed had stretched more than ten years, judging by the dates on his sketches.

Shinohara left behind more than eight hundred sketches for House in Tateshina. In addition to serving as a tool for hashing

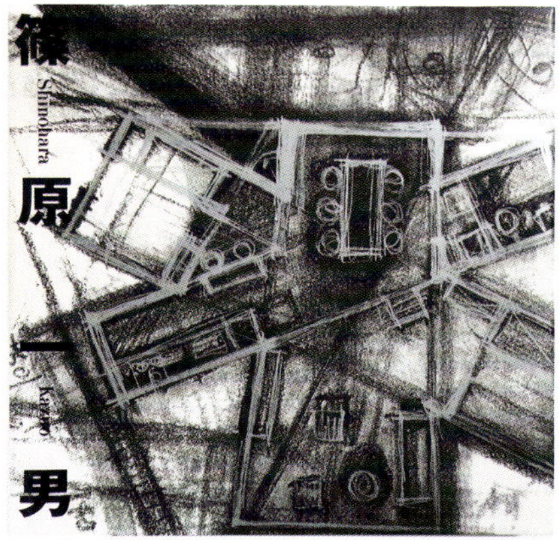

Cover of *Shinohara Kazuo* (Tokyo: TOTO shuppan, 1996).

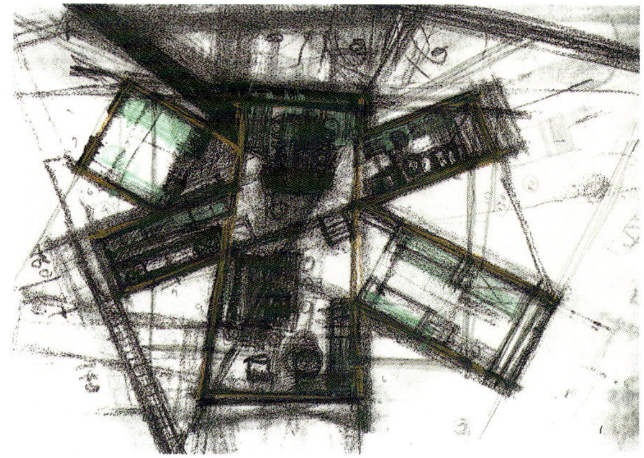

Shinohara Kazuo, sketch of House in Tateshina, unbuilt.

out the image within the mind of an architect, a sketch also helps one to then go about actually obtaining that image. I have always found a certain duality that inverts the subject and object in the exercise of making a sketch—discovering lines, shapes, and spaces that one is yet oblivious to, and noting the traces that are gradually left behind on a piece of paper by one's writing utensils. A sketch is a sort of avatar that functions through one's hand: although it is subordinate to you, it also possesses a kind of otherness with its own ego. As a result, sketching gives one the sensation that the sketch exists as an object that precedes the act of thinking. The texture and feel of Shinohara's sketches consist of an accumulation of lines; at the same time, they constantly seek out a kind of originary (*honrai no jibun no*) line that belongs to himself alone, out of this swelling bundle of lines. One can imagine that this is the sort of dialogue that emerges out of this confrontation between his abstract, inked diagrams that contain not a single wasted stroke, and the sketches persistently drawn over and over again. The cover of the monograph from TOTO Publishing (1996), which contains all of Shinohara's works except for House in Tateshina, presents an early sketch for this particular project. The staggering number of lines here, so numerous that one would expect them to bore a hole in the paper, is in fact a repeated quest to trace out just that one, "single" line.

Distinguished from these sketches that are quite particular to Shinohara, however, is another type of sketch that depicts on paper the geometries that are conjured up in the mind one after the other, even before one begins to think. A large volume of these discrete (*risanteki*) sketches, especially in relation to House in Tateshina, came to light after Shinohara passed away.

The discreteness of these sketches is perhaps not entirely unrelated to the discreteness with which Shinohara handled the geometrical forms found in his later works, such as House in Yokohama (1984). This character unfolded throughout all of these works, regardless of whether they were residential:

> This instantaneous visual coupling that is both autonomous and fragmentary is a central theme of this residence [House in Yokohama]. The main subject of the two works prior to this house was discrete forms—in two dimensions in the Japan Ukiyo-e Museum in Matsumoto, and in three dimensions in Higashi-Tamagawa Complex—or the coupling of volumes. This house was designed with two subjects in mind.... Each form and volume has been calculated like the component of a machine. One of the distinctive characteristics of the spatial situation that arises when these are coupled together, however, is what I would venture to define as random noise. I am particularly interested in exploring what these distinctive features are.[4]
>
> I am fond of the way that clusters of hard-edged primary geometric forms seem to flicker intensely, yet gently, in the light. I wait in anticipation of how a certain bright and radiant power appears, even within this dance-like movement.[5]

4 Shinohara Kazuo, "Hausu in Yokohama" *Shinkenchiku jūtaku tokushū*, no. 1 (May 1986): 133.

5 Shinohara Kazuo, *Shinohara Kazuo* (Tokyo: TOTO shuppan, 1996), 391.

6 Shinohara Kazuo, "Aru shōgyō toshi kikai," *Shinkenchiku* vol. 74, no. 1 (January 1989): 275.

> The terms that I have used mainly in the context of urban theory, such as "chaos" or "random noise," have, quite assuredly, absolutely nothing to do with the forms that have relinquished the possibility of any relationship between objects—such as you might find if you were to overturn a box of toys.[6]

The discreteness that Shinohara sought to achieve through his compositions of geometrical elements in his Fourth Style is generally considered to have reached its ultimate realization in House in Yokohama, while the formal development of his subsequent works has not been adequately assessed. In contrast to the exquisite balance with which multiple subvolumes are arranged with respect to the main geometric form in House in Yokohama and Centennial Hall at Tokyo Institute of Technology (1987), Shinohara's residential buildings after House in Yokohama, such as Tenmei House (1988) and Hanegi Complex (1988), contain multiple geometric elements that grapple with each other in an attempt to assert their dominance—they overlap with each other, while also seeming to be coupled together. This conjugation seems to resemble a sort of game, in which a certain degree of instability is retained. To me, however, this coupling of geometric forms seems to be preparing to transform itself into a new sort of geometry.

According to the diagrams, the gradient of the site on which House in Tateshina stands is approximately 4.2/10, or an angle of around 23 degrees—an angle at which one experiences the sensation of potentially slipping and falling if one is careless and does not hold onto something. Under current regulations, one would not be able to erect a residential building on such a steeply graded plot of land. Such a design was possible because of regulations in place when the land was first acquired. Shinohara obtained a long-term lease for this land at a time when he was still a junior faculty member at the Tokyo Institute of Technology. For the next half century he continued to pay rent as he waited for the right time to design the house.

In the sketches that Shinohara made over many years, one can see numerous, varied explorations of ways that geometric forms could hover over and collide with each other against this steep slope. This is undoubtedly an extrapolation of the discreteness that Shinohara had attempted to achieve with his Fourth Style. The impression that one receives from the final form of House in Tateshina, however, is less an art of discreteness that stirs the emotions by approaching the condition of music, than the quiet presence of multiple geometries in the process of transfiguring themselves into a new geometrical arrangement. The geometrical clusters of strong forms made to collide violently with each other in House in Yokohama and his subsequent works seem, in House in Tateshina, to have swallowed up all this energy and quietly transformed themselves into a new configuration. Furthermore, there is no question that the sloping mound of earth is a geometric element that constitutes a part of this newly transformed state.

A THIRTY-YEAR GAP

The aforementioned descriptions addressed the one commonality between Tanikawa House and House in Tateshina, namely an exposed earthen slope, but there are many differences between these two houses.

Tanikawa House (1974) was the first instance that featured this sloping earth. Some thirty years later, House in Tateshina, although plans for it were fully in place, remains unbuilt. While the earthen slope in Tanikawa House basically constituted a living room that people could walk around in, the slope in House in Tateshina protrudes out into part of the living room, with the upper second-storey portion hovering in space, on the assumption that nobody would actually be walking on the earth. The angle of the latter slope is also larger by a factor of about three. Whereas Tanikawa House was conceived as a holiday home for a poet, Tateshina is basically a personal residence meant for Shinohara's own family. Tanikawa House is one of the earliest examples of Shinohara's Third Style, while Tateshina is a posthumous work that came in the wake of his Fourth Style—accordingly, it features a style that has not been contextualized or positioned by Shinohara himself. While the earthen-floored (summer) living space alone in Tanikawa House measures 9 by 12 meters in floor area (108 meters square), House in Tateshina is Shinohara's smallest project, with a floor area of only 2.5 *ken* by 4 *ken,* or 10 *tsubo* (about 33 meters square). Although the two houses share the feature of the exposed structure protruding into the interior space, in Tanikawa House the pillars appear in the space, whereas those in Tateshina are not visible.

Nonetheless, it is highly likely that Shinohara was keenly aware of the relationship between these two projects in terms of the exposure of the earthen slope. As Shinohara had extremely exacting standards regarding the distances between people, things, and time, I used to have work discussions with him by relying purely on my personal sense of what the diagrams laid out. This was the kind of distance that our relationship was based on; asking about this, that, or the other was definitely out of the question. Thanks to this mode of working—or perhaps in spite of it—Shinohara would often tell me about his career as an architect and designer spanning nearly half a century. The design for House in Tateshina went back and forth between House in White (First Style, 1966) and House in Yokohama (Fourth Style), ultimately "taking its cue from the approach seen in House in White," according to him.

STYLE OF ONE'S FORERUNNERS

I would like to clarify my use of the term "style." As I have already mentioned, Shinohara organized and classified his own works according to their style. In other words, Shinohara's practice was essentially based on the premise that each work would be contextualized and positioned according to the style in which it was built. Typically, the term "style" is used in the sense of types or models, which does not display a great deal of variation. Style used in the context of architecture or art is applicable when it designates a range of objects capable of making reference to the archetypes of a particular era. If we say something like "akin to Gothic architecture," we understand the unique features that this phrase seeks to evoke, and we are able to imagine the particularities of something to which this metaphor applies, without requiring a specific instance to be raised. Accordingly, style is nothing other than a consolidated type arrived at by homing in on a nature that can be extracted once again. In this sense, style is an originary source type, as in the classics of antiquity, embodying a certain historical framework. Style is a form that can be found in what the forerunners of the past have created. According to

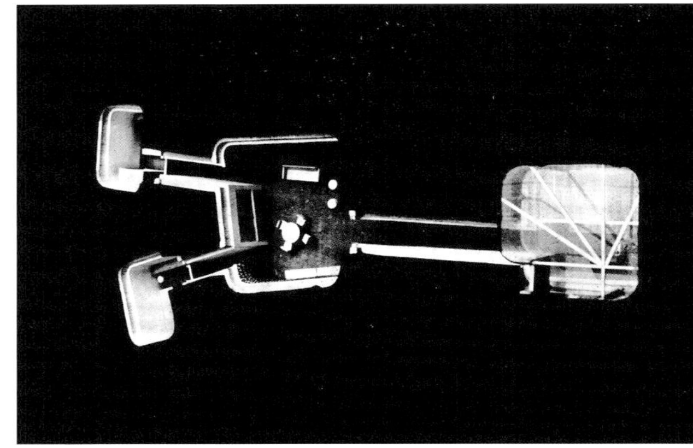

7 Kawamukai Masato, *Kingendai kenchiku-shi ron* (Tokyo: Chūō kōron bijutsu shuppansha, 2017), 46. Translated here from Japanese edition.

8 Kawamukai, *Kingendai kenchiku-shi ron*, 55.

Kawamukai Masato, who penned a thesis on modern and contemporary architectural history based on his reading of German architect and theorist Gottfried Semper's understanding of the term, "style" originally refers to "something that was rooted and ingrained." As Kawamukai elaborated:

> Style is born from the climate, region, environment, and local lifestyle and culture. Originally, style was something that was rooted and ingrained in these things. The idealized styles of the past also came about and continued to exist in this way.[7]

If we understand the notion of style in this way, can there possibly be a style that we can attribute to a single individual such as Shinohara? Here, it may be helpful to have recourse to the way in which figures like German architect Heinrich Hübsch dealt with the idea of style, in terms of a unique perspective that gazes on it, which is different to whatever distinguishes the style in question itself. For Hübsch, style is "something that is criticized through a process of reflection (*naisei*); the next style is then picked out." Again to quote Kawamukai's study:

> According to Nikolaus Pevsner, Hübsch observed and researched historical styles in order to criticize the styles that were in vogue at the time, and then picked out the styles of the past that he believed ought to replace them.[8]

The intervals between Shinohara's various styles must surely have seen him criticize his own style through a process of reflection—that is, a movement toward "anti-space." Shinohara first used the word "style" to apply to his work from the mid-1970s, in a bid to begin positioning and contextualizing these projects. During this time he twice ushered in a process of reflection; it was a stage where he was able to position relationships between each instance. Insofar as Shinohara's output consists of a series of works that resulted from repeated reflection, it was possible to organize and classify them according to an individual style that differed from the one that was assigned to one's predecessors.

STYLE OF ONE'S OWN

As previously mentioned, Shinohara saw his output in terms of permutations of four styles: the First Style is based on Japanese traditions, division and connection, frontality, and superfluous space; the Second on the creation of a sort of inorganic, cubic shell, or fissure space; the Third on naked things, savagery, gap, the city, and concreteness; and the Fourth on the notion of random noise and ModernNext. He started to categorize his own output using the word "style" in the mid-1970s, at a time when he had begun creating building in his Third Style. More than ten years earlier, however, at a time when he was tackling projects in his First Style, Shinohara wrote:

> A designer discovers his own style. By honing it sharply, he is able to escape a predilection toward typification. At the same time, the intense energy of that style fuels the assertion that one should struggle against and resist the old, anachronistic and backward styles that are being imposed from outside.... The style that we must create is not simply an aggregation of various design methods.

Shinohara Kazuo, House of Earth—Space in Black, 1964, unbuilt.

Shinohara Kazuo working on House in Yokohama's large clay site model, ca. 1982. Photo by Hosoe Eikō

> It consists in giving form to a single spirit that threads through the back of all of these methods.[9]

At this point, Shinohara had already begun to be conscious of giving a certain stylistic uniqueness to the development of his output. Around the time that he completed Tanikawa House (1974), he used the word "style" to describe the cubic spaces that distinguished his work prior to this project as "spaces meant to effect a conversion in my style," "a framework for my next style," or "a springboard." The anti-space to this approach, conversely, was positioned as "a naked space," or "cold, dry, and inorganic spaces," signaling how he was anticipating a sort of reversal:

> The cubes were spaces meant to effect a conversion in my style. At the same time, however, they were also a framework for my next style. Would it now be possible to discover a kind of anti-space that would serve as a springboard to the entirety of all the spaces I have created, which have been verified in this manner? A "naked space" is one of the signals for this. I will try to find a reversal of these spaces, of "hot" meaning toward cold, dry, and inorganic spaces, or of the totality of these spaces themselves.[10]

Around the time that he completed House in Uehara, which was designed around the same time as Tanikawa House, Shinohara made the following stipulations about his work using the word "style," which had for him become an ordinal sequence:

> I am beginning to feel empathy for the change in styles of expression as experienced by an artist like Pablo Picasso.... Just when a beautiful and distinctive style was established, he would embark on a new style that undermined it, and so on in sequence. I am now beginning to understand this mechanism.... The creation of any style will axiomatically encompass any force that is opposed to it and [the result] is the consequence of the struggle to resolve that opposition....
>
> I have always believed that the creation of new work is a two-tiers process. First, you must move yourself to an unknown domain, do some reconnaissance, and make it your own. Then you give whatever fresh nutrition is to be found in the new space, no matter how small it may be, back to the spaces of your past, operating in such a way that these old spaces do not remain isolated or negated.[11]

As one can see, there is something quite terrifying about Shinohara's obsessiveness when it comes to positioning and contextualizing his own works. As Okuyama Shin-ichi, who is also a contributing author to this volume, has pointed out, each of Shinohara's styles possesses a set of relationships: concepts and forms tested in styles from his late career are hinted at by prefatory allusions found in works and remarks belonging to other, earlier styles.[12]

Or perhaps this phenomenon is evident in the output of any architect. In the case of Shinohara, however, because these allusions take the form of preemptive, germ-like pronouncements that foreshadow an era, manifesting themselves later

9 Shinohara Kazuo, "Yōshiki ga tsukurareru toki," *Desain*, no. 32 (August 1962): 2–6.

10 Shinohara, "Ragyō no kūkan wo ōdan suru toki," 160.

11 Shinohara Kazuo, "Daisan no yōshiki" *Shinkenchiku* vol. 52, no. 1 (January 1977): 221–25. Translation used here from English-language version, "The Third Style, 1977," in *Kazuo Shinohara: Houses 2G*, no. 58/59, ed. David B. Stewart, Okuyama Shin-ichi, and Shiozaki Taishin (2011).

12 Okuyama Shin-ichi, "'Genkei jūtaku' no imi: bunkatsu, hi-bunkatsu soshite renketsu wo meguru kūkanteki shisaku," in *Shinohara Kazuo jūtaku zumen* (Tokyo: Shōkokusha, 2008), 134–35.

as extremely powerful forms, they seem to be the cunning connivance of one who has been concealing them all along, up until the times are able to catch up with him. For instance, the idea of a "fissure space" extracted from the Japanese *minka* commoner houses started to appear in works from Shinohara's First Style, where he pursued a form of abstraction by turning his attention to Japanese traditions. In the same manner, one can find remarks in his earliest writings on the subject of the "urban chaos" that he would later go on to pursue in his Fourth Style. The linkages between these terms speak eloquently of how Shinohara assembled his subjects by always taking style into account. Seen in this light, it becomes only natural to think of House in Tateshina as a kind of anti-space in relation to his Fourth Style; the distance between this project and Tanikawa House must also have been measured in advance.

This time, it was important that attention was focused on the "relationships between things" that united these two houses—or Shinohara's Third and Fourth styles. The fact that Shinohara was formerly a mathematician makes this stylistic connection even more significant. When a relationship exists between two numbers, a function is established. One can easily discover unique functions in the conflict and gap between naked things and concrete objects in the context of his Third Style, and the discrete geometric arrangements and combinations of his Fourth Style. When it comes to the relationships between functions, however, there is a sort of reversal that appears to be akin to a rupture. As is self-evident from the way Shinohara uses the term anti-space in relation to this meta-function, this is a sort of mapping that could only come about because of a similarity of perspective. When Shinohara ultimately decided to "take his cue from the approach seen in House in White," we can see that the hybridization and generation of geometries in House in Tateshina, having undergone two functions (his Third and Fourth Styles) and seeking the next relationship between things, eventually addressed one of the distinctive attributes of his First Style.

COLD SLOPING GROUND AND HOT SLOPING GROUND

As opposed to Tanikawa House, where natural earth is simply stripped of its meaning and left as is, producing a gap from the house, the earth in Tateshina is a new spatial form sublimated from a provisional form from Shinohara and various amalgamated geometries of his other houses. Although a superficial impression might suggest that the earth in Tanikawa House is wetter, and that in Tateshina drier, in fact the opposite is true. The earth in Tanikawa House is a cold, sloping ground that has been stripped of meaning. Conversely, although the earth in House in Tateshina has a more geometrical form, there is an element of heat to its essential nature that has been embedded in its geometry, and should perhaps be read as something superimposed onto the living space. Although the meaning of the background in each house is different, they both resemble the polished column placed in the abstracted space of House in White. In the following passage by Isozaki Arata, where he describes the column in House in White, if one replaces references to columns with sloping ground, and the context of historical Japanese houses with that of nature, one pretty much ends up with an explanation of House in Tateshina and its anti-space:

13 Shinohara and Isozaki, "Taidan: kenchiku ni tsuite," 141.

14 Shinohara, "Ragyō no kūkan wo ōdan suru toki," 159.

In my own reading, that sense of gloom in a Japanese house symbolizes the meaning behind each of the elements the house is comprised of, as in if you remove one column like the central post (*daikokubashira*) and alcove post (*tokobashira*). There are also the unique textures associated with the wood grain and the white walls. The range of architectural elements that were built into the context of traditional Japanese houses is extremely diverse. Deploying these unconsciously would mean that many elements of the past are dragged into the fray. With an exceptionally deft touch, however, as seen in the round columns of House in White, for instance, one can accomplish a two-layered operation that involves both temporarily cutting away traditional elements, while also incorporating them back into the mix. This is an extraordinary achievement. Here is a design that enables a metaphor to be created. In this respect, what Shinohara is probably seeking to do at this moment is to erase any trace of such a metaphor: in other words, to make everything *naked*, and to pick out another, different idea. This, to my mind, is probably what he has intended.[13]

It is perhaps to be expected that one would interpret Shinohara's remark that he had "returned once again to House in White" to refer to the abstraction and configuration of forms in a broader sense. Although it might seem incomprehensible, this strategy was in fact an exercise in discovering how styles circulate within Shinohara's output—based on the assumption that his "return" to House in White was in relation to how he dealt with the significance of earth. The sloping ground in House in Tateshina House lacks the concrete presence of the naked thing that appears in Tanikawa House: rather, it is a geometry in which nature has been abstracted. In Tanikawa House, the "accidental" angle of the sloping ground with some gradient or other has been scooped out, creating a concrete presence that produces a sense of gap. In contrast, at House in Tateshina, the scooped-out earth is temporarily abstracted in the form of a geometric element, before rejoining the space once again—just like the round column in House in White.

Reading Shinohara's remarks in relation to what Tanikawa Shuntarō said of the sloping ground in his own house encourages one to think that Shinohara was indeed preparing to reverse the meaning of this earth once again. This, after all, was an architect who managed to create a context while going around reversing his Four Styles. There is something of the literary scholar here, as well:

> He responded, saying that this was not a residence (*jūtaku*), but a house (*ie*). The title under which my houses are published in magazines has changed from "Something-House" to "Something-Residence." So it seems as if the opposite has happened, I replied.... I do feel, however, that I now have a grasp of the facts necessary to verify my own context.[14]

Translated by Darryl Wee

HOUSE IN TATESHINA, 2001–06
Chino, Nagano Prefecture
unbuilt

The last of Shinohara's works and intended for his own family, House in Tateshina is also the smallest in his oeuvre at only 10 *tsubo,* or about 33 square meters. Shinohara held a lease on this site for more than a half century without ever realizing anything on it, always in anticipation of the right moment. At 4.2/10 pitch or 23 degrees, the site's steep incline is debilitating to walk on and would not have been legal for any civilian construction. The roof pitch, at 60 degrees, is also the steepest in Shinohara's work. The incline inside the house, unlike at Tanikawa House (1974), is somewhat subdued. While many elements from earlier styles can be found in this scheme, there is a new level of intensity and asceticism that eludes full materialization.

Photo courtesy of
Shinohara Kazuo Archive

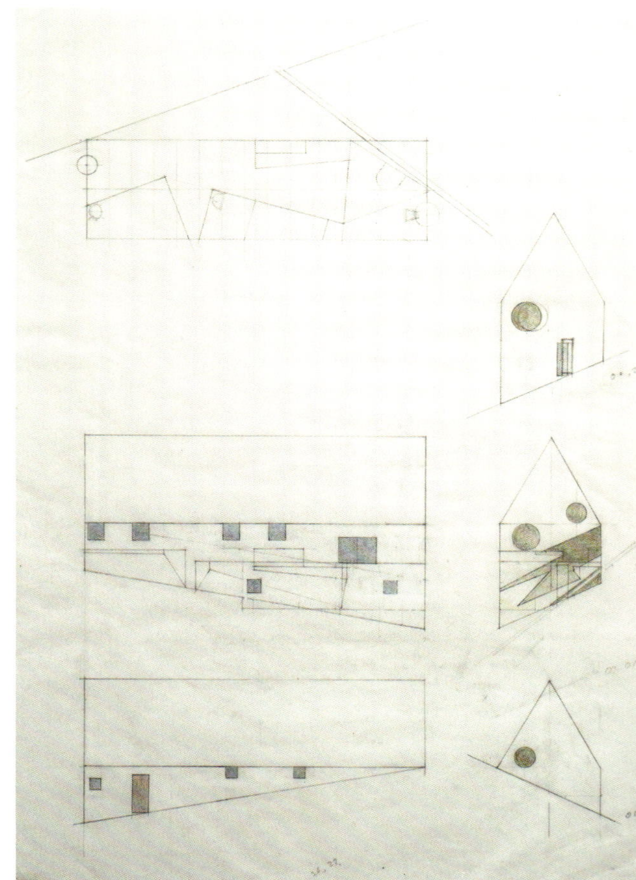

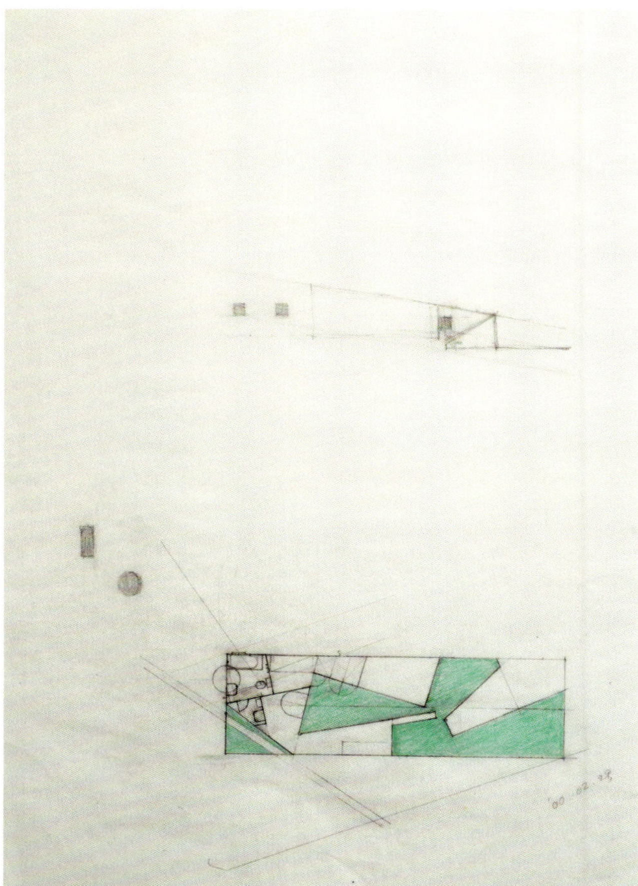

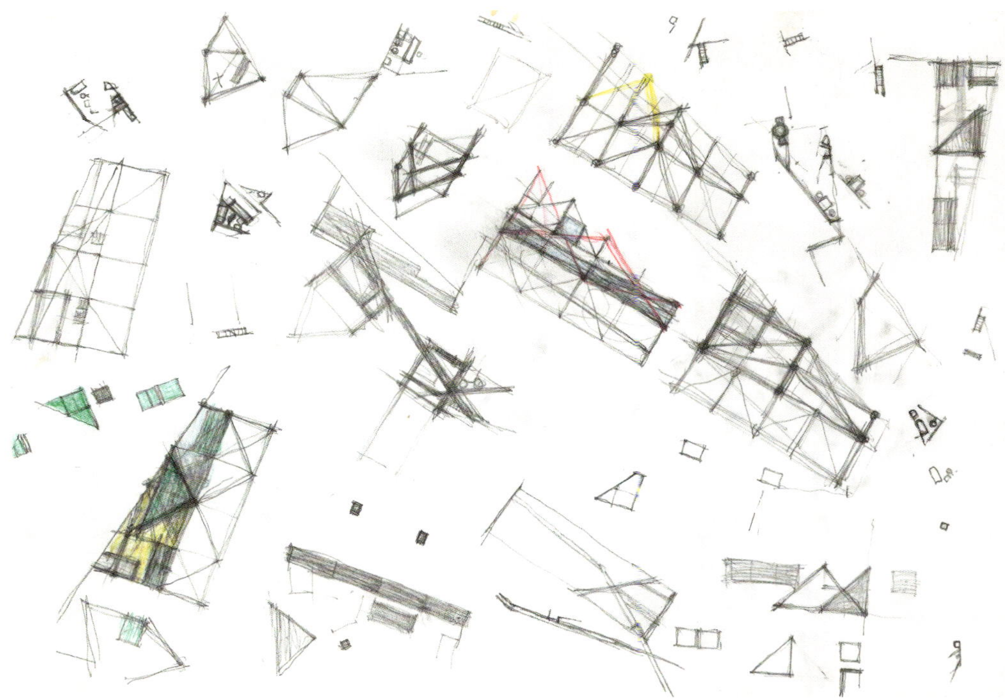

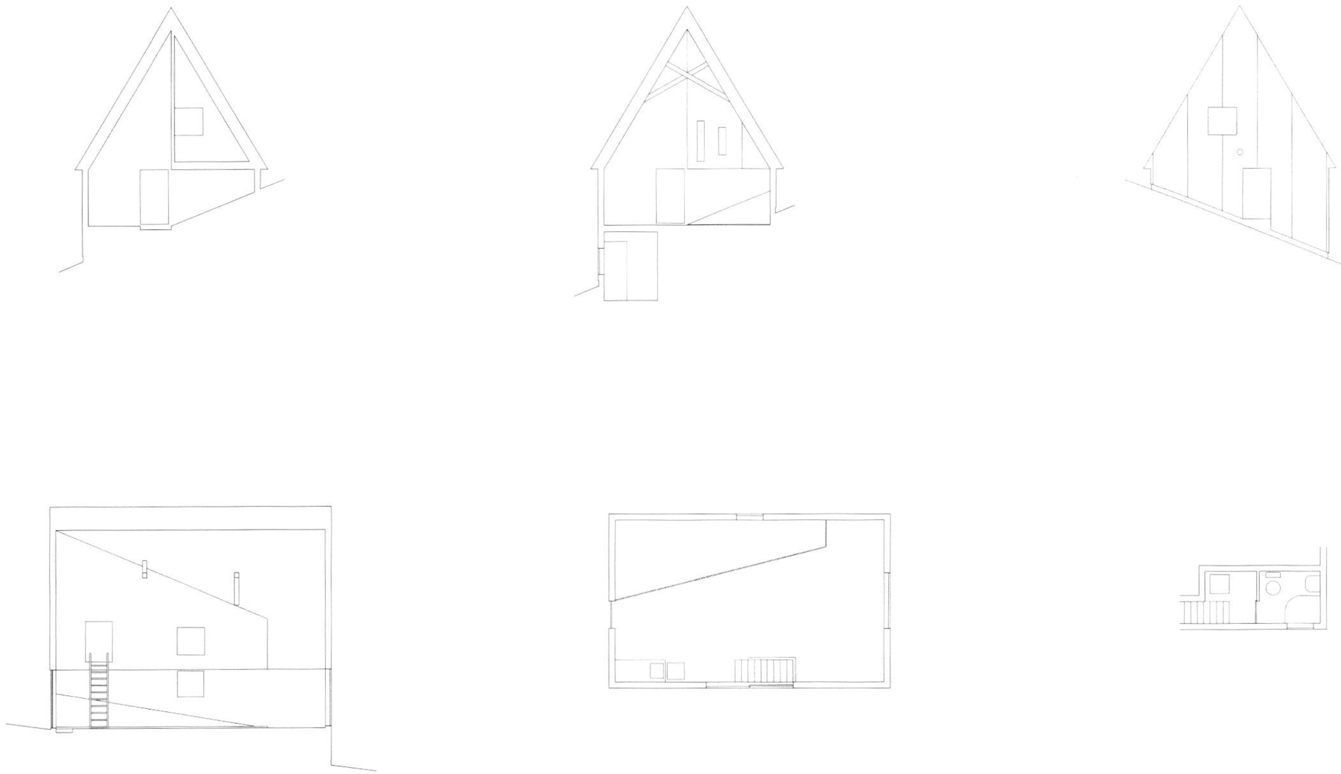

1:200

North elevation of 1:3 model.

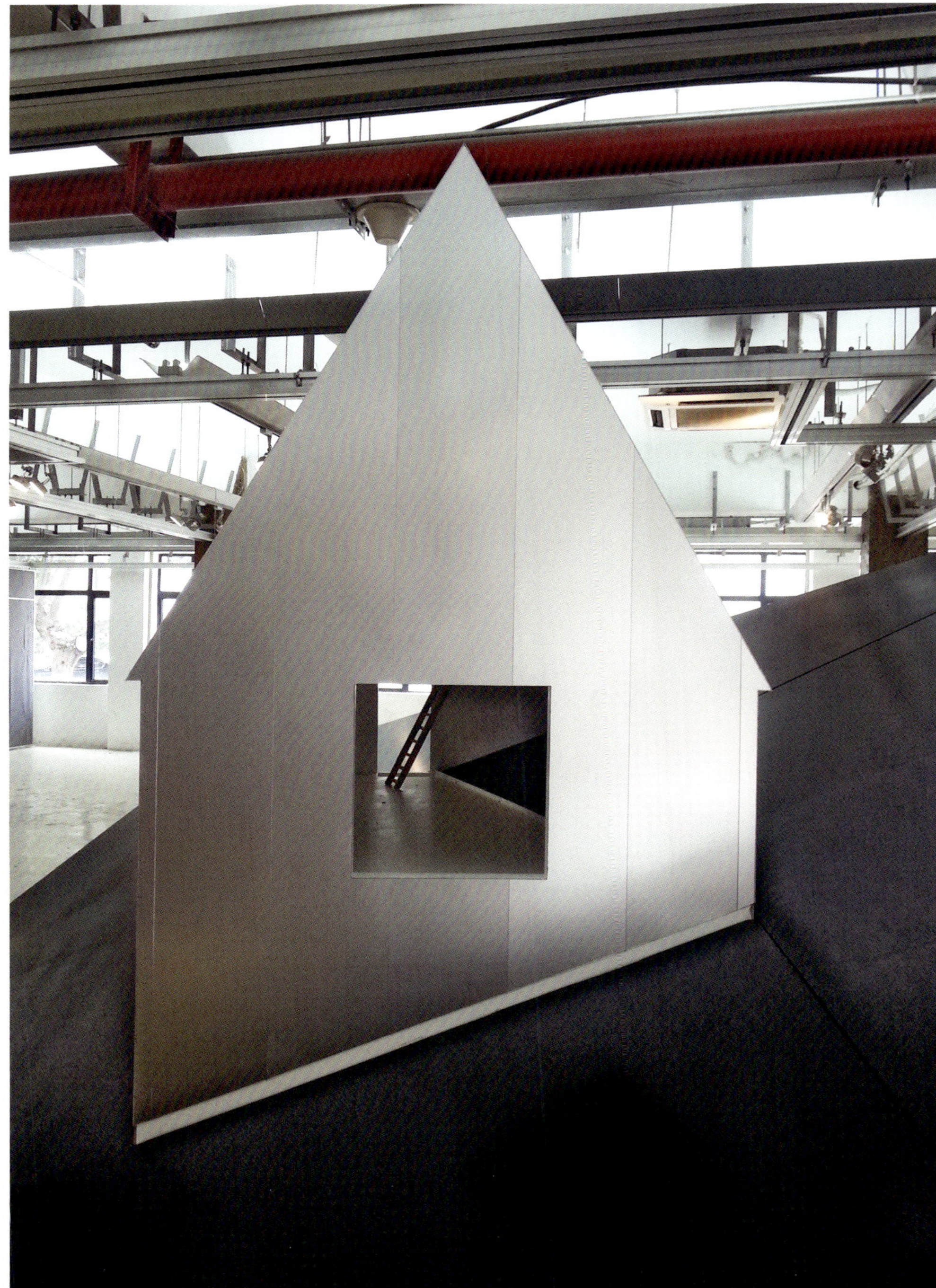

Kemper Art Museum, St. Louis, installation view. Photos by Whitney Curtis

ETH, Zurich, installation view. Photos by Angela Y. Pang and Martin Stollenwerk

Harvard Graduate School of Design, Cambridge, Massachusetts, installation view. Photos by Po Po and Justin Knight

Three Exhibitions

Angela Y. Pang

In the years between 2014 and 2019 a trilogy of exhibitions showcased Shinohara Kazuo's architecture with archival drawings, sketches, photographs, and scale models on loan from the Tokyo Institute of Technology. The first show, in St. Louis, surveyed Shinohara's earlier experimentations with tradition and abstraction and highlighted his influence on contemporary practices. The presentation in Zurich emphasized the Third Style. A small cabinet adjacent to the main gallery there displayed photos taken by Shinohara during his travels abroad in this period, suggesting connections between these visual cues and his design work. The third exhibition, in Cambridge, focused on his later works from the 1980s as an explicit dialogue between the space machine and the chaotic metropolis.

The St. Louis and Zurich iterations both employed tables, designed as picture frames extruded from the level ground, for the display of drawings and other objects on flat surfaces. The layout invited viewers to flow through the interstitial spaces between the objects on view and allowed for free traversals in the gallery space, encouraging viewers to make diachronic connections between Shinohara's works from different style periods. Fitted in a white cube gallery, the tables in St. Louis were arranged rectilinearly, while those in Zurich dissolved the boundaries with a soft grid. A very different approach was taken in Cambridge. As an homage to ModernNext, this exhibition design confronted the disjunct, porous gallery space with two strong and contrasting geometric figures projecting toward the two ends of the gallery.

On the Thresholds of Space Making: Shinohara Kazuo and His Legacy
Mildred Lane Kemper Art Museum, Washington University in St. Louis
January 31 to April 20, 2014

On the Thresholds of Space Making: Shinohara Kazuo
gta Exhibitions, Swiss Federal Institute of Technology (ETH), Zurich
September 21 to October 21, 2016

Shinohara Kazuo: ModernNext
Druker Design Gallery, Harvard Graduate School of Design, Cambridge, Massachusetts
August 26 to October 11, 2019

SHINOHARA KAZUO (1925–2006)

1943–47	studied mathematics at Tokyo School of Physics
1950–53	studied architecture at Tokyo Institute of Technology
1953	appointed assistant, Tokyo Institute of Technology
1962	promoted to associate professor in descriptive geometry, Tokyo Institute of Technology
1967	awarded doctor of engineering (dissertation title: "Study in Space Composition of Japanese Architecture")
1970	promoted to professor in descriptive geometry, Tokyo Institute of Technology
1972	awarded prize from Architectural Institute of Japan for the "series of houses from The Uncompleted House onward"
1979–83	featured in solo exhibitions in Europe and North America
1980	appointed professor in architecture, Tokyo Institute of Technology
1984	appointed Eero Saarinen Visiting Professor of Architecture, Yale University, United States
1986	retired from Tokyo Institute of Technology, established Shinohara Atelier
1990	awarded Medal with Purple Ribbon from the Government of Japan
1997	received Mainichi Art Special Award
2005	awarded Grand Prize from the Architectural Institute of Japan for "creating elegant architecture based on enduring theories of the house and the city"
2010	awarded Golden Lion in Memoriam, 12th Venice Architecture Biennale

CONTRIBUTORS

ANO DAICI is an architectural photographer based in Tokyo. As a student at University of Hokkaidō Graduate School, specializing in environmental engineering, he began documenting urban sceneries in his photographic work.

HOSAKA KENJIRŌ is director of the Museum of Modern Art, Shiga. He was previously curator of the National Museum of Modern Art, Tokyo, where he organized major exhibitions including *The Japanese House, Architecture and Life after 1945* (2017), *Francis Bacon* (2013), and *Where Is Architecture?: Seven Installations by Japanese Architects* (2010). He was trained in art history at Keio University.

CHRISTIAN KEREZ is professor of architecture at the Swiss Federal Institute of Technology in Zurich and obtained his degree in architecture from the same school. After extensive work in architectural photography, he opened his own architectural office in Zurich in 1993 and has been based in Berlin more recently. In 2012–13 he held the Kenzō Tange Visiting Professorship at Harvard Graduate School of Design. For the Swiss Pavilion at the Venice Architecture Biennale 2016 he participated with the project *Incidental Space*. He is currently working on several projects in various scales in Europe and the Middle East.

SENG KUAN is project associate professor and director of the International Architectural Education Platform at the University of Tokyo and teaches regularly at the Harvard Graduate School of Design. He has written extensively on Japan's postwar architectural culture. He is coeditor of *Kenzō Tange: Architecture for the World* (2012) and contributed to *Kiyonori Kikutake: Between Land and Sea* (2016). He previously taught at Washington University in St. Louis.

OKUYAMA SHIN-ICHI is professor of architecture at the Tokyo Institute of Technology, where he has been teaching since 1992. He received his bachelor's and doctoral degrees from the same school and has researched extensively on writing by architects in postwar Japan. He is editor of *Aphorisms: Shinohara Kazuo's Spatial Discourse* (2004). The architect of Midorigaoka Building No. 6 and Boat House at the Tokyo Institute of Technology, Okuyama is also principal of Atelier Okuyama.

KEN TADASHI OSHIMA is professor of architecture at the University of Washington, Seattle. Among his publications are *Kiyonori Kikutake: Between Land and Sea* (2016), *Architecturalized Asia* (2013), *GLOBAL ENDS: Towards the Beginning* (2012), *International Architecture in Interwar Japan: Constructing Kokusai Kenchiku* (2009), and *Arata Isozaki* (2009). He co-curated *Frank Lloyd Wright at 150: Unpacking the Archive* (Museum of Modern Art, New York, 2017) and *Crafting a Modern World: The Architecture and Design of Antonin and Noémi Raymond* (Kamakura Museum of Modern Art, 2007).

ANGELA Y. PANG is principal of PangArchitect. Her recent design work includes a new dormitory for the Chinese University of Hong Kong and renovations and extensions for the libraries of Hong Kong Polytechnic and Lingnan Universities. Pang has taught at the University of Hong Kong, Washington University in St. Louis, and Cornell University. She received a Special Award from the Hong Kong Institute of Architects.

SHIOZAKI TAISHIN is associate professor of architecture at the Tokyo Institute of Technology. He received his bachelor's and doctoral degrees from the same school. In 2003–06 he assisted Shinohara Kazuo on a series of design projects, including House in Tateshina. Together with Kobayashi Saeco, Shiozaki is principal of the firm Atelierco, which was recognized by *SD Review* in 2018 and by a Good Design Award in 2010. He was also coeditor of *The Japan Architect* no. 93, a monographic issue on Shinohara.

DAVID B. STEWART graduated from the University of Pennsylvania and subsequently took a PhD under Sir Nikolaus Pevsner at the Courtauld Institute of Art, University of London. He is professor at the Tokyo Institute of Technology. Author of *The Making of a Modern Japanese Architecture: 1868 to the Present* (1987/2002) as well as *Kazuo Shinohara: Centennial Hall, Tokyo* (1995), he produced the course MOOC: *Modern Japanese Architecture: From Meiji Restoration to Today* (TokyoTechX, edX, 2015).

TSUKAMOTO YOSHIHARU is, together with Kaijima Momoyo, principal of Atelier Bow-Wow. He is professor of architecture at the Tokyo Institute of Technology and received his bachelor's and doctoral degrees from the same school. He has served as guest professor at schools around the world, including the Harvard Graduate School of Design as the Kenzō Tange Visiting Professor; UCLA; Cornell; Rice; Columbia; and TU Delft.

CREDITS

Unless otherwise noted, all drawings and images are courtesy of the Shinohara Kazuo Archive. Used by permission.

Images drawn from previous publications are listed below.

30	*Kenchiku zasshi*, no. 689 (November 1941)
31	*Shinkenchiku* vol. 28, no. 5 (May 1953)
33	Sano Toshikata, *Kenchiku ron* (Tokyo: Bunka seikatsu kenkyūkai, 1925)
34	*Shinkenchiku* vol. 29, no. 11 (November 1954)
38	*Shinkenchiku* vol. 29, no. 11 (November 1954)
66.1	Exhibition catalogue for *Shinohara Kazuo & Asakura Setsu: Two Houses inside a Department Store* (Odakyū Department Store, Tokyo, 1964)
66.2	*Kindai kenchiku* vol. 18, no. 6 (June 1964)
66.3	*Kenchiku*, no. 45 (May 1964)
66.4	*Kindai kenchiku* vol. 18, no. 6 (June 1964)
66.5	*Kenchiku*, no. 45 (May 1964)
66.6	*Kenchiku*, no. 45 (May 1964)
68	Exhibition catalogue for *Shinohara Kazuo & Asakura Setsu: Two Houses inside a Department Store* (Odakyū Department Store, Tokyo, 1964)
223	Advertising campaign graphic for Nippon Telephone and Telegraph
228	The United States Navy
229	The National Aeronautics and Space Administration (NASA)
264.1–2	OMA
306	*Kenchiku*, no. 45 (May 1964)

ACKNOWLEDGMENTS

This book is indebted to numerous individuals and institutions. First to be thanked are the members of the architecture faculty at the Tokyo Institute of Technology. Professors Okuyama Shin-ichi, Shiozaki Taishin, David B. Stewart, Tsukamoto Yoshiharu, and Yamazaki Taisuke were all particularly patient and generous with their time, resources, and knowledge throughout the project's evolution.

This publication on Shinohara Kazuo is the third installment, following exhibitions and publications on Tange Kenzō and Kikutake Kiyonori, in what has become a series on Japanese masters of modern architecture. Initiated by Mohsen Mostafavi during his deanship at the Harvard Graduate School of Design (GSD), the series has been realized in collaboration with Lars Müller. Enthusiastic support from two successive chairs of the Department of Architecture, K. Michael Hays and Mark Lee, made possible this focus on Shinohara, especially the later works. Dean Sarah Whiting has warmly embraced this project and its pedagogical potential since her arrival at GSD. Toshiko Mori shared stories of her family's connection to Shinohara. Ken Stewart of the Office of Communications, Ann Whiteside and Alix Reiskind of the Frances Loeb Library, and Michael Voligny of the Office of Development and Alumni Relations offered invaluable advice and support.

A trilogy of exhibitions on Shinohara provided the foundations of this book, first at the Mildred Lane Kemper Art Museum at Washington University in St. Louis in spring 2014, followed by the Institute for the History and Theory of Architecture at the ETH in Zurich in fall 2016, and finally at the GSD's Druker Design Gallery in fall 2019. I wish to thank Sabine Eckmann, Rachel Keith, Jane Neidhardt, and Kristen Good at the Kemper; Fredi Fischli, Niels Olsen, and Daniel Sommer at the ETH; and Dan Borelli and the exhibition crew at the GSD. My proposal was awarded the Freund Faculty Curatorial Fellowship at Washington University in St. Louis, where Dean Carmon Colangelo of the Sam Fox School and Bruce Lindsey, Heather Woofter, Eric Mumford, Sung Ho Kim, and Robert McCarter all embraced a young faculty member's research agenda with warmth and enthusiasm.

Christian Kerez was instrumental in the development of this project, helping to bring the exhibition to Zurich and advocating for a closer examination of Shinohara's relationship with his artist clients. Rem Koolhaas, Nomiyama Gyōji, Ōtsuji Seiko and Ōtsuji Tetsuo, and Tanikawa Shuntarō generously shared their recollections of working with Shinohara. I am indebted to mentors, colleagues, and friends in Ano Daici, Iwan Baan, Barry Bergdoll, Hasegawa Yūko, Hiraiwa Yoshiyuki, Hosaka Kenjirō, Ishigami Junya, Kaijima Momoyo, Kobayashi Saeco, Andrea Leers, Matsushita Kiwa, Nishizawa Ryūe, Guy Nordenson, Ken Tadashi Oshima, Jordan Sand, Sakaushi Taku, Sasaki Mutsurō, Sejima Kazuyo, Shinohara Satoko, Melissa Vaughn, Cherie Wendelken, Yatsuka Hajime, and Yoshida Nobuyuki.

Early drafts to several chapters were first presented at a symposium held at Washington University in St. Louis, made possible by a faculty workshop grant and funding from the Association of Asian Studies' Northeast Asia Council, with the support of the Japan-US Friendship Commission. The Graham Foundation for Advanced Studies in the Fine Arts awarded grants first to the exhibition at the Kemper and again to this publication project.

I am also grateful to my colleagues at the University of Tokyo, in particular Kuma Kengo, Hirano Toshiki, and Katsu Hiroko for their advice, forbearance, and feedback. Chiba Manabu, Katō Kōichi, Noguchi Takafumi, Ōtsuki Toshio, and Yasuhara Motoki have all made Todai a welcoming and supportive base for my work.

Lars Müller stood by the project despite the many hiatuses and encouraged freedoms in reconceptualizing the project. Audrey Solomon, Helene Leuzinger, Maya Rüegg, and Esther Butterworth have been extraordinary collaborators. Álex Bueno, Michelle Hauk, Hattori Mari, and Amy Teschner embraced their charges with exceptional grace and diligence. Others who provided important assistance to the publication are Aikawa Kōji, Andō Satoshi, Michael Duckworth, Fujimoto Akiko, Hara Aya, Hoashi Terutaka, Inohana Mae, Kawai Emi, Kinoshita Hisako, Patricia Kohl, Kusunose Tomoyuki, Lei Hou, Mori Keiko, Murai Kumi, Nagashima Akio, Nishimaki Atsuko, Ōhashi Masanori, Ōta Yuma, Po Po, Saeki Yayoi, Florian Sauter, Shiba Michiko, Shiotani Keiko, Saki Yōsuke, Rita Varjabedian, Ueda Hiroshi, Watanabe Hiroshi, Darryl Wee, and Yoshimi Chiaki.

Angela Pang, together with Shin and Yun, have been part of my education of Shinohara every step along the way.

Seng Kuan

KAZUO SHINOHARA
Traversing the House and the City

Editor: Seng Kuan
Copyediting: Amy Teschner, Michael Duckworth
Proofreading: Amy Teschner
Photo assistance: Hattori Mari
Design: Integral Lars Müller / Lars Müller with Audrey Solomon and Helene Leuzinger
Lithography: prints professional, Berlin, Germany
Printing and binding: Offizin Scheufele, Stuttgart, Germany
Paper: Arto Satin, 150 g / m^2

Lars Müller Publishers is supported by the Swiss Federal Office of Culture with a structural contribution for the years 2021–2024.

Lars Müller Publishers
Zurich, Switzerland
www.lars-mueller-publishers.com

ISBN 978-3-03778-533-1

Distributed in North America by ARTBOOK | D.A.P.
www.artbook.com

Printed in Germany